GATT ACCORD

RESULTS OF URUGUAY ROUND OF MULTILATERAL TRADE NEGOTIATIONS

(Complete Text)

Edited by
K.R. GUPTA

ATLANTIC PUBLISHERS AND DISTRIBUTORS

Published by
ATLANTIC PUBLISHERS AND DISTRIBUTORS
B-2, Vishal Enclave, New Delhi-110 027
Phones 5413460, 5429987

Sales Office
4346/4C, Ansari Road, Darya Ganj,
New Delhi-110 002
Phones 3273880, 3285873
Fax 91-11-3285873

ISBN 81-7156-448-8

Typeset at
APD Computer Graphics, Delhi
Printed in India at
Tarun Offset Printers, Delhi

CONTENTS

Most Commonly-Used Abbreviations

BOP	:	Balance-of-Payments.
DS	:	Dispute Settlement.
DSU	:	Understanding on Rules and Procedures Governing the Settlement of Disputes.
GATS	:	General Agreement on Trade in Services.
GATT	:	General Agreement on Tariffs and Trade.
GDP	:	Government Procurement.
ISO	:	International Standards Organization.
ISO/IEC	:	ISO/International Electrotechnical Commission.
LLDCS	:	Least-Developed Countries.
WTO	:	**World Trade Organisation**
PSI	:	Preshipment Inspection.
SCM	:	Subsidies and Countervailing Measures.
SPS	:	Sanitary and Phytosanitary Measures.
TBT	:	Technical Barriers to Trade.
TRIMs	:	Trade-Related Investment Measures.
TRIPs	:	Trade-Related Aspects of Intellectual Property Rights, Including Trade in Counterfeit Goods.
TPRM	:	Trade Policy Review Mechanism.

must first have concluded negotiations for their accession to the GATT 1947 and become contracting parties thereto. For participants who are not contracting parties to the GATT 1947 as of the date of the Final Act, the Schedules are not definitive and shall be subsequently completed for the purpose of their accession to GATT 1947 and acceptance of the Agreement establishing the WTO

6. This Final Act and the texts of the instruments set out in the Annexes shall be deposited with the Director-General to the CONTRACTING PARTIES to the General Agreement on Tariffs and Trade who shall promptly furnish to each participant in the Uruguay Round of Multilateral Trade Negotiations a certified copy thereof.

DONE at [.........] this [.........] day of [.....] one thousand nine hundred and ninety-four in a single copy, in the English, French and Spanish languages, each text being authentic.

PART II

AGREEMENT ESTABLISHING THE WORLD TRADE ORGANISATION

The *Parties* to this Agreement,

Recognizing that their relations in the field of trade and economic endeavour should be conducted with a view to raising standards of living, ensuring full employment and a large and steadily growing volume of real income and effective demand, and expanding the production and trade in goods and services, while allowing for the optimal use of the world's resources in accordance with the objective of sustainable development, seeking both to protect and preserve the environment and enhance the means for doing so in a manner consistent with their respective needs and concerns at different levels of economic development,

Recognizing further that there is need for positive efforts designed to ensure that developing countries, and especially the least developed among them, secure a share in the growth in international trade commensurate with the needs of their economic development,

Being desirous of contributing to these objectives by entering into reciprocal and mutually advantageous arrangements directed to the substantial reduction of tariffs and other barriers to trade and to the elimination of discriminatory treatment in international trade relations,

Resolved, therefore, to develop an integrated, more viable and durable multilateral trading system encompassing the General Agreement on Tariffs and Trade, the results of past trade liberalization efforts, and all of the results of the Uruguay Round of multilateral trade negotiations,

PART I

FINAL ACT EMBODYING THE RESULTS OF THE URUGUAY ROUND OF MULTILATERAL TRADE NEGOTIATIONS

1. Having met in order to conclude the Uruguay Round of Multilateral Trade Negotiations, the representatives of the Governments and of the European Communities, members of the Trade Negotiations Committee (hereinafter referred to as "participants"), *agree* that the Agreement Establishing the **World Trade Organisation** and the Ministerial Declarations and Decisions, as set out in the annexes attached hereto (hereinafter referred to as "instruments"), embody the results of their negotiations and form an integral part of this Final Act.

2. By adopting the present Final Act, participants *agree*

(a) to adopt the Ministerial Declarations and Decisions; and

(b) to submit, as appropriate, the Agreement Establishing the **World Trade Organisation** for the consideration of their respective competent authorities with a view to seeking approval of this Agreement in accordance with appropriate procedures of the participant concerned.

3. Participants *agree* on the desirability of acceptance of the Agreement Establishing the **World Trade Organisation** by all participants with a view to its entry into force as early as possible and not later than [1 July 1995]. Not later than [early 1995], Ministers will meet, in accordance with the final paragraph of the Punta del Este Ministerial Declaration, to decide on the international implementation of the results including the timing of their entry into force.

4. Participants *agree* that the Agreement Establishing the **World Trade Organisation** shall be open for acceptance as a whole, by signature or otherwise, by all participants in the Uruguay Round of Multilateral Trade Negotiations pursuant to Article XIV of the Agreement Establishing the **World Trade Organisation**. The acceptance and entry into force of a Plurilateral Trade Agreement, included in Annex 4 of the Agreement Establishing the **World Trade Organisation**, shall be governed by the provisions of that Agreement.

5. Before accepting the Agreement Establishing the **World Trade Organisation**, participants who are not contracting parties to the GATT 1947

Determined to preserve the basic principles and to further the objectives underlying this multilateral trading system,

Agree as follows :

Article I
Establishment of the Organization

The **World Trade Organisation** (hereinafter referred to as "the WTO ") is hereby established.

Article II
Scope of the WTO

1. The WTO shall provide the common institutional framework for the conduct of trade relations among its Members in matters related to the agreements and associated legal instruments included in the Annexes to this Agreement.

2. The agreements and associated legal instruments included in Annexes 1, 2 and 3 (hereinafter referred to as "Multilateral Trade Agreements") are integral parts of this Agreement, binding on all Members.

3. The agreements and associated legal instruments included in Annex 4 (hereinafter referred to as 'Plurilateral Trade Agreements") are also part of this Agreement for those Members that have accepted them, and are binding on those Members. 'The Plurilateral Trade Agreements do not create either obligations or rights for Members that have not accepted them.

4. The General Agreement on Tariffs and Trade in Annex IA (hereinafter referred to as "GATT 1994") is legally distinct from the General Agreement on Tariffs and Trade, dated 30 October 1947, as subsequently rectified, amended or modified (hereinafter referred to as "GATT 1947").

Article III
Functions of the WTO

1. The WTO shall facilitate the implementation, administration, operation, and further the objectives, of this Agreement and of the Multilateral Trade Agreements, and shall also provide the framework for the implementation, administration and operation of the Plurilateral Trade Agreements.

2. The WTO shall provide the forum for negotiations among its Members concerning their multilateral trade relations in matters dealt with under the agreements in the annexes to this Agreement. The WTO may also provide a forum for further negotiations among its Members concerning their multilateral trade, relations and a framework for the implementation of the results of such negotiations, as may be decided by the Ministerial Conference.

3. The WTO shall administer the Understanding on Rules and Procedures Governing the Settlement of Disputes in Annex 2 to this Agreement.

4. The WTO shall administer the Trade Policy Review Mechanism provided for in Annex 3 to this Agreement.

5. With a view to achieving greater coherence in global economic policy-making, the WTO shall cooperate, as appropriate, with the International Monetary Fund and with the International Bank for Reconstruction and Development and its affiliated agencies.

Article IV
Structure of the WTO

1. There shall be a Ministerial Conference composed of representatives of all the Members, which shall meet at least once every two years. The Ministerial Conference shall carry out the functions of the WTO, and take actions necessary to this effect. The Ministerial Conference shall have the authority to take decisions on all matters under any of the Multilateral Trade Agreements, if so requested by a Member, in accordance with the specific requirements for decision-making in this Agreement and in any Multilateral Trade Agreement.

2. There shall be a General Council composed of representatives of all the Members, which shall meet as appropriate. In the intervals between meetings of the Ministerial Conference, its functions shall be conducted by the General Council. The General Council shall also carry out the functions assigned to it by this Agreement. The General Council shall establish its rules of procedure and approve the rules of procedure for the Committees provided for in paragraph 7.

3. The General Council shall convene as appropriate to discharge the responsibilities of the dispute Settlement Body provided for in the Understanding on Rules and Procedures Governing the Settlement of Disputes in Annex 2. The Dispute Settlement Body may have its own chairman and shall establish such rules of procedure as it deems necessary for the fulfilment of those responsibilities.

4. The General Council shall convene as appropriate to discharge the responsibilities of the Trade Policy Review Body provided for in the Trade Policy Review Mechanism in Annex 3. The Trade Policy Review Body may have its own chairman and shall establish such rules of procedure as it deems necessary for the fulfilment of those responsibilities.

5. There shall be a Council for Trade in Goods, a Council for Trade in Services and a Council for Trade-Related Aspects of Intellectual Property Rights (TRIPs), which shall operate under the general guidance of the

General Council. The Council for Trade in Goods shall oversee the functioning of the Multilateral Trade Agreements in Annex 1A, the Council for Trade in Services shall oversee the functioning of the Multilateral Trade Agreement in Annex 1B, and the Council for Trade-Related Aspects of Intellectual Property Rights shall oversee the functioning of the Multilateral Trade Agreement in Annex 1C. These Councils shall carry out the functions assigned to them by their respective agreements and by the General Council. They shall establish their respective rules of procedure subject to the approval of the General Council. Membership in these Councils shall be open to representatives of all Members. These Councils shall meet as necessary to carry out their functions.

6. The Council for Trade in Goods, the Council for Trade in Services and the Council for Trade-Related Aspects of Intellectual Property Rights shall establish subsidiary bodies as required. These subsidiary bodies shall establish their respective rules of procedure subject to the approval of their respective Councils.

7. The Ministerial Conference shall establish a Committee on Trade and Development, a Committee on Balance-of-Payments Restrictions and a Committee on Budget, Finance and Administration, which shall carry out the functions assigned to them by this Agreement and by the Multilateral Trade Agreements, and any additional functions assigned to them by the General Council, and may establish such additional Committees with such functions as it may deem appropriate. As part of its functions, the Committee on Trade and Development shall periodically review the special provisions in the Multilateral Trade Agreements in favour of the least-developed countries Members and report to the General Council for appropriate action. Membership in these Committees shall be open to representatives of all Members.

8. The bodies provided for under the Plurilateral Trade Agreements shall carry out the functions assigned to them under those Agreements and shall operate within the institutional framework of the WTO. These bodies shall keep the General Council informed of their activities on a regular basis.

Article V

1. The General Council shall make appropriate arrangements for effective cooperation with other intergovernmental organizations that have responsibilities related to those of the WTO

2. The General Council may make appropriate arrangements for consultation and cooperation with non-governmental organizations concerned with matters related to those of the WTO

Article VI

1. There is established a Secretariat of the WTO headed by a Director-General.

2. The Ministerial Conference shall appoint the Director-General and adopt regulations setting out the powers, duties, conditions of service and terms of office of the Director-General.

3. The Director-General shall appoint the members of the staff of the Secretariat and determine their duties and conditions of service in accordance with regulations adopted by the Ministerial Conference.

4. The responsibilities Of the Director-General and the staff of the Secretariat shall be exclusively international in character. In the discharge of their duties. the Director-General and the staff of the Secretariat shall not seek or accept instructions from any government or any other authority external to the WTO They shall refrain from any action which might adversely reflect on their position as international officials. The Members of the WTO shall respect the international character of the responsibilities of the Director-General and the staff of the Secretariat and shall not seek to influence them in the discharge of their duties.

Article VII
Budget and Contributions

1. The Director-General shall present to the Committee on Budget, Finance and Administration the annual budget estimate and financial statement of the WTO The Committee on Budget, Finance and Administration shall review the annual budget estimate and the financial statement presented by the Director-General and make recommendations thereon to the General Council. The annual budget estimates shall be subject to approval by the General Council.

2. The Committee on Budget, Finance and Administration shall propose to the General Council financial regulations which shall include provisions setting out:

(a) the scale of contributions apportioning the expenses of the WTO among its Members; and

(b) the measures to be taken in respect of Members in arrears.

The financial regulations shall be based, as far as practicable, on the regulations and practices of the GATT 1947.

3. The General Council shall adopt the financial regulations and the annual budget estimates by a two-thirds majority comprising more than half of the Members of the WTO

4. Each Member shall promptly contribute to the WTO its share in the expenses of the WTO in accordance with the financial regulations adopted by the General Council.

Article VIII
Status of the WTO

1. The WTO shall have legal personality, and shall be accorded by each of its Members such legal capacity as may be necessary for the exercise of its functions.

2. The WTO shall be accorded by each of its Members such privileges and immunities as are necessary for the exercise of its functions.

3. The officials of the WTO and the representatives of the Members shall similarly be accorded by each of its Members such privileges and immunities as are necessary for the independent exercise of their functions in connection with the WTO.

4. The privileges and immunities to be accorded by a Member to the WTO, its officials, and the representatives of its Members shall be similar to the privileges and immunities stipulated in the Convention on the Privileges and Immunities of the Specialized Agencies, approved by the General Assembly of the United Nations on 21 November 1947.

5. The WTO may conclude a headquarters agreement.

Article IX
Decision-Making

1. The WTO shall continue the practice of decision-making by consensus followed under the GATT 1947.[1] Except as otherwise provided, where a decision cannot be arrived at by consensus, the matter at issue shall be decided by voting. At meetings of the Ministerial Conference and the General Council, each Member of the WTO shall have one vote. Where the European Communities exercise their right to vote, they shall have a number of votes equal to the number of their Member States[2] which are Members of the WTO Decisions of the Ministerial Conference and the General Council shall be taken by a majority of the votes cast, unless otherwise provided in this Agreement or the Multilateral Trade Agreements.[3]

2. The Ministerial Conference and the General Council shall have the exclusive authority to adopt interpretations of this Agreement and of the Multilateral Trade Agreements. In the case of an interpretation of a Multilateral

---

[1] The body concerned shall be deemed to have decided by consensus on a matter submitted for its consideration, if no Member, present at the meeting where the decision is taken, formally objects to the proposed decision.

[2] The number of votes of the European Communities and their Member States shall in no case exceed the number of the Member States of the European Communities.

[3] Decisions by the General Council when convened as the Dispute Settlement Body shall be made only in accordance with the provisions of paragraph 2.4 of the Understanding on Rules and Procedures Governing the Settlement of Disputes.

Trade Agreement in Annex 1, they shall exercise their authority on the basis of a recommendation by the Council overseeing the functioning of that Agreement. The decision to adopt an interpretation shall be taken by a three-fourths majority of the Members. This paragraph shall not be used in a manner that would undermine the amendment provisions in Article X.

3. In exceptional circumstances, the Ministerial Conference[4] may decide to waive an obligation imposed on a Member by this Agreement or any of the Multilateral Trade Agreements; provided that any such decision shall be approved by three-fourths[5] of the Members.

(i) A request for a waiver concerning this Agreement shall be submitted to the Ministerial Conference for consideration pursuant to the practice of decision-making by consensus. The Ministerial Conference shall establish a time-period which shall not exceed ninety days to consider the request. If consensus is not reached during the time period, any decision to grant a waiver shall be taken by three-fourths of the Members.

(ii) A request for a waiver concerning the Multilateral Trade Agreements in Annexes 1A or 1B or 1C and their annexes, shall be submitted initially to the Councils for Trade in Goods, the Council for Trade in Services or the Council for TRIPs, respectively, for consideration during a time-period which shall not exceed ninety days. At the end of the time period, the relevant Council shalf submit a report to the Ministerial Conference.

4. A decision by Ministerial Conference granting a waiver shall state the exceptional circumstances justifying the decision, the terms and conditions governing the application of the waiver, and the date on which the waiver shall terminate. Any waiver granted for a period of more than one year shall be reviewed by the Ministerial Conference not later than one year after it is granted, and thereafter annuallly until the waiver terminates. In each review, the Ministerial Conference shall examine whether the exceptional circumstances justifying the waiver still exist and whether the terms and conditions attached to the waiver have been met. The Ministerial Conference, on the basis of the annual review, may extend, modify or terminate the waiver.

5. Decisions under a Plurilateral Trade Agreement, including any decision on interpretations and waivers, shall be governed by the provisions of that Agreement.

---

[4] References to the Ministerial Conference include the General Council.

[5] A decision to grant a waiver in respect of any obligation subject to a transition period or a period for staged implementation that the requesting Member has not performed by the end of the relevant period, shall be made only by consensus.

Article X
Amendments

1. Any Member of the WTO may initiate a proposal to amend the provisions of this Agreement or the Multilateral Trade Agreements in Annex 1 by submitting such proposal to the Ministerial Conference.[6] The Councils listed in Article IV may also submit to the Ministerial Conference proposals to amend the provisions of the corresponding Multilateral Trade Agreements in Annex 1 whose functioning they oversee. For a period of ninety days after the proposal has been tabled formally at the Ministerial Conference, unless the Ministerial Conference decides on a longer period, any decision by the Ministerial Conference to submit the proposed amendment to the Members for acceptance shall be taken by consensus. Unless the provisions of paragraphs 2, 5 or 6 apply, that decision shall specify whether the provisions of paragraphs 3 or 4 shall apply. If consensus is reached the Ministerial Conference shall forthwith submit the proposed amendment to the Members for acceptance. if consensus is not reached at a meeting of the Ministerial Conference within the established period, the Ministerial Conference shall decide by a two-thirds majority of the Members whether to submit the proposed amendment to the Members for acceptance. Except as provided in paragraphs 2, 5 and 6, the provisions of paragraph 3 shall apply to the proposed amendment, unless the Ministerial Conference decides by a three-fourths majority of the Members that the provisions of paragraph 4 shall apply.

2. Amendments to the provisions of this Article and to the provisions of the following enumerated Articles shall take effect only upon acceptance by all Members :

Article IX of this Agreement;

Articles I and II of the GATT 1994, in Annex IA;

Article II : 1 of the General Agreement on Trade in Services, in Annex 1B,

Article 4 of the Agreement on Trade-Related Aspects of Intellectual Property Rights, including Trade in Counterfeit Goods, in Annex 1C.

3. Amendments to provision of this Agreement, or the Multilateral Trade Agreements in Annexes IA and 1 C, other than those listed in paragraphs 2 and 6. of a nature that would alter the rights and obligations of the Members, shall take effect for the Members that have accepted them upon acceptance by two-thirds of the Members and thereafter for each other Member upon acceptance by it. The Ministerial Conference may decide by a

---

[6] References to the Ministerial Conference include the General Council.

three-fourths majority of the Members that any amendment made effective under this paragraph is of such a nature that any Member which has not accepted it within a period specified by the Ministerial Conference in each case. shall be free to withdraw from the WTO or to remain a Member with the consent of the Ministerial Conference.

4. Amendments to provisions of this Agreement or the Multilateral Trade Agreements in Annexes IA and IC, other than those listed in paragraphs 2 and 6, of a nature that would not alter the rights and obligations of the Members, shall take effect for all Members upon acceptance by two-thirds of the Members.

5. Except as provided in paragraph 2 above, amendments to Parts I, II and III of the General Agreement on Trade in Services, in Annex lB, and the respective annexes shall take effect for the Members that have accepted them upon acceptance by two-thirds of the Members and thereafter for each Member upon acceptance by it. The Ministerial Conference may decide by a three-fourths majority of the Members that any amendment made effective under the preceding provision is of such a nature that any Member which has not accepted it within a period specified by the Ministerial Conference in each case shall be free to withdraw from the WTO or to remain a Member with the consent of the Ministerial Conference. Amendments to Parts IV, V and VI of the General Agreement on Trade in Services, in Annex lB, and the respective annexes shall take effect for all Members upon acceptance by two-thirds of the Members.

6. Notwithstanding the other provisions of this Article, amendments to the Agreement on Trade-Related Aspects of Intellectual Property Rights, including Trade in Counterfeit Goods, in Annex 1C, meeting the requirements of Article 71, paragraph 2, of that Agreement may be adopted by the Ministerial Conference without further formal acceptance process.

7. Any Member accepting an amendment to this Agreement or a Multilateral Trade Agreement in Annex 1 shall deposit an instrument of acceptance with the Director-General of the WTO within the period of acceptance specified by the Ministerial Conference.

8. Any Member of the WTO may initiate a proposal to amend the provisions of the Multilateral Trade Agreements in Annexes 2 and 3 by submitting such proposal to the Ministerial Conference. The decision to approve amendments to the Multilateral Trade Agreement in Annex 2 shall be made by consensus and these amendments shall take effect for all Members upon approval by the Ministerial Conference. Decisions to approve amendments to the Multilateral Trade Agreement in Annex 3 shall take effect for all Members upon approval by the Ministerial Conference.

9. The Ministerial Conference, upon the request of the Members parties to a trade Agreement, may decide exclusively by consensus to add that Agreement to Annex 4. The Ministerial Conference, upon the request of the Members parties to a Plurilateral Trade Agreement in Annex 4, may decide to delete that Agreement from Annex 4.

10. Amendments to a Plurilateral Trade Agreement in Annex 4 shall be governed by the provisions of that Agreement.

Article XI

Original Membership

1. The contracting parties to the GATT 1947 as of the date of entry into force of this Agreement and the European Communities which accept this Agreement and the Multilateral Trade Agreements and for which Schedules of Concessions and Commitments are annexed to the GATT 1994 and for which Schedules of Specific Commitments are annexed to the General Agreement on Trade in Services in Annex lB shall become original Members of the WTO

2. The least developed countries recognized as such by the United Nations will only be required to undertake commitments and concessions to the extent consistent with their individual development, financial and trade needs or their administrative and institutional capabilities.

Article XII

Accession

1. Any state or separate customs territory possessing full autonomy in the conduct of its external commercial relations and of the other matters provided for in this Agreement and the Multilateral Trade Agreements may accede to this Agreement, on terms to be agreed between it and the WTO Such accession shall apply to this Agreement and the Multilateral Trade Agreements annexed thereto.

2. Decisions on accession shall be taken by the Ministerial Conference. The Ministerial Conference shall approve the agreement on the terms of accession by a two-thirds majority of the Members of the WTO

3. Accession to a Plurilateral Trade Agreement shall be governed by the provisions of that Agreement.

Article XIII

Non-Application of Multilateral Trade Agreements between Particular Members

1. This Agreement and the Multilateral Trade Agreements in Annexes 1

and 2 shall not apply as between any Member and any other Member if either of the Members, at the time either becomes a Member, does not consent to such application.

2. Paragraph 1 may be invoked between original Members of the WTO who were Contracting parties to the General Agreement on Tariffs and Trade 1947 only where Article XXXV of that Agreement had been invoked earlier and was effective as between those contracting parties at the time of entry into force for them of this Agreement.

3. Paragraph 1 shall apply between a Member and another Member which accedes under Article XII only if the Member not consenting to the application has so notified the Ministerial Conference before the approval of the agreement on the terms of accession by the Ministerial Conference.

4. The Ministerial Conference may review the operation of this Article in particular cases at the request of any Member and make appropriate recommendations.

5. Non-application of a Plurilateral Trade Agreement between parties to that Agreement shall be governed by the provisions of that Agreement.

Article XIV

Acceptance, Entry into Force and Deposit

1. This Agreement shall be open for acceptance, by signature or otherwise, by contracting parties to the GATT 1947 and the European Communities which are eligible to become original Members of the WTO in accordance with Article X1 of this Agreement. Such acceptance shall apply to this Agreement and the Multilateral Trade Agreements annexed thereto.

This Agreement and the Multilateral Trade Agreements annexed thereto shall enter into force on the date determined by Ministers in accordance with paragraph 3 of the Final Act Embodying the Results of the Uruguay Round of Multilateral Trade Negotiations and shall remain open for acceptance for a period of two years following that date unless the Ministers decide otherwise. An acceptance following the entry into force of this Agreement shall enter into force on the thirtieth day following the deposit of the instrument of acceptance.

2. A Member which accepts this Agreement after its entry into force shall implement those concessions and obligations in the Multilateral Trade Agreements that are to be implemented over a period of time starting with the entry into force of this Agreement as if it had accepted this Agreement on the date of its entry into force.

3. Until the entry into force of this Agreement, the text of this Agreement and the Multilateral Trade Agreements shall be deposited with the Director-

General to the CONTRACTING PARTIES to the GATT 1947. The Director-General shall promptly furnish a certified true copy of this Agreement and the Multilateral Trade Agreements, and a notification of each acceptance thereof, to each signatory of this Agreement. This Agreement and the Multilateral Trade Agreements, and any amendments thereto, shall, upon the entry into force of this Agreement, be deposited with the Director-General of the WTO

4. The acceptance and entry into force of a Plurilateral Trade Agreement shall be governed by the provisions of that Agreement. Such Agreements shall be deposited with the Director-General of the WTO.

Article XV
Withdrawal

1. Any Member may withdraw from this Agreement. Such withdrawal shall apply both to this Agreement and the Multilateral Trade Agreements and shall take effect upon the expiration of six months from the date on which written notice of withdrawal is received by the Director-General of the WTO.

2. Withdrawal from a Plurilateral Trade Agreement shall be governed by the provisions of that Agreement.

Article XVI
Miscellaneous Provisions

1. Except as otherwise provided for under this Agreement or the Multilateral Trade Agreements, the WTO shall be guided by the decisions, procedures and customary practices followed by the CONTRACTING PARTIES of the GATT 1947 and the bodies established in the framework of the GATT 1947.

2. To the extent practicable, the Secretariat of the GATT 1947 shall become the Secretariat of the WTO, and the Director-General to the CONTRACTING PARTIES to the GATT 1947, until such time as the Ministerial Conference has appointed a Director-General in accordance with Article VI:2 of this Agreement, shall serve as Director-General of the MTO.

3. In the event of a conflict between the provisions of this Agreement and the provisions of any of the Multilateral Trade Agreements, the provisions of this Agreement shall prevail.

4. Each Member shall ensure the conformity of its laws, regulations and administrative procedures with its obligations as provided in the annexed Agreements.

5. No reservations may be made in respect of any provisions of this Agreement. Reservations in respect of any of the provisions of the Multilateral Trade Agreements may only be made in accordance with the provisions set

out in those Agreements. Reservations in respect of a provision of a Plurilateral Trade Agreement shall be governed by the provisions of that Agreement.

6. This Agreement shall be registered in accordance with the provisions of Article 102 of the Charter of the United Nations.

Done at – this – day of – one thousand nine hundred and ninety –, in a single copy, in the English, French and Spanish languages, each text being authentic.

ANNEXES

Annex 1A

General interpretative note to Annex 1A :

In the event of conflict between a provision of the General Agreement on Tariffs and Trade 1994 and a provision of another agreement in Annex IA, the provision of the other agreement shall take precedence to the extent of the conflict.

1. General Agreement on Tariffs and Trade 1994

The General Agreement on Tariffs and Trade 1994 (hereinafter referred to as GATT 1994) consisting of:

(a) The provisions in the General Agreement on Tariffs and Trade dated 30 October 1947 annexed to the Final Act of the second session of the Preparatory Committee of the United Nations Conference on Trade and Employment (excluding the Protocol of Provisional Application), as rectified, amended or otherwise modified by the terms of legal instruments which have entered into force before the date of entry into force of the Agreement Establishing the **World Trade Organisation** Agreement are hereby made an integral part of this Annex.

(b) The provisions of the legal instruments that have entered into force under the GATT 1947 before the date of entry into force of the Agreement Establishing the WTO as set forth below:

i. protocols and certifications relating to tariff concessions;

ii. protocols of accession [excluding the provisions (a) concerning

---

Explanatory Notes:

The terms ' country' or ' countries' as used in this Agreement and the Multilateral Trade Agreements are to be understood to include any separate custom territory Member of the WTO.

In the case of a separate customs territory Member of the WTO where an expression in this Agreement and the Multilateral Trade Agreements is qualified by the term 'national', such expression shall be read as pertaining to that customs territory, unless otherwise specified.

provisional application and providing that Part 11 of the GATT 1947 shall be applied provisionally to the fullest extent not inconsistent with legislation existing on the date of the Protocol];

iii. waivers granted under Article XXV of the GATT 1947 and still in force on the date of entry into force of the Agreement Establishing the WTO ; and

iv. other decisions of the CONTRACTING PARTIES to the GATT 1947.

(c) The Understandings set out in sub-paragraphs (i) through (vii) below shall be deemed to be an integral part of the GATT 1994.

---

[7] Waivers covered by this provision are the following: 1. Argentina (Establishment of a new Schedule XIV, L/7271. 31.12.93); 2. Australia (Base dates under Article I:4. BISD 9S/46, no time-limit); 3. Australia (Treatment of Products of Papua New Guinea. BISD 8S/28, no time-limit); 4. Australia (Tariff preference for less developed countries, BISD 14S/23, no time-limit); 5. Bangladesh (Establishment of a new Schedule LXX, L/7272, 31.12.93); 6. Bolivia (Renegotiation of Schedule LXXXIV, L/7151.31.12.93); 7. Brazil (Establishment of a new Schedule III. L/72 73, 31.12.93); 8. Canada (CARIBBEAN, BISD 33S/97. 15.6.98); 9. Chile (Establishment of a new Schedule VII. L/7274, 31.12.93); 10. Cuba (Provisions of Article XV:6 BISD 13S/23, no time-limit); 11. Egypt (Renegotiation of Schedule LXIII; L/7281, 31.12.93); 12. European Coal and Steel Community (Waiver granted in connection with the ECSC, BISD 1S/17, no time-limit); 13. European Communities (Transitional measures to take account of the external economic impact of German unification, L/7246, 31.12.93); 14. France (Trading Arrangements with Morocco. BISD 9S/39, no time-limit); 15. Israel (Establishment of a new Schedule XLII, L/7275, 31.12.93); 16. Jamaica (Margins of preference, BISD 18S/33, no time-limit); 17. Jamaica (Establishment of a new Schedule LXVI, L/7291, 31.7.94); 18. Malawi (Base dates under Article I:4, BISD 9S/46, no time-limit); 19. Malawi (Renegotiation of Schedule LVIII, L/7152, 31.12.93); 20. Mexico (Establishment of a new Schedule LXXVII, L/7275, 31.12.93); 21. Morocco (Establishment of a new Schedule LXXXI, 7277, 31.12.93); 22. Pakistan (Establishment of a new Schedule XV, L/7278. 31.12.93); 23. Peru (Establishment of a new Schedule XXXV, LF/245, 31.12.93); 24. Senegal (Renegotiation of Schedule XLIX, L/7282, 31.12.93); 25. South Africa (Base dates under Article I:4. BISD 9S/46. no time-limit; 26. Sri Lanka (Establishment of a new Schedule VI. L/7279, 31.12.93); 27. Trinidad and Tobago (Establishment of a new Schedule LXVII, L/7290, 31.7.94); 28. United Kingdo.n (Items traditionally admitted free of duty from countries of the Commonwealth, BISD 3S/25, no time-limit); 29. United Kingdom (Special problems of dependent overseas territories, BISD 3S/21, no time-limit); 30. United States (Waiver in respect of products of the Trust Territory of Pacific Islands, BISD Vol. II, page 9, no time-limit); 31. United States (Imports of Automotive Products, BISD 14S/37, no time-limit); 32. United States (Caribbean Basin Economic Recovery Act. BISD 31S/20, 30.9.95); 33. United States (Andean Trade Preference Act. L/6961, 4.12.2001); 34. Uruguay (Renegotiation of Schedule XXXI, LF/280, 31.12.93); 35. Venezuela (Establishment of a new Schedule LXXXVI, L/7316, 30.6.94); 36. Zaire (Renegotiation of Schedule LXVIII L/7283, 31.12.93); 37. Zambia (Renegotiation of Schedule LXXVIII, L/7329, 30.11.95); 38. Zimbabwe (Customs treatment for products of United Kingdom territories, BISD 9S/47, no time-limit); 39. Zimbabwe (Bace dates under Article I:4, BISD 9S/46, no time-limit). This list will be modified to take into account waivers granted under the GATT 1947 up to the date of entry into force of this Agreement and waivers hereby listed which will have expired by that time.

i. Understanding on the Interpretation of Article III(b) of the General Agreement on Tariffs and Trade (text)

ii. Understanding on the Interpretation of Article XVII of the General Agreement on Tariffs and Trade (text)

iii. Understanding on Balance-of-Payments Provisions of the General Agreement on Tariffs and Trade (text)

iv. Understanding on the Interpretation of Article XXIV of the General Agreement on Tariffs and Trade (text)

v. Understanding in respect of waivers of obligations under the General Agreement on Tariffs and Trade (text)

vi. Understanding on the Interpretation of Article XXVIII of the General Agreement on Tariffs and Trade (text)

vii. Understanding on the Interpretation of Article XXXV of the General Agreement on Tariffs and Trade (text).

(d) Explanatory Notes:

i. The references to "contracting party' in the provisions of the GATT 1994 shall be deemed to read "Member". The references to "less-developed contracting party" and "developed contracting party" shall be deemed to read "developing country Member" and "developed country Member". The references to "Executive Secretary" shall be deemed to read "Director-General of the WTO"

ii. The references to the CONTRACTING PARTIES acting jointly in Articles XV: 1, XV:2, XV:8, XXXVIII and the Notes and Article XII and XVIII; and in the provisions on special exchange agreements in Articles XV:2, XV:3 XV:6, XV:7 and XV:9 of the GATT 1994 shall be deemed to be references to the. WTO The other functions that the provisions of the GATT 1994 assign to the CONTRACTING PARTIES acting jointly shall be allocated by the Ministerial Conference.

e. i. The provisions of Part 1I of the GATT 1994 shall not apply to measures taken by a Member under specific mandatory legislation, enacted by that Member before it became a contracting party to the GATT 1947, that prohibits the use, sale or lease of foreign-built or foreign-reconstructed vessels in commercial applications between points in national waters or the waters of an exclusive economic zone. This exemption applies to: (a) the continuation or prompt renewal of a non-conforming provision of such legislation; and (b) the amendment to a non-conforming provision of such legislation to the extent that the amendment does not decrease the conformity of the provision with Part II of the GATT 1947. This exemption is limited to measures taken under legislation described above that is notified and specified prior to the entry into force of the Agreement Establishing the WTO. If such legislation is subsequently modified to decrease its conformity with Part II of the GATT 1994, it will no longer qualify for coverage under this paragraph.

ii. The Ministerial Conference shall review this exemption not later than five years after the entry into force of the Agreement Establishing the WTO and thereafter every two years for as long as the exemption is in force for the purpose of examining whether the conditions which created the need for the exemption still prevail.

iii. A Member whose measures are covered by this exemption shall annually submit a detailed statistical notification consisting of a five-year moving average of actual and expected deliveries of relevant vessels as well as additional information on the use, sale, lease or repair of relevant vessels covered by this exemption.

iv. A Member that considers that this exemption operates in such a manner as to justify a reciprocal and proportionate limitation on the use, sale, lease or repair of vessels constructed in the territory of the Member invoking the exemption shall be free to introduce such a limitation subject to prior notification to the Ministerial Conference.

v. This exemption is without prejudice to solutions concerning specific aspects of the legislation covered by this exemption negotiated in sectoral agreements or in other fora.

2. The Uruguay Round Protocol to the General Agreement on Tariffs and Trade 1994 shall also be deemed to be an integral part of the GATT 1994 (text)

3. Agreement on Agriculture (text)

4. Agreement on Sanitary and Phytosanitary Measures (text)

5. Agreement on Textiles and Clothing (text)

6. Agreement on Technical Barriers to Trade (text)

7. Agreement as Trade-Related Aspects of Investment Measures (text)

8. Agreement on Implementation of Article VI of the General Agreement on Tariffs and Trade (text)

9. Agreement on Implementation of Article VII of the General Agreement on Tariffs and Trade (text)

10. Agreement on Preshipment Inspection (text)

11. Agreement on Rules of Origin (text)

12. Agreement on Import Licensing Procedures (text)

13. Agreement on Subsidies and Countervailing Measures (text)

14. Agreement on Safeguards (text).

Annex lB

General Agreement on Trade in Services (text) *Annex IC*

Annex 1C

Agreement on Trade-Related Aspects of Intellectual Property Rights, Including Trade in Counterfeit Goods (text)

Annex 2

Understanding on Rules and Procedures Covering the Settlement of Disputes (text)

Annex 3

Trade Policy Review Mechanism (text)

Annex 4

Agreement on Trade in Civil Aircraft (text)

Agreement on Government Procurement (text)

International Dairy Arrangement (text)

Arrangement Regarding Bovine Meat (text).

GATT 1994

GENERAL AGREEMENT ON TARIFFS AND TRADE 1994

URUGUAY ROUND AGREEMENTS ON TRADE IN GOODS (ANNEX IA)

The following Agreements, Understandings, Decisions, the texts of which are set out below, are an integral part of the Uruguay Round Agreements.

UNDERSTANDING ON THE INTERPRETATION ON ARTICLE III : 1 (B) OF THE GENERAL AGREEMENT ON TARIFFS AND TRADE 1994

1. It is agreed that in order to ensure transparency of the legal rights and obligations deriving from Article 1I:1 (b), the nature and level of any "other duties or charges" levied on bound tariff items, as referred to in that provision, shall be recorded in the Schedules of tariff concessions against the tariff item

to which they apply. It is understood that such recording does not change the legal character of "other duties or charges".

2. The date as of which "other-duties or charges" are bound, for the purposes of Article II, shall be the date of entry into force of the Agreement Establishing the WTO. "Other duties or charges" shall therefore be recorded in the Schedules of concessions at the levels applying on this date. At each subsequent renegotiation of a concession or negotiation of a new concession the applicable date for the tariff item in question shall become the date of the incorporation of the new concession in the Schedules of concessions. However, the date of the instrument by which a concession on any particular tariff item was first incorporated into the GATT 1947 or GATT 1994 shall also continue to be recorded in column 6 of the loose-leaf Schedules.

3. "Other duties or charges" shall be recorded in respect of all tariff bindings.

4. Where a tariff item has previously been the subject of a concession, the level of "other duties or charges" recorded in the Schedules of concessions shall not be higher than the level obtaining at the time of the first incorporation of the concession in the Schedules. It will be open to any Member to challenge the existence of an "other duty or charge", on the ground that no such "other duty or charge" existed at the time of the original binding of the item in question, as well as the consistency of the recorded level of any "other duty or charge" with the previously bound level, for a period of three years after the date of entry into force of the Agreement Establishing the WTO or three years after the date of deposit of the Schedule in question with the Director-General of the WTO, if that is a later date.

5. It is agreed that the recording of "other duties or charges" in the Schedules of concessions is without prejudice to their consistency with rights and obligations under the GATT 1994 other than those affected by paragraph 4 above. All Members retain the right to challenge, at any time, the consistency of any "other duty or charge" with such obligations.

6. For the purposes of this Understanding, the provisions of Articles XXII and XXIII of the GATT 1994 as elaborated and applied by the Understanding on Rules and Procedures Governing the Settlement of Disputes will apply.

7. It is agreed that "other duties or charges" omitted from a Schedule at the time of its deposit with, until the entry into force of the Agreement Establishing the WTO, the Director-General to the CONTRACTING PARTIES to the GATT or, thereafter, with the Director-General of the WTO, shall not subsequently be added to it and that any "other duty or charge" recorded at a level lower than that prevailing on the applicable date shall not be restored to that level unless such additions or changes are made within six months of the deposit of the Schedule.

8. The decision in paragraph 2 above regarding the date applicable to each concession for the purposes of Article 11: l(b) supersedes the decision regarding the applicable date taken by the GATT 1947 Council on 26 March 1980 (BISD 27S/22).

UNDERSTANDING ON THE INTRPRETATION OF ARTICLE XVII OF THE GENERAL AGREEMENT ON TARIFFS AND TRADE 1994

Noting that Article XVII provides for obligations on Members in respect of the activities of the state trading enterprises referred to in Article XVII: 1, which are required to be consistent with the general principles of non-discriminatory treatment prescribed in the GATT 1994 for governmental measures affecting imports or exports by private traders;

Noting further that Members are subject to their GATT 1994 obligations in respect of those governmental measures affecting state trading enterprises;

Recognizing that this Understanding is without prejudice to the substantive disciplines prescribed in Article XVII;

1. It is agreed that in order to ensure the transparency of the activities of state trading enterprises, such enterprises shall be notified to the Council for Trade in Goods, for review by the working party to be set up under paragraph 5 below, in accordance with the following working definition:

> "Governmental and non-governmental enterprises, including marketing boards, which have been granted exclusive or special rights or privileges, including statutory or constitutional powers, in the exercise of which they influence through their purchases or sales the level or direction of imports or exports."

This notification requirement does not apply to imports of products for immediate or ultimate consumption in governmental use or in use by an enterprise as specified above and not otherwise for resale or use in the production of goods for sale.

2. It is agreed that each Member shall conduct a review of its policy with regard to the submission of notifications on state trading enterprises to the Council for Trade in Goods, taking account of the provisions of this Understanding. In carrying out such a review, each Member should have regard to the need to ensure the maximum transparency possible in its notifications so as to permit a clear appreciation of the manner of operation of the enterprises notified and the effect of their operations on international trade.

3. Notifications shall be made in accordance with the 1960 questionnaire on State trading (BISD, 9S/184), it being understood that Members shall

notify the enterprises referred to in paragraph 1 above whether or not imports or exports have in fact taken place.

4. Any Member which has reason to believe that another Member has not adequately met its notification obligation may raise the matter with the Member concerned. If the matter is not satisfactorily resolved it may make a counter-notification to the Council for Trade in Goods, for consideration by the working party set up under paragraph 5 below, simultaneously informing the Member concerned.

5. A working party shall be set up, on behalf of the Council for Trade in Goods, to review notifications and counter-notifications. In the light of this review and without prejudice to Article XVII:4(c), the Council for Trade in Goods may make recommendations with regard to the adequacy of notifications and the need for further information. The working party shall also review, in the light of the notifications received, the adequacy of the 1960 questionnaire on state trading and the coverage of state trading enterprises notified under paragraph 1 above. It shall also develop an illustrative list showing the kinds of relationships between governments and enterprises, and the kinds of activities, engaged in by these enterprises, which may be relevant for the purposes of Article XVII. It is understood that the WTO Secretariat will provide a general background paper for the working party on the operations of state trading enterprises as they relate to international trade. Membership of the working party shall be open to all Members indicating their wish to serve on it. It shall meet within a year of the entry into force of the Agreement Establishing the WTO and thereafter at least once a year. It shall report annually to the Council for Trade in Goods.[8]

UNDERSTANDING ON THE BALANCE-OF-PAYMENTS OF THE GENERAL AGREEMENT ON TARIFFS AND TRADE 1994

Members,

Recognizing the provisions of Articles XII, XVIII.B of the GATT 1994 and of the 1979 Declaration on Trade Measures taken for Balance-of-Payments Purposes (hereafter referred to as the "1979 Declaration") and in order to clarify such provisions[9];

---

[8] The activities of this working party shall be co-ordinated with those of the working group provided for in section III of the Ministerial Decision on Notification Procedures.

[9] Nothing in this Understanding is intended to modify the rights and obligations of Members under Articles XII or XVIII:B of the GATT 1994. The provisions of Articles XXII and XXIII of the GATT 1994 as elaborated and applied by the Understanding on Rules and Procedures Governing the Settlement of Disputes may be invoked with respect to any matters arising from the application of restrictive import measures taken for balance-of-payments reasons.

Hereby agree as follows:

Application of Measures

1. Members confirm their commitment to publicly announce, as soon as possible, time-schedules for the removal of restrictive import measures taken for balance-of-payments purposes. It is understood that such time-schedules may be modified as appropriate to take into account changes in the balance-of payments situation. Wherever a time-schedule is not publicly announced justification shall be provided as to the reasons therefor.

2. Members confirm their commitment to give preference to those measures which have the least disruptive effect on trade. Such measures (hereafter referred to as "price-based measures") shall be understood to include import surcharges, import deposit requirements or other equivalent trade measures with an impact on the price of imported goods. It is understood that, notwithstanding the provisions of Article II, price-based measures taken for balance-of-payments purposes may be applied in excess of the duties inscribed in the schedule of a Member. Furthermore, the amount by which the price-based measure exceeds the bound duty shall be clearly and separately indicated under the notification procedures of this Understanding.

3. Members shall seek to avoid the imposition of new quantitative restrictions for balance-of payments purposes unless, because of a critical balance-of-payments situation, price-based measures cannot arrest a sharp deterioration in the external payments position. In those cases in which a Member applies quantitative restrictions, justification shall be provided as to the reasons why price-based measures are not an adequate instrument to deal with the balance-of-payments situation. A Member maintaining quantitative restrictions shall indicate in successive consultations the progress made in significantly reducing the incidence and restrictive effect of such measures. It is understood that not more than one type of restrictive import measure taken for balance-of-payments reasons may be applied on the same product.

4. Members confirm that restrictive import measures taken for balance-of-payments reasons may only be applied to control the general level of imports and may not exceed what is necessary to address the balance-of-payments situation. In order to minimise any incidental protective effects, restrictions shall be administered in a transparent manner. The authorities of the importing Member shall provide adequate justification as to the criteria used to determine which products are subject to restriction. As provided in Articles XII:3 and XVIII:B: 10, Members may, in the case of certain essential products, exclude or limit the application of surcharges applied across the board or other measures applied for balance-of-payments reasons. The term essential products shall be understood to mean products which meet basic

consumption needs or which contribute to the Member's effort to improve its balance-of payments situation, such as capital goods or inputs needed for production. In the administration of quantitative restrictions, discretionary licensing shall be used only when unavoidable and be progressively phased out. Appropriate justification shall be provided as to the criteria used to determine allowable import quantities or values.

Procedures for Balance-of-Payments Consultations

5. The Committee on Balance-of-Payments Restrictions (hereafter referred to as "Committee") shall carry out consultations in order to review all restrictive import measures taken for balance-of payments purposes. The membership of the Committee is open to all Members indicating their wish to serve in it. The Committee shall follow the procedures for consultations on balance-of-payments restrictions approved by the GATT 1947 Council on 28 April 1970 and set out in BISD, Eighteenth Supplement, pages 48-53 (hereafter referred to as "Full consultation Procedures"), subject to the provisions set out below.

6. A Member applying new restrictions or raising the general level of its existing restrictions by a substantial intensification of the measures shall enter into consultations with the Committee within four months of the adoption of such measures. The Member adopting such measures may request that a consultation be held under Article XII:4(a) or Article XVIII: 12(a) as appropriate. If no such request has been made, the Chairman of the Committee shall invite the Member to hold such consultation. Factors that may be examined in the consultation would include, *inter alia,* the introduction of new types of restrictive measures for balance-of-payments purposes, or an increase in the level or product coverage of restrictions.

7. All restrictions applied for balance-of-payments purposes shall be subject to periodic review in the Committee under paragraph 4(b) of Article XII or under paragraph 12(b) of Article XVIII, subject to the possibility of altering the periodicity of consultations in agreement with the consulting Member or pursuant to any specific review procedure that may be recommended by the General Council.

8. Consultations may be held under simplified procedures in the case of least-developed country Members or in the case of developing country Members which are pursuing liberalisation efforts in conformity with the schedule presented to the Committee in previous consultations. Simplified consultations may also be held when the Trade Policy Review of a developing country Member is scheduled for the same calendar year as the date fixed for the consultations. In such cases the decision as to whether a full consultation should be held will be made on the basis of the factors enumerated in

paragraph 8 of the 1979 Declaration. Except in the case of least-developed country Members, no more than two successive consultations may be held under simplified procedures.

Notification and Documentation

9. A Member shall notify to the General Council the introduction of or any changes in the application of restrictive import measures taken for balance-of-payments purposes as well as any modifications in time schedules for the removal of such measures as announced under paragraph 1. Significant changes shall be notified to the General Council prior to or not later than 30 days after their announcement. A consolidated notification, including all changes in laws, regulations, policy statements or public notices, shall be made available to the WTO Secretariat on a yearly basis for examination by Members. Notifications shall include full information, as far as possible, at the tariff line level, on the type of measures applied, the criteria used for their administration, product coverage and trade flows affected.

10. At the request of any Member, notifications may be reviewed by the Committee. Such reviews would be limited to the clarification of specific issues raised by a notification or examination of whether a consultation under Article XII:4(a) or Article XVIII: 12(a) is required. Members which have reasons to believe that a restrictive import measure applied by another Member was taken for balance-of-payments reasons may bring the matter to the attention of the Committee. The Chairman of the Committee shall request information on the measure and make it available to all Members. Without prejudice to the right of any member of the Committee to seek appropriate clarifications in the course of consultations, questions may be submitted in advance for consideration by the consulting Member.

11. The consulting Member shall prepare a Basic Document for the consultations which, in addition to any other information considered to be relevant, should include: (a) an overview of the balance-of payments situations and prospects, including a consideration of the internal and external factors having a bearing on the balance-of-payments situation and the domestic policy measures taken in order to restore equilibrium on a sound and lasting basis; (b) a full description of the restrictions applied for balance-of payments reasons, their legal basis and steps taken to reduce incidental protective effects; (c) measures taken since the last consultation to liberalise import restrictions, in the light of the conclusions of the Committee; (d) plan for the elimination and progressive relaxation of remaining restrictions. References may be made, when relevant, to the information provided in other notifications or reports made to the WTO. Under Simplified Consultations, the consulting Member shall submit a written statement containing essential information on the elements covered by the Basic Document.

12. The WTO Secretariat shall, with a view to facilitating the consultations in the Committee, prepare a factual background paper dealing with the different aspects of the plan for consultations. In the case of developing country Members, the Secretariat document will include relevant background and analytical material on the incidence of the external trading environment on the balance-of-payments situation and prospects of the consulting Member. The technical assistance services of the WTO Secretariat shall, at the request of a developing country Member, assist in preparing the documentation for the consultations.

Conclusions of Balance-of-Payments Consultations

13. The Committee shall report on its consultations to the General Council. in the case of full consultations, the report should indicate the Committee's conclusions on the different elements of the plan for consultations, as well as the facts and reasons on which they are based. The Committee shall endeavour to include in its conclusions proposals for recommendations aimed at promoting the implementation of Articles XII, XVIII:B, the 1979 Declaration and this Understanding. In those cases in which a time-schedule has been presented for the removal of restrictive measures taken for balance-of payments reasons, the General Council may recommend that, in adhering to such a time-schedule, a Member shall be deemed to be in compliance with its GATT 1994 obligations. Whenever the General Council has made specific recommendations, the rights and obligations of Members shall be assessed in the light of such recommendations. In the absence of specific proposals for recommendations by the General Council, the Committee's conclusions should record the different views expressed in the Committee. In the case of simplified consultations, the report shall include a summary of the main elements discussed in the Committee and a decision on whether Full Consultations are required.

UNDERSTANDING ON THE INTERPRETATION OF ARTICLE XXIV OF THE GENERAL AGREEMENT ON TARIFFS AND TRADE 1994

Members,

Having regard to the provisions of Article XXIV of the GATT 1994;

Recognizing that customs unions and free trade areas have greatly increased in number and importance since the establishment of the GATT 1947 and today cover a significant proportion of world trade;

Recognizing the contribution to the expansion of world trade that may be made by closer integration between the economies of the parties to such agreements;

Recognizing also that such contribution is increased if the elimination between the constituent territories of duties and other restrictive regulations of commerce extends to all trade, and diminished if any major sector of trade is excluded;

Reaffirming that the purpose of such agreements should be to facilitate trade between the constituent territories and not to raise barriers to the trade of other Members with such territories; and that in their formation or enlargement the parties to them should to the greatest possible extent avoid creating adverse effects on the trade of other Members;

Convinced also of the need to reinforce the effectiveness of the role of the Council for Trade in Goods in reviewing agreements notified under Article XXIV, by clarifying the criteria and procedures for the assessment of new or enlarged agreements, and improving the transparency of all Article XXIV agreements;

Recognizing the need for a common understanding of the obligations of Members under Article XXIV: 12;

Hereby agree as follows :

1. Customs unions, free trade areas, and interim agreements leading to the formation of a customs union or free trade area, to be consistent with Article XXIV, must satisfy the provisions of its paragraphs 5, 6, 7 and 8 *inter alia.*

Article XXIV:5

2. The evaluation under Article XXIV:5(a) of the general incidence of the duties and other regulations of commerce applicable before and after the formation of a customs union shall in respect of duties and charges be based upon an overall assessment of weighted average tariff rates and of customs duties collected. This assessment shall be based on import statistics for a previous representative period to be supplied by the customs union, on a tariff line basis and in values and quantities, broken down by WTO country of origin. The WTO Secretariat shall compute the weighted average tariff rates and customs duties collected in accordance with the methodology used in the assessment of tariff offers in the Uruguay Round. For this purpose, the duties and charges to be taken into consideration shall be the applied rates of duty. It is recognised that for the purpose of the overall assessment of the incidence of other regulations of commerce for which quantification and aggregation are difficult, the examination of individual measures, regulations, products covered and trade flows affected may be required.

3. The "reasonable length of time" referred to, in Article XXIV:5(c) should exceed ten years only in exceptional cases. In cases where Members

believe that, ten-years would be insufficient they shall provide a full explanation to the Council for Trade in Goods of the need for a longer period.

Article XXIV:6

4. Paragraph 6 of Article XXIV establishes the procedure to be followed when a Member forming a customs union proposes to increase a bound rate of duty. In this regard it is reaffirmed that the procedure set forth m Article XXVIII, as elaborated in the guidelines adopted by the GATT 1947 CONTRACTING PARTIES on 10 November 1980 (27S/26) and in the Understanding on the Interpretation of Article XXVIII of the General Agreement on Tariffs and Trade 1994, must be commenced before tariff concessions are modified or withdrawn upon the formation of a customs union or an interim agreement leading to the formation of a customs union.

5. It is agreed that these negotiations will be entered into in good faith with a view to achieving mutually satisfactory compensatory adjustment. In such negotiations, as required by Article XXIV:6, due account shall be taken of reductions of duties on the same tariff line made by other constituents of the customs union upon its formation. Should such reductions not be sufficient to provide the necessary compensatory adjustment, the customs union would offer compensation, which may take the form of reductions of duties on other tariff lines. Such an offer shall be taken into consideration by the Members having negotiating rights in the binding being modified or withdrawn. Should the compensatory adjustment remain unacceptable, negotiations should be continued. Where, despite such efforts. agreement in negotiations on compensatory adjustment under Article XXVIII as elaborated by the Understanding on the Interpretation of Article XXVIII of the General Agreement on Tariffs and Trade 1994 cannot be reached within a reasonable period from the initiation of negotiations, the customs union shall, nevertheless, be free to modify or withdraw the concessions; affected Members shall then be free to withdraw substantially equivalent concessions in accordance with Article XXVIII.

6. The GATT 1994 imposes no obligation on Members benefiting from a reduction of duties consequent upon the formation of a customs union, or an interim agreement leading to the formation of a customs union, to provide compensatory adjustment to its constituents.

Review of Customs Unions and Free Trade Areas

7. All notifications made under Article XXIV : 7(a) shall be examined by a working party in the light of the relevant provisions of the GATT 1994 and of paragraph 1 of this Understanding. The working party shall submit a report to the Council for Trade in Goods on its findings in this regard. The Council

for Trade in Goods may make such recommendations to Members as it deems appropriate.

8. In regard to interim agreements, the working party may in its report make appropriate recommendations on the proposed time-frame and on measures required to complete the formation of the customs union or free trade area. It may if necessary provide for further review of the agreement.

9. Substantial changes in the plan and schedule included in an interim agreement shall be notified, and shall be examined by the Council for Trade in Goods if so requested.

10. Should an interim agreement notified under Article XXIV: 7(a) not include a plan and schedule, contrary to Article XXIV:5 (c), the working party shall in its report recommend such a plan and schedule. The parties shall not maintain or put into force, as the case may be, such agreement if they are not prepared to modify it in accordance with these recommendations. Provision shall be made for subsequent review of the implementation of the recommendations.

11. Customs unions and constituents of free trade areas shall report periodically to the Council for Trade in Goods, as envisaged by the GATT 1947 CONTRACTING PARTIES in their instruction to the GATT 1947 Council concerning reports on regional agreements (BISD 18S/38), on the operation of the relevant agreement. Any significant changes and/or developments in the agreements should be reported as they occur.

Dispute Settlement

12. The provisions of Articles XXII and XXIII of the GATT 1994 as elaborated and applied by the Understanding on Rules and Procedures Governing the Settlement of Disputes may be invoked with respect to any matters arising from the application of those provisions of Article XXIV relating to customs unions, free trade areas or interim agreements leading to the formation of a customs union or free trade area.

Article XXIV:12

13. Each Member is fully responsible under the GATT 1994 for the observance of all provisions of the GATT 1994, and shall take such reasonable measures as may be available to it to ensure such observance by regional and local governments and authorities within its territory.

14. The provisions of Articles XXII and XXIII of the GATT 1994 as elaborated and applied by the Understanding on Rules and Procedures Governing the Settlement of Disputes may be invoked in respect of measures affecting its observance taken by regional or local governments or authorities within the territory of a Member. When the Dispute Settlement Body has

ruled that a provision of the GATT 1994 has not been observed, the responsible Member shall take such reasonable measures as may be available to it to ensure its observance. The provisions relating to compensation and suspension of concessions or other obligations apply in cases where it has not been possible to secure such observance.

15. Each Member undertakes to accord sympathetic consideration to and afford adequate opportunity for consultation regarding any representations made by another Member concerning measures affecting the operation of the GATT 1994 taken within the territory of the former.

UNDERSTANDING IN RESPECT OF WAIVERS OF OBLIGATIONS UNDER THE GENERAL AGREEMENT ON TARIFFS AND TRADE 1994

1. It is agreed that a request for a waiver or for an extension of an existing waiver shall describe the measures which the Member proposes to take, the specific policy objectives which the Member seeks to pursue and the reasons which prevent the Member from achieving its policy objectives by measures consistent with its obligations under the GATT 1994.
2. Any waiver in effect on the date of entry into force of the Agreement Establishing the WTO shall terminate, unless extended in accordance with the procedures above and those of Article IX of the Agreement Establishing the WTO; on the date of its expiry or two years from the date of entry into force of the Agreement Establishing the WTO whichever is earlier.
3. Any Member considering that a benefit accruing to it under the GATT 1994 is being nullified or impaired as a result of
   (a) the failure of the Member to whom a waiver was granted to observe the terms or conditions of the waiver, or
   (b) the application of a measure consistent with the terms and conditions of the waiver may invoke the provisions of Article XXIII of the GATT 1994 as elaborated and applied by the Understanding on Rules and Procedures Governing the Settlement of Disputes.

UNDERSTANDING ON THE INTERPRETATION OF ARTICLE XXVIII OF THE GENERAL AGREEMENT ON TARIFFS AND TRADE 1994

1. For the purposes of modification or withdrawal of a concession, the Member which has the highest ratio of exports affected by the concession (*i.e.*, exports of the product to the market of the Member modifying or withdrawing the concession) to its total exports shali be deemed to have a principal supplying interest if it does not already have an initial negotiating

right or a principal supplying interest as provided for in Article XXVIII:1. It is however agreed that this paragraph will be reviewed by the Council for Trade in Goods five years from the date of the entry into force of the Agreement Establishing the WTO with a view to deciding whether this criterion has worked satisfactorily in securing a redistribution of negotiating rights in favour of small and medium-sized exporting Members. If this is not the case consideration will be given to possible improvements, including, in the light of the availability of adequate data, the adoption of a criterion based on the ratio of exports affected by the concession to exports to all markets of the product in question.

2. Where a Member considers that it has a principal supplying interest in terms of paragraph 1 above, it should communicate its claim in writing, with supporting evidence, to the Member proposing to modify or withdraw a concession, and at the same time inform the WTO Secretariat. Paragraph 4 of the "Procedures for Negotiations under Article XXVIII" (BISD 27S/26) shall apply in these cases.

3. In the determination of Members with a principal supplying interest (whether as provided for in paragraph 1 above or in Article XXVIII:1) or substantial interest, it is agreed that only trade in the affected product which has taken place on an m.f.n. basis shall be taken into consideration. However, trade in the affected product which has taken place under non-contractual preferences shall also be taken into account if the trade in question has ceased to benefit from such preferential treatment, thus becoming MFN trade, at the time of the renegotiation or will do so by its conclusion.

4. When a tariff concession is modified or withdrawn on a new product (*i.e.*, a product for which three years' trade statistics are not available) the Member possessing initial negotiating rights on the tariff line where the product is or was formerly classified shall be deemed to have an initial negotiating right in the concession in question. The determination of principal supplying and substantial interests and the calculation of compensation shall take into account *inter alia* production capacity and investment in the affected product in the exporting Member and estimates of export growth, as well as forecasts of demand for the product in the importing Member. For the purposes of this paragraph "new product" is understood to include a tariff item created by means of a breakout from an existing tariff line.

5. Where a Member considers that it has a principal supplying or a substantial interest in terms of paragraph 4 above, it should communicate its claim in writing, with supporting evidence, to the Member proposing to modify or withdraw a concession, and at the same time inform the WTO Secretariat. Paragraph 4 of the 'Procedures for Negotiations under Article XXVIII" (BISD 27S/26) shall apply in these cases.

6. When an unlimited tariff concession is replaced by a tariff rate quota, the amount of compensation provided should exceed the amount of the trade actually affected by the modification of the concession. The basis for the calculation of compensation should be the amount by which future trade prospects exceed the level of the quota. It is understood that the calculation of future trade prospects should be based on the greater of :

(i) the average annual trade in the most recent representative three year period, increased by the average annual growth rate of imports in that same period, or by ten per cent, whichever is the greater; or

(ii) trade in the most recent year increased by ten per cent.

In no case shall the liability for compensation exceed that which would be entailed by complete withdrawal of the concession.

7. Any Member having a principal supplying interest, whether as provided for in paragraph 1 above or in Article XXVIIII. in a concession which is modified or withdrawn shall be accorded an initial negotiating right in the compensatory concessions, unless another form of compensation is agreed by the Members concerned.

UNDERSTANDING ON THE INTERPRETATION OF ARTICLE XXXV OF THE GENERAL AGREEMENT ON TARIFFS AND TRADE 1947

THE CONTRACTING PARTIES,

Having regard to the interlinked provisions of paragraph 1 of Article XXXV of the General Agreement on Tariffs and Trade 1947;

Noting that by invoking Article XXXV a contracting party on the one hand, or a government acceding to GATT 1947 on the other, declines to apply GATT 1947, or alternatively Article II of that Agreement, to the other party;

Desiring to ensure that tariff negotiations between contracting parties and a government acceding to GATT 1947 are not inhibited by unwillingness to accept an obligation to apply GATT 1947 as a consequence of entry into such negotiations;

Agree as follows:

A contracting party and a government acceding to GATT 1947 may engage in negotiations relating to the establishment of a GATT schedule of concessions by the acceding government without prejudice to the right of either to invoke Article XXXV in respect of the other.

URUGUAY ROUND PROTOCOL TO THE GENERAL AGREEMENT ON TARIFFS AND TRADE 1994

Members,

Having carried out negotiations within the framework of the General Agreement on Tariffs and Trade 1947, pursuant to the Ministerial Declaration on the Uruguay Round,

Hereby *agree as* follows:

1. The schedule annexed to this Protocol relating to a Member shall become a Schedule to the GATT 1994 relating to that Member on the day on which the Agreement Establishing the WTO enters into force for that Member. Any schedule submitted in accordance with the Ministerial Decision on measures in favour of least-developed countries shall be deemed to be annexed to this Protocol.

2. The tariff reductions agreed upon by each Member shall be implemented in five equal rate reductions, except as may be otherwise specified in a Member's Schedule. The first such reduction shall be made effective on the date of entry into force of the Agreement Establishing the WTO each successive reduction shall be made effective on 1 January of each of the following years, and the final rate shall become effective not later than the date four years after the date of entry into force of the Agreement Establishing the WTO except as may be otherwise specified in that Member's Schedule. Unless otherwise specified in its Schedule, a Member that accepts the Agreement Establishing the WTO after its entry into force shall, on the date this Agreement enters into force for it, make effective all rate reductions that have already taken place together with the reductions which it would under the preceding sentence have been obligated to make effective on 1 January of the year following, and shall make effective all remaining rate reductions on the schedule specified in the previous sentence. The reduced rate should in each stage be rounded off to the first decimal. For agricultural products, as defined in Article 2 of the Agreement on Agriculture, the staging of reductions shall be implemented as specified in the relevant parts of the schedules.

3. The implementation of the concessions and commitments contained in the schedules annexed to this Protocol shall, upon request, be subject to multilateral examination by the Members. This would be without prejudice to the rights and obligations of Members under Agreements in Annex 1-A of the Agreement Establishing the WTO

4. After the schedule annexed to this Protocol relating to a Member has

become a Schedule to the GATT 1994 pursuant to the provisions of paragraph 1, such Member shall be free at any time to withhold or to withdraw in whole or in part the concession in such Schedule with respect to any product for which the principal supplier is any other Uruguay Round participant the schedule of which has not yet become a Schedule to the GATT 1994. Such action can, however, only be taken after written notice of any such withholding or withdrawal of a concession has been given to the Council for Trade in Goods and after consultations have been held, upon request, with any Member, the relevant Schedule relating to which has become a Schedule to the GATT 1994 and which has a substantial interest in the product involved. Any concessions so withheld or withdrawn shall be applied on and after the day on which the schedule of the Member which has the principal supplying interest becomes a Schedule to the GATT 1994.

5. (a) Without prejudice to the provisions of Article 4:2 of the Agreement on Agriculture, for the purpose of the reference in Article II : 1 (b) and (c) of the GATT 1994 to the date of that Agreement, the applicable date in respect of each product which is the subject of a concession provided for in a schedule of concessions annexed to this Protocol shall be the date of this Protocol.

(b) For the purpose of the reference in Article Il: 6(a) of the GATT 1994 to the date of that Agreement, the applicable date in respect of a schedule of concessions annexed to this Protocol shall be the date of this Protocol.

6. In cases of modification or withdrawal of concessions relating to non-tariff measures as contained in Part III of the schedules, the provisions of Article XXVIII of the GATT 1994 and the Procedures for Negotiations under Article XXVIII (BISD 27S/26) shall apply. This would be without prejudice to the rights and obligations of Members under the GATT 1994.

7. In each case in which a schedule annexed to this Protocol results for any product in treatment less favourable than was provided for such production the Schedules of the General Agreement 1947 prior to the entry into force of this Protocol, the Member to whom the schedule relates shall be deemed to have taken appropriate action as would have been otherwise necessary under the relevant provisions of Article XXVIII of the GATT 1947 or 1994. The provisions of this paragraph shall apply to the Schedules of Members listed by agreement in the Annex to this Protocol.

8. The Schedules annexed hereto are authentic in the English, French and Spanish language as specified in each Schedule.

9. The date of this Protocol shall be the date of the adoption of the Final Act Embodying the Results of the Uruguay Round Multilateral Trade Negotiations.

Appendix I

SCHEDULE ... (Name of Member)

This schedule is authentic only in the [English] [French] [Spanish] language

PART I : MOST-FAVOURED-NATION TARIFF
SECTION I – Agricultural Products
SECTION I-A Tariffs

Tariff item number	Description of products	Base rate of duty	Bound rate of duty	Implementation period from/to	Special safeguard	Initial negotiating right	Other duties and charges
1	2	3	4	5	6	7	8

PART I (continued)
SECTION I-B Tariff Quotas

Description of Products	Tarrif item number (s)	Initial quota quantity and inquota tariff rate	Final quota quantity and inquota tariff quota	Implementation period from/to	Initial negotiating right	Other terms and conditions
1	2	3	4	5	6	7

Appendix II

SCHEDULE .... (Name of Member)

This schedule is authentic only in the [English] [French] [Spanish] language

PART I- MOST-FAVOURED-NATION TARIFF

SECTION II – Other Product

Tariff number	Description of products	Base rate of duty (U/B)	Bound rate of duty	Initial negotiating right	other duties and charges
1	2	3	4	5	6
00.00.00 (at appropriate level)	Manufactured etc...	24% [U] [B]	12%	CA	

Appendix III

SCHEDULE ... (Name of Member)

PART II – PREFERENTIAL TARIFF

(If applicable)

Appendix IV

SCHEDULE ... (Name of Member)

PART III – NON-TARIFF CONCESSIONS

Tariff item number	Description of products	Concessions

Appendix V

SCHEDULE ... (Name of Member)

This schedule is authentic only in the [English] [French] [Spanish] language

PART IV: AGRICULTURE PRODUCTS: COMMITMENTS LIMITING SUBSIDIZATION

(Article 3 of the Agreement on Agriculture)

SECTION I – Domestic Support: Total AMS Commitments

BASE TOTAL AMS	Annual and final bound commitment levels 199X-200Y	Relevant Supporting Tables and document reference
1	2	3

PART IV (continued)

SECTION II – Export Subsidies: Budgetary Outlay and Quantity Reduction Commitments

Description of products and tariff item numbers at HS six digit level	Base outlay level	Calendar/ other year applied	Annual and final outlay 199X-200Y	Base quantity	Calendar/ other year applied	Annual and final quantity commitment levels	Relevant Supporting Tables and document reference
1	2	3	4	5	6	7	8

PART IV (Continued)

SECTION III – Commitments Limiting the Scope of Export Subsidies

Description of products	Nature of commitments
1	2

AGREEMENT ON AGRICULTURE

Members,

Having decided to establish a basis for initiating a process of reform of trade in agriculture in line with the objectives of the negotiations as set out in the Punta del Este Declaration;

Recalling that the long-term objective as agreed at the Mid-Term Review "is to establish a fair and market-oriented agricultural trading system and that a reform process should be initiated through the negotiation of commitments on support and protection and through the establishment of strengthened and more operationally effective GATT rules and disciplines";

Recalling further that "the above-mentioned long-term objective is to provide for substantial progressive reductions in agricultural support and protection sustained over an agreed period of time, resulting in correcting and preventing restrictions and distortions in world agricultural markets";

Committed to achieving specific binding commitments in each of the following areas: market access; domestic support; export competition; and to reaching an agreement on sanitary and phytosanitary issues;

Having agreed that in implementing their commitments on market access, developed country Members would take fully into account the particular needs and conditions of developing country Members by providing for a greater improvement of opportunities and terms of access for agricultural products of particular interest to these Members, including the fullest liberalization of trade in tropical agricultural products as agreed at the Mid-Term Review, and products of particular importance to the diversification of production from the growing of illicit narcotic crops;

Noting that commitments under the reform programme should be made in an equitable way among all Members, having regard to non-trade concerns, including food security and the need to protect the environment; having regard to the agreement that special and differential treatment to developing countries is an integral element of the negotiations, and taking into account the possible negative effects of the implementation of the reform programme on least-developed and net food-importing developing countries;

Hereby agree, as follows:

Part I

Article I – Definition of Terms

In this Agreement, unless the context otherwise requires:

(a) "Aggregate Measurement of Support" and "AMS" mean the annual level of support, expressed in monetary terms, provided for an agricultural product in favour of the producers of the basic agricultural product or non-product-specific support provided in favour of agricultural producers in general, other than support provided under programmes that qualify as exempt from reduction under Annex 2 to this Agreement, which is:

(i) with respect to support provided during the base period, specified in the relevant tables of supporting material incorporated by reference in Part IV of a Member's Schedule; and

(ii) with respect to support provided during any year of the implementation period and thereafter, calculated in accordance with the provisions of Annex 3 of this Agreement and taking into account the constituent data and methodology used in the tables of supporting material incorporated by reference in Part IV of the Member's Schedule;

(b) "basic product" in relation to domestic support commitments is defined as the product as close as practicable to the point of first sale as specified in a Member's Schedule and in the related supporting material;

(c) "budgetary outlays" or "outlays" include revenue foregone;

(d) "Equivalent Measurement of Support" means the annual level of support, expressed in monetary terms, provided to producers of a basic agricultural product through the application of one or more measures, the calculation of which in accordance with the AMS methodology is impracticable, other than support provided under programmes that qualify as exempt from reduction under Annex 2 to this Agreement, and which is:

(i) with respect to support provided during the base period, specified in the relevant tables of supporting material incorporated by reference in Part IV of a Member's Schedule; and

(ii) with respect to support provided during any year of the implementation period and thereafter, calculated in accordance with the provisions of Annex 4 of this Agreement and taking into account the constituent data and methodology used in the tables of supporting material incorporated by reference in Part IV of the Member's Schedule;

(e) "export subsidies" refer to subsidies contingent upon export performance including the export subsidies listed in Article 9 of this Agreement;

(f) "implementation period" means the six-year period commencing in the year 1995, except that, for the purposes of Article 13, it means the nine-year period commencing in 1995;

(g) "market access concessions" include all market access commitments undertaken pursuant to this Agreement;

(h) "Total Aggregate Measurement of Support" and "Total AMS" mean the sum of all domestic support provided in favour of agricultural producers, calculated as the sum of all aggregate measurements of support for basic agricultural products, all non-product-specific aggregate measurements of support and all equivalent measurements of support for agricultural products, and which is:

(i) with respect to support provided during the base period (*i.e.*, the "Base Total AMS") and the maximum support permitted to be provided during any year of the implementation period or thereafter (*i.e.*, the "Annual and Final Bound Commitment Levels"), as specified in Part IV of a Member's Schedule; and

(ii) with respect to the level of support actually provided during any year of the implementation period and thereafter (*i.e.*, the "Current Total AMS"), calculated in accordance with the provisions of this Agreement, including Article 6, and with the constituent data and methodology used in the tables of supporting material incorporated by reference in Part IV of the Member's Schedule;

(i) "year" in (f) above and in relation to the specific commitments of a Member refers to the calendar, financial or marketing year specified in the Schedule relating to that Member.

Article 2 – Product Coverage

This Agreement applies to the products listed in Annex 1 to this Agreement, hereinafter referred to as agricultural products.

Part II

Article 3 – Incorporation of Concessions and Commitments

1. The domestic support and export subsidy commitments in Part IV of each Member's Schedule constitute commitments limiting subsidization and are hereby made an integral part of the GATT 1994.

2. Subject to the provisions of Article 6 of this Agreement, a Member shall not provide support in favour of domestic producers in excess of the commitment levels specified in Section I of Part IV of its Schedule.

3. Subject to the provisions of paragraphs 2(b) and 4 of Article 9 of this Agreement, a Member shall not provide export subsidies listed in paragraph 1 of Article 9 in respect of the agricultural products or groups of products specified in Section II of Part IV of its Schedule in excess of the budgetary outlay and quantity commitment levels specified therein and shall not provide such subsidies in respect of any agricultural product not specified in that Section of its Schedule.

Part III

Article 4 – Market Access

1. Market access concessions contained in Schedules relate to bindings and reductions of tariffs, and to other market access commitments as specified therein.

2. Members shall not maintain, resort to, or revert to any measures of the kind which have been required to be converted into ordinary customs duties[10], except as otherwise provided for in Article 5 and Annex 5 hereof.

Article 5 – Special Safeguard Provisions

1. Notwithstanding the provisions of Article II: l(b) of the GATT 1994, any Member may take recourse to the provisions of paragraphs 4 and 5 below in connection with the importation of an agricultural product, in respect of which measures referred to in paragraph 2 of Article 4 have been converted into an ordinary customs duty and which is designated in its Schedule with the symbol "SSG" as being the subject of a concession in respect of which the provisions of this Article may be invoked, if:

(i) the volume of imports of that product entering the customs territory of the Member granting the concession during any year exceeds a trigger level which relates to the existing market access opportunity as set out in paragraph 4 below; or, but not concurrently:

(ii) the price at which imports of that product may enter the

---

[10] These measures include quantitative import restrictions, variable import levies, minimum import prices, discretionary import licensing, non-tariff measures maintained through state trading enterprises, voluntary export restraints and similar border measures other than ordinary customs duties, whether or not the measures are maintained under country-specific derogations from the provisions of the GATT 1947. but not measures maintained under balance-of-payments provisions or under other general, non-agriculture-specific provisions of the GATT 1994 or of the other Multilateral Trade Agreements in Annex IA to the WTO -

customs territory of the Member granting the concession, as determined on the basis of the c.i.f. import price of the shipment concerned expressed in terms of its domestic currency, falls below a trigger price equal to the average 1986 to 1988 reference price[11] for the product concerned.

2. Imports under current and minimum access commitments established as part of a concession referred to in paragraph 1 above shall be counted for the purpose of determining the volume of imports required for invoking the provisions of sub-paragraph 1 (i) and paragraph 4, but imports under such commitments shall not be affected by any additional duty imposed under either paragraph 4 or paragraph 5 below.

3. Any supplies of the product in question which were *en route* on the basis of a contract settled before the additional duty is imposed under sub-paragraph l (i) above and paragraph 4 below shall be exempted from any such additional duty provided that they may be counted in the volume of imports of the product in question during the following year for the purposes of triggering the provisions of sub-paragraph l (i) in that year.

4. Any additional duty imposed under sub-paragraph l(i) above shall only be maintained until the end of the year in which it has been imposed, and may only be levied at a level which shall not exceed one-third of the level of the ordinary customs duty in effect in the year in which the action is taken. The trigger level shall be set according to the following schedule based on market access opportunities defined as imports as a percentage of the corresponding domestic consumption[12] during the three preceding years for which data are available:

(a) where such market access opportunities for a product are less than or equal to 10 per cent, the base trigger level shall equal 125 per cent;

(b) where such market access opportunities for a product are greater than 10 per cent but less than or equal to 30 per cent, the base trigger level shall equal 110 per cent;

(c) where such market access opportunities for a product are greater than 30 per cent, the base trigger level shall equal 105 per cent.

---

[11] The reference price used to invoke the provisions of this sub-paragraph shall, in general, be the average c.i.f. unit value of the product concerned, or otherwise shall be an appropriate price in terms of the quality of the product and its stage of processing. It shall, following its initial use, be publicly specified and available to the extent necessary to allow other Members to assess the additional duty that may be levied.

[12] Where domestic consumption is not taken into account, the base trigger level under (a) below shall apply.

In all cases the additional duty may be imposed in any year where the absolute volume of imports of the product concerned entering the customs territory of the Member granting the concession exceeds the sum of (x) the base trigger level set out above multiplied by the average quantity of imports during the three preceding years for which data are available and (y) the absolute volume change in domestic consumption of the product concerned in the most recent year for which data are available compared to the preceding year, provided that the trigger level shall not be less than 105 per cent of the average quantity of imports in (x) above.

5. The additional duty imposed under sub-paragraph 1(ii) above shall be set according to the following schedule:

(a) if the difference between c.i.f. import price of the shipment expressed in terms of the domestic currency (hereinafter referred to as the "import price") and the trigger price as defined under that sub-paragraph is less than or equal to 10 per cent of the trigger price, no additional duty shall be imposed,

(b) if the difference between the import price and the trigger price (hereinafter referred to as the "difference") is greater than 10 per cent but less than or equal to 40 per cent of the trigger price, the additional duty shall equal 30 per cent of the amount by which the difference exceeds 10 per cent;

(c) if the difference is greater than 40 per cent but less than or equal to 60 per cent of the trigger price, the additional duty shall equal 50 per cent of the amount by which the difference exceeds 40 per cent, plus the additional duty allowed under (b);

(d) if the difference is greater than 60 per cent but less than or equal to 75 per cent, the additional duty shall equal 70 per cent of the amount by which the difference exceeds 60 per cent of the trigger price, plus the additional duties allowed under (b) and (c);

(e) if the difference is greater than 75 per cent of the trigger price, the additional duty shall equal 90 per cent of the amount by which the difference exceeds 75 per cent, plus the additional duties allowed under (b), (c) and (d).

6. For perishable and seasonal products, the conditions set out above shall be applied in such a manner as to take account of the specific characteristics of such products. In particular, shorter time periods under paragraph 1(i) and paragraph 4 may be used in reference to the corresponding periods in the base period and different reference prices for different periods may be used under paragraph 1 (ii).

7. The operation of the special safeguard shall be carried out in a transparent

manner. Any Member taking action under paragraph 1 (i) above shall give notice in writing, including relevant data, to the Committee on Agriculture as far in advance as may be practicable and in any event within 10 days of the implementation of such action. In cases where changes in consumption volumes must be allocated to individual tariff lines subject to action under paragraph 4, relevant data shall include the information and methods used allocate these changes. A Member taking action under paragraph 4 shall afford any interested Members the opportunity to consult with it in respect of the conditions of application of such action. Any Member taking action under paragraph 1 (ii) above shall give notice in writing, including relevant data, to the Committee on Agriculture within 10 days of the implementation of the first such action or, for perishable and seasonal products, the first action in any period. Members undertake, as far as practicable, not to take recourse to the provisions of paragraph 1 (ii) where the volume of imports of the products concerned are declining. In either case a Member taking such action shall afford any interested Members the opportunity to consult with it in respect of the conditions of application of such action.

8. Where measures are taken in conformity with paragraphs 1 through 7 above, Members undertake not to have recourse, in respect of such measures, to the provisions of Article XIX: 1(a) and XIX:3 of the GATT 1994 or paragraph 17 of the Agreement on Safeguards.

9. The provisions of this Article shall remain in force for the duration of the reform process as determined under Article 20.

Part IV

Article 6 – Domestic Support Commitments

1. The domestic support reduction commitments of each Member contained in Part IV of its Schedule shall apply to all of its domestic support measures in favour of agricultural producers with the exception of domestic measures which are not subject to reduction in terms of the criteria set out in this Article and in Annex 2 to this Agreement. The commitments are expressed in terms of Total Aggregate Measurement of Support and "Annual and Final Bound Commitment Levels".

2. In accordance with the Mid-Term Review Agreement that government measures of assistance, whether direct or indirect, to encourage agricultural and rural development are an integral part of the development programmes of developing countries, investment subsidies which are generally available, to agriculture in developing country Members and agricultural input subsidies generally available to low-income or resource poor producers in developing country Members shall be exempt from domestic support reduction commitments that would otherwise be applicable to such measures, as shall

domestic support to producers in developing country Members to encourage diversification from growing illicit narcotic crops. Domestic support meeting the criteria of this paragraph shall not be required to be included in a Member's calculation of its Current Total AMS.

3. A Member shall be considered to be in compliance with its domestic support reduction commitments in any year in which its domestic support in favour of agricultural producers expressed in terms of Current Total AMS does not exceed the corresponding annual or final bound commitment level specified in Part IV of the Member's Schedule.

4. (a) A Member shall not be required to include in the calculation of its Current Total AMS and shall not be required to reduce:

(i) product-specific domestic support which would otherwise be required to be included in a Member's calculation of its Current AMS where such support does not exceed 5 per cent of that Member's total value of production of a basic product during the relevant year; and

(ii) non-product-specific domestic support which would otherwise be required to be included in a Member's calculation of its Current AMS where such support does not exceed 5 per cent of the value of that Member's total agricultural production.

(b) For developing country Members, the *de minimis* percentage under this paragraph shall be 10 per cent.

5. (a) Direct payments under production-limiting programmes shall not be subject to the commitment to reduce domestic support if:

(i) such payments are based on fixed area and yields; or

(ii) such payments are made on 85 per cent or less of the base level of production; or

(iii) livestock payments are made on a fixed number of head.

(b) The exemption from the reduction commitment for direct payments meeting the above criteria shall be reflected by the exclusion of the value of those direct payments in a Member's calculation of its Current Total AMS.

Article 7 – General Disciplines on Domestic Support

1. Each Member shall ensure that any domestic support measures in favour of agricultural producers which are not subject to reduction commitments because they qualify under the criteria set out in Annex 2 to this Agreement are maintained in conformity therewith.

2. (a) Any domestic support measure in favour of agricultural producers, including any modification to such measure, and any measure that is subsequently

introduced that cannot be shown to satisfy the criteria in Annex 2 to this Agreement or to be exempt from reduction by reason of any other provision of this Agreement shall be included in the Member's calculation of its Current Total AMS.

(b) Where no Total AMS commitment exists in Part IV of a Member's Schedule, the Member shall not provide support to agricultural producers in excess of the relevant *de minimis* level set out in paragraph 4 of Article 6.

Part V

Article 8 – Export Competition Commitments

Each Member undertakes not to provide export subsidies otherwise than in conformity with this Agreement and with the commitments as specified in that Member's Schedule.

Article 9 – Export Subsidy Commitments

1. The following export subsidies are subject to reduction commitments under this Agreement:

(a) The provision by governments or their agencies of direct subsidies, including payments-in-kind, to a firm to an industry, to producers of an agricultural product, to a cooperative or other association of such producers, or to a marketing board, contingent on export performance.

(b) The sale or disposal for export by governments or their agencies of non-commercial stocks of agricultural products at a price lower than the comparable price charged for the like product to buyers in the domestic market.

(c) Payments on the export of an agricultural product that are financed by virtue of governmental action, whether or not a charge on the public account is involved, including payments that are financed from the proceeds of a levy imposed on the agricultural product concerned or on an agricultural product from which the exported product is derived.

(d) The provision of subsidies to reduce the costs of marketing exports of agricultural products (other than widely available export promotion and advisory services) including handling, upgrading and other processing costs, and the costs of international transport and freight.

(e) Internal transport and freight charges on export shipments, provided or mandated by governments, on terms more favourable than for domestic shipments.

(f) Subsidies on agricultural products contingent on their incorporation in exported products.

2. (a) Except as provided in sub-paragraph (b), the export subsidy commitment levels for each year of the implementation period, as specified in a Member's Schedule, represent with respect to the export subsidies listed in paragraph 1 of this Article:

(i) in the case of budgetary outlay reduction commitments, the maximum level of expenditure for such subsidies that may be allocated or incurred in that year; and

(ii) in the case of export quantity reduction commitments, the maximum quantity of an agricultural product, or group of such products, in respect of which such export subsidies may be granted in that year.

(b) In any of the second through fifth years of the implementation period, a Member may provide export subsidies listed in paragraph 1 above in a given year in excess of the corresponding annual commitment levels in respect of the products or groups of products specified in Part IV of the Member's Schedule, provided that:

(i) the cumulative amounts of budgetary outlays for such subsidies, from the beginning of the implementation period through the year in question, does not exceed the cumulative amounts that would have resulted from full compliance with the relevant annual outlay commitment levels specified in the Member's Schedule by more than 3 per cent of the base period level of such budgetary outlays;

(ii) the cumulative quantities exported with the benefit of such export subsidies, from the beginning of the implementation period through the year in question, does not exceed the cumulative quantities that would have resulted from full compliance with the relevant annual quantity commitment levels specified in the Member's Schedule by more than 1.75 per cent of the base period quantities;

(iii) the total cumulative amounts of budgetary outlays for such export subsidies and the quantities benefiting from such export subsidies over the entire implementation period are no greater than the totals that would have resulted from full compliance with the relevant annual commitment levels specified in the Member's Schedule; and

(iv) the Member's budgetary outlays for export subsidies and the quantities benefiting from such subsidies, at the conclusion of the implementation period, are no greater than 64 per cent and 79 per cent of the 1986-1990 base period levels, respectively. For developing country Members these percentages shall be 76 and 86 per cent, respectively.

3. Commitments relating to limitations on the extension of the scope of export subsidization are as specified in Schedules.

4. During the implementation period developing country Members shall not be required to undertake commitments in respect of the export subsidies listed in sub-paragraphs (d) and (e) of paragraph 1 above provided that these are not applied in a manner that would circumvent reduction commitments.

Article 10 – Prevention of Circumvention of Export Subsidy Commitments

1. Export subsidies not listed in Article 9(1) of this Agreement shall not be applied in a manner which results in, or which threatens to lead to, circumvention of export subsidy commitments; nor shall non-commercial transactions be used to circumvent such commitments.

2. Members undertake to work toward the development of internationally agreed disciplines to govern the provision of export credits, export credit guarantees or insurance programmes and, after agreement on such disciplines, to provide export credits, export credit guarantees or insurance programmes only in conformity therewith.

3. Any Member which claims that any quantity exported in excess of a reduction commitment level is not subsidized must establish that no export subsidy, whether listed in Article 9 or not, has been granted in respect of the quantity of exports in question.

4. Members donors of international food aid shall ensure:

(a) that the provision of international food aid is not tied directly or indirectly to commercial exports of agricultural products to recipient countries;

(b) that international food aid transactions, including bilateral food aid which is monetised, shall be carried out in accordance with the FAO "Principles of Surplus Disposal and Consultative Obligations" including, where appropriate, the system of Usual Marketing Requirements (UMRs); and

(c) that such aid shall be provided to the extent possible in fully grant form or on terms no less concessional than those provided for in Article IV of the Food Aid Convention 1986.

Article 11 – Incorporated Products

In no case may the per unit subsidy paid on an incorporated agricultural primary product exceed the per unit export subsidy that would be payable on exports of the primary product as such.

Part VI

Article 12 – Disciplines on Export Prohibitions and Restrictions

1. Where any Member institutes any new export prohibition or restriction on foodstuffs in accordance with paragraph 2 (a) of Article XI of the GATT 1994, the Member shall observe the following provisions:

(i) the Member instituting the export prohibition or restriction shall give due consideration to the effects of such prohibition or restriction on importing Members' food security;

(ii) before any Member institutes an export prohibition or restriction, it shall give notice in writing, as far in advance as practicable, to the Committee on Agriculture comprising such information as the nature and the duration of such measure, and shall consult, upon request, with any other Member having a substantial interest as an importer with respect to any matter related to the measure in question. The Member instituting such export prohibition or restriction shall provide, upon request, such a Member with necessary information.

2. The provisions of this Article shall not apply to any developing country Member, unless the measure is taken by a developing country Member which is a net-food expert of the specific foodstuff concerned.

Part VII

Article 13 – Due Restraint

During the implementation period, notwithstanding the provisions of the GATT 1994 and the Agreement on Subsidies and Countervailing Measures ('Subsidies Agreement") :

1. Domestic support measures that conform fully to the provisions of Annex 2 to this Agreement shall be:

(a) non-actionable subsidies for purposes of countervailing duties[13];

(b) exempt from actions based on Article XVI of the GATT 1994 and Part III of the Subsidies Agreement; and

(c) exempt from actions based on non-violation nullification or impairment of the benefits of tariff concessions accruing to another

[13] "Countervailing duties" where referred to in this Article are those covered by Article VI of the GATT 1994 and Part V of the Agreement on Subsidies and Countervailing Duties.

Member under Article II of the GATT 1994, in the sense of Article XXIII:1(b) of the GATT 1994.

2. Domestic support measures that conform fully to the provisions of Article 6 of this Agreement including direct payments that conform to the requirements of paragraph 5 thereof, as reflected in each Member's Schedule, as well as domestic support within *de minimis* levels and in conformity with paragraph 2 of Article 6, shall be:

(a) exempt from the imposition of countervailing duties unless a determination of injury or threat thereof is made in accordance with Article VI of the GATT 1994 and Part V of the Subsidies Agreement, and due restraint shall be shown in initiating any countervailing duty investigations;

(b) exempt from actions based on Article XVI:1 of the GATT 1994 or Articles 5 and 6 of the Subsidies Agreement, provided that such measures do not grant support to a specific commodity in excess of that decided during the 1992 marketing year; and

(c) exempt from actions based on non-violation nullification or impairment of the benefits of tariff concessions accruing to another Member under Article II of the GATT 1994, in the sense of Article XXIII: l(b) of the GATT 1994, provided that such measures do not grant support to a specific commodity in excess of that decided during the 1992 marketing year.

3. Export subsidies that conform fully to the provisions of Part V of this Agreement, as reflected in each Member's Schedule of Commitments, shall be:

(a) subject to countervailing duties only upon a determination of injury or threat thereof based on volume, effect on prices, or consequent impact in accordance with Article VI of the GATT 1994 and Part V of the Subsidies Agreement, and due restraint shall be shown in initiating any countervailing duty investigations; and

(b) exempt from actions based on Article XVI of the GATT 1994 or Articles 3, 5 and 6 of the Subsidies Agreement.

Part VIII

Article 14 – Sanitary and Phytosanitary Measures

Members agree to give effect to the Agreement on Sanitary and Phytosanitary Measures.

Part IX

Article 15 – Special and Differential Treatment

1. In keeping with the recognition that differential and more favourable treatment for developing country Members is an integral part of the negotiation, special and differential treatment in respect of commitments shall be provided as set out in the relevant provisions of this Agreement and embodied in the Schedules of concessions and commitments.

2. Developing countries shall have the flexibility to implement reduction commitments over a period of up to 10 years. Least developed country Members shall not be required to undertake reduction commitments.

Part X

Article 16 – Least-developed and Net Food-Importing Developing Countries

1. Developed country Members shall take such action as is provided for within the framework of the Decision on Measures Concerning the Possible Negative Effects of the Reform Programme on Least-developed and Net Food-Importing Developing Countries.

2. The Committee on Agriculture shall monitor, as appropriate, the follow-up to this Decision.

Part XI

Article 17 – Committee on Agriculture

A Committee on Agriculture shall be established.

Article 18 – Review of the Implementation of Commitments

1. Progress in the implementation of commitments negotiated under the Uruguay Round reform programme shall be reviewed by the Committee on Agriculture.

2. The review process shall be undertaken on the basis of notifications submitted by Members in relation to such matters and at such intervals as shall be determined, as well as on the basis of such documentation as the MTO Secretariat may be requested to prepare in order to facilitate the review process.

3. In addition to the notifications to be submitted under paragraph 2, any new domestic support measure, or modification of an existing measure, for which exemption from reduction is claimed shall be notified promptly. This notification shall contain details of the new or modified measure and its conformity with the agreed criteria as set out either in Article 6 or in Annex 2 to this Agreement.

4. In the review process Members shall give due consideration to the

influence of excessive rates of inflation on the ability of any Member to abide by its domestic support commitments.

5. Members agree to consult annually in the Committee on Agriculture with respect to their participation in the normal growth of world trade in agricultural products within the framework of the commitments on export subsidies under this Agreement.

6. The review process shall provide an opportunity for Members to raise any matter relevant to the implementation of commitments under the reform programme as set out in this Agreement

7. Any Member may bring to the attention of the Committee on Agriculture any measure which it considers ought to have been notified by another Member.

Article 19 – Consultation and Dispute Settlement

The provisions of Articles XXII and XXIII of the GATT 1994, as elaborated and applied by the Understanding on Rules and Procedures Governing the Settlement of Disputes, shall apply to consultations and the settlement of disputes under this Agreement.

Part XII

Article 20 – Continuation of the Reform Process

Recognizing that the long-term objective of substantial progressive reductions in support and protection resulting in fundamental reform is an on-going process, Members agree that negotiations for continuing the process will be initiated one year before the end of the implementation period, taking into account:

- the experience to that date from implementing the reduction commitments;
- the effects of the reduction commitments on world trade in agriculture;
- non-trade concerns, special and differential treatment to developing country Members, and the objective to establish a fair and market-oriented agricultural trading system, and the. other objectives and concerns mentioned in the preamble to this Agreement; and
- what further commitments are necessary to achieve the above mentioned long-term objectives.

Part XIII

Article 21 – Final Provisions

1. The provisions of the GATT 1994 and of other Multilateral Trade

Agreements in Annex IA to the WTO shall apply subject to the provisions of this Agreement.

2. The Annexes to this Agreement are hereby made an integral part of this Agreement.

ANNEX 1

Product Coverage

1. This Agreement shall cover the following products:

(i) HS Chapters 1 to 24 less fish and fish products, plus

(ii)			
(ii)	HS Code	29.05.43	(mannitol)
	HS Code	29.05.44	(sorbitol)
	HS Heading	33.01	(essential oils)
	HS Headings	35.01 to 35.05	(albuminoidal substances, modified starches, glues)
	HS Code	38.09.10	(finishing agents)
	HS Code	38.23.60	(sorbitol n.e.p.)
	HS Headings	41.01 to 41.03	(hides and skins)
	HS Heading	43.01	(raw furskins)
	HS Headings	50.01 to 50.03	(raw silk and silk waste)
	HS Headings	51.01 to 51.03	(wool and animal hair)
	HS Headings	52.01 to 52.03	(raw cotton, waste and cotton carded or combed)
	HS Heading	53.01	(raw flax)
	HS Heading	53.02	(raw hemp)

2. The foregoing shall not limit the product coverage of the Agreement on Sanitary and Phytosanitary Measures.

ANNEX 2

Domestic Support : The Basis for Exemption from the Reduction Commitments

1. Domestic support policies for which exemption from the reduction commitments is claimed shall meet the fundamental requirement that they have no, or at most minimal, trade distortion effects or effects on production. Accordingly, all policies for which exemption is claimed shall conform to the following basic criteria:

(i) the support in question shall be provided through a publicly-funded government programme (including government revenue foregone) not involving transfers from consumers; and

(ii) the support in question shall not have the effect of providing price support to producers; plus policy-specific criteria and conditions as set out below.

Government Service Programmes

2. General services

Policies in this category involve expenditures (or revenue foregone) in relation to programmes which provide services or benefits to agriculture or the rural community. They shall not involve direct payments to producers or processors. Such programmes, which include but are not restricted to the following list. shall meet the general criteria in paragraph 1 above and policy-specific conditions where set out below:

(i) research, including general research, research in connection with environmental programmes, and research pro-grammes relating to particular products;

(ii) pest and disease control, including general and product-specific pest and disease control measures, such as early warning systems, quarantine and eradication;

(iii) training services, including both general and specialist training facilities;

(iv) extension and advisory services, including the provision of means to facilitate the transfer of information and the results of research to producers and consumers;

(v) inspection services, including general inspection services and the inspection of particular products for health, safety, grading or standardization purposes;

(vi) marketing and promotion services, including market information, advice and promotion relating to particular products but excluding expenditure for unspecified purposes that could be used by sellers to reduce their selling price or confer a direct economic benefit to purchasers; and

(vii) infrastructural services, including: electricity reticulation, roads and other means of transport, market and port facilities, water supply facilities, dams and drainage schemes, and infrastructural works associated with environmental programmes. In all cases the expenditure shall be directed to the provision or construction of capital works only, and shall exclude the subsidized provision of on-farm facilities other than for the reticulation of generally-available public utilities. It shall not include subsidies to inputs or operating costs, or preferential user charges.

3. Public stockholding for food security purposes[14]

Expenditures (or revenue foregone) in relation to the accumulation and holding of stocks of products which form an integral part of a food security programme identified in national legislation. This may include government aid to private storage of products as part of such a programme.

The volume and accumulation of such stocks shall correspond to predetermined targets related solely to food security. The process of stock accumulation and disposal shall be financially transparent. Food purchases by the government shall be made at current market prices and sales from food security stocks shall be made at no less than the current domestic market price for the product and quality in question.

4. Domestic food aid[15]

Expenditures (or revenue foregone) in relation to the provision of domestic food aid to sections of the population in need.

Eligibility to receive the food aid shall be subject to clearly-defined criteria related to nutritional objectives. Such aid shall be in the form of direct provision of food to those concerned or the provision of means to allow eligible recipients to buy food either at market or at subsidized prices. Food purchases by the government shall be made at current market prices and the financing and administration of the aid shall be transparent.

5. Direct payments to producers

Support provided through direct payments (or revenue foregone, including payments in kind) to producers for which exemption from reduction commitments is claimed shall meet the basic criteria set out in paragraph 1 above, plus specific criteria applying to individual types of direct payment as set out in paragraphs 6 to 13 below. Where exemption from reduction is

---

[14] For the purposes of paragraph 3 of this Annex, Governmental stockholding programmes for food security purposes in developing countries whose operation is transparent and conducted in accordance with officially published objective criteria or guidelines shall be considered to be in conformity with the provisions of this paragraph including programmes under which stocks of foodstuffs for food security purposes are acquired and released at administered prices; provided that the difference between the acquisition price and the external reference price is accounted for in the AMS.

[14&15] For the purposes of paragraphs 3 and 4 of this Annex, the provision of foodstuffs at subsidized prices with the objective of meeting food requirements of urban and rural poor in developing countries on a regular basis at reasonable prices shall be considered to be in conformity with the provisions of this paragraph.

claimed for any existing or new type of direct payment other than those specified in paragraphs 6 to 13, it shall conform to criteria (ii) to (v) of paragraph 6 in addition to the general criteria set out in paragraph 1.

6. De coupled income support

(i) Eligibility for such payment shall be determined by clearly-defined criteria such as income, status as a producer or landowner, factor use or production level in a defined and fixed base period.

(ii) The amount of such payments in any given year shall not be related to, or based on, the type or volume of production (including livestock units) undertaken by the producer in any year after the base period.

(iii) The amount of such payments in any given year shall not be related to, or based on, the prices, domestic or international, applying to any production under-taken in any year after the base period.

(iv) The amount of such payments in any given year shall not be related to, or based on, the factors of production employed in any year after the base period.

(v) No production shall be required in order to receive such payments.

7. Government financial participation in income insurance and income safety-net programmes

(i) Eligibility for such payments shall be determined by an income loss, taking into account only income derived from agriculture, which exceeds 30 per cent of average gross income or the equivalent in net income terms (excluding any payments from the same or similar schemes) in the preceding three-year period or a three-year average based on the preceding five-year period excluding the highest and the lowest entry. Any producer meeting this condition shall he eligible to receive the payments.

(ii) The amount of such payments shall compensate for less than 70 per cent of the producer's income loss in the year the producer becomes eligible to receive this assistance.

(iii) The amount of any such payments shall relate solely to income; it shall not relate to the type or volume of production (including livestock units) undertaken by the producer; or to the prices, domestic or international, applying to such production; or to the factors of production employed.

(iv) Where a producer receives in the same year payments under this paragraph and under paragraph 8 below (relief from natural disasters), the total of such payments shall be less than 100 per cent of the producer's total loss.

8. Payments (made either directly or by way of government financial participation in crop schemes) for relief flora natural disasters

(i) Eligibility for such payments shall arise only following a formal recognition by government authorities that a natural or like disaster (including disease outbreaks, pest infestations, nuclear accidents, and war on the territory of the Member concerned) has occurred or is occurring; and shall be determined by a production loss which exceeds 30 per cent of the average of production in the preceding three-year period or a three year average based on the preceding five-year period, excluding the highest and the lowest entry.

(ii) Payments made following a disaster shall be applied only in respect of losses of income, livestock (including payments in connection with the veterinary treatment of animals), land or other production factors due to the natural disaster in question.

(iii) Payments shall compensate for not more than the total cost of replacing such losses and shall not require or specify the type or quantity of future production.

(iv) Payments made during a disaster shall not exceed the level required to prevent or alleviate further loss as defined in criterion (ii) above.

(v) Where a producer receives in the same year payments under this paragraph and under paragraph 7 above (income insurance and income safety-net programmes), the total of such payments shall be less than 100 per cent of the producer's total loss.

9. Structural adjustment assistance provided through producer retirement programmes

(i) Eligibility for such payments shall be determined by reference to clearly-defined criteria in programmes designed to facilitate the retirement of persons engaged in marketable agricultural production, or their movement to non-agricultural activities.

(ii) Payments shall be conditional upon the total and permanent retirement of the recipients from marketable agricultural production.

10. Structural adjustment assistance provided through resource retirement programmes:

(i) Eligibility for such payments shall be determined by reference to clearly-defined criteria in programmes designed to remove land or other resources, including livestock, from marketable agricultural production.

(ii) Payments shall be conditional upon the retirement of land from marketable agricultural production for a minimum of 3 years, and in the case of livestock on its slaughter or definitive permanent disposal.

(iii) Payments shall not require or specify any alternative use for such land or other resources which involves the production of marketable agricultural products.

(iv) Payments shall not be related to either the type or quantity of production or to the prices, domestic or international, applying to production undertaken using the land or other resources remaining in production.

11. Structural adjustment assistance provided through investment aids

(i) Eligibility for such payments shall be determined by reference to clearly-defined criteria in government programmes designed to assist the financial or physical restructuring of a producer's operations in response to objectively demonstrated structural disadvantages. Eligibility for such programmes may also be based on a clearly-defined government programme for the reprivatization of agricultural land.

(ii) The amount of such payments in any given year shall not be related to, or based on, the type or volume of production (including livestock units) undertaken by the producer in any year after the base period other than as provided for under (v) below.

(iii) The amount of such payments in any given year shall not be related to, or based on, the prices, domestic or international, applying to any production undertaken in any year after the base period.

(iv) The payments shall be given only for the period of time necessary for the realization of the investment in respect of which they are provided.

(v) The payments shall not mandate or in any way designate the agricultural products to be produced by the recipients except to require them not to produce a particular product.

(vi) The payments shall be limited to the amount required to compensate for the structural disadvantage.

12. Payments under environmental programmes

  (i) Eligibility for such payments shall be determined as part of a clearly-defined government environmental or conservation programme and be dependent on the fulfilment of specific conditions under the government programme, including conditions related to production methods or inputs.

  (ii) The amount of payment shall be limited to the extra costs or loss of income involved in complying with the government programme.

13. Payments under regional assistance programmes

  (i) Eligibility for such payments shall be limited to producers in disadvantaged regions. Each such region must be a clearly designated contiguous geographical area with a definable economic and administrative identity, considered as disadvantaged on the basis of neutral and objective criteria clearly spelt out in law or regulation and indicating that the region's difficulties arise out of more than temporary circumstances.

  (ii) The amount of such payments in any given year shall not be related to, or based on, the type or volume of production (including livestock units) undertaken by the producer in any year after the base period other than to reduce that production.

  (iii) The amount of such payments in any given year shall not be related to, or based on, the prices, domestic or international, applying to any production undertaken in any year after the base period.

  (iv) Payments shall be available only to producers in eligible regions, but generally available to all producers within such regions.

  (v) Where related to production factors, payments shall be made at a degressive rate above a threshold level of the factor concerned.

  (vi) The payments shall be limited to the extra costs or loss of income involved in undertaking agricultural production in the prescribed area.

ANNEX 3

Domestic Support : Calculation of Aggregate Measurement of Support

1. Subject to the provisions of Article 6, an Aggregate Measurement of

Support (AMS) shall be calculated on a product-specific basis for each basic product (defined as the product as close as practicable to the point of first sale) receiving market price support, non-exempt direct payments, or any other subsidy not exempted from the reduction commitment ("other non-exempt policies"). Support which is non-product specific shall be totalled into one non-product-specific AMS in total monetary terms.

2. Subsidies under paragraph 1 shall include both budgetary outlays and revenue foregone by governments or their agents.

3. Support at both the national and sub-national level shall be included.

4. Specific agricultural levies or fees paid by producers shall be deducted from the AMS.

5. The AMS calculated as outlined below for the base period shall constitute the base level for the implementation of the reduction commitment on domestic support.

6. For each basic product, a specific AMS shall be established, expressed in total monetary value terms.

7. The AMS shall be calculated as close as practicable to the point of first sale of the product concerned. Policies directed at agricultural processors shall be included to the extent that such policies benefit the producers of the basic products.

8. Market price support: market price support shall be calculated using the gap between a fixed external reference price and the applied administered price multiplied by the quantity of production eligible to receive the applied administered price. Budgetary payments made to maintain this gap such as buying-in or storage costs, shall not be included in the AMS.

9. The fixed external reference price shall be based on the years 1986 to 1988 and shall generally be the average f.o.b. unit value for the product concerned in a net exporting country and the average c.i.f. unit value for the product concerned in a net importing country in the base period. The fixed reference price may be adjusted for quality differences as necessary.

10. Non-exempt direct payments : non-exempt direct payments which are dependent on a price gap shall be calculated either using the gap between the fixed reference price and the applied administered price multiplied by the quantity of production eligible to receive the administered price, or using budgetary outlays.

11. The fixed reference price shall be based on the years 1986 to 1988 and shall generally be the actual price used for determining payment rates.

12. Non-exempt direct payments which are based on factors other than price shall be measured using budgetary outlays.

13. Other non-exempt policies, including input subsidies and other policies such as marketing cost reduction measures: the value of such policies shall be measured using government budgetary outlays or, where the use of budgetary outlays does not reflect the full extent of the subsidy concerned, the basis for calculating the subsidy shall be the gap between the price of the subsidised good or service and a representative market price for a similar good or service multiplied by the quantity of the good or service.

ANNEX 4

Domestic Support : Calculation of Equivalent Measurement of Support

1. Subject to the provisions of Article 6, equivalent measurements of support shall be calculated in respect of all products where market price support as defined in Annex 3 exists but for which calculation of this component of the AMS is not practicable. For such products the base level for implementation of the domestic support reduction commitments shall consist of a market price support component expressed in terms of equivalent measurements of support under paragraph 2 below, as well as any non-exempt direct payments and other non-exempt support, which shall be evaluated as provided for under paragraph 3 below. Support at both national and sub-national level shall be included.

2. The equivalent measurements of support provided for in paragraph 1 shall be calculated on a product-specific basis for all products as close as practicable to the point of first sale ("basic products") receiving market price support and for which the calculation of the market price support component of the AMS is not practicable. For those basic products, equivalent measurements of market price support shall be made using the applied administered price and the quantity of production eligible to receive that price or, where this is not practicable, on budgetary outlays used to maintain the producer price.

3. Where products falling under paragraph 1 above are the subject of non-exempt direct payments or any other product-specific subsidy not exempted from the reduction commitment, the basis for equivalent measurements of support concerning these measures shall be calculations as for the corresponding AMS components (specified in paragraphs 10 to 13 of Annex 3).

4. Equivalent measurements of support shall be calculated on the amount of subsidy as close as practicable to the point of first sale of the product concerned. Policies directed at agricultural processors shall be included to the extent that such policies benefit the producers of the basic products. Specific agricultural levies or fees paid by producers shall reduce the equivalent measurements of support by a corresponding amount.

ANNEX 5

Special Treatment Under Article 4:2

Section A

1. The provisions of Article 4:2 of this Agreement shall not apply with effect from the entry into force of this Agreement to any primary agricultural product and its worked and/or prepared products ("designated products") in respect of which the following conditions are complied with (hereinafter referred to as "special treatment"):

(a) imports of the designated products comprised less than 3 per cent of corresponding domestic consumption in the base period 1986-1988 ("the base period");

(b) no export subsidies have been provided since the beginning of the base period for the designated products;

(c) effective production restricting measures are applied to the primary agricultural product;

(d) such products are designated with the symbol "ST-Annex 5" in Section IB of Part I of a Member's Schedule annexed to the Uruguay Round (1994) Protocol as being subject to special treatment reflecting factors of non-trade concerns, such as food security and environmental protection; and

(e) minimum access opportunities in respect of the designated products correspond, as specified in Section IB of Part I of the Schedule of the Member concerned, to 4 per cent of base period domestic consumption of the designated products from the beginning of the first year of the implementation period and, thereafter, are increased by 0.8 per cent of corresponding domestic consumption in the base period per year for the remainder of the implementation period.

2. At the beginning of any year of the implementation period a Member may cease to apply special treatment in respect of the designated products by complying with the provisions of paragraph 6 below. In such a case, the Member concerned shall maintain the minimum access opportunities already in effect at such time and increase the minimum access opportunities by 0.4 per cent of corresponding domestic consumption in the base period per year for the remainder of the implementation period. Thereafter, the level of minimum access opportunities resulting from this formula in the final year of the implementation period shall be maintained in the Schedule of the Member concerned.

3. Any negotiation on the question of whether there can be a continuation of the special treatment as set out in paragraph 1 above after the end of the implementation period shall be completed within the time-frame of the implementation period itself as a part of the negotiations set out in Article 20 of this Agreement, taking into account the factors of non-trade concerns.

4. If it is agreed as a result of the negotiation referred to in paragraph 3 above that a Member may continue to apply the special treatment, such Member shall confer additional and acceptable concessions as determined in that negotiation.

5. Where the special treatment is not to be continued at the end of the implementation period, the Member concerned shall implement the provisions of paragraph 6 below. In such a case, after the end of the implementation period the minimum access opportunities for the designated products shall be maintained at the level of 8 per cent of corresponding domestic consumption in the base period in the Schedule of the Member concerned.

6. Border measures other than ordinary customs duties maintained in respect of the designated products shall become subject to the provisions of Article 4:2 of this Agreement with effect from the beginning of the year in which the special treatment ceases to apply. Such products shall be subject to ordinary customs duties, which shall be bound in the Schedule of the Member concerned and applied, from the beginning of the year in which special treatment ceases and thereafter, at such rates as would have been applicable had a reduction of at least 15 per cent been implemented over the implementation period in equal annual instalments. These duties shall be established on the basis of tariff equivalents to be calculated in accordance with the guidelines prescribed in the attachment hereto.

Section B

7. The provisions of Article 4:2 of this Agreement shall also not apply with effect from the entry into force of this Agreement to a primary agricultural product that is the predominant staple in the traditional diet of a developing country Member and in respect of which the following conditions, in addition to those specified in paragraph 1 (a) through 1 (d) above, as they apply to the products concerned, are complied with :

- minimum access opportunities in respect of the products concerned, as specified in Section IB of Part I of the Schedule of the developing country Member concerned, correspond to 1 per cent of base period domestic consumption of the products concerned from the beginning of the first year of the implementation period and are increased in equal annual instalments to 2 per cent of corresponding domestic consumption in the base period at the beginning of the fifth year of the implementation period. From the beginning of the sixth year of the implementation period, minimum access opportunities in respect of the products concerned correspond to 2 per cent of corresponding domestic consumption in the base period and are increased in equal annual instalments to 4 per cent of corresponding domestic consumption in the base period until the beginning of the tenth year. Thereafter, the level of minimum access opportunities resulting from this formula in the tenth year shall be maintained in the Schedule of the developing country Member concerned.

- appropriate market access opportunities have been provided for in other products under this Agreement.

8. Any negotiation on the question of whether there can be a continuation of the special treatment as set out in paragraph 7 above after the end of the tenth year following the beginning of the implementation period shall be initiated and completed within the time-frame of the tenth year itself following the beginning of the implementation period.

9. If it is agreed as a result of the negotiation referred to in paragraph 8 above that a Member may continue to apply the special treatment, such Member shall confer additional and acceptable concessions as determined in that negotiation.

10. In the event that special treatment under paragraph 7 above is not to be continued beyond the tenth year following the beginning of the implementation period, the products concerned shall be subject to ordinary customs duties, established on the basis of a tariff equivalent to be calculated in accordance with the guidelines prescribed in the attachment hereto, which shall be bound in the Schedule of the Member concerned. In other respects, the provisions of paragraph 6 above shall apply as modified by the relevant special and differential treatment accorded to developing country Members under this Agreement.

Attachment to Annex 5

Guidelines for the Calculation of Tariff Equivalents for the Specific Purpose Specified in Paragraphs 6 and 10 of this Annex

1. The calculation of the tariff equivalents, whether expressed as *ad valorem* or specific rates, shall be made using the actual difference between internal and external prices in a transparent manner. Data used shall be for the years 1986 to 1988. Tariff equivalents:

(i) shall primarily be established at the four-digit level of the HS;

(ii) shall be established at the six-digit or a more detailed level of the HS wherever appropriate;

(iii) shall generally be established for worked and/or prepared products by multiplying the specific tariff equivalent(s) for the primary agricultural product(s) by the proportion(s) in value terms or in physical terms as appropriate of the primary agricultural product(s) in the worked and/or prepared products, and take account, where necessary, of any additional elements currently providing protection to industry.

2. External prices shall be, in general, actual average c.i.f. unit values for the importing country. Where average c.i.f. unit values are not available or appropriate, external prices shall be either:

(i) appropriate average c.i.f. unit values of a near country; or

(ii) estimated from average f.o.b. unit values of (an) appropriate major exporter(s) adjusted by adding an estimate of insurance, freight and other relevant costs to the importing country.

3. The external prices shall generally be converted to domestic currencies using the annual average market exchange rate for the same period as the price data.

4. The internal price shall generally be a representative wholesale price ruling in the domestic market or an estimate of that price where adequate data is not available.

5. The initial tariff equivalents may be adjusted, where necessary, to take account of differences in quality or variety using an appropriate coefficient.

6. Where a tariff equivalent resulting from these guidelines is negative or lower than the current bound rate, the initial tariff equivalent may be established at the current bound rate or on the basis of national offers for that product.

7. Where an adjustment is made to the level of a tariff equivalent which would have resulted from the above guidelines, the Member concerned shall afford, on request, full opportunities for consultation with a view to negotiating appropriate solutions.

AGREEMENT ON THE APPLICATION OF SANITARY AND PHYTOSANITARY MEASURES

Members,

Reaffirming that no Member should be prevented from adopting or enforcing measures necessary to protect human, animal or plant life or health, subject to the requirement that they are not applied in a manner which would constitute a means of arbitrary or unjustifiable discrimination between

Members where the same conditions prevail or a disguised restriction on international trade;

Desiring to improve the human health, animal health and Phytosanitary situation in all Members;

Noting that sanitary and phytosanitary measures are often applied on the basis of bilateral agreements or protocols;

Desiring the establishment of a multilateral framework of rules and disciplines to guide the adoption, development and the enforcement of sanitary and phytosanitary measures in order to minimize their negative effects on trade;

Recognizing the important contribution that international standards, guidelines and recommendations can make in this regard;

Desiring to further the use of harmonized sanitary and phytosanitary measures between Members, on the basis of international standards, guidelines and recommendations developed by the relevant international organizations, including the Codex Alimentarius Commission, the International Office of Epizootics, and the relevant international and regional organizations operating within the framework of the International Plant Protection Convention, without requiring Members to change their appropriate level of protection of human, animal or plant life or health;

Recognizing that developing country Members may encounter special difficulties in complying with the sanitary or phytosanitary measures of importing Members, and as a consequence, in access to markets, and also in the formulation and application of sanitary or phytosanitary measures in their own territories, and desiring to assist them in their endeavours in this regard;

Desiring therefore to elaborate rules for the application of the provisions of the GATT 1994 which relate to the use of sanitary or phytosanitary measures, in particular the provisions of Article XX(b)[16];

Agree as follows:

1. This Agreement applies to all sanitary and phytosanitary measures which may, directly or indirectly, affect international trade. Such measures shall be developed and applied in accordance with the provisions of this Agreement.

2. For the purposes of this Agreement, the definitions provided in Annex A shall apply.

3. The annexes are an integral part of this Agreement.

---

[16] In this Agreement. reference to Article XX(b) includes also the chapeau of that Article.

4. Nothing in this Agreement shall affect the rights of Members under the Agreement on Technical Barriers to Trade with respect to measures not within the scope of this Agreement.

Basic Rights and Obligations

5. Members have the right to take sanitary and phytosanitary measures necessary for the protection of human, animal or plant life or health, provided that such measures are not inconsistent with the provisions of this Agreement.

6. Members shall ensure that any sanitary or phytosanitary measure is applied only to the extent necessary to protect human, animal or plant life or health, is based on scientific principles and is not maintained without sufficient scientific evidence, except as provided for in paragraph 22.

7. Members shall ensure that their sanitary and phytosanitary measures do not arbitrarily or unjustifiably discriminate between Members where identical or similar conditions prevail, including between their own territory and other Members. Sanitary and phytosanitary measures shall not be applied in a manner which would constitute a disguised restriction on international trade.

8. Sanitary or phytosanitary measures which conform to the relevant provisions of this Agreement shall be presumed to be in accordance with the obligations of the Members under the provisions of the GATT 1994 which relate to the use of sanitary or phytosanitary measures, in particular the provisions of Article XX(b).

Harmonization

9. To harmonize sanitary and phytosanitary measures on as wide a basis as possible, Members shall base their sanitary or phytosanitary measures on international standards, guidelines or recommendations, where they exist, except as otherwise provided for in this Agreement, and in particular in paragraph 11.

10. Sanitary or phytosanitary measures which conform to international standards, guidelines or recommendations shall be deemed to be necessary to protect human, animal or plant life or health, and presumed to be consistent with the relevant provisions of this Agreement and of the GATT 1994.

11. Members may introduce or maintain sanitary or phytosanitary measures which result in a higher level of sanitary or phytosanitary protection than would be achieved by measures based on the relevant international standards, guidelines or recommendations, if there is a scientific justification, or as a consequence of the level of protection a Member determines to be appropriate in accordance with the relevant provisions of paragraphs 16

through 23.[17] Notwithstanding the above, all measures which result in a level of sanitary or phytosanitary protection different from that which would be achieved by measures based on international standards, guidelines or recommendations shall not be inconsistent with any other provision of this Agreement.

12. Members shall play a full part within the limits of their resources in the relevant international organizations and their subsidiary bodies, in particular the Codex Alimentarius Commission, the International Office of Epizootics, and in the international and regional organizations operating within the framework of the International Plant Protection Convention, to promote within these organizations the development and periodic review of standards, guidelines and recommendations with respect to all aspects of sanitary and phytosanitary measures.

13. The Committee on Sanitary and Phytosanitary Measures, as provided for in paragraphs 38 and 41, shall develop a procedure to monitor the process of international harmonization and co-ordinate efforts in this regard with the relevant international organizations.

Equivalence

14. Members shall accept the sanitary or phytosanitary measures of other Members as equivalent, even if these measures differ from their own or from those used by other Members trading in the same product, if the exporting Member objectively demonstrates to the importing Member that its measures achieve the importing Member's appropriate level of sanitary or phytosanitary protection. For this purpose, reasonable access shall be given, upon request, to the importing Member for inspection, testing and other relevant procedures.

15. Members shall, upon request, enter into consultations with the aim of achieving bilateral and multilateral agreements on recognition of the equivalence of specified sanitary or phytosanitary measures.

Assessment of Risk and Determination of the Appropriate Level of Sanitary or Phytosanitary Protection

16. Members shall ensure that their sanitary or phytosanitary measures are based on an assessment, as appropriate to the circum-stances, of the risks to human, animal or plant life or health, taking into account risk assessment techniques developed by the relevant international organizations.

---

[17] For the purposes of paragraph 11, there is a scientific justification if, on the basis of an examination and evaluation of available scientific information in conformity with the relevant provisions of this Agreement, a Member determines that the relevant international standards, guidelines or recommendations are not sufficient to achieve its appropriate level of protection.

17. In the assessment of risks, Members shall take into account available scientific evidence; relevant processes and production methods; relevant inspection, sampling and testing methods; prevalence of specific diseases or pests; existence of pest- or disease-free areas; relevant ecological and environmental conditions; and quarantine or other treatment.

18. In assessing the risk to animal or plant life or health and determining the measure to be applied for achieving the appropriate level of sanitary or Phytosanitary protection from such risk, Members shall take into account as relevant economic factors: the potential damage in terms of loss of production or sales in the event of the entry, establishment or spread of a pest or disease; the costs of control or eradication in the territory of the importing Member; and the relative cost effectiveness of alternative approaches to limiting risks.

19. Members should, when determining the appropriate level of sanitary or phytosanitary protection, take into account the objective of minimizing negative trade effects.

20. With the objective of achieving consistency in the application of the concept of appropriate level of sanitary and phytosanitary protection against risks to human life or health, or to animal and plant life or health, each Member shall avoid arbitrary or unjustifiable distinctions in the levels it considers to be appropriate in different situations, if such distinctions result in discrimination or a disguised restriction on international trade. Members shall co-operate in the Committee on Sanitary and Phytosanitary Measures in accordance with paragraphs 38, 39 and 40 of this Agreement to develop guidelines to further the practical implementation of this provision. In developing the guidelines the Committee shall take into account all relevant factors, including the exceptional character of human health risks to which people voluntarily expose themselves.

21. Without prejudice to paragraph 10, when establishing or maintaining sanitary or phytosanitary measures to achieve the appropriate level of sanitary or phytosanitary protection, Members shall ensure that such measures are not more trade restrictive than required to achieve their appropriate level of protection, taking into account technical and economic feasibility.[18]

22. In cases where relevant scientific evidence is insufficient, a Member may provisionally adopt sanitary or phytosanitary measures on the basis of available pertinent information, including that from the relevant international organizations as well as from sanitary or phytosanitary measures applied by other Members. In such circumstances, Members shall seek to obtain the

---

[18] For purposes of paragraph 21, a measure is not more trade restrictive than required unless there is another measure, reasonably available taking into account technical and economic feasibility, that achieves the appropriate level of protection and is significantly less restrictive to trade.

additional information necessary for a more objective assessment of risk and review the sanitary or phytosanitary measure accordingly within a reasonable period of time.

23. When a Member has reason to believe that a specific sanitary or phytosanitary measure introduced or maintained by another Member is constraining, or has the potential to constrain, its exports and the measure is not based on the relevant international standards, guidelines or recommendations, or such standards, guidelines or recommendations do not exist, an explanation of the reasons for such sanitary or phytosanitary measure may be requested and shall be provided by the Member maintaining the measure.

Adaptation to Regional Conditions, including Pest- or Disease-Free Areas and Areas of Low Pest or Disease Prevalence

24. Members shall ensure that their sanitary or phytosanitary measures are adapted to the sanitary or phytosanitary characteristics of the area – whether a country, part of a country, or areas of several countries – from which the product originated and to which the product is destined. In assessing the sanitary or phytosanitary characteristics of a region, Members shall take into account, *inter alia,* the level of prevalence of specific diseases or pests, the existence of eradication or control programmes, and appropriate criteria or guidelines which may be developed by the relevant international organizations.

25. Members shall in particular, recognize the concepts of pest- or disease-free areas and areas or disease prevalence. Determination of such areas shall be based on factors such as geography, ecosystems, epidemiological surveillance, and the effectiveness of sanitary or phytosanitary controls.

26. Exporting Members claiming that areas within their territories are pest- or disease-free or areas of low pest or disease prevalence shall provide the necessary evidence thereof in order to objectively demonstrate to the importing Member that such areas are, and are likely to remain, pest- or disease-free or areas of low pest or disease prevalence, respectively. For this purpose, reasonable access shall be given, upon request, to the importing Member for inspection, testing and other relevant procedures.

Transparency

27. Members shall notify changes in their sanitary or phytosanitary measures and shall provide information on their sanitary or phytosanitary measures in accordance with the provisions of Annex B.

Control, Inspection and Approval Procedures

28. Members shall observe the provisions of Annex C in the operation of control, inspection and approval procedures, including national systems for

approving the use of additives or for establishing tolerances for contaminants in foods, beverages or feedstuffs, and otherwise ensure that their procedures are not inconsistent with the provisions of this Agreement.

Technical Assistance

29. Members agree to facilitate the provision of technical assistance to other Members, especially developing country Members, either bilaterally or through the appropriate international organizations. Such assistance may be, *inter alia,* in the areas of processing technologies, research and infrastructure, including in the establishment of national regulatory bodies, and may take the form of advice, credits, donations and grants, including for the purpose of seeking technical expertise, training and equipment to allow such countries to adjust to, and comply with, sanitary or Phytosanitary measures necessary to achieve the appropriate level of sanitary or phytosanitary protection in their export markets.

30. Where substantial investments are required in order for an exporting developing country Member to fulfil the sanitary or Phytosanitary requirements of an importing Member, the latter shall consider providing such technical assistance as will permit the developing country Member to maintain and expand its market access opportunities for the product involved.

Special and Differential Treatment

31. In the preparation and application of sanitary or phytosanitary measures, Members shall take account of the special needs of developing country Members, and in particular of the least-developed ones.

32. Where the appropriate level of sanitary or phytosanitary protection allows scope for the phased introduction of new sanitary or phytosanitary measures, longer time-frames for compliance should be accorded on products of interest to developing country Members so as to maintain opportunities for their exports.

33. With a view to ensuring that developing country Members are able to comply with the provisions of this Agreement, the Committee on Sanitary and Phytosanitary Measures, provided for below, is enabled to grant to such countries, upon request, specified, time-limited exceptions in whole or in part, from obligations under this Agreement, taking into account their financial, trade and development needs.

34. Members should encourage and facilitate the active participation of developing country Members in the relevant international organizations.

Consultations and Dispute Settlement

35. The provisions of Articles XXII and XXIII of the GATT 1994 as

elaborated and applied by the MTO Understanding on Rules and Procedures Governing the Settlement of Disputes shall apply to consultations and the settlement of disputes under this Agreement, except as otherwise specifically provided herein.

36. In a dispute under this Agreement involving scientific or technical issues, a panel should seek advice from experts chosen by the panel in consultation with the parties to the dispute. To this end, the panel may, when it deems it appropriate, establish an advisory technical experts group, or consult the relevant international organizations, at the request of either party to the dispute or on its own initiative.

37. Nothing in this Agreement shall impair the rights of Members under other international agreements, including the rights to resort to the good offices or dispute settlement mechanisms of other international organizations or established under any international agreement.

Administration

38. A Committee on Sanitary and Phytosanitary Measures shall be established to provide a regular forum for consultations. It shall carry out the functions necessary to implement the provisions of this Agreement and the furtherance of its objectives, in particular with respect to harmonization. The Committee shall reach its decisions by consensus.

39. The Committee shall encourage and facilitate *ad hoc* consultations or negotiations among its Members on specific sanitary or phytosanitary issues. The Committee shall encourage the use of international standards, guidelines or recommendations by all Members and, in this regard, shall sponsor technical consultation and study with the objective of increasing coordination and integration between international and national systems and approaches for approving the use of food additives or for establishing tolerances for contaminants in foods, beverages and feedstuffs.

40. The Committee shall maintain close contact with the relevant international organizations in the field of sanitary and phytosanitary protection, especially with the Codex Alimentarius Commission, the International Office of Epizootics, and the Secretariat of the International Plant Protection Convention, with the objective of securing the best available scientific and technical advice for the administration of this Agreement and in order to ensure that unnecessary duplication of effort is avoided.

41. The Committee shall develop a procedure to monitor the process of international harmonization and the use of international standards, guidelines or recommendations. For this purpose, the Committee should, in conjunction with the relevant international organizations, establish a list of international standards, guidelines or recommendations relating to sanitary or phytosanitary

measures which the Committee determines to have a major trade impact. The list should include an indication by Members of those international standards, guidelines or recommendations which they apply as conditions for import or on the basis of which imported products conforming to these standards can enjoy access to their markets. For those cases in which a Member does not apply an international standard, guideline or recommendation as a condition for import, the Member should provide an indication of the reason thereof. and, in particular. if it considers that the standard is not stringent enough to provide the appropriate level of sanitary or phytosanitary protection. If a Member revises its position, following its indication of the use of a standard, guideline or recommendation as a condition for import, it should provide an explanation for its change and so inform the WTO Secretariat as well as the relevant international organizations, unless such notification and explanation is given according to the procedures of Annex B.

42. In order to avoid unnecessary duplication, the Committee may decide, as appropriate, to use the information generated by the procedures, particularly for notification, which are in operation in the relevant international organizations.

43. The Committee may, on the basis of an initiative from one of the Members, through appropriate channels invite the relevant international organizations or their subsidiary bodies to examine specific matters with respect to a particular standard, guideline or recommendation, including the basis of explanations for non-use given according to paragraph 41 above.

44. The Committee shall review the operation and implementation of this Agreement three years after entry into force of the Agreement Establishing the WTO, and thereafter as the need arises. Where appropriate, the Committee may submit to the Council for Trade in Goods proposals to amend the text of this Agreement having regard, *inter alia,* to the experience gained in its implementation.

Implementation

45. Members are fully responsible under this Agreement for the observance of all obligations set forth herein. Members shall formulate and implement positive measures and mechanisms in support of the observance of the provisions of this Agreement by other than central government bodies. Members shall take such reasonable measures as may be available to them to ensure that non-governmental entities within their territories, as well as regional bodies in which relevant entities within their territories are Members, comply with the relevant provisions of this Agreement. In addition, Members shall not take measures which have the effect of, directly or indirectly, requiring or encouraging such regional or non-governmental entities, or local governmental bodies, to act in a manner inconsistent with the provisions of this Agreement.

Members shall ensure that they rely on the services of non-governmental entities for implementing sanitary or phytosanitary measures only if these entities comply with the provisions of this Agreement.

Final Provisions

46. The least developed country Members may delay application of the provisions of this Agreement for a period of 5 years following the date of entry into force of the WTO with respect to their sanitary or phytosanitary measures affecting importation or imported products. Other developing country Members may delay application of the provisions of this Agreement, other than paragraphs 23 and 27, for 2 years following the date of entry into force of the Agreement establishing the WTO with respect to their existing sanitary or phytosanitary measures affecting importation or imported products where such application is prevented by a lack of technical expertise, technical infrastructure or resources.

ANNEX A

Definitions[19]

For the purposes of this Agreement, the following definitions shall apply:

1. *Sanitary or phytosanitary measure* – Any measure applied:

   - to protect animal or plant life or health within the territory of the Member from: risks arising from the entry, establishment or spread of pests, diseases, disease-carrying organisms or disease-causing organisms;
   - to protect human or animal life or health within the territory of the Member from risks arising from additives, contaminants, toxins or disease-causing organisms in foods, beverages or feedstuffs;
   - to protect human life or health within the territory of the Member from risks arising from diseases carried by animals, plants or products thereof, or from the entry, establishment or spread of pests;
   - or to prevent or limit other damage within the territory of the Member from the entry, establishment or spread of pests.

Sanitary or phytosanitary measures include all relevant laws, decrees, regulations, requirements and procedures including, *inter alia,* end product criteria; processes and production methods; testing, inspection, certification and approval procedures; quarantine treatments including relevant requirements associated

---

[19] For the purpose of these definitions "animal" includes fish and wild fauna; "plant" includes forests and wild flora; "pests" include weeds; "contaminants" include pesticide and veterinary drug residues and extraneous matter.

with the transport of animals or plants, or with the materials necessary for their survival during transport; provisions on relevant statistical methods, sampling procedures and methods of risk assessment; and packaging and labelling requirements directly related to food safety.

2. *Harmonization* – The establishment, recognition and application of common sanitary and phytosanitary measures by different Members.

3. *International standards, guidelines and recommendations* –

– for food safety the standards, guidelines and recommendations established by the Codex Alimentarius Commission relating to food additives, veterinary drug and pesticide residues, contaminants, methods of analysis and sampling, and codes and guidelines of hygienic practice;

– for animal health and zoonoses, the standards, guidelines and recommendations developed under the auspices of the International Office of Epizootics;

– for plant health, the international standards, guidelines and recommendations developed under the auspices of the Secretariat of the International Plant Protection Convention in co-operation with regional organizations operating within the framework of the International Plant Protection Convention; and for matters not covered by the above organizations, appropriate standards, guidelines and recommendations promulgated by other relevant international organizations open for Membership to all Members, as identified by the Committee on Sanitary and Phytosanitary Measures.

4. *Risk assessment* – The evaluation of the likelihood of entry, establishment or spread of a pest or disease within the territory of an importing Member according to the sanitary or phytosanitary measures which might be applied, and of the associated potential biological and economic consequences; or the evaluation of the potential for adverse effects on human or animal health arising from the presence of additives, contaminants, toxins or disease-causing organisms in food, feedstuffs and beverages.

5. *Appropriate Level of Sanitary or Phytosanitary Protection* – The level of protection deemed appropriate by the Member establishing a sanitary or phytosanitary measure to protect human animal or plant life or health within its territory.

NOTE: Many Members otherwise refer to this concept as the "acceptable level of risk".

6. *Pest- or Disease-Free Area* – An area, whether all of a country, part of

a country, or all or parts of several countries, as identified by the competent authorities, in which a specific pest or disease does not occur.

NOTE: A pest- or disease-free area may surround, be surrounded by, or be adjacent to an area – whether within part of a country or in a geographic region which includes parts of or all of several countries – in which a specific pest or disease is known to occur but is subject to regional control measures such as the establishment of protection, surveillance and buffer zones which will confine or eradicate the pest or disease in question.

7. *Area of low pest or disease prevalence* – An area, whether all of a country, part of a country, or all or parts of several countries, as identified by the competent authorities, in which a specific pest or disease occurs at low levels and which are subject to effective surveillance, control or eradication measures.

ANNEX B

Transparency of Sanitary and Phytosanitary Regulations

1. Publication of regulations

1.1 Members shall ensure that all sanitary and phytosanitary regulations[20] which have been adopted are published promptly in such a manner as to enable interested Members to become acquainted with them.

1.2 Except in urgent circumstances, Members shall allow a reasonable interval between the publication of a sanitary or phytosanitary regulation and its entry into force in order to allow time for producers in exporting Members, and particularly in developing country Members, to adapt their products and methods of production to the requirements of the importing Member.

2. Enquiry points

2.1 Each Member shall ensure that one enquiry point exists which is responsible for the provision of answers to all reasonable questions from interested Members as well as for the provision of relevant documents regarding:

(a) any sanitary or phytosanitary regulations adopted or proposed within its territory;

(b) any control and inspection procedures, production and quarantine treatment, pesticide tolerance and food additive approval procedures, which are operated within its territory;

(c) risk assessment procedures, factors taken into consi-deration, as

[20] Sanitary and phytosanitary measures such as laws, decrees or ordinances which are applicable generally.

well as the determination of the appropriate level of sanitary and phytosanitary protection;

(d) the Membership and participation of the Member, or of relevant bodies within its territory, in international and regional sanitary and Phytosanitary organizations and systems, as well as in bilateral and multilateral agreements and arrangements within the scope of this Agreement, and the texts of such agreements and arrangements.

2.2 Members shall ensure that where copies of documents are requested by interested Members, they are supplied at the same price (if any), apart from the cost of delivery, as to the nationals[21] of the Member concerned.

3. Notification procedures

3.1 Whenever an international standard, guideline or recommen-dation does not exist or the content of a proposed sanitary or phytosanitary regulation is not substantially the same as the content of an international standard, guideline or recommendation, and if the regulation may have a significant effect on trade of other Members, Members shall:

(a) publish a notice at an early stage in such a manner as to enable interested Members to become acquainted with the proposal to introduce a particular regulation;

(b) notify other Members, through the WTO Secretariat, of the products to be covered by the regulation together with a brief indication of the objective and rationale of the proposed regulation. Such notifications shall take place at an early stage, when amendments can still be introduced and comments taken into account;

(c) provide upon request to other Members copies of the proposed regulation and, whenever possible, identify the parts which in substance deviate from international standards, guidelines or recommendations;

(d) without discrimination, allow reasonable time for other Members to make comments in writing, discuss these comments upon request, and take the comments and the results of the discussions into account.

3.2 However, where urgent problems of health protection arise or threaten to arise for a Member, that Member may omit such of the steps

[21] When "nationals" are referred to in this Agreement, they shall be deemed, in the case of a separate customs territory Member of the WTO to mean persons, natural or legal, who are domiciled or who have a real and effective commercial establishment in that customs territory.

enumerated in paragraph 3.1 of this Annex as it finds necessary, provided that the Member:

(a) immediately notifies other Members, through the WTO Secretariat, of the particular regulation and the products covered, with a brief indication of the objective and the rationale of the regulation, including the nature of the urgent problem(s);

(b) provides upon request to other Members copies of the regulation;

(c) allows other Members to make comments in writing, discusses these comments upon request, and takes the comments and the results of the discussions into account.

3.3 Notifications to the WTO Secretariat shall be in English, French or Spanish.

3.4 Developed country Members shall, if requested by other Members, provide copies of the documents or, in case of voluminous documents, summaries of the documents covered by a specific notification in English, French or Spanish.

3.5 The WTO Secretariat shall promptly circulate copies of the notification to all Members and interested international organizations and draw the attention of developing country Members to any notifications relating to products of particular interest to them.

3.6 Members shall designate one single central government authority as responsible for the implementation, on the national level. of the provisions concerning notification procedures according to paragraphs 3.1, 3.2, 3.3 and 3.4 of this Annex.

4. General reservations

4.1 Nothing in this Agreement shall be construed as requiring:

(a) the provision of particulars or copies of drafts or the publication of texts other than in the language of the Member except as stated in paragraph 3.4 of this Annex; or

(b) Members to disclose confidential information which would impede enforcement of sanitary or phytosanitary legislation or which would prejudice the legitimate commercial interests of particular enterprises.

ANNEX C

Control, Inspection and Approval Procedures[22]

1. Members shall ensure, with respect to any procedure to check and ensure the fulfilment of sanitary or phytosanitary measures, that:

(a) such procedures are undertaken and completed without undue delay and in no less favourable mariner for imported products than for like domestic products;

(b) the standard processing period of each procedure is published or that the anticipated processing period is communicated to the applicant upon request; when receiving an application, the competent body promptly examines the completeness of the documentation and informs the applicant in a precise and complete manner of all deficiencies; the competent body transmits as soon as possible the results of the procedure in a precise and complete manner to the applicant so that corrective action may be taken if necessary; even when the application has deficiencies, the competent body proceeds as far as practicable with the procedure if the applicant so requests; and that upon request, the applicant is informed of the stage of the procedure, with any delay being explained;

(c) information requirements are limited to what is necessary for appropriate control, inspection and approval procedures, including for approval of the use of additives or for the establishment of tolerances;

(d) the confidentiality of information about imported products arising from or supplied in connection with control, inspection and approval is respected in a way no less favourable than for domestic products and in such a manner that legitimate commercial interests are protected;

(e) any requirements for control, inspection and approval of individual specimens of a product are limited to what is reasonable and necessary;

(f) any fees imposed for the procedures on imported products are

---

[22] Control inspection and approval procedures include, *inter alia*, procedures for sampling testing and certification.

equitable in relation to any fees charged on like domestic products or products originating in any other Member and should be no higher than the actual cost of the service;

(g) the same criteria should be used in the siting of facilities used in the procedures and the selection of samples of imported products as for domestic products so as to minimize the inconvenience to applicants, importers, exporters or their agents;

(h) whenever specifications of a product are changed subsequent to its control and inspection in light of the applicable regulations, the procedure for the modified product is limited to what is necessary to determine whether adequate confidence exists that the product still meets the regulations concerned: and

(i) a procedure exists to review complaints concerning the operation of such procedures and to take corrective action when a complaint is justified.

Where an importing Member operates a system for the approval of the use of food additives or for the establishment of tolerances for contaminants in food, feedstuffs or beverages which prohibits or restricts access to its domestic markets for products based on the absence of an approval, the importing Member shall consider the use of a relevant international standard as the basis for access until a final determination is made.

2. Where a sanitary or phytosanitary measure specifies control at the level of production, the Member in whose territory the production takes place shall provide the necessary assistance to facilitate such control and the work of the controlling authorities.

3. Nothing in this Agreement shall prevent Members from carrying out reasonable inspection within their own territories.

AGREEMENT ON TEXTILES AND CLOTHING

Recalling that Ministers agreed at Punta del Este that "negotiations in the area of textiles and clothing shall aim to formulate modalities that would permit the eventual integration of this sector into GATT on the basis of strengthened GATT rules and disciplines, thereby also contributing to the objective of further liberalization of trade":

Recalling also that in the April 1989 Decision of the Trade Negotiations Committee it was agreed that the process of integration should commence following the conclusion of the Uruguay Round and should be progressive in character.

Recalling further that it was agreed that special treatment should be accorded to the least developed country Members;

Members hereby *agree* as follows:

Article I

1. This Agreement 'sets out provisions to be applied by Members during a transition period for the integration of the textiles and clothing sector into the GATT 1994.

2. Members agree to use the provisions of paragraph 18 of Article 2 and paragraph 6(b) of Article 6 of this Agreement in such a way as to permit meaningful increases in access possibilities for small suppliers and the development of commercially significant trading opportunities for new entrants in the field of textiles and clothing trade.[23]

3. Members shall have due regard to the situation of those Members which have not participated in the Protocols extending the Arrangement Regarding International Trade in Textiles (MFA) since 1986 and, to the extent possible, shall afford them special treatment in applying the provisions of this Agreement.

4. Members agree that the particular interests of the cotton producing exporting Members should, in consultation with them, be reflected in the implementation of the provisions of this Agreement.

5. In order to facilitate the integration of the textiles and clothing sector into the GATT 1994, Members should allow for continuous autonomous industrial adjustment and increased competition in their markets.

6. Unless otherwise provided in this Agreement, its provisions shall not affect the rights and obligations of Members under the provisions of the Agreement Establishing the WTO and the multilateral trade agreements annexed thereto.

7. The textile and clothing products to which this Agreement applies are set out in the Annex to this Agreement (hereafter referred to as the Annex).

Article 2

1. All quantitative restrictions within bilateral agreements maintained under Article 4 or notified under Article 7 or 8 of the MFA in force on the day before the entry into force of this Agreement, shall, within 60 days following its entry into force, be notified in detail, including the restraint levels, growth rates and flexibility provisions, by the Members maintaining such restrictions, to the Textiles Monitoring Body (herein referred to as the TMB) established under Article 8. Members agree that as of the date of entry into force of this Agreement, all such restrictions maintained between GATT 1947 contracting

---

[23] To the extent possible, exports from a least-developed country may also benefit from this provision.

parties, and in place on the day before its entry into force, shall be governed by the provisions of this Agreement.

2. The TMB shall circulate these notifications to all Members for their information. It is open to any Member to bring to the attention of the TMB, within 60 days of the circulation of the notifications, any observations it deems appropriate with regard to such notifications. Such observations shall be circulated to the other Members for their information. The TMB may make recommendations, as appropriate, to the Members concerned.

3. When the twelve-month period of restrictions to be notified under paragraph 1 above does not coincide with the 12-month period immediately preceding the entry into force of this Agreement, the Members concerned should mutually agree on arrangements to bring the period of restrictions into line with the agreement year[24], and to establish notional base levels of such restrictions in order to implement the provisions of this Article. Concerned Members agree to enter consultations promptly upon request with a view to reaching such mutual agreement. Any such arrangements shall take into account, *inter alia*, seasonal patterns of shipments in recent years. The results of these consultations shall be notified to the TMB which shall make such recommendations as it deems appropriate to the Members concerned.

4. The restrictions notified under paragraph 1 above shall be deemed to constitute the totality of such restrictions applied by the respective Members on the day before the entry into force of this Agreement. No new restrictions in terms of products or Members shall be introduced except under the provisions of this Agreement or relevant GATT 1994 provisions.[25] Restrictions not notified within 60 days of the entry into force of this Agreement shall be terminated forthwith.

5. Any unilateral measure taken under Article 3 of the MFA prior to the date of entry into force of this Agreement may remain in effect for the duration specified therein, but not exceeding 12 months, if it has been reviewed by the Textiles Surveillance Body (TSB) established under the MFA. Should the TSB not have had the opportunity to review any such unilateral measure it shall be reviewed by the TMB in accordance with the rules and procedures governing Article 3 measures under the MFA. Any measure applied under an MFA Article 4 agreement prior to the date of entry into force of this Agreement that is the subject of a dispute which the TSB has not had the opportunity to review shall also be reviewed by the TMB in accordance with the MFA rules and procedures applicable for such a review.

---

[24] The agreement year is defined to mean a 12-month period beginning from the date of entry into force of this Agreement and at the subsequent 12-month intervals.

[25] The relevant GATT 1994 provisions shall not include Article XIX in respect of products not yet integrated into GATT 1994, except as specifically provided in the Note to the Annex.

6. On the date of entry into force of this Agreement, each Member shall integrate into GATT 1994 products which, in 1990, accounted for not less than 16 per cent of the total volume of imports in 1990 of the products in the Annex, in terms of HS lines or categories. The products to be integrated shall encompass products from each of the following four groups: tops and yarns, fabrics, made-up textile products, and clothing.

7. Full details of the actions to be taken pursuant to paragraph 6 above shall be notified by the Members concerned according to the following:

- Members maintaining restrictions failing under paragraph 1 above undertake, notwithstanding the date of the entry into force of this Agreement, to notify such details to the GATT Secretariat not later than (1 July 1992).[26] The GATT Secretariat shall promptly circulate these notifications to the other Members for information. These notifications will be made available to the TMB, when established, for the purposes of paragraph 21 below;
- Members which have, pursuant to paragraph 1 of Article 6, retained the right to use the provisions of Article 6, shall notify such details to the TMB not later than 60 days following the entry into force of this Agreement, or, in the case of those Members covered by paragraph 3 of Article 1, not later than at the end of the twelfth month that this Agreement is in effect. The TMB shall circulate these notifications to the other Members for information and review them as provided in paragraph 21 below.

8. The remaining products, *i.e.*, the products not integrated into GATT 1994 under paragraph 6 above, shall be integrated, in terms of HS lines or categories, in three stages, as follows:

A. On the first day of the 37th month that this Agreement is in effect, products which, in 1990. accounted for not less than 17 per cent of the total volume of 1990 imports of the products in the Annex. The products to be integrated by the Members shall encompass products from each of the following four groups: tops and yarns, fabrics, made-up textile products, and clothing.

B. On the first day of the 85th month that this Agreement is in effect, products which, in 1990, accounted for not less than 18 per cent of the total volume of 1990 imports of the products in the Annex. The products to be integrated by the Members shall encompass products from each of the following four groups: tops and yarns, fabrics, made-up textile products, and clothing.

---

[26] Participants agreed to examine, in the first quarter of 1994, the date and the technical and administrative aspects related to the implementation of this provision.

C. On the first day of the 121st month that the Agreement Establishing the WTO is in effect, the textiles and clothing sector shall stand integrated into GATT 1994, all restrictions under this Agreement having been eliminated.

9. Members which have notified, pursuant to paragraph 1 of Article 6, their intention not to retain the right to use the provisions of Article 6 shall, for the purposes of this Agreement, be deemed to have integrated their textiles and clothing products into the GATT 1994. Such Members shall, therefore, be exempted from complying with the provisions of paragraphs 6 to 8 above and 11 below.

10. Nothing in this Agreement shall prevent a Member which has submitted an integration programme pursuant to paragraph 6 or 8 above from integrating products into the GATT 1994 earlier than provided for in such a programme. However, any such integration of products shall take effect at the beginning of an agreement year, and details shall be notified to the TMB at least three months prior thereto for circulation to all Members.

11. The respective programmes of integration, in pursuance of paragraph 8 above, shall be notified in detail to the TMB at least 12 months before their coming into effect and circulated by the TMB to all Members.

12. The base levels of the restrictions on the remaining products, mentioned in paragraph 8 above, shall be the restraint levels referred to in paragraph 1 above.

13. During Stage 1 of this Agreement (from the date of entry into force of this Agreement to the 36th month that it is in effect, inclusive) the level of each restriction under MFA bilateral agreements in force for the 12-month period prior to its entry into force shall be increased annually by not less than the growth rate established for the respective restrictions, increased by 16 per cent.

14. Except where the Council for Trade in Goods or the Dispute Settlement Body decides otherwise under paragraph 12 of Article 8, the level of each remaining restriction shall be increased annually during subsequent stages of the Agreement by not less than the following:

(i) for Stage 2 (from the 37th to the 84th month that this Agreement is in effect, inclusive), the growth rate for the respective restrictions during Stage 1, increased by 25 per cent;

(ii) for Stage 3 (from the 85th to the 120th month that this Agreement is in effect, inclusive), the growth rate for the respective restrictions during Stage 2, increased by 27 per cent.

15. Nothing in this Agreement shall prevent a Member from eliminating

any restriction maintained pursuant to this Article, effective at the beginning of any agreement year during the transition period, provided the exporting Member concerned and the TMB are notified at least three months prior to the elimination coming into effect. The period for prior notification might be shortened to 30 days with the agreement of the restrained Member. The TMB shall circulate such notifications to all Members. In considering the elimination of restrictions as envisaged in this paragraph, the Members concerned shall take into account the treatment of similar exports from other Members.

16. Flexibility provisions, *i.e.*, swing, carryover and carry forward, applicable to all quantitative restrictions in force in accordance with the provisions of this Article, shall be the same as those provided for in MFA bilateral agreements for the 12-month period prior to the entry into force of this Agreement. No quantitative limits shall be placed or maintained on the combined use of swing, carryover and carry forward.

17. Administrative arrangements, as deemed necessary in relation to the implementation of any provision of this Article, shall be a matter for agreement between the Members concerned. Any such arrangements shall be notified to the TMB.

18. As regards those Members whose exports are subject to restrictions on the day before the entry into force of this Agreement and whose restrictions represent 1.2 per cent or less of the total volume of the restrictions applied by an importing Member as of 31 December 1991 and notified under this Article, meaningful improvement in access for their exports shall be provided at the entry into force of this Agreement and for its duration through advancement by one stage of the growth rates set out in paragraphs 13 and 14 above, or through at least equivalent changes as may be mutually agreed with respect to a different mix of base levels, growth and flexibility provisions. Such improvements shall be notified to the TMB.

19. In any case, during the validity of this Agreement, in which a safeguard measure is initiated by a Member under Article XIX of the GATT 1994 in respect of a particular product during a period of one year immediately following the integration of that product into GATT 1994 in accordance with the provisions of this Article, the provisions of Article XIX, as interpreted by the Agreement on Safeguards, will apply save as set out in paragraph 20 below.

20. Where such a measure is applied using non-tariff means, the importing Member concerned shall apply the measure in a manner as set forth in paragraph 2(d) of Article XIII of the GATT 1994 at the request of any exporting Member whose exports of such products were subject to restrictions under this Agreement at any time in the one-year period immediately prior to

the initiation of the safeguard measure. The concerned exporting Member shall administer such a measure. The applicable level shall not reduce the relevant exports below the level of a recent representative period, which shall normally be the average of exports from the concerned Member in the last three representative years for which statistics are available. Further, when the safeguard measure is applied for more than one year, the applicable level shall be progressively liberalised at regular intervals during the period of application. In such cases the concerned exporting Member shall not exercise the right of suspending substantially equivalent concessions or other obligations under the GATT 1994 as provided for under paragraph 3(a) of Article XIX of the GATT 1994.

21. The TMB shall keep under review the implementation of this Article. It shall, at the request of any Member, review any particular matter with reference to the implementation of the provisions of this Article. It shall make appropriate recommendations or findings within 30 days to the Member or Members concerned, after inviting the participation of such Members.

Article 3

1. Within 60 days following the entry into force of this Agreement, Members maintaining restrictions[27] on textile and clothing products (other than restrictions maintained under the MFA and covered by the provisions of Article 2), whether consistent with GATT 1994 or not, shall (a) notify them in detail to the TMB, or (b) provide to the TMB notifications with respect to them which have been submitted to any other WTO body. The notifications should, wherever applicable, provide information with respect to any GATT 1994 justification for the restrictions, including GATT 1994 provisions on which they are based.

2. All restrictions falling under paragraph 1 above, except those justified under a GATT 1994 provision, shall be either:

(a) brought into conformity with the GATT 1994 within one year following the entry into force of this Agreement, and be notified to the TMB for its information; or

(b) phased out progressively according to a programme to be presented to the TMB by the Member maintaining the restrictions not later than six months after the date of entry into force of this Agreement. This programme shall provide for all restrictions to be phased out within a period not exceeding the duration of this Agreement. The TMB may make recommendations to the Member concerned with respect to such a programme.

[27] Restrictions denote all unilateral quantitative restrictions, bilateral arrangements and other measures having a similar effect.

3. During the validity of this Agreement, Members shall provide to the TMB, for its information, notifications submitted to any other WTO bodies with respect to any new restrictions or changes in existing restrictions on textile and clothing products, taken under any GATT 1994 provision, within 60 days of their coming into effect.

4. It shall be open to any Member to make reverse notifications to the TMB, for its information, in regard to the GATT 1994 justification, or in regard to any restrictions that may not have been notified under the provisions of this Article. Actions with respect to such notifications may be pursued by any Member under relevant GATT 1994 provisions or procedures in the appropriate MTO body.

5. The TMB shall circulate the notifications made pursuant to this Article to all Members for their information.

Article 4

1. Restrictions referred to in Article 2, and those applied under Article 6, shall be administered by the exporting Members. Importing Members shall not be obliged to accept shipments in excess of the restrictions notified under Article 2, and of restrictions applied pursuant to Article 6.

2. Members agree that the introduction of changes, such as changes in practices, rules, procedures and categorization of textile and clothing products, including those changes relating to the Harmonized System, in the implementation or administration of those restrictions notified or applied under this Agreement should not upset the balance of rights and obligations between the Members concerned under this Agreement; adversely affect the access available to a Member; impede the full utilization of such access; or disrupt trade under this Agreement.

3. If a product which constitutes only part of a restriction is notified for integration pursuant to the provisions of Article 2, Members agree that any change in the level of that restriction shall not upset the balance of rights and obligations between the Members concerned under this Agreement.

4. When changes mentioned in paragraphs 2 and 3 above are necessary, however, Members agree that the Member initiating such changes shall inform and, wherever possible, initiate consultations with the affected Member or Members prior to the implementation of such changes, with a view to reaching a mutually acceptable solution regarding appropriate and equitable adjustment. Members further agree that where consultation prior to implementation is not feasible, the Member initiating such changes will, at the request of the affected Member, consult within 60 days if possible, with the Members concerned with a view to reaching a mutually satisfactory solution regarding appropriate and equitable adjustments. If a mutually

satisfactory solution is not reached, any Member involved may refer the matter to the TMB for recommendations as provided in Article 8. Should the TSB not have had the opportunity to review a dispute concerning such changes introduced prior to the entry into force of this Agreement, it shall be reviewed by the TMB in accordance with the rules and procedures of the MFA applicable for such a review.

Article 5

1. Members agree that circumvention by transhipment, rerouting, false declaration concerning country or place of origin, and falsification of official documents, frustrates the implementation of this Agreement to integrate the textiles and clothing sector into the GATT 1994. Accordingly, Members should establish the necessary legal provisions and/or administrative procedures to address and take action against such circumvention. Members further agree that, consistent with their domestic laws and procedures, they will cooperate fully to address problems arising from circumvention.

2. Should any Member believe that this Agreement is being circumvented by transshipment, re-routing, false declaration concerning country or place of origin, or falsification of official documents, and that no, or inadequate, measures are being applied to address or to take action against such circumvention, that Member should consult with the Member or Members concerned with a view to seeking a mutually satisfactory solution. Such consultations should be held promptly, and within 30 days when possible. If a mutually satisfactory solution is not reached, the matter may be referred by any Member involved to the TMB for recommendations.

3. Members agree to take necessary action, consistent with their domestic laws and procedures, to prevent, to investigate and, where appropriate, to take legal and/or administrative action against circumvention practices within their territory. Members agree to cooperate fully, consistent with their domestic laws and procedures, in instances of circumvention or alleged circumvention of this Agreement, to establish the relevant facts in the places of import, export and, where applicable, transshipment. It is agreed that such cooperation, consistent with domestic laws and procedures, will include investigation of circumvention practices which increase restrained exports to the Member maintaining such restraints; exchange of documents, correspondence, reports and other relevant information to the extent available; and facilitation of plant visits and contacts, upon request and on a case-by-case basis. Members should endeavour to clarify the circumstances of any such instances of circumvention or alleged circumvention, including the respective roles of the exporters or importers involved.

4. Where, as a result of investigation, there is sufficient evidence that

circumvention has occurred (*e.g.*, where evidence is available concerning the country or place of true origin, and the circumstances of such circumvention) Members agree that appropriate action, to the extent necessary to address the problem, should be taken. Such action may include the denial of entry of goods or, where goods have entered, having due regard to the actual circumstances and the involvement of the country or place of true origin, the adjustment of charges to restraint levels to reflect the true country or place of origin. Also, where there is evidence of the involvement of the territories of the Members through which the goods have been transshipped, such action may include the introduction of restraints with respect to such Members. Any such actions, together with their timing and scope, may be taken after consultations held with a view to arriving at a mutually satisfactory solution between the concerned Members and shall be notified to the TMB with full justification. The Members concerned may agree on other remedies in consultation. Any such agreement shall also be notified to the TMB, and the TMB may make such recommendations to the Members concerned as it deems appropriate. If a mutually satisfactory solution is not reached, any Member concerned may refer the matter to the TMB for prompt review and recommendations.

5. Members note that some cases of circumvention may involve shipments transiting through countries or places with no changes or alterations made to the goods contained in such shipments in the places of transit. They note that it may not be generally practicable for such places of transit to exercise control over such shipments.

6. Members agree that false declaration concerning fibre content, quantities, description or classification of merchandise also frustrates the objective of this Agreement. Where there is evidence that any such false declaration has been made for purposes of circumvention, Members agree that appropriate measures, consistent with domestic laws and procedures, should be taken against the exporters or importers involved. Should any Member believe that this Agreement is being circumvented by such false declaration and that no, or inadequate, administrative measures are being applied to address and/or to take action against such circumvention, that Member should consult promptly with the Member involved with a view to seeking a mutually satisfactory solution. If such a solution is not reached, the matter may be referred by any Member involved to the TMB for recommendations. This provision is not intended to prevent Members from making technical adjustments when inadvertent errors in declarations have been made.

Article 6

1. Members recognise that during the transition period it may be necessary

to apply a specific transitional safeguard mechanism (hereinafter referred to as "transitional safeguard"). The transitional safeguard may be applied by any Member, to products covered by the Annex to this Agreement, except those integrated into the GATT 1994 under the provisions of Article 2. Members not maintaining restrictions falling under Article 2 shall notify the TMB within 60 days following the entry into force of this Agreement, whether or not they wish to retain the right to use the provisions of this Article. Members which have not participated in the Protocols extending the MFA since 1986, shall make such notification within 6 months following the entry into force of this Agreement. The transitional safeguard should be applied as sparingly as possible, consistently with the provisions of this Article and the effective implementation of the integration process under this Agreement.

2. Safeguard action may be taken under this Article when, on the basis of a determination by a Member[28], it is demonstrated that a particular product is being imported into its territory in such increased quantities as to cause serious damage, or actual threat thereof, to the domestic industry producing like and/or directly competitive products. Serious damage or actual threat thereof must demonstrably be caused by such increased quantities in total imports of that product and not by such other factors as technological changes or changes in consumer preference.

3. In making a determination of serious damage, or actual threat thereof, as referred to in paragraph 2 above, the Member shall examine the effect of those imports on the state of the particular industry, as reflected in changes in such relevant economic variables as output, productivity, utilization of capacity, inventories, market share, exports, wages, employment, domestic prices, profits and investment; none of which, either alone or combined with other factors, can necessarily give decisive guidance.

4. Any measure invoked pursuant to the provisions of this Article shall be applied on a Member-by-Member basis. The Member or Members to whom serious damage, or actual threat thereof, referred to in paragraphs 2 and 3 above, is attributed, shall be determined on the basis of a sharp and substantial increase in imports, actual or imminent[29], from such a Member or Members

---

[28] A Customs union may apply a safeguard measure as a single unit or on behalf of a member State. When a customs union applies a safeguard measure as a single unit, all the requirements for the determination of serious damage or actual threat thereof under this Agreement shall be based on the conditions existing in the customs union as a whole. When a safeguard measure is applied on behalf of a member State, all the requirements for the determination of serious damage, or actual threat thereof, shall be based on the conditions existing in that member State and the measure shall be limited to that member State.

[29] Such an imminent increase shall be a measureable one and shall not be determined to exist on the basis of allegation, conjecture or mere possibility arising, for example, from the existence of production capacity in the exporting Members.

individually, and on the basis of the level of imports as compared with imports from other sources, market share, and import and domestic prices at a comparable stage of commercial transaction; none of these factors, either alone or combined with other factors, can necessarily give decisive guidance. Such safeguard measure shall not be applied to the exports of any Member whose exports of the particular product are already under restraint under this Agreement.

5. The period of validity of a determination of serious damage or actual threat thereof for the purpose of invoking safeguard action shall not exceed 90 days from the date of initial notification as set forth in paragraph 7 below.

6. In the application of the transitional safeguard, particular account shall be taken of the interests of exporting Members as set out below:

(a) Least-developed country Members shall be accorded treatment significantly more favourable than that provided to the other groups of Members referred to in this paragraph, preferably in all its elements but, at least, on overall terms.

(b) Members whose total volume of textile and clothing exports is small in comparison with the total' volume of exports of other Members and who account for only a small percentage of total imports of that product into the importing Member shall be accorded differential and more favourable treatment in the fixing of the economic terms provided in paragraphs 8, 13 and 14 below. For those suppliers, due account will be taken, pursuant to paragraphs 2 and 3 of Article 1, of the future possibilities for the development of their trade and the need to allow commercial quantities of imports from them.

(c) With respect to wool products from wool producing developing Members whose economy and textiles and clothing trade are dependent on the wool sector, whose total textile andclothing exports consist almost exclusively of wool products, and whose volume of textiles and clothing trade is comparatively small in the markets of the importing Members, special consideration shall be given to the export needs of such Members when considering quota levels, growth rates and flexibility.

(d) More favourable treatment shall be accorded to reimports by a Member of textile and clothing products which that Member has exported to another Member for processing and subsequent reimportation, as defined by the laws and practices of the importing Member, and subject to satisfactory control and certification procedures, when these products are imported from a Member for which this type of trade represents a significant proportion of its total exports of textiles and clothing.

7. The Member proposing to take safeguard action shall seek consultations with the Member or Members which would be affected by such action. The request for consultations shall be accompanied by specific and relevant factual information, as up-to-date as possible, particularly in regard to: (a) the factors; referred to in paragraph 3 above, on which the Member invoking the action has based its determination of the existence of serious damage or actual threat thereof; and (b) the factors, referred to in paragraph 4 above, on the basis of which it proposes to invoke the safeguard action with respect to the Member or Members concerned. In respect of requests made under this paragraph, the information shall be related, as closely as possible, to identifiable segments of production and to the reference period set out in paragraph 8 below. The Member invoking the action shall also indicate the specific level at which imports of the product in question from the Member or Members concerned are proposed to be restrained; such level shall not be lower than the level referred to in paragraph 8 below. The Member seeking consultations shall, at the same time, communicate to the Chairman of the TMB the request for consultations, including all the relevant factual data outlined in paragraphs 3 and 4 above, together with the proposed restraint level. The Chairman shall inform the members of the TMB of the request for consultations, indicating the requesting Member, the product in question and the Member having received the request. The Member or Members concerned shall respond to this request promptly and the consultations shall be held without delay and normally be completed within 60 days of the date on which the request has been received.

8. If, in the consultations, there is mutual understanding that the situation calls for restraint on the exports of the particular product from the Member or Members concerned, the level of such restraint shall be fixed at a level not lower than the actual level of exports or imports from the Member concerned during the twelve-month period terminating two months preceding the month in which the request for consultation was made.

9. Details of the agreed restraint measure shall be communicated to the TMB within 60 days from the date of conclusion of the agreement. The TMB shall determine whether the agreement is justified in accordance with the provisions of this Article. In order to make its determination, the TMB shall have available to it the factual data provided to the Chairman of the TMB, referred to in paragraph 7 above, as well as any other relevant information provided by the Members concerned. The TMB may make such recommendations as it deems appropriate to the Members concerned.

10. If, however, after the expiry of the period of 60 days from the date on

which the request for consultations was received, there has been no agreement between the Members, the Member which proposed to take safeguard action may apply the restraint by date of import or date of export, in accordance with the provisions of this Article, within 30 days following the 60 days period for consultations, and at the same time refer the matter to the TMB. It shall be open to either Member to refer the matter to the TMB before the expiry of the period of 60 days. In either case, the TMB shall promptly conduct an examination of the matter including the determination of serious damage, or actual threat thereof, and its causes, and make appropriate recommendations to the Members concerned within 30 days. In order to conduct such examination, the TMB shall have available to it the factual data provided to the Chairman of the TMB, referred to in paragraph 7 above, as well as any other relevant information provided by the Members concerned.

11. In highly unusual and critical circumstances, where delay would cause damage which would be difficult to repair, action under paragraph 10 above may be taken provisionally on the condition that the request for consultations and notification to the TMB shall be effected within no more than 5 working days after taking the action. In the case that consultations do not produce agreement, the TMB shall be notified at the conclusion of consultations, but in any case no later than 60 days from the date of the implementation of the action. The TMB shall promptly conduct an examination of the matter, and make appropriate recommendations to the Members concerned within 30 days. In the case that consultations do produce agreement, Members shall notify the TMB upon conclusion but, in any case, no later than 90 days from the date of the implementation of the action. The TMB may make such recommendations as it deems appropriate to the Members concerned.

12. Measures invoked pursuant to the provisions of this Article may remain in place: (a) for up to three years without extension, or (b) until the product is integrated into GATT 1994, whichever comes first.

13. Should the restraint measure remain in force for a period exceeding one year, the level for subsequent years shall be the level specified for the first year increased by a growth rate of not less than 6 per cent per annum, unless otherwise justified to the TMB. The restraint level for the product concerned may be exceeded in either year of any two subsequent years by carry forward and/or carryover of 10 per cent of which carry forward shall not represent more than 5 per cent. No quantitative limits shall be placed on the combined use of carryover, carry forward and the provision of paragraph 14 below.

14. When more than one product from another Member is placed under restraint under this Article by a Member, the level of restraint agreed, pursuant to the provisions of this Article, for each of these products may be exceeded by 7 per cent, provided that the total exports subject to restraint do

not exceed the total of the levels for all products so restrained under this Article, on the basis of agreed common units. Where the periods of application of restraints of these products do not coincide with each other, this provision shall be applied to any overlapping period on a *pro rata* basis.

15. If a safeguard action is applied under this Article to a product for which a restraint was previously in place under the MFA during the 12-month period prior to the entry into force of this Agreement, or pursuant to the provisions of Article 2 or 6 of this Agreement, the level of the new restraint shall be the level provided for in paragraph 8 of this Article unless the new restraint comes into force within one year of:

(a) the date of notification referred to in paragraph 15 of Article 2 for the elimination of the previous restraint; or

(b) the date of removal of the previous restraint put in place pursuant to the provisions of this Article or of the MFA

in which case the level shall not be less than the higher of (i) the level of restraint for the last twelve-month period during which the product was under restraint, or (ii) the level of restraint provided for in paragraph 8 of this Article.

16. When a Member which is not maintaining a restraint under Article 2 decides to apply a restraint pursuant to the provisions of this Article, it shall establish appropriate arrangements which: (a) take full account of such factors as established tariff classification and quantitative units based on normal commercial practices in export and import transactions, both as regards fibre composition and in terms of competing for the same segment of its domestic market, and (b) avoid over-categorisation. The request for consultations referred to in paragraph 7 or 11 above shall include full information on such arrangements.

Article 7

1. As part of the integration process and with reference to the specific commitments undertaken by the Members as a result of the Uruguay Round, all Members shall take such actions as may be necessary to abide by GATT 1994 rules and disciplines so as to:

(i) achieve improved access to markets for textile and clothing products through such measures as tariff reductions and bindings, reduction or elimination of non-tariff barriers, and facilitation of customs, administrative and licensing formalities;

(ii) ensure the application of policies relating to fair and equitable trading conditions as regards textiles and clothing in such areas as dumping and anti-dumping rules and procedures, subsidies and countervailing measures, and protection of intellectual property rights; and

(iii) avoid discrimination against imports in the textiles and clothing sector when taking measures for general trade policy reasons.

Such actions shall be without prejudice to the rights and obligations of Members under GATT 1994.

2. Members shall notify to the TMB the actions referred to in paragraph 1 above which have a hearing on the implementation of this Agreement. To the extent that these have been notified to other WTO committees or bodies, a summary, with reference to the original notification, shall be sufficient to fulfil the requirements under this paragraph. It shall be open to any Member to make reverse notifications to the TMB.

3. Where any Member considers that another Member has not taken the actions referred to in paragraph 1 above, and that the balance of rights and obligations under this Agreement has been upset, that Member may bring the matter before the relevant WTO committees and bodies and inform the TMB. Any subsequent findings or conclusions by the WTO committees and bodies concerned shall form a part of the TMB's comprehensive report.

Article 8

1. In order to supervise the implementation of this Agreement, to examine all measures taken under its provisions and their conformity therewith, and to take the actions specifically required of it in the Articles of this Agreement, there shall be established by the Council for Trade in Goods a Textiles Monitoring Body (TMB). The TMB shall consist of a Chairman and 10 members. Its membership shall be balanced and broadly representative of the Members and shall provide for rotation of its members at appropriate intervals. The members shall be appointed by Members designated by the Council for Trade in Goods to serve on the TMB, discharging their function on an *ad personam* basis.

2. The TMB will develop its own working procedures. It is understood, however, that consensus within the TMB does not require the assent or concurrence of members appointed by Members involved in an unresolved issue under review by the Body.

3. The TMB shall be considered as a standing body and shall meet as necessary to carry out the functions required of it under this Agreement. It shall rely on notifications and information supplied by the Members under the relevant Articles of this Agreement, supplemented by any additional information or necessary details they may submit or it may decide to seek from them. It may also rely on notifications to and reports from other WTO committees and bodies and from such other sources as it may deem appropriate.

4. Members shall afford to each other adequate opportunity for consultations with respect to any matters affecting the operation of this Agreement.

5. In the absence of any mutually agreed solution in the bilateral consultations provided for in this Agreement, the TMB shall, at the request of either Member, and following a thorough and prompt consideration of the matter, make recommendations to the Members concerned.

6. At the request of any Member, the TMB shall review promptly any particular matter which that Member considers to be detrimental to its interests under this Agreement and where consultations between it and the Member or Members concerned have failed to produce a mutually satisfactory solution. On such matters, the TMB may make such observations as it deems appropriate to the Members concerned and for the purposes of the review provide for in paragraph 11 below.

7. Before formulating its recommendations or observations, the TMB shall invite participation of such Members as may be directly affected by the matter in question.

8. Whenever the TMB is called upon to make recommendations or findings, it shall do so, preferably within a period of 30 days, unless a different time period is specified in this Agreement. All such recommendations or findings shall be communicated to the Members directly concerned. All such recommendations or findings shall also be communicated to the Council for Trade in Goods for its information.

9. The Members shall endeavour to accept in full the recommendations of the TMB, which shall exercise proper surveillance of the implementation of such recommendations.

10. If a Member considers itself unable to conform with the recommendations of the TMB, it shall provide the TMB with the reasons therefor not later than one month after receipt of such recommendations. Following thorough consideration of the reasons given, the TMB shall issue any further recommendations it considers appropriate forthwith. If, after such further recommendations, the matter remains unresolved, either Member may bring the matter before the Dispute Settlement Body and invoke paragraph 2 of Article XXIII of GATT 1994 and the relevant provisions of the Understanding on Rules and Procedures Governing the Settlement of Disputes.

11. In order to oversee the implementation of the Agreement, the Council for Trade in Goods shall conduct a major review before the end of each stage of the integration process. To assist in this review, the TMB shall, at least five months before the end of each stage, transmit to the Council for Trade in Goods a comprehensive report on the implementation of this Agreement

during the stage under review, in particular in matters with regard to the integration process, the application of the transitional safeguard mechanism, and relating to the application of GATT 1994 rules and disciplines as defined in Articles 2, 3, 6 and 7 of this Agreement, respectively. The TMB's comprehensive report may include any recommendation as deemed appropriate by the TMB to the Council for Trade in Goods.

12. In the light of its review the Council for Trade in Goods shall by consensus take such decisions as it deems appropriate to ensure that the balance of rights and obligations embodied in this Agreement is not being impaired. For the resolution of any disputes that may arise with respect to matters referred to in Article 7 of this Agreement, the Dispute Settlement Body may authorize, without prejudice to the final dates set out under Article 9 of this Agreement, an adjustment to paragraph 14 of Article 2, for the stage subsequent to the review, with respect to any Member found not to be complying with its obligations under this Agreement.

Article 9

1. This Agreement and all restrictions thereunder shall stand terminated on the first day of the 121st month that the Agreement Establishing the WTO is in effect, on which date the textiles and clothing sector shall be fully integrated into the GATT 1994. There shall be no extension of this Agreement.

ANNEX

List of Products Covered by this Agreement

1. This Annex lists textile and clothing products identified by Harmonised Commodity Description and Coding System (HS) codes at the six digit level.

2. Actions under the safeguard provisions in Article 6 will be taken on particular textile and clothing products and not on the basis of the HS lines *per se*.

NOTE : Actions under the safeguard provisions in Article 6 of this Agreement shall not apply to:

1. developing Members' exports of handloom fabrics of the cottage industry, or hand-made cottage industry products made of such handloom fabrics, or traditional folklore handicraft textile and clothing products, provided that such products are properly certified under arrangements established between the Members concerned;
2. historically traded textile products which were internationally traded in commercially significant quantities prior to 1982, such as bags, sacks, carpetbacking, cordage, luggage, mats, mattings and carpets

typically made from fibres such as jute, coir, sisal, abaca, maguey and henequen;

3. products made of pure silk.

For such products, the provisions of Article XIX of the GATT 1994, as interpreted by the Agreement on Safeguards, shall be applicable.

HS No.	**Product description**
	Section 11
Ch. 50	**Silk.**
5004 00	Silk yarn (other than yarn spun from silk waste) not put up for retail sale
5005 00	Yarn spun from silk waste, not put up for retail sale.
5006 00	Silk yarn & yarn spun from silk waste, put up f retail sale; silk-worm gut
5007 10	Woven fabrics of noil silk
5007 20	Woven fabrics of silk/silk waste, other than noil silk, 85%/ more of such fibres
5007 90	Woven fabrics of silk, nes
Ch. 51	**Wool, fine/coarse animal hair, horsehair yarn & fabric.**
5105 10	Carded wool
5105 21	Combed wool in fragments
5105 29	Wool tops and other combed wool, other than combed wool in fragments
5105 30	Fine animal hair, carded or combed
5106 10	Yarn of carded wool, > / = 85 % by weight of wool, not put up for retail sale
5106 20	Yarn of carded wool, < 85 % by weight of wool, not put up for retail sale
5107 10	Yarn of combed wool, > /=85 % by weight of wool, not put up for retail sale
5107 20	Yarn of combed wool, < 85 % by weight of wool, not put up for retail sale
5108 10	Yarn of carded fine animal hair, not put up for retail sale
5108 20	Yarn of combed fine animal hair, not put up for retail sale
5109 10	Yarn of wool/of fine animal hair, > / = 85 % by weight of such fibres, put up

HS No.	Product Description
5109 90	Yarn of wool/of fine animal hair, < 85 % by weight of such fibres, put up
5110 00	Yarn of coarse animal hair or of horsehair
5111 11	Woven fabrics of carded wool/fine animal hair, > / = 85 % by weight, < / = 300 g/m2
5111 19	Woven fabrics of carded wool/fine animal hair, > / = 85 % by weight, > 300 g/m2
5111 20	Woven fabric of carded wool/fine animal hair, > / = 85 % by wt, mixd w m-m fib
5111 30	Woven fabric of carded wool/fine animal halr, > / = 85 % by wt, mixd w m-m fib
5111 90	Woven fabrics of carded wool/fine animal hair, > / = 85 % by weight, nes
5112 11	Woven fabric of combed wool/fine animal hair, > / = 85 % by weight, < / = 200 g/m2
5112 19	Woven fabrics of combed wool/fine animal hair, >/= 85 % by weight, > 200 g/m2
5112 20	Woven fabrics of combed wool/fine animal hair, < 85 % by wt, mixd w m-m fib
5112 30	Woven fabrics of combed wool/fine animal hair, < 85 % by wt, mixd w m-m fib
5112 90	Woven fabrics of combed wool/fine animal hair, < 85% by weight, nes
5113 00	Woven fabrics of coarse animal hair or of horsehair
Ch. 52	**Cotton**
5204 11	Cotton sewing thread, >/= 85 % by weight of cotton, not put up for retail sale
5204 19	Cotton sewing thread, < 85 % by weight of cotton, not put up for retail sale
5204 20	Cotton sewing thread, put up for retail sale
5205 11	Cotton yarn, > / = 85 % single, uncombed, > / =.714.29 dtex, not put up
5205 12	Cotton yarn, >/=85%, single, uncombed, 714.29 >dtex>/ =232.56, not put up
5205 13	Cotton yarn,>/=85%, single, uncombed, 232.56 > dtex>/ =192.31, not put up

HS No.	Product description
5205 14	Cotton yarn, >/=85%, single, uncombed, 192.31 > dtex>/=125, not put up
5205 15	Cotton yarn, > / = 85 %, single, uncombed, < 125 dtex, not put up for retail sale
5205 21	Cotton yarn, >/=85%, single, combed, >/=714.29, not put up
5205 22	Cotton yarn, >/=85%, single, combed, 714.29> dtex>/=232.56, not put up
5205 23	Cotton yarn, >/=85%, single, combed, 232.56> dtex>/=192.31, not put up
5205 24	Cotton yarn, >/=85%, single, combed, 192.31 >dtex>/=125, not put up
5205 25	Cotton yarn, >/= 85 %, single, combed, < 125 dtex, not put up for retail sale
5205 31	Cotton yarn, >/= 85 %, multi, uncombed, >/= 714.29 dtex, not put up, nes
5205 32	Cotton yarn, >/=85%, multi, uncombed, 714.29 >dtex>/=232.56, not put up, nes
5205 33	Cotton yarn, >/=85%, multi, uncombed, 232.56> dtex>/=192.31, not put up, nes
5205 34	Cotton yarn, >/=85%, multi, uncombed, 192.31> dtex>/=125, not put up, nes
5205 35	Cotton yarn, > / = 85 %, multi, uncombed, < 125 dtex, not put up, nes
5205 41	Cotton yarn, > / = 85 %, multiple, combed, > / = 714.29 dtex, not put up, nes
5205 42	Cotton yarn, > / = 85 %, multi, combed, 714.29 > dtex > / = 232.56, not put up, nes
5205 43	Cotton yarn, >/=85%, multi, combed, 232.56 >dtex>/=192.31, not put up, nes
5205 44	Cotton yarn, >/=85%, multiple, combed, 192.31 >dtex>/=125, not put up, nes
5205 45	Cotton yarn, > / = 85 %, multiple, combed, < 125 dtex, not put up, nes
5206 11	Cotton yarn, <85%, single, uncombed, >/=714.29, not put up

HS No.	Product Description
5206 12	Cotton yarn, <85%, single, uncombed, 714.29 >dtex>/=232.56, not put up
5206 13	Cotton yarn, <85%, single, uncombed, 232.56 >dtex>/=192.31, not put up
5206 14	Cotton yarn, <85%, single, uncombed, 192.31 >dtex>/=125, not put up
5206 15	Cotton yarn, < 85 %, single, uncombed, < 125 dtex, not put up for retail sale
5206 21	Cotton yarn, < 85 %, single, combed, >/=714.29 dtex, not put up
5206 22	Cotton yarn, <85%, single, combed, 714.29 >dtex>/=232.56, not put up
5206 23	Cotton yarn, <85%, single, combed, 232.56 >dtex>/=192.31, not put up
5206 24	Cotton yarn, <85%, single, combed, 192.31 >dtex>/=125, not put up
5206 25	Cotton yarn, < 85 %, single, combed, < 125 dtex, not put up for retail sale
5206 31	Cotton yarn, < 85 %, multiple, uncombed, > / = 714.29, not put up, nes
5206 32	Cotton yarn, < 85 %, multiple, uncombed, 714.29 > dtex > / = 232.56, not put up, nes
5206 33	Cotton yarn, <85%, multiple, uncombed, 232.56 >dex>/=192.31, not put up. nes
5206 34	Cotton yarn, <85%, multiple, uncombed, 192.31 >dtex>/=125, not put up, nes
5206 35	Cotton yarn, < 85 %, multiple, uncombed, < 125 dtex, not put up, nes
5206 41	Cotton yarn, <85%, multiple, combed, >/=714.29, not put up, nes
5206 42	Cotton yarn, < 85 %, multiple, combed, 714.29 > dtex > /=232.56, not put up, nes
5206 43	Cotton yarn, <85%, multiple, combed, 232.56 >dtex>/=192.31, not put up, nes
5206 44	Cotton yarn, <85%, multiple, combed, 192.31 >dtex>/=125, not put up, nes

HS No.	Product Description
5206 45	Cotton yarn, < 85 %, multiple, combed, < 125 dtex, not put up, nes
5207 10	Cotton yarn (other than' sewing thread) >/= 85% by weight of cotton, put up
5207 90	Cotton yarn (other than sewg thread) < 85 % by wt of cotton, put up for retail sale
5208 11	Plain weave cotton fabric, >/=85%, not more than 100 g/m2, unbleached
5208 12	Plain weave cotton fabric, >/= 85%, > 100 g/m2 to 200 g/m2, unbleached
5208 13	Twill weave cotton fabric, >/=85%, not more than 200 g/m2, unbleached
5208 19	Woven fabrics of cotton, > / = 85%, not more than 200 g/m2, unbleached, nes
5208 21	Plain weave cotton fabrics, >/=85 %, not more than 100 g/m2, bleached
5208 22	Plain weave cotton fabric, >/= 85 %, > 100 g/m2 to 200 g/m2, bleached
5208 23	Twill weave cotton fabric, >/= 85 %, not more than 200 g/m2, bleached
5208 29	Woven fabrics of cotton, >/=85 %, not more than 200 g/m2, bleached, nes
5208 31	Plain weave cotton fabric, >/=85%, not more than 100 g/m2, dyed
5208 32	Plain weave cotton fabric, > / = 85%, > 100g/m = to 200g/m =, dyed
5208 33	Twill weave cotton fabrics., >/= 85 not, not more than 200 g/m2, dyed
5208 39	Woven fabrics of cotton, > / = 85 %, not more than 200 g/m2, dyed, nes
5208 41	Plain weave cotton fabric, >/= 85 %, not more than 100 g/m2, yarn dyed
5208 42	Plain weave cotton fabrics, >/= 85 %, > 100 g/m2 to 200 g/m2, yarn dyed
5208 43	Twill weave cotton fabric, >/= 85 %, not more than 200 g/m2, yarn dyed

HS No.	Product Description
5208 49	Woven fabrics of cotton, > / = 85 %, not more than 200 g/m2, yarn dyed, nes
5208 51	Plain weave cotton fabrics, >/=85%, not more than 100 g/m2, printed
5208 52	Plain weave cotton fabric, >/= 85 %, > 100 g/m2 to 200 g/m2, printed
5208 53	Twill weave cotton fabric, >/=85 %, not more than 200 g/m2, printed
5208 59	Woven fabrics of cotton, > / = 85 %, not more than 200 g/m2, printed, nes
5209 11	Plain weave cotton fabric, > / = 85 %, more than 200 g/m2, unbleached
5209 12	Twill weave cotton fabric, >/=85%, more than 200 g/m2, unbleached
5209 19	Woven fabrics of cotton, > /= 85%, more than 200 g/m2, unbleached, nes
5209 21	Plain weave cotton fabric, >/= 85%, more than 200 g/m2, bleached
5209 22	Twill weave cotton fabrics, >/= 85%, more than 200 g/m2, bleached
5209 29	Woven fabrics of cotton, > / = 85%, more than 200 g/m2, bleached, nes
5209 31	Plain weave cotton fabrics, >/= 85%, more than 200 g/m2, dyed
5209 32	Twill weave cotton fabrics, >/= 85%, more than 200 g/m2, dyed
5209 39	Woven fabrics of cotton, > / = 85%, more than 200 g/m2, dyed, nes
5209 41	Plain weave cotton fabrics, >/= 85%, more than 200 g/m2, yarn dyed
5209 42	Denim fabrics of cotton, > / = 85%, more than 200 g/m2
5209 43	Twill weave cotton fab, other than denim, > / = 85%, more than 200 g/m2, yarn dyed
5209 49	Woven fabrics of cotton, > / = 85 %, more than 200 g/m2, yarn dyed, nes
5209 51	Plain weave cotton fabrics, >/= 85 %, more than 200 g/m2, printed

HS No.	Product Description
5209 52	Twill weave cotton fabrics, >/= 85 %. more than 200 g/m2, printed
5209 59	Woven fabrics of cotton, > / = 85 %, more than 200 g/m2, printed, nes
5210 11	Plain weave cotton fab, < 85 % mixd w m-m fib, not more than 200 g/m2, unbl
5210 12	Twill weave cotton fab,<85% mixd w m-m fib, not more than 200 g/m2, unbl
5210 19	Woven fab of cotton, < 85 % mixd with m-m fib, </=200 g/m2, unbl, nes
5210 21	Plain weave cotton fab,<85% mixd w m-m fib, not more than 200 g/m2, bl
5210 22	Twill weave cotton fab, < 85 % mixd w m-m fib, not more than 200 g/m2, bl
5210 29	Woven fabrics of cotton. < 85% mixd with m-m fib, </=200 g/m2, bl, nes
5210 31	Plain weave cotton fab, < 85 % mixd w m-m fib. not more than 200 g/m2, dyed
5210 32	Twill weave cotton fab, < 85 % mixd w m-m fib, not more than 200 g/m2, dyed
5210 39	Woven fabrics of cotton, < 85 % mixd with m-m fib, </=200 g/m2, dyed, nes
5210 41	Plain weave cotton fab, < 85 % mixd w m-m fib, not more than 200g/m2, yarn dyed
5210 42	Twill weave cotton fab, < 85 % mixd w m-m fib, not more thn 200g/m2, yarn dyed
5210 49	Woven fabrics of cotton, < 85% mixed w m-m fib, </=200g/m2, yarn dyed, nes
5210 51	Plain weave cotton fab, < 85% mixd w m-m fib, not more than 200 g/m2, printed
5210 52	Twill weave cotton fab, < 85% mixd w m-m fib, not more than 200g/m2, printed
5210 59	Woven fabrics of cotton, < 85% mixed with m-m fib, </=200g/m2, printed, nes
5211 11	Plain weave cotton fab, < 85 % mixd w m-m fib, more than 200 g/m2, unbleachd

HS No.	Product Description
5211 12	Twill weave cotton fab, < 85% mixed with m-m fib, more than 200 g/m2, unbl
5211 19	Woven fabrics of cotton, <85% mixd w m-m fib, more than 200g/m2, unbl, nes
5211 21	Plain weave cotton fab, < 85 % mixd w m-m fib, more than 200 g/m2, bleached
5211 22	Twill weave cotton fab, < 85 % mixd w m-m fib, more than 200 g/m2, bleached
5211 29	Woven fabrics of cotton, < 85% mixd w m-m fib, more than 200 g/m2, bl, nes
5211 31	Plain weave cotton fab, < 85% mixed with m-m fib, more than 200 g/m2, dyed
5211 32	Twill weave cotton fab, < 85% mixed with m-m fib, more than 200 g/m2, dyed
5211 39	Woven fabrics of cotton, < 85% mixd w m-m fib, more than 200 g/m2, dyed, nes
5211 41	Plain weave cotton fab, < 85% mixd w m-m fib, more than 200 g/m2, yarn dyed
5211 42	Denim fabrics of cotton, < 85% mixed with m-m fib, more than 200 g/m2
5211 43	Twill weave cotton fab, other than denim, < 85% mixd w m-m fib, > 200g/m2, yarn dyed
5211 49	Woven fabrics of cotton, < 85 % mixd with m-m fib, > 200 g/m2, yarn dyed, nes
5211 51	Plain weave cotton fab, < 85 % mixd w m-m' fib, more than 200 g/m2, printed
5211 52	Twill weave cotton fab, <85% mixd w m-m fib, more than 200 g/m2, printed
5211 59	Woven fabrics of cotton, < 85 % mixd w m-m fib, more thn 200g/m2, printed, nes
5212 11	Woven fabrics of cotton, weighing not more than 200 g/m2, unbleached, nes
5212 12	Woven fabrics of cotton, weighing not more than 200 g/m2, bleached, nes
5212 13	Woven fabrics of cotton, weighing not more than 200 g/m2, dyed, nes

HS No.	Product Description
5212 14	Woven fabrics of cotton, </=200g/m2, of yarns of different colours, nes
5212 15	Woven fabrics of cotton, weighing not more than 200 g/m2, printed, nes
5212 21	Woven fabrics of cotton, weighing more than 200 g/m2, unbleached, nes
5212 22	Woven fabrics of cotton, weighing more than 200 g/m2, bleached, nes
5212 23	Woven fabrics of cotton, weighing more than 200 g/m2, dyed, nes
5212 24	Woven fabrics of cotton, > 200 g/m2. of yarns of different colours, nes
5212 25	Woven fabrics of cotton, weighing more than 200 g/m2, printed, nes
Ch. 53	**Other vegetable textile fibres; paper yarn & woven fab.**
5306 10	Flax yarn, single
5306 20	Flax yarn, multiple (folded) or cabled
5307 10	Yarn of jute or of other textile bast fibres, single
5307 20	Yarn of jute or of other textile bast fibres, multiple (folded) or cabled
5308 20	True hemp yarn
5308 90	Yarn of other vegetable textile fibres
5309 11	Woven fabrics, containg 85 % or more by weight of flax, unbleached or bl
5309 19	Woven fabrics, containing 85% or more by weight of flax, other than unbl or bl
5309 21	Woven fabrics of flax, containg < 85 % by weight of flax, unbleached or bl
5309 29	Woven fabrics of flax, containing < 85 % by weight of flax, other than unbl or bl
5310 10	Woven fabrics of jute or of other textile bast fibres, unbleached
5310 90	Woven fabrics of jute or of other textile bast fibres, other than unbleached
5311 00	Woven fabrics of both vegetable textile fibres; woven fab of paper yarn

HS No.	Product Description
Ch. 54	**Man-made filaments**
5401 10	Sewing thread of synthetic filaments
5401 20	Sewing thread of artificial filaments
5402 10	High tenacity yarn (other than sewing thread), nylon/other polyamides fi, not put up
5402 20	High tenacity yarn (other than sewing thread), of polyester filaments, not put up
5402 31	Textured yarn nes, of nylon/other polyamides fi, < / = 50tex/s. y., not put up
5402 32	Textured yarn nes, of nylon/other polyamides fi, > 50 tex/s.y., not put up
5402 33	Textured yarn nes, of polyester filaments, not put up for retail sale
5402 39	Textured yarn of synthetic filaments, nes, not put up
5402 41	Yarn of nylon or other polyamides fi, single, untwisted, nes, not put up
5402 42	Yarn of polyester filaments, partially oriented, single, nes, not put up
5402 43	Yarn of polyester filaments, single, untwisted, nes, not put up
5402 49	Yarn of synthetic filaments, single, untwisted, nes, not put up
5402 51	Yarn of nylon or other polyamides fi, single, > 50 turns/m, not put up
5402 52	Yarn of polyester filaments, single; > 50 turns per metre, not put up
5402 59	Yarn of synthetic filaments, single, > 50 turns per metre, nes, not put up
5402 61	Yarn of nylon or other polyamides fi, multiple, nes, not put up
5402 62	Yarn of polyester filaments, multiple, nes, not put up
5402 69	Yarn of synthetic filaments, multiple, nes, not put up
5403 10	High tenacity yarn (other than sewing thread), of viscose rayon filament, not put up
5403 20	Textured yarn nes, of artificial filaments, not put up for retail sale

HS No.	Product Description
5403 31	Yarn of viscose rayon filaments, single, untwisted, nes, not put up
5403 32	Yarn of viscose rayon filaments, single, > 120 turns per m, nes, not put up
5403 33	Yarn of cellulose acetate filaments, single, nes, not put up
5403 39	Yarn of artificial filaments, single, nes, not put up
5403 41	Yarn of viscose rayon filaments, multiple, nes, not put up
5403 42	Yarn of cellulose acetate filaments, multiple, nes, not put up
5403 49	Yarn of artificial filaments, multiple, nes, not put up
5404 10	Synthetic mono, >/=67dtex, no cross sectional dimension exceeds 1 mm
5404 90	Strip & the like of syn tex material of an apparent width not exceeding 5mm
5405 00	Artificial mono, 67 dtex, cross-sect > mm; strip of arti tex mat w </=5mm
5406 10	Yarn of synthetic filament (other than sewing thread), put up for retail sale
5406 20	Yarn of artificial filament (other than sewing thread),put up for retail sale
5407 10	Woven fab of high tenacity fi yarns of nylon other polyamides/polyesters
5407 20	Woven fab obtaind from strip/the like of synthetic textile materials
5407 30	Fabrics specified in Note 9 Section XI (layers of parallel syn tex yarn)
5407 41	Woven fab, >/= 85 % of nylon/other polyamides filaments, unbl or bl, nes
5407 42	Woven fabrics, > / = 85 % of nylon/other polyamides filaments, dyed, nes
5407 43	Woven fab, > / = 85 % of nylon/other polyamides filaments, yarn dyed, nes
5407 44	Woven fabrics, > / = 85 % of nylon/other polyamides filaments, printed, nes
5407 51	Woven fabrics, >/= 85 % of textured polyester filaments, unbl or bl, nes

HS No.	Product Description
5407 52	Woven fabrics, > / = 85 % of textured polyester filaments, dyed, nes
5407 53	Woven fabrics, > / = 85 % of textured polyester filaments, yarn dyed, nes
5407 54	Woven fabrics, > / = 85 % of textured polyester filaments, printed, nes
5407 60	Woven fabrics, > / = 85 % of non-textured polyester filaments, nes
5407 71	Woven lab, > / = 85 % of synthetic filaments, unbleached or bleached, nes
5407 72	Woven fabrics, >/= 85% of synthetic filaments, dyed, nes
5407 73	Woven fabrics, > /= 85% of synthetic filaments, yarn dyed, nes
5407 74	Woven fabrics, > / = 85% of synthetic filaments, printed, nes
5407 81	Woven fabrics of synthetic filaments, < 85% mixd w cotton, unbl or bl, nes
5407 82	Woven/fabrics of synthetic filaments, < 85% mixed with cotton, dyed, nes
5407 83	Woven fabrics of synthetic filaments, < 85% mixd w cotton, yarn dyd, nes
5407 84	Woven fabrics of synthetic filaments, < 85% mixd with cotton, printed, nes
5407 91	Woven fabrics of synthetic filaments, unbleached or bleached, nes
5407 92	Woven fabrics of synthetic filaments, dyed, nes
5407 93	Woven fabrics of synthetic filaments, yarn dyed, nes
5407 94	Woven fabrics of synthetic filaments, printed, nes
5408 10	Woven fabrics of high tenacity filament yarns of viscose rayon
5408 21	Woven fab, > / = 85 % of artificial fi or strip of art tex mat, unbl/bl, nes
5408 22	Woven fab, > / = 85 % of artificial fi or strip of art tex mat, dyed, nes
5408 23	Woven fab, > / = 85 % of artificial fi or strip of art tex mat, yarn dyed, nes

HS No.	Product Description
5408 24	Woven lab, > / = 85 % of artificial fi or strip of art rex mat, printed, nes
5408 31	Woven fabrics of artificial filaments, unbleached or bleached, nes
5408 32	Woven fabrics of artificial filaments, dyed, nes
5408 33	Woven fabrics of artificial filaments, yarn dyed, nes
5408 34	Woven fabrics of artificial filaments, printed, nes
Ch. 55	**Man-made staple fibres**
5501 10	Filament tow of nylon or other polyamides
5501 20	Filament tow of polyesters
5501 30	Filament tow of acrylic or modacrylic
5501 90	Synthetic filament tow, nes
5502 00	Artificial filament tow
5503 10	Staple fibres of nylon or other polyamides, not carded or combed
5503 20	Staple fibres of polyesters, not carded or combed
5503 30	Staple fibres of acrylic or modacrylic, not carded or combed
5503 40	Staple fibres of polypropylene, not carded or combed
5503 90	Synthetic staple fibres, not carded or combed, nes
5504 10	Staple fibres of viscose, not carded or combed
5504 90	Artificial staple fibres, other than viscose, not carded or combed
5505 10	Waste of synthetic fibres
5505 20	Waste of artificial fibres
5506 10	Staple fibres of nylon or other polyamides, carded or combed
5506 20	Staple fibres of polyesters, carded or combed
5506 30	Staple fibres of acrylic or modacrylic, carded or combed
5506 90	Synthetic staple fibres, carded or combed, nes
5507 00	Artificial staple fibres, carded or combed
5508 10	Sewing thread of synthetic staple fibres
5508 20	Sewing thread of artificial staple fibres
5509 11	Yarn, >/= 85 % nylon or other polyamides staple fibres, single, not put up

HS No.	Product Description
5509 12	Yarn,>/=85% nylon or other polyamides staple fibres, multi, not put up, nes
5509 21	Yarn, > / = 85 % of polyester staple fibres, single, not put up
5509 22	Yarn, >/= 85 % of polyester staple fibres, multiple, not put up, nes
5509 31	Yarn, >/= 85 % of acrylic or modacrylic staple fibres, single, not put up
5509 32	Yarn, >/=85 % acrylic/modacrylic staple fibres, multiple, not put up, nes
5509 41	Yarn, >/= 85 % of other synthetic staple fibres, single, not put up
5509 42	Yarn, > / = 85 % of other synthetic staple fibres, multiple, not put up, nes
5509 51	Yarn of polyester staple fibres mixd w arti staple fib, not put up, nes
5509 52	Yarn of polyester staple fib mixd w wool/fine animal hair, not put up, nes
5509 53	Yarn of polyester staple fibres mixed with cotton, not put up, nes
5509 59	Yarn of polyester staple fibres, not put up, nes
5509 61	Yarn of acrylic staple fib mixd w wool/fine animal hair, not put up, nes
5509 62	Yarn of acrylic staple fibres mixed with cotton, not put up, nes
5509 69	Yarn of acrylic staple fibres, not put up, nes
5509 91	Yarn of other synthetic staple fibres mixed w wool/fine animal hair, nes
5509 92	Yarn of other synthetic staple fibres mixed with cotton, not put up, nes
5509 99	Yarn of other synthetic staple fibres, not put up, ness
5510 11	Yarn, >/=85% of artificial staple fibres, single, not put up
5510 12	Yarn, > / = 85 % of artificial staple fibres, multiple, not put up, nes
5510 20	Yarn of artificial staple fib mixed w wool/fine animal hair, not put up, nes

HS No.	Product Description
5510 30	Yarn of artificial staple fibres mixed with cotton, not put up, nes
5510 90	Yarn of, artificial staple fibres, not put up, nes
5511 10	Yarn, > / = 85% of synthetic staple fibres, other than sewing thread, put up
5511 20	Yarn, < 85% of synthetic staple fibres, put up for retail sale, nes
5511 30	Yarn of artificial fibres (other than sewing thread), put up for retail sale
5512 11	Woven fabrics, containing >/=85% of polyester staple fibres, unbl or bl
5512 19	Woven fabrics, containing >/= 85 % of polyester staple fibres, other than unbl or bl
5512 21	Woven fabrics, containing >/=85% of acrylic staple fibres, unbleached or bl
5512 29	Woven fabrics, containing >/= 85% of acrylic staple fibres, other than unbl or bl
5512 91	Woven fabrics, containing >/= 85% of other synthetic staple fibres, unbl/bl
5512 99	Woven fabrics, containing > / = 85% of other synthetic staple fib, other than unbl/bl
5513 11	Plain weave polyest stapl fib fab, < 85% mixed w cotton, </=170g/m2, unbl/bl
5513 12	Twill weave polyest stapl fib fab, < 85%, mixed w cotton, < / = 170g/m2, unbl/bl
5513 13	Woven fab of polyest staple fib, < 85% mixed w cot, </=170g/m2, unbl/bl, nes
5513 19	Woven fabrics of other syn staple fib, < 85% mixed w cot, </=170g/m2, unbl/bl
5513 21	Plain weave polyester staple fib fab, < 85 %, mixed w cotton, < / = 170g/m2, dyed
5513 22	Twill weave polyest staple fib fab, < 85%, mixed w cotton, </=170g/m2, dyed
5513 23	Woven fab of polyester staple fib, <85%, mixed w/cot, </=170 g/m2, dyed, nes

HS No.	Product Description
5513 29	Woven fabrics of other syn staple fib, < 85 % mixed w cotton, < / = 170g/m2, dyed
5513 31	Plain weave polyest stapl fib fab, < 85% mixd w/cot, < / = 170g/m2, yarn dyed
5513 32	Twill weave polyest stapl fib fab, < 85% mixed w/cot, < / = 170g/m2, yarn dyed
5513 33	Woven fab of polyest staple fib, < 85% mixd w/cot, </= 170 g/m2, dyed nes
5513 39	Woven fab of both syn staple fib, < 85% mixd w/cot, < / = 170g/m2, yarn dyed
5513 41	Plain weave polyester stapl fib fab, < 85%, mixed w/cot, </= 170g/m2, printed
5513 42	Twill weave polyest staple fib fab, < 85%, mixed w/cot, < =/170g/m2, printed
5513 43	Woven fab of polyester staple fib, < 85 % mixed w/cot, < / = 170g/m2, ptd, nes
5513 49	Woven fab of both syn staple fib, < 85%, mixed w/cot, </ = 170g/m2, printed
5514 11	Plain weave polyest staple fib fab, < 85%, mixed w/cotton, > 170g/m2, unbl/bl
5514 12	Twill weave polyest stapl fib fab, < 85%, mixed w/cotton, > 170g/m2, unbl/bl
5514 13	Woven fab of polyester staple fib, < 85%, mixed w/cot, > 170g/m2, unbl/bl, nes
5514 19	Woven fabrics of other syn staple fib, < 85%, mixed w/cot, > 170 g/m2, unbl/bl
5514 21	Plain weave polyester staple fibre fab, < 85% mixed w/ cotton, > 170g/m2, dyed
5514 22	Twill weave polyester staple fibre lab, < 85 % .mixd w/ cotton, > 170g/m2, dyed
5514 23	Woven fabrics of polyester staple fib, < 85%, mixed w/cot, > 170 g/m2, dyed
5514 29	Woven fabrics of other synthetic staple fib, < 85%, mixed w/cot, > 170g/m2, dyed
5514 31	Plain weave polyester staple fib fab, < 85% mixd w/cot, > 170g/m2, yarn dyed

HS No.	Product Description
5514 32	Twill weave polyester staple fib fab, < 85%, mixed w/cot, > 170g/m2, yarn dyed
5514 33	Woven fab of polyester stapl fib, < 85%, mixed w/cot, > 170g/m2, yarn dyed nes
5514 39	Woven fabrics of other syn staple fib, < 85%, mixed w/cot, > 170 g/m2, yarn dyed
5514 41	Plain weave polyester staple fibre fab. < 85%, mixed w/cot, > 170g/m2, printed
5514 42	Twill weave polyester staple fibre fab, < 85%, mixed w/cot, > 170g/m2, printed
5514 43	Woven fab of polyester staple fibres < 85%, mixed w/cot, > 170g/m2, ptd, nes
5514 49	Woven fabrics of other syn staple fib, < 85%, mixed w/cot, > 170 g/m2, printed
5515 11	Woven fab of polyester staple fib mixed w viscose rayon staple fib, nes
5515 12	Woven fabrics of polyester staple fibres mixed w man-made filaments, nes
5515 13	Woven fab of polyester staple fibres mixed w/wool/fine animal hair, nes
5515 19	Woven fabrics of polyester staple fibres, nes
5515 21	Woven fabrics of acrylic staple fibres, mixd w/man-made filaments, nes
5515 22	Woven fab of acrylic staple fibres, mixd w/wool/fine animal hair, nes
5515 29	Woven fabrics of acrylic or modacrylic staple fibres, nes
5515 91	Woven fabrics of other syn staple fib, mixed with man-made filaments, nes
5515 92	Woven fabrics of other syn staple fib, mixed w/wool of fine animal hair, nes
5515 99	Woven fabrics of synthetic staple fibres, nes
5516 11	Woven fabrics, containing > / = 85% of artificial staple fibres, unbleached/bl
5516 12	Woven fabrics, containing >/= 85% of artificial staple fibres, dyed
5516 13	Woven fabrics, containing >/= 85% of artificial staple fib, yarn dyed

HS No.	Product Description
5516 14	Woven fabrics, containing >/=85% of artificial staple fibres, printed
5516 21	Woven fabrics of artificial staple fib, < 85%, mixed w/ man-made fi, unbl/bl
5516 22	Woven fabrics of artificial staple fib, < 85 %, mixed with man-made fi, dyed
5516 23	Woven fabrics of artificial staple fib, < 85 %, mixed with m-m fi, yarn dyed
5516 24	Woven fabrics of artificial staple fib, <85%, mixed w/man-made fi, printed
5516 31	Woven fab of arti staple fib, < 85% mixed w/wool/fine animal hair, unbl/bl
5516 32	Woven fabrics of arti staple fib, < 85% mixed w/wool/fine animal hair, dyed
5516 33	Woven fab of arti staple fib, < 85% mixed w/wool/fine animal hair, yarn dyed
5516 34	Woven fab of arti staple fib, < 85% mixd w/wool/fine animal hair, printed
5516 41	Woven fabrics of artificial staple fib, < 85% mixed with cotton, unbl or bl
5516 42	Woven fabrics of artificial staple fib, < 85% mixed with cotton, dyed
5516 43	Woven fabrics of artificial staple fib, < 85% mixed with cotton, yarn dyed
5516 44	Woven fabrics of artificial staple fib, < 85% mixed with cotton, printed
5516 91	Woven fabrics of artificial staple fibres, unbleached or bleached, nes
5516 92	Woven fabrics of artificial staple fibres, dyed, nes
5516 93	Woven fabrics of artificial staple fibres, yarn, dyed, nes
5516 94	Woven fabrics of artificial staple fibres, printed, nes
Ch. 56	**Wadding, felt & non woven; yarns; twine, cordage, etc.**
5601 10	Sanitary articles of wadding of textile mat *i.e.* sanitary towels, tampons
5601 21	Wadding of cotton and articles thereof, other than sanitary articles

HS No.	Product Description
5601 22	Wadding of man-made fibres and articles thereof, other than sanitary articles
5601 29	Wadding of other textile materials & articles thereof, other than sanitary articles
5601 30	Textile flock and dust and mill neps
5602 10	Needleloom felt and stitch-bonded fibre fabrics
5602 21	Felt other than needleloom, of wool or fine animal hair, not impreg, ctd, cov etc
5602 29	Felt other than needleloom, of other textile materials, not impreg, ctd, cov etc
5602 90	Felt of textile materials, nes
5603 00	Non-wovens, whether or not impregnated, coated, covered or laminated
5604 10	Rubber thread and cord, textile covered
5604 20	High tenacity yarn of polyest, nylon other polyamid, viscose rayon, ctd etc.
5604 90	Textile yarn, Strip & the like, impreg ctd/cov with rubber or plastics, nes
5605 00	Metallised yarn, beg textile yarn combind w/metal thread, strip/powder
5606 00	Gimped yarn nes; chenille yam; loop wale-yarn
5607 10	Twine, cordage, ropes and cables, of jute or other, textile bast fibres
5607 21	Binder or baler twine, of sisal or other textile fibres of the genus Agave
5607 29	Twine nes, cordage, ropes and cables, of sisal textile fibres
5607 30	Twine, cordage, ropes and cables, of abaca or other hard (leaf) fibres
5607 41	Binder or baler twine, of polyethylene or polypropylene
5607 49	Twine nes, cordage, ropes and cables, of polyethylene or polypropylene
5607 50	Twine, cordage, ropes and cables, of other synthetic fibres
5607 90	Twine, cordage, ropes and cables, of other materials
5608 11	Made up fishing nets, of man-made textile materials

HS No.	Product Description
5608 19	Knotted netting of twine/cordage/rope, and other made up nets of m-m tex mat
5608 90	Knotted netintg of twine/cordage/rope, nes, and made up nets of other tex mat
5609 00	Articles of yarn, strip, twine, cordage, rope and cables, nes
Ch. 57	**Carpets and other textile floor coverings**
5701 10	Carpets of wool or fine animal hair, knotted
5701 90	Carpets of other textile materials, knotted
5702 10	Kelem, Schumacks, Karamanie and similar textile hand-woven rugs
5702 20	Floor coverings of coconut fibres (coir)
5702 31	Carpets of wool/fine animal hair, of woven pile construction, not made up nes
5702 32	Carpets of man-made textile mat, of woven pile construction, not made up, nes
5702 39	Carpets of other textile mat, of woven pile construction, not made up, nes
5702 41	Carpets of wool/fine animal hair, of woven pile construction, made up, nes
5702 42	Carpets of man-made textile mat, of woven pile construction, made up, nes
5702 49	Carpets of other textile materials, of woven pile construction, made up, nes
5702 51	Carpets of wool or fine animal hair, woven, not made up, nes
5702 52	Carpets of man-made textile materials, woven, not made up, nes
5702 59	Carpets of other textile materials, woven, not made up, nes
5702 91	Carpets of wool or fine animal hair, woven, made up, nes
5702 92	Carpets of man-made textile materials, woven, made up, nes
5702 99	Carpets of other textile materials, woven, made up, nes
5703 10	Carpets of wool or fine animal hair, tufted
5703 20	Carpets of nylon or other polyamides, tufted

HS No.	Product Description
5703 30	Carpets of other man-made textile materials, tufted
5703 90	Carpets of other textile materials, tufted
5704 10	Tiles of felt of textile materials, having a max surface area of 0.3 m2
5704 90	Carpets of felt of textile materials, nes
5705 00	Carpets and other textile floor coverings, nes
Ch. 58	**Special woven fab; tufted tex fab; lace; tapestries etc.**
5801 10	Woven pile fabrics of wool/fine animal hair, other than terry & narrow fabrics
5801 21	Woven uncut weft pile fabrics of cotton, other than terry and narrow fabrics
5801 22	Cut corduroy fabrics of cotton, other than narrow fabrics
5801 23	Woven weft pile fabrics of cotton, nes
5801 24	Woven warp pile fab of cotton, pingl (uncut), other than terry & narrow fab
5801 25	Woven warp pile fabrics of cotton, cut, other than terry and narrow fabrics
5801 26	Chenille fabrics of cotton, other than narrow fabrics
5801 31	Woven uncut weft pile fabrics of man-made fibres, other than terry & narrow fab
5801 32	Cut corduroy fabrics of man-made fibres, other than narrow fabrics
5801 33	Woven weft pile fabrics of man-made fibres, nes
5801 34	Woven warp pile fab of man-made fib, pingl (uncut), other than terry & narrow fab
5801 35	Woven warp pile fabrics of man-made fib, cut, other than terry & narrow fabrics
5801 36	Chenille fabrics of man-made fibres, other than narrow fabrics
5801 90	Woven pile fab & chenille fab of other tex mat, other than terry & narrow fabrics
5802 11	Terry towelling & similar woven terry fab of cotton, other than narrow fab, unbl
5802 19	Terry towelling & similar woven terry fab of cotton, other than unbl & other than nat fab

HS No.	Product Description
5802 20	Terry towelling & sim woven terry fab of other rex mat, other than narrow fabrics
5802 30	Tufted textile fabrics, other than products of heading No. 57.03
5803 10	Gauze of cotton, other than narrow fabrics
5803 90	Gauze of other textile material, other than narrow fabrics
5804 10	Tulles & other net fabrics, not incl woven, knitted or crocheted fabrics
5804 21	Mechanically made lace of man-made fib, in the piece, in strips/motifs
5804 29	Mechanically made lace of other rex mat. in the piece, in strips/in motifs
5804 30	Hand-made lace, in the piece, in strips or in motifs
5805 00	Hand-woven tapestries & needle-worked tapestries, whether or not made up
5806 10	Narrow woven pile fabrics and narrow chenille fabrics
5806 20	Narrow woven fab, cntg by wt >/= 5 % elastomeric yarn/ rubber thread nes
5806 31	Narrow woven fabrics of cotton, nes
5806 32	Narrow woven fabrics of man-made fibres, nes
5806 39	Narrow woven fabrics of other textile materials, nes
5806 40	Fabrics consisting of warp w/o weft assembled by means of an adhesive
5807 10	Labels, badges and similar woven articles of textile materials
5807 90	Labels, badges and similar articles, not woven, of textile materials, nes
5808 10	Braids in the piece
5808 90	Ornamental trimmings in the piece, other than knit; tassels, pompons & similar art
5809 00	Woven fabrics of metal thread/of metallised yarn, for apparel, etc., nes
5810 10	Embroidery without visible ground, in the piece, in strips or in motifs
5810 91	Embroidery of cotton, in the piece, in strips or in motifs, nes

HS No.	Product Description
5810 92	Embroidery of man-made fibres, in the piece, in strips or in motifs, nes
5810 99	Embroidery of other textile materials, in the piece, in strips/motifs, nes
5811 00	Quilted textile products in the piece
Ch. 59	**Impregnated, coated, cover/laminated textile fabric etc.**
5901 10	Textile fabrics coated with gum, of a kind usd for outer covers of books
5901 90	Tracg cloth; prepared paintg canvas; stifflened textile fab: for hats etc.
5902 10	Tire cord fabric made of nylon or other polyamides high tenacity yarns
5902 20	Tire cord fabric made of polyester high tenacity yarns
5902 90	Tire cord fabric made of viscose rayon high tenacity yarns
5903 10	Textile fab impregnated, ctd, cov, or laminatd polyvinyl chloride, nes
5903 20	Textile fabrics impregnated, ctd, cov, or laminated with polyurethane, nes
5903 90	Textile fabrics impregnated, ctd, cov, or laminated with plastics, nes
5904 10	Lineoleum, whether or not cut to shape
5904 91	Floor coverings, other than linoleum, with a base of needleloom felt/nonwovens
5904 92	Floor coverings, other than linoleum, with other textile base
5905 00	Textile wall coverings
5906 10	Rubberised textile adhesive tape of a width not exceeding 20 cm
5906 91	Rubberised textile knitted or crocheted fabrics, nes
5906 99	Rubberised textile fabrics, nes
5907 00	Textile fab impreg, ctd, cov nes painted canvas (*e.g.* threatrical scenery)
5908 00	Textile wicks for lamps, stoves, etc; gas mantles & knitted gas mantle fabric
5909 00	Textile hosepiping and similar textile tubing

HS No.	Product Description
5910 00	Transmission or conveyor belts or belting of textile material
5911 10	Textile fabrics usd f card clothing, and sim fabric for technical uses
5911 20	Textile bolting cloth, whether or not made up
5911 31	Textile fabrics used in paper-making or similar machines, <650 g/m2
5911 32	Textile fabrics used in paper-making or similar mach, weighing >/=650 g/m2
5911 40	Textile straing cloth used in oil presses or the like, incl of human hair
5911 90	Textile products and articles for technical uses, nes
Ch. 60	**Knitted or crocheted fabrics**
6001 10	Long pile knitted or crocheted textile fabrics
6001 21	Looped pile knitted or crocheted fabrics, of cotton
6001 22	Looped pile knitted or crocheted fabrics, of man-made fibres
6001 29	Looped pile knitted or crocheted fabrics, of other textile materials
6001 91	Pile knitted or crocheted fabrics, of cotton, nes
6001 92	Pile knitted or crocheted fabrics, of man-made fibres, nes
6001 99	Pile knitted or crocheted fabrics, of other textile materials. nes
6002 10	Knittd or crochetd tex lab, w < / = 30 cm, > / = 5% of elastomeric/rubber, nes
6002 20	Knitted or crocheted textile fabrics, of a width not exceeding 30 cm, nes
6002 30	Knitted/crocheted tex fab, width > 30 cm, > / = 5% of elastomeric/rubber, nes
6002 41	Warp knitted fabrics, of wool or fine animal hair, nes
6002 42	Warp knitted fabrics, of cotton, nes
6002 43	Warp knitted fabrics, of man-made fibres, nes
6002 49	Warp knitted fabrics, of other materials, nes
6002 91	Knitted or crocheted fabrics, of wool or of fine animal hair, nes

HS No.	Product Description
6002 92	Knitted or crocheted fabrics, of cotton, nes
6002 93	Knitted or crocheted fabrics, of man-made fibres, nes
6002 99	Knitted or crocheted fabrics, of other materials, nes
Ch. 61	**Art of apparel & clothing access, knitted or crocheted**
6101 10	Men/boys overcoats, anoraks etc. of wool or fine animal hair, knitted
6101 20	Men/boys overcoats, anoraks etc. of cotton, knitted
6101 30	Men/boys overcoats, anoraks etc. of man-made fibres, knitted
6101 90	Men/boys overcoats, anoraks etc. of other textile materials, knitted
6102 10	Women/girls overcoats, anoraks etc. of wool or fine animal hair, knitted
6102 20	Women/girls overcoats, anoraks etc. of cotton, knitted
6102 30	Women/girls overcoats, anoraks etc. of man-made fibres, knitted
6102 90	Women/girls overcoats, anoraks etc. of other textile materials, knitted
6103 11	Men/boys suits, of wool or fine animal hair, knitted
6103 12	Men/boys suits, of synthetic fibres, knitted
6103 19	Men/boys suits, of other textile materials, knitted
6103 21	Men/boys ensembles, of wool or fine animal hair, knitted
6103 22	Men/boys ensembles, of cotton, knitted
6103 23	Men/boys ensembles, of synthetic fibres, knitted
6103 29	Men/boys ensembles, of other textile materials, knitted
6103 31	Men/boys jackets and blazers, of wool or fine animal hair, knitted
6103 32	Men/boys jackets and blazers, of cotton, knitted
6103 33	Men/boys jackets and blazers, of synthetic fibres, knitted
6103 39	Men/boys jackets and blazers, of other textile materials, knitted
6103 41	Men/boys trousers and shorts, of wool or fine animal hair, knitted
6103 42	Men/boys trousers and shorts, of cotton, knitted

HS No.	Product Description
6103 43	Men/boys trousers and shorts, of synthetic fibres, knitted
6103 49	Men/boys trousers and shorts, of other textile materials, knitted
6104 11	Women/girls suits, of wool or fine animal hair, knitted
6104 12	Women/girls suits, of cotton, knitted
6104 13	Women/girls suits, of synthetic fibres, knitted
6104 19	Women/girls suits, of other textile materials, knitted
6104 21	Women/girls ensembles, of wool or fine animal hair, knitted
6104 22	Women/girls ensembles, of cotton, knitted
6104 23	Women/girls ensembles, of synthetic fibres, knitted
6104 29	Women/girls ensembles, of other textile materials, knitted
6104 31	Women/girls jackets, of wool or fine animal hair, knitted
6104 32	Women/girls jackets, of cotton, knitted
6104 33	Women/girls jackets, of synthetic fibres, knitted
6104 39	Women/girls jackets, of other textile materials, knitted
6104 41	Women/girls dresses, of wool or fine animal hair, knitted
6104 42	Women/girls dresses, of cotton, knitted
6104 43	Women/girls dresses, of synthetic fibres, knitted
6104 44	Women/girls dresses, of artificial fibres, knitted
6104 49	Women/girls dresses, of other textile materials, knitted
6104 51	Women/girls skirts, of wool or fine animal hair, knitted
6104 52	Women/girls skins, of cotton, knitted
6104 53	Women/girls skins, of synthetic fibres, knitted
6104 59	Women/girls skirts, of other textile materials, knitted
6104 61	Women/girls trousers and shorts, of wool or fine animal hair, knitted
6104 62	Women/girls trousers and shorts, of cotton, knitted
6104 63	Women/girls trousers and shorts, of synthetic fibres, knitted
6104 69	Women/girls trousers and shorts, of other textile materials, knitted
6105 10	Men/boys shirts, of cotton, knitted
6105 20	Men/boys shirts, of man-made fibres, knitted

HS No.	Product Description
6105 90	Men/boys shirts, of other textile materials, knitted
6106 10	Women/girls blouses and shirts, of cotton, knitted
6106 20	Women/girls blouses and shirts, of man-made fibres, knitted
6106 90	Women/girls blouses and shirts, of other materials, knitted
6107 11	Men/boys underpants and briefs, of cotton, knitted
6107 12	Men/boys underpants and briefs, of man-made fibres, knitted
6107 19	Men/boy underpants and briefs, of other textile materials, knitted
6107 21	Men/boys night-shirts and pyjamas, of cotton, knitted
6107 22	Men/boys night-shirts and pyjamas, of man-made fibres, knitted
6107 29	Men/boys night-shirts and pyjamas, of other textile materials, knitted
6107 91	Men/boys bathrobes, dressing gowns etc. of cotton, knitted
6107 92	Men/boys bathrobes, dressing gowns, etc. of man-made fibres, knitted
6107 99	Men/boys bathrobes, dressing gowns, etc. of other textile materials, knitted
6108 11	Women/girls slips and petticoats, of man-made fibres, knitted
6108 19	Women/girls slips and petticoats, of other textile materials, knitted
6108 21	Women/girls briefs and panties, of cotton, knitted
6108 22	Women/girls briefs and panties, of man-made fibres, knitted
6108 29	Women/girls briefs and panties, of other textile materials, knitted
6108 31	Women/girls night-dresses and pyjamas, of cotton, knitted
6108 32	Women/girls night-dresses and pyjamas, of man-made fibres, knitted
6108 39	Women/girls night-dresses & pyjamas, of other textile materials, knitted
6108 91	Women/girls bathrobes, dressing gowns, etc. of cotton, knitted
6108 92	Women/girls bathrobes, dressing gowns, etc. of man-made fibres, knitted

HS No.	Product Description
6108 99	Women/girls bathrobes, dressing gowns, etc. of other textile materials, knitted
6109 10	T-shirts, singlets and other vests, of cotton, knitted
6109 90	T-shirts, singlets and other vests, of other textile materials, knitted
6110 10	Pullovers, cardigans & similar article of wool or fine animal hair, knitted
6110 20	Pullovers, cardigans and similar articles of cotton, knitted
6110 30	Pullovers, cardigans and similar articles of man-made fibres, knitted
6110 90	Pullovers, cardigans & similar articles of other textile materials, knitted
6111 10	Babies garments & clothing accessories of wool or fine animal hair, knitted
6111 20	Babies garments and clothing accessories of cotton, knitted
6111 30	Babies garments and clothing accessories of synthetic fibres, knitted
6111 90	Babies garments & clothing accessories of other textile materials, knitted
6112 11	Track suits, of cotton, knitted
6112 12	Track suits, of synthetic fibres, knitted
6112 19	Track suits, of other textile materials, knitted
6112 20	Ski suits, of textile materials, knitted
6112 31	Men/boys swimwear, of synthetic fibres, knitted
6112 39	Men/boys swimwear, of other textile materials, knitted
6112 41	Women/girls swimwear, of synthetic fibres, knitted
6112 49	Women/girls swimwear, of other textile materials, knitted
6113 00	Garments made up of impreg, coated, covered or laminated textile knitted fab
6114 10	Garments nes, of wool or fine animal hair, knitted
6114 20	Garments nes, of cotton, knitted
6114 30	Garments nes, of man-made fibres, knitted
6114 90	Garments nes, of other textile materials, knitted
6115 11	Panty hose & tights, of synthetic fibre yarns < 67 dtex/ single yarn knitted

HS No.	Product Description
6115 12	Panty hose & tights, of synthetic fib yarns >/=67 dtex/ single yarn knitted
6115 19	Panty hose and tights, of other textile materials, knitted
6115 20	Women full-I/knee-l hosiery, of textile yarn < 67 dtex/ single yarn knitted
6115 91	Hosiery nes, of wool or fine animal hair, knitted
6115 92	Hosiery nes, of cotton, knitted
6115 93	Hosiery nes, of synthetic fibres, knitted
6115 99	Hosiery nes, of other textile materials, knitted
6116 10	Gloves impregnated, coated or covered with plastics or rubber, knitted
6116 91	Gloves, mittens and mitts, nes, of wool or fine animal hair, knitted
6116 92	Gloves, mittens and mitts, nes. of cotton, knitted
6116 93	Gloves, mittens and mitts, nes, of synthetic fibres, knitted
6116 99	Gloves, mittens and mitts, nes, of other textile materials, knitted
6117 10	Shawls, scarves, veils and the like, of textile materials, knitted
6117 20	Ties, bow ties and cravats, of textile materials, knitted
6117 80	Clothing accessories nes, of textile materials, knitted
6117 90	Parts of garments/of clothing accessories, of textile materials, knitted
Ch. 62	**Art of apparel & clothing access, not knitted/crocheted**
6201 11	Men/boys overcoats&similar articles of wool/fine animal hair, not knit
6201 12	Men/boys overcoats and similar articles of cotton, not knitted
6201 13	Men/boys overcoats & similar articles of man-made fibres, not knitted
6201 19	Men/boys overcoats & similar articles of other textile materials, not knitted
6201 91	Men/boys anoraks & similar articles, of wool/fine animal hair, not knitted

HS No.	Product Description
6201 92	Men/boys anoraks and similar articles, of cotton, not knitted
6201 93	Men/boys anoraks and similar articles, of man-made fibres, not knitted
6201 99	Men/boys anoraks & similar articles, of other textile materials, not knitted
6202 11	Women/girls overcoats & similar articles of wool/fine animal hair not knit
6202 12	Women/girls overcoats and similar articles of cotton, not knitted
6202 13	Women/girls overcoats & similar articles of man-made fibres, not knitted
6202 19	Women/girls overcoats & similar articles of other textile mat, not knit
6202 91	Women/girls anoraks & similar article of wool/fine animal hair, not knit
6202 92	Women/girls anoraks and similar article of cotton, not knitted
6202 93	Women/girls anoraks & similar article of man-made fibres, not knitted
6202 99	Women/girls anoraks & similar article of other textile materials, not knit
6203 11	Men/boys suits, of wool or fine animal hair, not knitted
6203 12	Men/boys suits, of synthetic fibres, not knitted
6203 19	Men/boys suits, of other textile materials, not knitted
6203 21	Men/boys ensembles, of wool or fine animal hair, not knitted
6203 22	Men/boys ensembles, of cotton, not knitted
6203 23	Men/boys ensembles, of synthetic fibres, not knitted
6203 29	Men/boys ensembles, of other textile materials, not knitted
6203 31	Men/boys jackets and blazers, of wool or fine animal hair, not knitted
6203 32	Men/boys jackets and blazers, of cotton, not knitted
6203 33	Men/boys jackets and blazers, of synthetic fibres, not knitted

HS No.	Product Description
6203 39	Men/boys jackets and blazers, of other textile materials, not knitted
6203 41	Men/boys trousers and shorts, of wool or fine animal hair, not knitted
6203 42	Men/boys trousers and shorts, of cotton, not knitted
6203 43	Men/boys trousers and shorts, of synthetic fibres, not knitted
6203 49	Men/boys trousers and shorts, of other textile materials, not knitted
6204 11	Women/girls-suits, of wool or fine animal hair, not knitted
6204 12	Women/girls suits, of cotton, not knitted
6204 13	Women/girls suits, of synthetic fibres, not knitted
6204 19	Women/girls suits, of other textile materials, not knitted
6204 21	Women/girls ensembles, of wool or fine animal hair, not knitted
6204 22	Women/girls ensembles, of cotton, not knitted
6204 23	Women/girls ensembles, of synthetic fibres, not knitted
6204 29	Women/girls ensembles, of other textile materials, not knitted
6204 31	Women/girls jackets, of wool or fine animal hair, not knitted
6204 32	Women/girls jackets, of cotton, not knitted
6204 33	Women/girls jackets, of synthetic fibres, not knitted
6204 39	Women/girls jackets, of other textile materials, not knitted
6204 41	Women/girls dresses, of wool or fine animal hair, not knitted
6204 42	Women/girls dresses, of cotton, not knitted
6204 43	Women/girls dresses, of synthetic fibres, not knitted
6204 44	Women/girls dresses, of artificial fibres, not knitted
6204 49	Women/girls dresses, of other textile materials, not knitted
6204 51	Women/girls skirts, of wool or fine animal hair, not knitted
6204 52	Women/girls skirts, of cotton, not knitted
6204 53	Women/girls skirts, of synthetic fibres, not knitted
6204 59	Women/girls skirts, of other textile materials, not knitted

HS No.	Product Description
6204 61	Women/girls trousers & shorts, of wool or fine animal hair, not knitted
6204 62	Women/girls trousers and shorts, of cotton, not knitted
6204 63	Women/girls trousers and shorts, of synthetic fibres, not knitted
6204 69	Women/girls trousers & shorts, of other textile materials, not knitted
6205 10	Men/boys shirts, of wool or fine animal hair, not knitted
6205 20	Men/boys shirts, of cotton, not knitted
6205 30	Men/boys shirts, of man-made fibres, not knitted
6205 90	Men/boys shirts, of other textile materials, not knitted
6206 10	Women/girls blouses and shirts, of silk or silk waste, not knitted
6206 20	Women/girls blouses & shirts, of wool or fine animal hair, not knitted
6206 30	Women/girls blouses and shirts, of cotton, not knitted
6206 40	Women/girls blouses and shirts, of man-made fibres, not knitted
6206 90	Women/girls blouses and shirts, of other textile materials, not knitted
6207 11	Men/boys underpants and briefs, of cotton, not knitted
6207 19	Men/boys underpants and briefs, of other textile materials, not knitted
6207 21	Men/boys night-shirts and pyjamas, of cotton, not knitted
6207 22	Men/boys night-shirts and pyjamas, of man-made fibres, not knitted
6207 29	Men/boys night-shirts & pyjamas, of other textile materials, not knitted
6207 91	Men/boys bathrobes, dressing gowns, etc. of cotton, not knitted
6207 92	Men/boys bathrobes, dressing gowns, etc. of man-made fibres, not knitted
6207 99	Men/boys bathrobes, dressing gowns, etc. of other textile materials, not knitted
6208 11	Women/girls slips and petticoats, of man-made fibres, not knitted

HS No.	Product Description
6208 19	Women/girls slips & petticoats, of other textile materials, not knitted
6208 21	Women/girls night-dresses and pyjamas, of cotton, not knitted
6208 22	Women/girls night-dresses and pyjamas, of man-made fibres, not knitted
6208 29	Women/girls nightdresses & pyjamas, of other textile materials, not knitted
6208 91	Women/girls panties, bathrobes, etc. of cotton not knitted
6208 92	Women/girls panties, bathrobes, etc. of man-made fibres, not knitted
6208 99	Women/girls panties, bathrobes, etc. of other textile materials, not knitted
6209 10	Babies garments & clothing accessories of wool or fine animal hair, not knitted
6209 20	Babies garments and clothing accessories of cotton, not knitted
6209 30	Babies garments & clothing accessories of synthetic fibres, not knitted
6209 90	Babies garments & clothing accessories of other textile materials, not knitted
6210 10	Garments made up of textile felts and of non-woven textile fabrics
6210 20	Men/boys evercoats & similar articles of impreg, ctd, cov etc., tex wov fab
6210 30	Women/girls overcoats & similar articles, of impreg, ctd, etc., tex wov fab
6210 40	Men/boys garments nes, made up of impreg, ctd, cov, etc., textile woven fab
6210 50	Women/girls garments nes, of impregnated, ctd, cov, etc., textile woven fab
6211 11	Men/boys swimwear, of textile materials not knitted
6211 12	Women/girls swimwear, of textile materials, not knitted
6211 20	Ski suits, of textile materials, not knitted
6211 31	Men/boys garments nes, of wool or fine animal hair, not knitted

HS No.	Product Description
6211 32	Men/boys garments nes, of cotton, not knitted
6211 33	Men/boys garments nes, of man-made fibres, not knitted
6211 39	Men/boys garments nes, of other textile materials, not knitted
6211 41	Women/girls garments nes, of wool or fine animal hair, not knitted
6211 42	Women/girls garments nes, of cotton, not knitted
6211 43	Women/girls garments nes, of man-made fibres, not knitted
6211 49	Women/girls garments nes, of other textile materials, not knitted
6212 10	Brassieres and parts thereof, of textile materials
6212 20	Girdles, panty girdles and parts thereof, of textile materials
6212 30	Corselettes and parts thereof, of textile materials
6212 90	Corsets, braces & similar articles & parts thereof, of textile materials
6213 10	Handkerchiefs, of silk or silk waste, not knitted
6213 20	Handkerchiefs, of cotton, not knitted
6213 90	Handkerchiefs, of other textile materials, not knitted
6214 10	Shawls, scarves, veils and the like, of silk or silk waste, not knitted
6214 20	Shawls, scarves, veils & the like, of wool or fine animal hair, not knitted
6214 30	Shawls, scarves, veils and the like, of synthetic fibres, not knitted
6214 40	Shawls, scarves, veils and the like, of artificial fibres, not knitted
6214 90	Shawls, scarves, veils & the like, of other textile materials, not knitted
6215 10	Ties, bow ties and cravats, of silk or silk waste, not knitted
6215 20	Ties, bow ties and cravats, of man-made fibres, not knitted
6215 90	Ties, bow ties and cravats, of other textile materials, not knitted
6216 00	Gloves, mittens and mitts, of textile materials, not knitted
6217 10	Clothing accessories nes, of textile materials, not knitted

HS No.	Product Description
6217 90	Parts of garments or of clothing accessories nes, of tex mat, not knitted
Ch. 63	**Other made up textile articles; sets; worn clothing etc.**
6301 10	Electric blankets, of textile materials
6301 20	Blankets (other than electric) & travelling rugs, of wool or fine animal hair
6301 30	Blankets (other than electric) and travelling rugs, of cotton
6301 40	Blankets (other than electric) and travelling rugs, of synthetic fibres
6301 90	Blankets (other than electric) and travelling rugs, of other textile materials
6302 10	Bed linen, of textile knitted or crocheted materials
6302 21	Bed linen, of cotton, printed, not knitted
6302 22	Bed linen, of man-made fibres, printed, not knitted
6302 29	Bed linen, of other textile materials, printed, not knitted
6302 31	Bed linen, of cotton, nes
6302 32	Bed linen, of man-made fibres, nes
6302 39	Bed linen, of other textile materials, nes
6302 40	Table linen, of textile knitted or crocheted materials
6302 51	Table linen, of cotton, not knitted
6302 52	Table linen, of flax, not knitted
6302 53	Table linen, of man-made fibres, not knitted
6302 59	Table linen, of other textile materials, not knitted
6302 60	Toilet&kitchen linen, of terry towellg or similar terry fab, of cotton
6302 91	Toilet and kitchen linen, of cotton, nes
6302 92	Toilet and kitchen linen, of flax
6302 93	Toilet and kitchen linen, of man-made fibres
6302 99	Toilet and kitchen linen, of other textile materials
6303 11	Curtains, drapes, interior blinds & curtain or bed valances, of cotton, knit
6303 12	Curtains, drapes, interior blinds & curtain/bed valances, of syn fib, knitted

HS No.	Product Description
6303 19	Curtains, drapes, interior blinds & curtain/bed valances, other tex mat, knit
6303 91	Curtains/drapes/interior blinds & curtain/bed valances, of cotton, not knit
6303 92	Curtains/drapes/interior blinds curtain/bed valances, of syn fib, not knit
6303 99	Curtain/drape/interior blind curtainr/bed valance, of other tex mat, not knit
6304 11	Bedspreads of textile materials, nes, knitted or crocheted
6304 19	Bedspreads of textile materials, nes, not knitted or crocheted
6304 91	Furnishing articles nes, of textile materials, knitted or crocheted
6304 92	Furnishing articles nes, of cotton, not knitted or crocheted
6304 93	Furnishing articles nes, of synthetic fibres, not knitted or crocheted
6304 99	Furnishg articles nes, of other textile materials, not knitted or crocheted
6305 10	Sacks & bags, for packing of goods, of jute or of other textile bast fibres
6305 20	Sacks and bags, for packing of goods, of cotton
6305 31	Sacks & bags, for packing of goods, of polyethylene or polypropylene strips
6305 39	Sacks & bags, for packing of goods, of other man-made textile materials
6305 90	Sacks and bags, for packing of goods, of other textile materials
6306 11	Tarpaulins, awnings and sunblinds, of cotton
6306 12	Tarpaulins, awnings and sunblinds, of synthetic fibres
6306 19	Tarpaulins, awnings and sunblinds, of other textile materials
6306 21	Tents, of cotton
6306 22	Tents, of synthetic fibres
6306 29	Tents, of other textile materials
6306 31	Sails, of synthetic fibres
6306 39	Sails, of other textile materials
6306 41	Pneumatic mattresses, of cotton
6306 49	Pneumatic mattresses, of other textile materials

HS No.	Product description
6306 91	Camping goods nes, of cotton
6306 99	Camping goods nes, of other textile materials
6307 10	Floor-cloths, dish-cloths, dusters & similar cleaning cloths, of tex mat
6307 20	Life jackets and life belts, of textile materials
6307 90	Made up articles, of textile materials, nes, including dress patterns
6308 00	Sets consisting of woven fab & yarn, for making up into rugs, tapestries etc.
6309 00	Worn clothing and other worn articles

Textile and clothing products in Chapters 30-49, 64-96

HS No.	Product description
3005 90	Wadding, gauze, bandages and the like
ex 3921 12	)
ex 3921 13	(Woven, knitted or non-woven fabrics coated, covered or laminated with plastics
ex 3921 90	)
ex 4202 12	) ex 4202 22 (Luggage, handbags and flatgoods with an outer surface predominantly of textile materials
ex 4202 32	)
ex 4202 92	)
ex 6405 20	Footwear with soles and uppers of wool felt
ex 6406 10	Footwear uppers of which 50% or more of the external surface area is textile material
ex 6406 99	Leg warmers and gaiters of textile material
6501 00	Hat-forms, hat bodies and hoods of felt; plateaux and manchons of felt
6502 00	Hat-shapes, plaited or made by assembling strips of any material
6503 00	Felt hats and other felt headgear
6504 00	Hats & other headgear, plaited or made by assembling strips of any material
6505 90	Hats & other headgear, knitted or made up from lace, or other textile material
6601 10	Umbrellas and sun umbrellas, garden type

6601 91		Other umbrella types, telescopic shaft
6601 99		Other umbrellas
ex 7019 10		Yams of fibre glass
ex 7019 20		Woven fabrics of fibre glass
8708 21		Safety seat belts for motor vehicles
8804 00		Parachutes; their parts and accessories
9113 90		Watch straps, bands and bracelets of textile materials
ex 9404 90		Pillow and cushions of cotton; quilts; eiderdowns; comforters and similar articles of textile materials
9502 91		Garments for dolls
ex 9612 10		Woven ribbons, of man-made fibres, other than those measuring less than 30 mm in width and permanently put up in cartridges

AGREEMENT ON TECHNICAL BARRIERS TO TRADE

Having regard to the Multilateral Trade Negotiations,

Desiring to further the objectives of the GATT 1994;

Recognizing the important contribution that international standards and conformity assessment systems can make in this regard by improving efficiency of production and facilitating the conduct of international trade;

Desiring therefore to encourage the development of such international standards and conformity assessment systems;

Desiring however to ensure that technical regulations and standards, including packaging, marking and labelling requirements, and procedures for assessment of conformity with technical regulations and standards do not create unnecessary obstacles to international trade;

Recognizing that no country should be prevented from taking measures necessary to ensure the quality of its exports, or for the protection of human, animal or plant life or health, of the environment, or for the prevention of deceptive practices, at the levels it considers appropriate, subject to the requirement that they are not applied in a manner which would constitute a means of arbitrary or unjustifiable discrimination between countries where the same conditions prevail or a disguised restriction on international trade, and are otherwise in accordance with the provisions of this Agreement.

Recognizing that no country should be prevented from taking measures necessary for the protection of its essential security interest;

Recognizing the contribution which international standardization can make to the transfer of technology from developed to developing countries;

Recognizing that developing countries may encounter special difficulties in the formulation and application of technical regulations and standards and procedures for assessment of conformity with technical regulations and standards, and desiring to assist them in their endeavours in this regard;

Members *hereby* agree as follows:

Article 1

General Provisions

1.1 General terms for standardization and procedures for assessment of conformity shall normally have the meaning given to them by definitions adopted within the United Nations system and by international standardizing bodies taking into account their context and in the light of the object and purpose of this Agreement.

1.2 However, for the purposes of this Agreement the meaning of the terms given in Annex 1 applies.

1.3 All products including industrial and agricultural products, shall be subject to the provisions of this Agreement.

1.4 Purchasing specifications prepared by governmental bodies for production or consumption requirements of governmental bodies are not subject to the provisions of this Agreement but are addressed in the Agreement on Government Procurement, according to its coverage.

1.5 The provisions of this Agreement do not apply to sanitary and phytosanitary measures as defined in Annex A of the Agreement on Sanitary and Phytosanitary measures.

1.6 All references in this Agreement to technical regulations, standards and conformity assessment procedures shall be construed to include any amendments thereto and any additions to the rules or the product coverage thereof, except amendments and additions of an insignificant nature.

TECHNICAL REGULATIONS AND STANDARDS

Article 2

Preparation, Adoption and Application of Technical Regulations by Central Government Bodies

With respect to their central government bodies:

2.1 Members shall ensure that in respect of technical regulations, products imported from the territory of any Member shall be accorded treatment no less favourable than that accorded to like products of national origin and to like products originating in any other country.

2.2 Members shall ensure that technical regulations are not prepared, adopted or applied with a view to or with the effect of creating unnecessary obstacles to international trade. For this purpose, technical regulations shall not be more trade-restrictive than necessary to fulfil a legitimate objective, taking account of the risks non-fulfilment would create. Such legitimate objectives are, *inter alia,* national security requirements; the prevention of deceptive practices; protection of human health or safety, animal or plant life or health, or the environment. In assessing such risks, relevant elements of consideration are, *inter alia,* available scientific and technical information, related processing technology or intended end uses of products.

2.3 Technical regulations shall not be maintained if the circumstances or objectives giving rise to their adoption no longer exist or if the changed circumstances or objectives can be addressed in a less trade-restrictive manner.

2.4 Where technical regulations are required and relevant international standards exist or their completion is imminent, Members shall use them, or the relevant parts of them, as a basis for their technical regulations except when such international standards or relevant parts would be an ineffective or inappropriate means for the fulfilment of the legitimate objectives pursued, for instance because of fundamental climatic or geographical factors or fundamental technological problems.

2.5 A Member preparing, adopting or applying a technical regulation which may have a significant effect on trade of other Members shall, upon the request of another Member, explain the justification for that technical regulation in terms of the provisions of paragraphs 2 to 4 of Article 2. Whenever a technical regulation is prepared, adopted or applied for one of the legitimate objectives explicitly mentioned in paragraph 2 of Article 2, and is in accordance with relevant international standards, it shall be rebuttably presumed not to create an unnecessary obstacle to international trade.

2.6 With a view to harmonizing technical regulations on as wide a basis as possible, Members shall play a full part, within the limits of their resources, in the preparation by appropriate international standardizing bodies of international standards for products for which they either have adopted, or expect to adopt, technical regulations.

2.7 Members shall give positive consideration to accepting as equivalent technical regulations of other Members, even if these regulations differ from their own, provided they are satisfied that these regulations adequately fulfil the objectives of their own regulations.

2.8 Wherever appropriate, Members shall specify technical regulations based on product requirements in terms of performance rather than design or descriptive characteristics.

2.9 Whenever a relevant international standard does not exist or the technical content of a proposed technical regulation is not in accordance with the technical content of relevant international standards, and if the technical regulation may have a significant effect on trade of other Members, Members shall:

2.9.1 publish a notice in a publication at an early appropriate stage, in such a manner as to enable interested parties in other Members to become acquainted with it, that they propose to introduce a particular technical regulation;

2.9.2 notify other Members through the WTO Secretariat of the products to be covered by the proposed technical regulation, together with a brief indication of its objective and rationale; such notifications shall take place at an early appropriate stage, when amendments can still be introduced' and comments taken into account;

2.9.3 upon request, provide to other Members, particulars or copies of the proposed technical regulation and, whenever possible, identify the parts which in substance deviate from relevant international standards;

2.9.4 without discrimination, allow reasonable time for other Members to make comments in writing, discuss these comments upon request, and take these written comments and the results of these discussions into account.

2.10 Subject to the provisions in the lead-in to Article 2, paragraph 9, where urgent problems of safety, health, environmental protection or national security arise or threaten to arise for a Member, that Member may omit such of the steps enumerated in Article 2, paragraph 9, as it finds necessary provided that the Member, upon adoption of a technical regulation, shall:

2.10.1 notify immediately other Members through the WTO Secretariat of the particular technical regulation and the products covered, with a brief indication of the objective and the rationale of the technical regulation, including the nature of the urgent problems;

2.10.2 upon request, provide other Members with copies of the technical regulation;

2.10.3 without discrimination, allow other Members to present their comments in writing, discuss these comments upon request, and take these written comments and the results of these discussions into account.

2.11 Members shall ensure that all technical regulations which have been adopted are published promptly or otherwise made available in such a manner as to enable interested parties in other Members to become acquainted with them.

2.12 Except in those urgent circumstances referred to in Article 2, paragraph 10, Members shall allow a reasonable interval between the publication of a technical regulation and its entry into force in order to allow time for producers in exporting Members, and particularly in developing country Members, to adapt their products or methods of production to the requirements of the importing Member.

Article 3

Preparation, Adoption and Application of Technical Regulations by Local Government Bodies and Non-Governmental Bodies

With respect to their local government and non-governmental bodies within their territories:

3.1 Members shall take such reasonable measures as may be available to them to ensure compliance by such bodies with the provisions of Article 2, with the exception of the obligation to notify as referred to in paragraphs 9.2 and 10.1 of Article 2.

3.2 Members shall ensure that the technical regulations of local governments on the level directly below that of the central government in Members are notified in accordance with the provisions of Article 2, paragraphs 9.2 and 10.1, noting that notification shall not be required for technical regulations the technical content of which is substantially the same as that of previously notified technical regulations of central government bodies of the Member concerned.

3.3 Members may require contact with other Members, including the notifications, provision of information, comments and discussions referred to in paragraphs 9 and 10 of Article 2, to take place through the central government.

3.4 Members shall not take measures which require or encourage local government bodies or non-governmental bodies within their territories to act in a manner inconsistent with the provisions of Article 2.

3.5 Members are fully responsible under this Agreement for the observance of all provisions of Article 2. Members shall formulate and implement positive measures and mechanisms in support of the observance of the provisions of Article 2 by other than central government bodies.

Article 4

Preparation, Adoption and Application of Standards

4.1 Members shall ensure that their central government standardizing bodies accept and comply with the Code of good practice for the preparation, adoption and application of standards in Annex 3 to this Agreement. They shall take such reasonable measures as may be available to them to ensure that local government and non-governmental standardizing bodies within their territories as well as regional standardizing bodies of which they or one or more bodies within their territories are members, accept and comply with this Code of good practice. In addition, Members shall not take measures which have the effect of, directly or indirectly, requiring or encouraging such standardizing bodies to act in a manner inconsistent with the Code of good practice in Annex 3. The obligations of Members with respect to compliance of standardizing bodies with the provisions of the Code of good practice shall apply irrespective of whether or not a standardizing body has accepted the Code of good practice.

4.2 Standardizing bodies that have accepted and are complying with the Code of good practice in Annex 3 shall be acknowledged by the Members as complying with the principles of this Agreement.

COMFORMITY WITH TECHNICAL REGULATIONS AND STANDARDS

Article 5

Procedures for Assessment of Conformit by Central Government Bodies

5.1 Members shall ensure that, in cases where a positive assurance of conformity with technical regulations or standards is required, their central government bodies apply the following provisions to products originating in the territories of other Members:

5.1.1 conformity assessment procedures are prepared, adopted and applied so as to grant access for suppliers of like products originating in the territories of other Members under conditions no less favourable than those accorded to suppliers of like products of national origin or originating in any other country, in a comparable situation; access entails suppliers' right to an assessment of conformity under the rules of the procedure, including, when foreseen by this procedure, the possibility to have conformity assessment activities undertaken at the site of facilities and to receive the mark of the system;

5.1.2 conformity assessment procedures are not prepared, adopted or applied with a view to or with the effect of creating unnecessary obstacles to international trade. This means, *inter alia,* that conformity assessment procedures shall not be more strict or be applied more strictly than is necessary to give the importing Member adequate confidence that products conform with the applicable technical regulations or standards, taking account of the risks non-conformity would create.

5.2 When implementing the provisions of paragraph 1 of Article 5, Members shall ensure that:

5.2.1 conformity assessment procedures are undertaken and completed as expeditiously as possible and in a no less favourable order for products originating in the territories of other Members than for like domestic products;

5.2.2 the standard processing period of each conformity assessment procedure is published or that the anticipated processing period is communicated to the applicant upon request; when receiving an application, the competent body promptly examines the completeness of the documentation and informs the applicant in a precise and complete manner of all deficiencies; the competent body transmits as soon as possible the results of the assessment in a precise and complete manner to the applicant so that corrective action may be taken if necessary; even when the application has deficiencies, the competent body proceeds as far as practicable with the conformity assessment if the applicant so requests; and that, upon request, the applicant is informed of the stage of the procedure, with any delay being explained;

5.2.3 information requirements are limited to what is necessary to assess conformity and determine fees;

5.2.4 the confidentiality of information about products originating in the territories of other Members arising from or supplied in connection with such conformity assessment procedures is respected in the same way as for domestic products and in such a manner that legitimate commercial interests are protected;

5.2 5 any fees imposed for assessing the conformity of products originating in the territories of other Members are equitable in relation to any fees chargeable for assessing the conformity of like products of national origin or originating in any other country, taking into account communication, transportation and other costs arising from differences between location of facilities of the applicant and the conformity assessment body;

5.2.6 the siting of facilities used in conformity assessment procedures and the selection of samples are not such as to cause unnecessary inconvenience to applicants or their agents;

5.2.7 whenever specifications of a product are changed subsequent to its determination of conformity to the applicable technical regulations or standards, the conformity assessment procedure for the modified product is limited to what is necessary to determine whether adequate confidence exists that the product still meets the technical regulations or standards concerned;

5.2.8 a procedure exists to review complaints concerning the operation of a conformity assessment procedure and to take corrective action when a complaint is justified.

5.3 Nothing in paragraphs 1 and 2 of Article 5 shall prevent Members from carrying out reasonable spot checks within their territories.

5.4 In cases where a positive assurance is required that products conform with technical regulations or standards, and relevant guides or recommendations issued by international standardizing bodies exist or their completion is imminent, Members shall ensure that central government bodies use them, or the relevant parts of them, as a basis for their conformity assessment procedures, except where, as duly explained upon request, such guides or recommendations or relevant parts are inappropriate for the Members concerned, for, *inter alia,* such reasons as national security requirements; the prevention of deceptive practices; protection of human health or safety, animal or plant life or health, or the environment; fundamental climatic or other geographical factors: fundamental technological or infrastructural problems.

5.5 With a view to harmonizing conformity assessment procedures on as wide a basis as possible, Members shall play a full part within the limits of their resources in the preparation by appropriate international standardizing bodies of guides and recommendations for conformity assessment procedures.

5.6 Whenever a relevant guide or recommendation issued by an international standardizing body does not exist or the technical content of a proposed conformity assessment procedure is not in accordance with relevant guides and recommendations issued by international standardizing bodies, and if the conformity assessment procedure may have a significant effect on trade of other Members, Members shall:

5.6.1 publish a notice in a publication at an early appropriate stage, in such a manner as to enable interested parties in other Members to become acquainted with it, that they propose to introduce a particular conformity assessment procedure;

5.6.2 notify other Members through the WTO Secretariat of the products to be covered by the proposed conformity assessment procedure, together with a brief indication of its objective and rationale. Such notifications shall take place at an early appropriate stage, when amendments can still be introduced and comments taken into account;

5.6.3 upon request, provide to other Members particulars or copies of the proposed procedure and, whenever possible, identify the parts which in substance deviate from relevant guides or recommendations issued by international standardizing bodies;

5.6.4 without discrimination, allow reasonable time for other Members to make comments in writing, discuss these comments upon request, and take these written comments and the results of these discussions into account.

5.7 Where urgent problems of safety, health, environmental protection or national security arise or threaten to arise for a Member, that Member may omit such of the steps enumerated in paragraph 6 of Article 5 as it finds necessary provided that the Member, upon adoption of the procedure, shall:

5.7.1 notify immediately other Members through the WTO Secretariat of the particular procedure and the products covered, with a brief indication of the objective and the rationale of the procedure, including the nature of the urgent problems;

5.7.2 upon request, provide other Members with copies of the rules of the procedure;

5.7.3 without discrimination, allow other Members to present their comments in writing, discuss these comments upon request, and take these written comments and the results of these discussions into account.

5.8 Members shall ensure that all conformity assessment procedures which have been adopted are published promptly or otherwise made available in such a manner as to enable interested parties in other Members to become acquainted with them.

5.9 Except in those urgent circumstances referred to in paragraph 7 of Article 5, Members shall allow a reasonable interval between the publication of requirements concerning conformity assessment procedures and their entry into force in order to allow time for producers in exporting Members, and particularly in developing country Members, to adapt their products or methods of production to the requirements of the importing Member.

Article 6

Recognition of Conformity Assessment by Central Government Bodies

With respect to their central government bodies:

6.1 Without prejudice to the provisions of Article 6, paragraphs 3 and 4, Members shall ensure, whenever possible, that results of conformity assessment procedures in other Members are accepted, even when those procedures differ from their own, provided they are satisfied that those procedures offer an assurance of conformity with applicable technical regulations or standards equivalent to their own procedures. It is recognized that prior consultations may be necessary in order to arrive at a mutually satisfactory understanding regarding, in particular:

(a) adequate and enduring technical competence of the relevant conformity assessment bodies in the exporting Member, so that confidence in the continued reliability of their conformity assessment results can exist; in this regard, verified compliance, for instance through accreditation, with relevant guides or recommendations issued by international standardizing bodies shall be taken into account as an indication of adequate technical competence;

(b) limitation of the acceptance of conformity assessment results to those produced by designated bodies in the exporting Member.

6.2 Members shall ensure that their conformity assessment procedures permit, as far as practicable, the implementation of the provisions in paragraph 1 of Article 6.

6.3 Members are encouraged, at the request of other Members, to be willing to enter into negotiations for the conclusion of agreements for the mutual recognition of results of each other's conformity assessment procedures. Members may require that such agreements fulfil the criteria of Article 6, paragraph 1, and give mutual satisfaction regarding their potential for facilitating trade in the products concerned.

6.4 Members are encouraged to permit participation of conformity assessment bodies located in the territories of other Members in their conformity assessment procedures under conditions no less favourable than those accorded to bodies located within their territory or the territory of any other country.

Article 7

Procedures for Assessment of Conformity by Local Government Bodies

With respect to their local government bodies within their territories:

7.1 Members shall take such reasonable measures as may be available to them to ensure compliance by such bodies with the provisions of Articles 5 and 6, with the exception of the obligation to notify as referred to in paragraphs 6.2 and 7.1 of Article 5.

7.2 Members shall ensure that the conformity assessment procedures of local governments on the level directly below that of the central government in Members are notified in accordance with the provisions of paragraphs 6.2 and 7.1 of Article 5, noting that notifications shall not be required for conformity assessment procedures the technical content of which is substantially the same as that of previously notified conformity assessment procedures of central government bodies of the Members concerned.

7.3 Members may require contact with other Members, including the notifications, provision of information, comments and discussions referred to in paragraphs 6 and 7 of Article 5, to take place through the central government.

7.4 Members shall not take measures which require or encourage local government bodies within their territories to act in a manner inconsistent with the provisions of Articles 5 and 6.

7.5 Members are fully responsible under this Agreement for the observance of all provisions of Articles 5 and 6. Members shall formulate and implement positive measures and mechanisms in support of the observance of the provisions of Articles 5 and 6 by other than central government bodies.

Article 8

Procedures for Assessment of Conformity by Non-Governmental Bodies

8.1 Members shall take such reasonable measures as may be available to them to ensure that non-governmental bodies within their territories which operate conformity assessment procedures comply with the provisions of Articles 5 and 6, with the exception of the obligation to notify proposed conformity assessment procedures. In addition, Members shall not take measures which have the effect of, directly or indirectly, requiring or encouraging such bodies to act in a manner inconsistent with the provisions of Articles 5 and 6.

8.2 Members shall ensure that their central government bodies rely on conformity assessment procedures operated by non-governmental bodies only if these latter bodies comply with the provisions of Articles 5 and 6, with the exception of the obligation to notify proposed conformity assessment procedures.

Article 9

International and Regional Systems

9.1 Where a positive assurance of conformity with a technical regulation or standard is required, Members shall, wherever practicable, formulate and adopt international systems for conformity assessment and become members thereof or participate therein.

9.2 Members shall take such reasonable measures as may be available to them to ensure that international and regional systems for conformity assessment, in which relevant bodies within their territories are members or participants, comply with the provisions of Articles 5 and 6. In addition, Members shall not take any measures which have the effect of, directly or indirectly, requiring or encouraging such systems to act in a manner inconsistent with any of the provisions of Articles 5 and 6.

9.3 Members shall ensure that their central government bodies rely on international or regional conformity assessment systems only to the extent that these systems comply with the provisions of Articles 5 and 6, as applicable.

INFORMATION AND ASSISTANCE

Article 10

Information About Technical Regulations, Standards and Conformity Assessment Procedures

10.1 Each Member shall ensure that an enquiry point exists which is able to answer all reasonable enquiries from other Members and interested parties in other Members as well as to provide the relevant documents regarding:

10.1.1 any technical regulations adopted or proposed within its territory by central or local government bodies, by non-governmental bodies which have legal power to enforce a technical regulation, or by regional standardizing bodies of which such bodies are members or participants;

10.1.2 any standards adopted or proposed within its territory by central or local government bodies, or by regional standardizing bodies of which such bodies are members or participants;

10.1.3 any conformity assessment procedures, or proposed conformity assessment procedures, which are operated within its territory by central or local government bodies, or by non-governmental bodies which have legal power to enforce a technical regulation, or by regional bodies of which such bodies are members or participants;

10.1.4 the membership and participation of the Member, or of relevant central or local government bodies within its territory, in international and regional standardizing bodies and conformity assessment systems, as well as in bilateral and multilateral arrangements within the scope of this Agreement; they shall also be able to provide reasonable information on the provisions of such systems and arrangements;

10.1.5 the location of notices published pursuant to this Agreement, or the provision of information as to where such information can be obtained; and

10.1.6 the location of the enquiry points mentioned in paragraph 3 of Article 10.

10.2 If, however, for legal or administrative reasons more than one enquiry point is established by a Member, that Member shall provide to the other Members complete and unambiguous information on the scope of responsibility of each of these enquiry points. In addition, that Member shall ensure that any enquiries addressed to an incorrect enquiry point shall promptly be conveyed to the correct enquiry point.

10.3 Each Member shall take such reasonable measures as may be available to it to ensure that one or more enquiry points exist which are able to answer all reasonable enquiries from other Members and interested parties in other Members as well as to provide the relevant documents or information as to where they can be obtained regarding:

10.3.1 any standards adopted or proposed within its territory by non-governmental standardizing bodies, or by regional standardizing bodies of which such bodies are members or participants; and

10.3.2 any conformity assessment procedures, or proposed conformity assessment Procedures, which are operated within its territory by non-governmental bodies, or by regional bodies of which such bodies are members or participants;

10.3.3 the membership and participation of relevant non-governmental bodies within its territory in international and regional standardizing bodies and conformity assessment systems, as well as in bilateral and multilateral arrangements within the scope of this Agreement; they shall also be able to provide reasonable information on the provisions of such systems and arrangements.

10.4 Members shall take such reasonable measures as may be available to them to ensure that where copies of documents are requested by other Members or by interested parties in other Members, in accordance with the provisions of this Agreement, they are supplied at an equitable price (if any) which shall, apart from the real cost of delivery, be the same for the nationals[30] of the Member concerned or of any other Member.

10.5 Developed country Members shall, if requested by other Members, provide, in English, French or Spanish, translations of the documents covered by a specific notification or, in case of voluminous documents, of summaries of such documents.

10.6 The WTO Secretariat will, when it receives notifications in accordance with the provisions of this Agreement, circulate copies of the notifications to all Members and interested international standardizing and conformity assessment bodies, and draw the attention of developing country Members to any notifications relating to products of particular interest to them.

---

[30] 'Nationals' here shall be deemed, in the case of a separate customs territory Member of the WTO to mean persons, natural or legal, who are domiciled or who have a real and effective industrial or commercial establishment in that customs territory.

10.7 Whenever a Member has reached an agreement with any other country or countries on issues related to technical regulations, standards or conformity assessment procedures which may have a significant effect on trade, at least one Member to the agreement shall notify other Members through the WTO Secretariat of the products to be covered by the agreement. and include a brief description of the agreement Members concerned are encouraged to enter, upon request, into consultations with other Members for the purposes of concluding similar agreements or of arranging for their participation in such agreements.

10.8 Nothing in this Agreement shall be construed as requiring:

10.8.1 the publication of texts other than in the language of the Member;

10.8.2 the provision of particulars or copies of drafts other than in the language of the Member except as stated in paragraph 5 of Article 10; or

10.8.3 Members to furnish any information, the disclosure of which they consider contrary to their essential security interests.

10.9 Notifications to the WTO Secretariat shall be in English, French or Spanish.

10.10 Members shall designate a single central government authority that is responsible for the implementation on the national level of the provisions concerning notification procedures under this Agreement except those included in Annex 3.

10.11 If, however, for legal or administrative reasons the responsibility for notification procedures is divided among two or more central government authorities, the Member concerned shall provide to the other Members complete and unambiguous information on the scope of responsibility of each of these authorities.

Article 11

Technical Assistance to Other Members

11.1 Members shall, if requested, advise other Members, especially the developing country Members, on the preparation of technical regulations.

11.2 Members shall, if requested, advise other Members, especially the developing country Members and shall grant them technical assistance on mutually agreed terms and conditions regarding the establishment of national standardizing bodies, and participation in the international standardizing bodies, and shall encourage their national standardizing bodies to do likewise.

11.3 Members shall, if requested, take such reasonable measures as may be available to them to arrange for the regulatory bodies within their territories to advise other Members, especially the developing country Members, and shall grant them technical assistance on mutually agreed terms and conditions regarding:

11.3.1 the establishment of regulatory bodies, or bodies for the assessment of conformity with technical regulations; and

11.3.2 the methods by which their technical regulations can best be met.

11.4 Members shall, if requested, take such reasonable measures as may be available to them to arrange for advice to be given to other Members, especially the developing country Members, and shall grant them technical assistance, on mutually agreed terms and conditions, regarding the establishment of bodies for the assessment of conformity with standards adopted within the territory of the requesting Member.

11.5 Members shall, if requested, advise other Members, especially the developing country Members, and shall grant them technical assistance, on mutually agreed terms and conditions, regarding the steps that should be taken by their producers if they wish to have access to systems for conformity assessment operated by governmental or non-governmental bodies within the territory of the Member receiving the request.

11.6 Members which are members or participants of international or regional systems for conformity assessment shall, if requested, advise other Members, especially the developing country Members, and shall grant them technical assistance, on mutually agreed terms and conditions, regarding the establishment of the institutions and legal framework which would enable them to fulfil the obligations of membership or participation in such systems.

11.7 Members shall, if so requested, encourage bodies within their territories which are members or participants of international or regional systems for conformity assessment to advise other Members, especially the developing country Members, and should consider requests for technical assistance from them regarding the establishment of the institutions which would enable the relevant bodies within their territories to fulfil the obligations of membership or participation.

11.8 In providing advice and technical assistance to other Members in terms of Article 11, paragraphs 1 to 7, Members shall give priority to the needs of the least-developed country Members.

Article 12

Special and Differential Treatment of Developing Country Members

12.1 Members shall provide differential and more favourable treatment to developing country Members to this Agreement, through the following provisions as well as through the relevant provisions of other Articles of this Agreement.

12.2 Members shall give particular attention to the provisions of this Agreement concerning developing country Members' rights and obligations and shall take into account the special development, financial and trade needs of developing country Members in the implementation of this Agreement, both nationally and in the operation of this Agreement's institutional arrangements.

12.3 Members shall, in the preparation and application of technical regulations, standards and conformity assessment procedures, take account of the special development, financial and trade needs of developing country Members, with a view to ensuring that such technical regulations, standards and conformity assessment procedures do not create unnecessary obstacles to exports from developing country Members.

12.4 Members recognize that, although international standards, guides or recommendations may exist, in their particular technological and socio-economic conditions, developing country Members adopt certain technical regulations, standards or conformity assessment procedures aimed at preserving indigenous technology and production methods and processes compatible with their development needs. Members therefore recognize that developing country Members should not be expected to use international standards as a basis for their technical regulations or standards, including test methods, which are not appropriate to their development, financial and trade needs.

12.5 Members shall take such reasonable measures as may be available to them to ensure that international standardizing bodies and international systems for conformity assessment are organized and operated in a way which facilitates active and representative participation of relevant bodies in all Members, taking into account the special problems of developing country Members.

12.6 Members shall take such reasonable measures as may be available to them to ensure that international standardizing bodies, upon request of developing country Members, examine the possibility of, and, if practicable, prepare-international standards concerning products of special interest to developing country Members.

12.7 Members shall, in accordance with the provisions of Article 11, provide technical assistance to developing country Members to ensure that the preparation and application of technical regulations, standards and conformity assessment procedures do not create unnecessary obstacles to the expansion and diversification of exports from developing country Members.

In determining the terms and conditions of the technical assistance, account shall be taken of the stage of development of the requesting Members and in particular of the least-developed country Members.

12.8 It is recognized that developing country Members may face special problems, including institutional and infrastructural problems, in the field of preparation and application of technical regulations, standards and conformity assessment procedures. It is further recognized that the special development and trade needs of developing country Members, as well as their stage of technological development, may hinder their ability to discharge fully their obligations under this Agreement. Members, therefore, shall take this fact fully into account. Accordingly, with a view to ensuring that developing country Members are able to comply with this Agreement, the Committee is enabled to grant, upon request, specified, time-limited exceptions in whole or in part from obligations under this Agreement. When considering such requests the Committee shall take into account the special problems, in the field of preparation and application of technical regulations, standards and conformity assessment procedures, and the special development and trade needs of the developing country Member, as well as its stage of technological development, which may hinder its ability to discharge fully its obligations under this Agreement. The Committee shall, in particular, take into account the special problems of the least-developed country Members.

12.9 During consultations, developed country Members shall bear in mind the special difficulties experienced by developing country Members in formulating and implementing standards and technical regulations and conformity assessment procedures, and in their desire to assist developing country Members with their efforts in this direction, developed country Members shall take account of the special needs of the former in regard to financing, trade and development.

12.10 The Committee shall examine periodically the special and differential treatment, as laid down in this Agreement, granted to developing country Members on national and international levels.

INSTITUTIONS, CONSULTATION AND DISPUTE SETTLEMENT

Article 13

The Committee on Technical Barriers to Trade

There shall be established under this Agreement:

13.1 A Committee on Technical Barriers to Trade composed of representatives from each of the Members (hereinafter referred to as "the Committee"). The Committee shall elect its own Chairman and shall meet as necessary, but no less than once a year for the purpose of affording Members the opportunity of consulting on any matters relating to the operation of this Agreement or the furtherance of its objectives, and shall carry out such responsibilities as assigned to it under this Agreement or by the Members.

13.2 Working parties or other bodies as may be appropriate, which shall carry out such responsibilities as may be assigned to them by the Committee in accordance with the relevant provisions of this Agreement.

13.3 It is understood that unnecessary duplication should be avoided between the work under this Agreement and that of governments in other technical bodies. The Committee shall examine this problem with a view to minimizing such duplication.

Article 14
Consultation and Dispute Settlement

14.1 Consultations and the settlement of disputes with respect to any matter affecting the operation of this Agreement shall take place under the auspices of the Dispute Settlement Body and shall follow, *mutatis mutandis, the* provisions of Articles XXII and XXIII of the GATT 1994, as elaborated and applied by the Understanding Governing the Rules and Procedures for Settlement of Disputes.

14.2 At the request of a party to a dispute, or at its own initiative, a panel may establish a technical expert group to assist in questions of a technical nature, requiring detailed consideration by experts.

14.3 Technical expert groups shall be governed by the procedures of Annex 2.

14.4 The dispute settlement provisions set out above can be invoked in cases where a Member considers that another Member has not achieved satisfactory results under Articles 3, 4, 7, 8 and 9 and its trade interests are significantly affected. In this respect, such results shall be equivalent to those as if the body in question were a Member.

FINAL PROVISIONS

Article 15
Final Provisions

Reservations

15.1 Reservations may not be entered in respect of any of the provisions of this Agreement without the consent of the other Members.

Review

15.2 Each Member shall, promptly after the date on which the Agreement Establishing the WTO enters into force for it, inform the Committee of measures in existence or taken to ensure the implementation and administration of this Agreement. Any changes of such measures thereafter shall also be notified to the Committee.

15.3 The Committee shall review annually the implementation and operation of this Agreement taking into account the objectives thereof.

15.4 Not later than the end of the third year from the entry into force of the Agreement Establishing the WTO and at the end of each three-year period thereafter, the Committee shall review the operation and implementation of this Agreement, including the provisions relating to transparency, with a view to recommending an adjustment of the rights and obligations of this Agreement where necessary to ensure mutual economic advantage and balance of rights and obligations, without prejudice to the provisions of Article 12. Having regard, *inter alia,* to the experience gained in the implementation of the Agreement, the Committee shall, where appropriate, submit proposals for amendments to the text of this Agreement to the Council for Trade in Goods.

Annexes

15.5 The annexes to this Agreement constitute an integral part thereof.

ANNEX 1

Terms and their definitions for the Purpose of this agreement

The terms presented in the sixth edition of the ISO/IEC Guide 2: 1991, General Terms and Their Definitions Concerning Standardization and Related Activities, shall, when used in this Agreement, have the same meaning as given in the definitions in the said Guide taking into account that services are excluded from the coverage of this Agreement.

For the purpose of this Agreement, however, the following definitions shall apply:

1. Technical regulation

Document which lays down product characteristics or their related processes and production methods, including the applicable administrative provisions, with which compliance is mandatory. It may also include or deal exclusively with terminology, symbols, packaging, marking or labelling requirements as they apply to a product, process or production method.

Explanatory note : The definition in ISO/IEC Guide 2 is not self-contained, but based on the so-called "building block" system.

2. Standard

For the term "Standard" the following definition shall apply:

Document approved by a recognized body, that provides, for common and repeated use, rules, guidelines or characteristics for products or related processes and production methods, with which compliance is not mandatory. It may also include or deal exclusively with terminology, symbols, packaging, marking or labelling requirements as they apply to a product, process or production method.

Explanatory note : The terms as defined in ISO/IEC Guide 2 cover products, processes and services. This agreement deals only with technical regulations, standards and conformity assessment procedures related to products or processes and production methods. Standards as defined by ISO/IEC Guide 2 may be mandatory or voluntary. For the purpose of this Agreement standards are defined as voluntary and technical regulations as mandatory documents. Standards prepared by the international standardization community are based on consensus. This Agreement covers also documents that are not based on consensus.

3. Conformity assessment procedures

Any procedure used, directly or indirectly, to determine that relevant requirements in technical regulations or standards are fulfilled.

Explanatory note: Conformity assessment procedures include, *inter alia,* procedures for sampling, testing and inspection; evaluation, verification and assurance of conformity; registration, accreditation and approval as well as their combinations.

4. International body or system

Body or system whose membership is open to the relevant bodies of at least all Members.

5. Regional body or system

Body or system whose membership is open to the relevant bodies of only some of the Members.

6. Central government body

Central government, its ministries and departments or any body subject to the control of the central government in respect of the activity in question.

Explanatory note : In the case of the European Communities the provisions governing central government bodies apply. However, regional bodies or conformity assessment systems may be established within the European Communities, and in such cases would be subject to the provisions of this Agreement on regional bodies or conformity assessment systems.

7. Local government body

Government other than a central government (*e.g.* states, provinces,

Länder, cantons, municipalities, etc.), its ministries or departments or any body subject to the control of such a government in respect of the activity in question.

8. Non-governmental body

Body other than a central government body or a local government body, including a non-governmental body which has legal power to enforce a technical regulation.

ANNEX 2

Technical Expert Gropus

The following procedures shall apply to technical expert groups established in accordance with the provisions of Article 14.

1. Technical expert groups are under the panel's authority. Their terms of reference and detailed working procedures shall be decided by the panel, and they shall report to the panel.

2. Participation in technical expert groups shall be restricted to persons of professional standing and experience in the field in question.

3. Citizens of parties to the dispute shall not serve on a technical expert group without the joint agreement of the parties to the dispute, except in exceptional circumstances when the panel considers that the need for specialized scientific expertise cannot be fulfilled otherwise. Government officials of parties to the dispute shall not serve on a technical expert group. Members of technical expert groups shall serve in their individual capacities and not as government representatives, nor as representatives of any organization. Governments or organizations shall therefore not give them instructions with regard to matters before a technical expert group.

4. Technical expert groups may consult and seek information and technical advice from any source they deem appropriate. Before a technical expert group seeks such information or advice from a source within the jurisdiction of a Member, it shall inform the government of that Member. Any Member shall respond promptly and fully to any request by a technical expert group for such information as the technical expert group considers necessary and appropriate.

5. The parties to a dispute shall have access to all relevant information provided to a technical expert group, unless it is of a confidential nature. Confidential information provided to the technical expert group shall not be released without formal authorization from the government, organization or person providing the information. Where such information is requested from the technical expert group but release of such information by the technical

expert group is not authorized, a non-confidential summary of the information will be provided by the government, organization or person supplying the information.

6. The technical expert group shall submit a draft report to the Members concerned with a view to obtaining their comments, and taking them into account, as appropriate, in the final report, which shall also be circulated to the Members concerned when it is submitted to the panel.

ANNEX 3

Code of Good Practice for the Preparation, Adoption and Application of Standards

General Provisions

A. For the purposes of this Code the definitions in Annex 1 of this Agreement shall apply.

B. This Code is open to acceptance by any standardizing body within the territory of a Member of the WTO, whether a central government body, a local government body, or a non-governmental body; to any governmental regional standardizing body one or more members of which are Member of the WTO; and to any non-governmental regional standardizing body one or more members of which are situated within the territory of a Member of the WTO (hereafter collectively called "standardizing bodies" and individually "the standardizing body").

C. Standardizing bodies that have accepted or withdrawn from this Code shall notify this fact to the ISO/IEC Information Centre in Geneva. The notification shall include the name and address of the body concerned and the scope of its current and expected standardization activities. The notification may be sent either directly to the ISO/IEC Information Centre, or through the national member body of ISO/IEC or, preferably, through the relevant national member or international affiliate of ISONET, as appropriate.

Substantive Provisions

D. In respect of standards, the standardizing body shall accord treatment to products originating in the territory of any other Member of the WTO no less favourable than that accorded to like products of national origin and to like products originating in any other country.

E. The standardizing body shall ensure that standards are not prepared, adopted or applied with a view to, or with the effect of, creating unnecessary obstacles to international trade.

F. Where international standards exist or their completion is imminent, the standardizing body shall use them, or the relevant parts of them, as a basis for the standards it develops, except where such international standards or relevant parts would be ineffective or inappropriate, for instance, because of an insufficient level of protection or fundamental climatic or geographical factors or fundamental technological problems.

G. With a view to harmonizing standards on as wide a basis as possible, the standardizing body shall, in an appropriate way, play a full part within the limits of its resources in the preparation by relevant international standardizing bodies of international standards regarding subject matter for which it either has adopted, or expects to adopt, standards. For standardizing bodies within the territory of a Member, participation in a particular international standardization activity shall, whenever possible, take place through one delegation representing all standardizing bodies in the territory that have adopted, or expect to adopt, standards for the subject matter to which the international standardization activity relates.

H. The standardizing body within the territory of a Member shall make every effort to avoid duplication of, or overlap with, the work of other standardizing bodies in the national territory or with the work of relevant international or regional standardizing bodies. They shall also make every effort to achieve a national consensus on the standards they develop. Likewise the regional standardizing body shall make every effort to avoid duplication of, or overlap with, the work of relevant international standardizing bodies.

I. Wherever appropriate, the standardizing body shall specify standards based on product requirements in terms of performance rather than design or descriptive characteristics.

J. At least once every six months, the standardizing body shall publish a work programme containing its name and address, the standards it is currently preparing and the standards which it has adopted in the preceding period. A standard is under preparation from the moment a decision has been taken to develop a standard until that standard has been adopted. The titles of specific draft standards shall, upon request, be provided in English, French or Spanish. A notice of the existence of the work programme shall be published in a national or, as the case may be, regional publication of standardization activities.

The work programme shall for each standard indicate, in accordance with any ISONET rules, the classification relevant to the subject matter, the stage attained in the standard's development, and the references of any international standards taken as a basis. No later than at the time of publication of its work programme, the standardizing body shall notify the existence thereof to the ISO/IEC Information Centre in Geneva.

The notification shall contain the name and address of the standardizing body, the name and issue of the publication in which the work programme is published, the period to which the work programme applies, its price (if any), and how and where it can be obtained. The notification may be sent directly to the ISO/IEC Information Centre, or, preferably, through the relevant national member or international affiliate of ISONET, as appropriate.

K. The national member of ISO/IEC shall make every effort to become a member of ISONET or to appoint another body to become a member as well as to acquire the most advanced membership type possible for the ISONET member. Other standardizing bodies shall make ever), effort to associate themselves with the ISONET member.

L. Before adopting a standard, the standardizing body shall allow a period of at least sixty days for the submission of comments on the draft standard by interested parties within the territory of a Member of the WTO. This period may, however, be shortened in cases where urgent problems of safety, health or environment arise or threaten to arise. No later than at the start of the comment period, the standardizing body shall publish a notice announcing the period for commenting in the publication referred to in paragraph J. Such notification shall include, as far as practicable, whether the draft standard deviates from relevant international standards.

M. On the request of any interested party within the territory of a Member of the WTO, the standardizing body shall promptly provide, or arrange to provide, a copy of a draft standard which it has submitted for comments. Any fees charged for this service shall, apart from the real cost of delivery, be the same for domestic and foreign parties.

N. The standardizing body shall take into account, in the further processing of the standard, the comments received during the period for commenting. Comments received through standardizing bodies that have accepted this Code of good practice shall, if so requested, be replied to as promptly as possible. The reply shall include an explanation why a deviation from relevant international standards is necessary.

O. Once the standard has been adopted, it shall be promptly published.

P. On the request of any interested party within the territory of a Member of the WTO, the standardizing body shall promptly provide or arrange to provide a copy of its most recent work programme or of a standard which it produced. Any fees charged for this service shall, apart from the real costs of delivery, be the same for foreign and domestic parties.

Q. The standardizing body shall afford sympathetic consideration to, and adequate opportunity for, consultation regarding representations with respect to the operation of this Code presented by standardizing bodies that have accepted this Code of good practice. It shall make an objective effort to solve any complaints.

AGREEMENT ON TRADE-RELATED INVESTMENT MEASURES

Members,

Considering that Ministers agreed in the Punta del Este Declaration that "Following an examination of the operation of GATT Articles related to the trade restrictive and distorting effects of investment measures, negotiations should elaborate, as appropriate, further provisions that may be necessary to avoid such adverse effects on trade";

Desiring to promote the expansion and progressive liberalisation of world trade and to facilitate investment across international frontiers so as to increase the economic growth of all trading partners, and particularly developing country Members while ensuring free competition;

Taking into account the particular trade, development and financial needs of developing country Members, particularly those of the least-developed country Members;

Recognizing that certain investment measures can cause trade restrictive and distorting effects;

Hereby agree as follows:

Article I
Coverage

This Agreement applies to investment measures related to trade in goods only (hereafter referred to as 'TRIMs").

Article 2
National Treatment and Quantitative Restrictions

1. Without prejudice to other rights and obligations under the GATT 1994, no Member shall apply any TRIM that is inconsistent with the provisions of Article III or Article XI of the GATT 1994.

2. An illustrative list of TRIMs that are inconsistent with the obligation of national treatment provided for in Article III:4 of the GATT 1994 and the obligation of the general elimination of quantitative restrictions provided for in Article XI: 1 of the GATT 1994 is contained in the Annex to this Agreement.

Article 3
Exceptions

All exceptions under the GATT 1994 shall apply, as appropriate, to the provisions of this Agreement.

Article 4
Developing Country Members

A developing country Member shall be freee to deviate temporarily from the provisions of Article 2 above to the extent and in such a manner as Article XVIII of GATT 1994, the Understanding on the Balance-of-Paymnets Provisions of the General Agreement on Tariffs and Trade 1994, and the 1979 Declaration on Trade Measures Taken for Balance-of-Paymnets Purposes permit the Member to deviate from the provisions of Articles III and XI of the GATT 1994.

Article 5
Notification and Transitional Arrangements

1. Members within ninety days of the entry into force of the Agreement Establishing the WTO, shall notify the Council for Trade in Goods of all TRIMs they are applying that are not in conformity with provisions of this Agreement. Such TRIMs of general or specific application shall be notified, along with their principal features.[31]

2. Each Member shall eliminate all TRIMs which are notified under paragraph 1 above within two years of the date of entry into force of the Agreement Establishing the WTO in case of a developed country Member, within five years in the case of a developing country Member, and within seven years in the case of a least-developed country Member.

3. On request, the Council for Trade in Goods may extend the transition period for the elimination of TRIMs notified under paragraph 1 above for a developing country Member, including a least-developed country Member, which demonstrates particular diffculties in implementing the provisions of this Agreement. In considering such a request, the Council for Trade in Goods shall take into account the individual development financial and trade needs of the Member in question.

4. During the transition period, a Member shall not modify the terms of any TRIM which it notifies under paragraph 1 above from those prevailing at the date of entry into force of the Agreement Establishing the WTO so as to increase the degree of inconsistency with the provisions of Article 2 above. TRIMs introduced less than 180 days before the entry into force of the Agreement Establsihing the WTO shall not benefit from the transitional arrangements provided in paragraph 2 above.

5. Notwithstanding the provisions of Article 2 above, a Member in order

[31] In the case of TRIMs applied under discretionary authority each specific application shall be notified. Information that would prejudice the legitimate commercial interests of particular enterprises need not be disclosed.

not to disadvantage established enterprises which are subject to a TRIM notified under paragraph 1 above may apply during the transition period the same TRIM to a new investment (i) where the products to those of the established enterprises, and (ii) where necessary to avoid distorting the conditions of competition between the new investment and the established enterprises. Any TRIM so applied to a new investment shall be notified to the Council for Trade in Goods. The terms of such a TRIM shall be equivalent in their competitive effect to those applicable to the established enterprises and it shall be terminated at the same time.

Article 6
Transparency

1. Members reaffirm, with respect to TRIMs, their commitment to obligations on transparency and notification in Article X of the GATT 1994, in the undertaking on "Notification" contained in the 1979 Understanding Regarding Notification, Consultation, Dispute Settlement and Surveillance and in the Ministerial Decision on Notification Procedures.

2. Each Member shall notify the WTO Secretariat of the publications in which TRIMs may be found, including those applied by regional and local governments and authorities within their territories.

3. Each Member shall accord sympathetic consideration to requests for information, and afford adequate opportunity for consultation, on any matter arising from this Agreement raised by another Member. In conformity with Article X of the GATT 1994 no Member is required to disclose information the disclosure of which would impede law enforcement or otherwise be contrary to the public interest or would prejudice the legitimate commercial interests of particular enterprises, public or private.

Article 7
Committee on TRIMs

1. A Committee on Trade-Related Investment Measures shall be established, open to all Members of the WTO. The Committee shall elect its own Chairman and Vice-Chairman, and shall meet not less than once a year and otherwise at the request of any Member.

2. The Committee shall carry out responsibilities assigned to it by the Council for Trade in Goods and shall afford Members the opportunity to consult on any matters relating to the operation and implementation of this Agreement.

3. The Committee shall monitor the operation and implementation of this Agreement and shall report thereon annually to the Council for Trade in Goods.

Article 8
Consultation and Dispute Settlement

The provisions of Articles XXII and XXIII of the GATT 1994, as elaborated and applied by the Understanding on Rules and Procedures Governing the Settlement of Disputes, shall apply to consultations and the settlement of disputes under this Agreement.

Article 9
Review by the Council for Trade in Goods

Not later than five years after the date of entry into force of the Agreement Establishing the WTO, the Council for Trade in Goods shall review the operation of this Agreement and, as appropriate, propose to the Ministerial Conference amendments to its text. In the course of this review, the Council for Trade in Goods shall consider whether it should be complemented with provisions on investment policy and competition policy.

ANNEX

Illustrative List

1. TRIMs that are inconsistent with the obligation of national treatment provided for in Article III:4 of the GATT 1994 include those which are mandatory or enforceable under domestic law or under administrative rulings, or compliance with which is necessary to obtain an advantage, and which require:

(a) the purchase or use by an enterprise of products of domestic origin or from any domestic source, whether specified in terms of particular products, in terms of volume or value of products, or in terms of a proportion of volume or value of its local production; or

(b) that an enterprise's purchases or use of imported products be limited to an amount related to the volume or value of local products that it exports.

2. TRIMs that are inconsistent with the obligation of the general elimination of quantitative restrictions provided for in Article XI: 1 of the GATT 1994 include those which are mandatory or enforceable under domestic law or under administrative rulings, or compliance with which is necessary to obtain an advantage, and which restrict:

(a) the importation by an enterprise of products used in or related to its local production, generally or to an amount related to the volume or value of local production that it exports;

(b) the importation by an enterprise of products used in or related to its local production by restricting its access to foreign exchange to an amount related to the foreign exchange inflows attributable to the enterprise; or

(c) the exportation or sale for export by an enterprise of products, whether specified in terms of particular products, in terms of volume or value of products, or in terms of a proportion of volume or value of its local production.

AGREEMENT ON IMPLEMENTATION OF ARTICLE VI OF GATT 1994

PART I

Article 1
Principles

An anti-dumping measure shall be applied only under the circumstances provided for in Article VI of the GATT 1994 and pursuant to investigations initiated[32] and conducted in accordance with the provisions of this Agreement. The following provisions govern the application of Article VI of the GATT 1994 in so far as action is taken under anti-dumping legislation or regulations.

Article 2
Determination of Dumping

2.1 For the purpose of this Agreement a product is to be considered as being dumped, *i.e.*, introduced into the commerce of another country at less than its normal value, if the export price of the product exported from one country to another is less than the comparable price, in the ordinary course of trade, for the like product when destined for consumption in the exporting country.

2.2 When there are no sales of the like product in the ordinary course of trade in the domestic market of the exporting country or when, because of the particular market situation or the low volume of the sales in the domestic market of the exporting country[33], such sales do not permit a proper comparison, the margin of dumping shall be determined by comparison with a comparable

[32] The term "initiated"as used hereinafter means the procedural action by which a Member formally commences an investigation as provided in Article 5.

[33] Sales of the like product destined for consumption in the domestic market of the exporting country shall normally be considered a sufficient quantity for the determination of the normal value if such sales constitute 5 per cent or more of the sales of the product under consideration to the importing country, provided that a lower ratio should be acceptable where the evidence demonstrates that domestic sales at such lower ratio are nonetheless of sufficient magnitude to provide for a proper comparison.

price of the like product when exported to an appropriate third country provided that this price is representative, or with the cost of production in the country of origin plus a reasonable amount for administrative, selling and any other costs and for profits.

2.2.1 Sales of the like product in the domestic market of the exporting country or sales to a third country at prices below per unit (fixed and variable) costs of production plus selling, general and administrative costs may be treated as not being in the ordinary course of trade by reason of price and may be disregarded in determining normal value only if the authorities[34] determine that such sales are made within an extended periodof time[35] in substantial quantities[36] and are at prices which do not provide for the recovery of all costs within a reasonable period of time. If prices which are below costs at the time of sale are above weighted average costs for the period of investigation, such prices shall be considered to provide for recovery of costs within a reasonable period of time.

2.2.1.1 For the purpose of paragraph 2 of this Article. costs shall normally be calculated on the basis of records kept by the exporter or producer under investigation, provided that such records are in accordance with the generally accepted accounting principles of the exporting country and reasonably reflect the costs associated with the production and sale of the product under consideration. Authorities shall consider all available evidence on the proper allocation of costs, including that which is made available by the exporter or producer in the course of the investigation provided that such allocations have been historically utilized by the exporter or producer, in particular in relation to establishing appropriate amortization and depreciation periods and allowances for capital expenditures and other development costs. Unless already reflected in the cost allocations under this sub-paragraph, costs shall be adjusted appropriately for those non-recurring items of cost which

---

[34] When in this Agreement the term "authorities" is used, it shall be interpreted as meaning authorities at an appropriate senior level.

[35] The extended period of time should normally be one year but shall in no case be less than six months.

[36] Sales below per unit cost are made in substantial quantities when the authorities establish that the weighted average selling price of the transactions under consideration for the determination of the normal value is below the weighted average unit cost or that the volume of sales below per unit costs represents not less than 20 per cent of the volume sold in transactions under consideration for the determination of the normal value.

benefit future and/or current production, or for circumstances in which costs during the period of investigation are affected by start-up operations.[37]

2.2.2 For the purpose of paragraph 2 of this Article, the amounts for administrative selling and any other costs and for profits shall be based on actual data pertaining to production and sales in the ordinary course of trade of the like product by the exporter or producer under investigation. When such amounts cannot be determined on this basis, the amounts may be determined on the basis of:

(i) the actual amounts incurred and realized by the exporter or producer in question in respect of production and sales in the domestic market of the country of origin of the same general category of products;

(ii) the weighted average of the actual amounts incurred and realized by other exporters or producers subject to investigation in respect of production and sales of the like product in the domestic market of the country of origin;

(iii) any other reasonable method, provided that the amount for profit so established shall not exceed the profit normally realized by other exporters or producers on sales of products of the same general category in the domestic market of the country of origin.

2.3 In cases where there is no export price or where it appears to the authorities concerned that the export price is unreliable because of association or a compensatory arrangement between the exporter and the importer or a third party, the export price may be constructed on the basis of the price at which the imported products are first resold to an independent buyer, or if the products are not resold to an independent buyer, or not resold in the condition as imported, on such reasonable basis as the authorities may determine.

2.4 A fair comparison shall be made between the export price and the normal value. This comparison shall be made at the same level of trade, normally at the ex-factory level, and in respect of sales made at as nearly as possible the same time. Due allowance shall be made in each case, on its merits, for differences which affect price comparability, including differences in conditions and terms of sale, taxation, levels of trade, quantities, physical characteristics and any other differences which are also demonstrated to

[37] The adjustment made for start-up operations shall reflect the costs at the end of the start-up period or, if that period extends beyond the period of investigation, the most recent costs which can reasonably be taken into account by the authorities during the investigation.

affect price comparability.[38] In the cases referred to in paragraph 3 of Article 2, allowances for costs, including duties and taxes, incurred between importation and resale, and for profits accruing, should also be made. If in these cases, price comparability has been affected, the authorities shall establish the normal value at a level of trade equivalent to the level of trade of the constructed export price, or make due allowance as warranted under this paragraph. The authorities shall indicate to the parties in question what information is necessary to ensure a fair comparison and shall not impose an unreasonable burden of proof on those parties.

2.4.1 When the price comparison under this paragraph requires a conversion of currencies, such conversion should be made using the rate of exchange on the date of sale[39], provided. that when a sale of foreign currency on forward markets is directly linked to the export sale involved, the rate of exchange in the forward sale shall be used. Fluctuations in exchange rates shall be ignored and, in an investigation the authorities shall allow exporters at least 60 days to have adjusted their export prices to reflect sustained movements during the period of investigation.

2.4.2 Subject to the provisions governing fair comparison in paragraph 4 of this Article, the existence of margins of dumping during the investigation phase shall normally be established on the basis of a comparison of a weighted average normal value with a weighted average of prices of all comparable export transactions or by a comparison of normal value and export prices on a transaction to transaction basis. A normal value established on a weighted average basis may be compared to prices of individual export transactions if the authorities find a pattern of export prices which differ significantly among different purchasers, regions or time periods and if an explanation is provided why such differences cannot be taken into account appropriately by the use of a weighted average-to-weighted average or transaction-to-transaction comparison.

2.5 In the case where products are not imported directly from the country of origin but are exported to the country of importation from an intermediate country, the price at which the products are sold from the country of export to the country of importation shall normally be compared with the comparable price in the country of export. However, comparison may be made with the

[38] It is understood that some of the above factors may overlap, and authorities shall ensure that they do not duplicate adjustments that have been already made under this provision.

[39] Normally. the date of sale would be the date of contract, purchase order. order confirmation, or invoice, whichever establishes the material terms of sale.

price in the country of origin, if, for example, the products are merely trans-shipped through the country of export, or such products are not produced in the country of export, or there is no comparable price for them in the country of export.

2.6 Throughout this Agreement the term "like product" ("produit similaire") shall be interpreted to mean a product which is identical, *i.e.*, alike in all respects to the product under consideration, or in the absence of such a product, another product which although not alike in all respects, has characteristics closely resembling those of the product under consideration.

2.7 This Article is without prejudice to the second Supplementary Provision to paragraph 1 of Article VI in Annex I to the GATT 1994.

Article 3

Determination of Injury[40]

3.1 A determination of injury for purposes of Article VI of the GATT 1994 shall be based on positive evidence and involve an objective examination of both (a) the volume of the dumped imports and the effect of the dumped imports on prices in the domestic market for like products, and (b) the consequent impact of these imports on domestic producers of such products.

3.2 With regard to the volume of the dumped imports, the investigating authorities shall consider whether there has been a significant increase in dumped imports, either in absolute terms or relative to production or consumption in the importing country. With regard to the effect of the dumped imports on prices, the investigating authorities shall consider whether there has been a significant price undercutting by the dumped imports as compared with the price of a like product of the importing country, or whether the effect of such imports is otherwise to depress prices to a significant degree or prevent price increases, which otherwise would have occurred, to a significant degree. No one or several of these factors can necessarily give decisive guidance.

3.3 Where imports of a product from more than one country are simultaneously subject to antidumping investigations, the investigating authorities may cumulatively assess effects of such imports only if they determine that (1) the margin of dumping established in relation to the imports from each country is more than *de minimis* as defined in paragraph 8 of Article 5 and that the volume of imports from each country is not negligible and (2) a cumulative assessment of the effects of the imports is appropriate in light of

---

[40] Under this Agreement the term "injury" shall, unless otherwise specified, be taken to mean material injury to a domestic industry threat of material injury to a domestic industry or material retardation of the establishment of such an industry and shall be interpreted in accordance with the provisions of this Article.

the conditions of competition between imported products and the conditions of competition between the imported products and the like domestic product.

3.4 The examination of the impact of the dumped imports on the domestic industry concerned shall include an evaluation of all relevant economic factors and indices having a bearing on the state of the industry, including actual and potential decline in sales, profits, output, market share, productivity, return on investments, or utilization of capacity; factors affecting domestic prices; the magnitude of the margin of dumping; actual and potential negative effects on cash flow, inventories, employment, wages, growth, ability to raise capital or investments. This list is not exhaustive, nor can one or several of these factors necessarily give decisive guidance.

3.5 It must be demonstrated that the dumped imports are, through the effects of dumping, as set forth in paragraphs 2 and 4 of this Article, causing injury within the meaning of this Agreement. The demonstration of a causal relationship between the dumped imports and the injury to the domestic industry shall be based on an examination of all relevant evidence before the authorities. The authorities shall also examine any known factors other than the dumped imports which at the same time are injuring the domestic industry, and the injuries caused by these other factors must not be attributed to the dumped imports. Factors which may be relevant in this respect include, *inter alia,* the volume and prices of imports not sold at dumping prices, contraction in demand or changes in the patterns of consumption, trade restrictive practices of and competition between the foreign and domestic producers, developments in technology and the export performance and productivity of the domestic industry.

3.6 The effect of the dumped imports shall be assessed in relation to the domestic production of the like product when available data permit the separate identification of that production on the basis of such criteria as the production process, producers' sales and profits. If such separate identification of that production is not possible, the effects of the dumped imports shall be assessed by the examination of the production of the narrowest group or range of products, which includes the like product, for which the necessary information can be provided.

3.7 A determination of a threat of material injury shall be based on facts and not merely on allegation, conjecture or remote possibility. The change in circumstances which would create a situation in which the dumping would cause injury must be clearly foreseen and imminent.[41] In making a determination

[41] One example, though not an exclusive one, is that there is convincing reason to believe that there will be, in the near future, substantially increased importations of the product at dumped prices.

regarding the existence of a threat of material injury, the authorities should consider, *inter alia,* such factors as:

(i) a significant rate of increase of dumped imports into the domestic market indicating the likelihood of substantially increased importations;

(ii) sufficient freely disposable or an imminent, substantial increase in capacity of the exporter indicating the likelihood of substantially increased dumped exports to the importing country's market, taking into account the availability of other export markets to absorb any additional exports;

(iii) whether imports are entering at prices that will have a significant depressing or suppressing effect on domestic prices, and would likely increase demand for further imports; and

(iv) inventories of the product being investigated.

No one of these factors by itself can necessarily give decisive guidance but the totality of the factors considered must lead to the conclusion that further dumped exports are imminent and that, unless protective action is taken, material injury would occur.

3.8 With respect to cases where injury is threatened by dumped imports, the application of antidumping measures shall be considered and decided with special care.

Article 4

Definition of Domestic Industry

4.1 For the purposes of this Agreement, the term "domestic industry" shall be interpreted as referring to the domestic producers as a whole of the like products or to those of them whose collective output of the products constitutes a major proportion of the total domestic production of those products, except that

(i) when producers are related[42] to the exporters or importers or are themselves importers of the allegedly dumped product, the term "domestic industry" may be interpreted as referring to the rest of the producers;

---

[42] For the purpose of this paragraph, producers shall be deemed to be related to exporters or importers only if (a) one of them directly or indirectly controls the other; or (b) both of them are directly or indirectly controlled by a third person; or (c) together they directly or indirectly control a third person, provided that there are grounds for believing or suspecting that the effect of the relationship is such as to cause the producer concerned to behave differently from non-related producers. For the purpose of this paragraph, one shall be deemed to control another when the former is legally or operationally in a position to exercise restraint or direction over the latter.

(ii) in exceptional circumstances the territory of a Member may, for the production in question, be divided into two or more competitive markets and the producers within each market may be regarded as a separate industry if (a) the producers within such market sell all or almost all of their production of the product in question in that market, and (b) the demand in that market is not to any substantial degree supplied by producers of the product in question located elsewhere in the territory. In such circumstances, injury may be found to exist even where a major portion of the total domestic industry is not injured, provided there is a concentration of dumped imports into such an isolated market and provided further that the dumped imports are causing injury to the producers of all or almost all of the production within such market.

4.2 When the domestic industry has been interpreted as referring to the producers in a certain area, *i.e.*, a market as defined in paragraph 1 (ii), anti-dumping duties shall be levied[43] only on the products in question consigned for final consumption to that area. When the constitutional law of the importing country does not permit the levying of anti-dumping duties on such a basis, the importing Member may levy the anti-dumping duties without limitation only if (1) the exporters shall have been given an opportunity to cease exporting at dumped prices to the area concerned or otherwise give assurances pursuant to Article 8 of this Agreement, and adequate assurances in this regard have not been promptly given, and (2) such duties cannot be levied only on products of specific producers which supply the area in question.

4.3 Where two or more countries have reached under the provisions of paragraph 8 (a) of Article XXIV of the GATT 1994 such a level of integration that they have the characteristics of a single, unified market, the industry in the entire area of integration shall be taken to be the domestic industry referred to in paragraph 1 above.

4.4 The provisions of paragraph 6 of Article 3 shall be applicable to this Article.

Article 5
Initiation and Subsequent Investigation

5.1 Except as provided for in paragraph 6 of Article 5, an investigation to determine the existence, degree and effect of any alleged dumping shall be initiated upon a written application by or on behalf of the domestic industry.

---

[43] As used in this Agreement "levy' shall mean the definitive or final legal assessment or collection of a duty or tax.

5.2 An application under paragraph 1 shall include evidence of (a) dumping, (b) injury within the meaning of Article VI of the GATT 1994 as interpreted by this Agreement and (c) a causal link between the dumped imports and the alleged injury. Simple assertion, unsubstantiated by relevant evidence, cannot be considered sufficient to meet the requirements of this paragraph. The application shall contain such information as is reasonably available to the applicant on the following:

(i) identity of the applicant and a description of the volume and value of the domestic production of the like product by the applicant. Where a written application is made on behalf of the domestic industry, the application shall identify the industry on behalf of which the application is made by a list of all known domestic producers of the like product (or associations of domestic producers of the like product) and, to the extent possible, a description of the volume and value of domestic production of the like product accounted for by such producers;

(ii) a complete description of the allegedly dumped product, the names of the country or countries of origin or export in question, the identity of each known exporter or foreign producer and a list of known persons importing the product in question;

(iii) information on prices at which the product in question is sold when destined for consumption in the domestic markets of the country or countries of origin or export (or, where appropriate, information on the prices at which the product is sold from the country or countries of origin or export to a third country or countries or on the constructed value of the product) and information on export prices or, where appropriate, on the prices at which the product is first resold to an independent buyer in the importing country;

(iv) information on the evolution of the volume of the allegedly dumped imports, the effect of these, imports on prices of the like product in the domestic market and the consequent impact of the imports on the domestic industry, as demonstrated by relevant factors and indices having a bearing on the state of the domestic industry, such as those listed in paragraphs 2 and 4 of Article 3.

5.3 The authorities shall examine the accuracy and adequacy of the evidence provided in the application to determine whether there is sufficient evidence to justify the initiation of an investigation.

5.4 An investigation shall not be initiated pursuant to paragraph 1 unless the authorities have determined, on the basis of an examination of the degree of support for, or opposition to, the application expressed[44] by domestic producers of the like product, that the application has been made by or on behalf of the domestic industry.[45] The application shall be considered to have been made "by or on behalf of the domestic industry" if it is supported by those domestic producers whose collective output constitutes more than 50 per cent of the total production of the like product produced by that portion of the domestic industry expressing either support for or opposition to the application. However, no investigation shall be initiated when domestic producers expressly supporting the application account for less than 25 per cent of total production of the like product produced by the domestic industry.

5.5 The authorities shall avoid, unless a decision has been made to initiate an investigation, any publicizing of the application for the initiation of an investigation. However, after receipt of a properly documented application and before proceeding to initiate an investigation, the authorities shall notify the government of the exporting country concerned.

5.6 If in special circumstances, the authorities concerned decide to initiate an investigation without having received a written application by or on behalf of a domestic industry for the initiation of such investigation, they shall proceed only if they have sufficient evidence of dumping, injury and a causal link, as described in paragraph 2, to justify the initiation of an investigation.

5.7 The evidence of both dumping and injury shall be considered simultaneously (a) in the decision whether or not to initiate an investigation, and (b) thereafter, during the course of the investigation, starting on a date not later than the earliest date on which in accordance with the provisions of this Agreement provisional measures may be applied.

5.8 An application under paragraph 1 shall be rejected and an investigation shall be terminated promptly as soon as the authorities concerned are satisfied that there is not sufficient evidence of either dumping or of injury to justify proceeding with the case. There shall be immediate termination in cases where the authorities determine that the margin of dumping is *de minimis,* or that the volume of dumped imports, actual or potential, or the injury, is negligible. The margin of dumping shall be considered to be *de minimis* if this margin is less than 2 per cent, expressed as a percentage of the export price.

---

[44] In the the case of fragmented industries involving an exceptionally large number of producers, authorities may determine support and opposition by using statistically valid sampling techniques.

[45] Members are aware that in the territory of certain Members, employees of domestic producers of the like product or representatives of those employees, may make or support an application for an investiagion under paragraph 1.

The volume of dumped imports shall normally be regarded as negligible if the volume of dumped imports from a particular country is found to account for less than 3 per cent of imports of the like product in the importing country unless countries which individually account for less than 3 per cent of the imports of the like product in the importing country collectively account for more than 7 per cent of imports of the like product in the importing country.

5.9 An anti-dumping proceeding shall not hinder the procedures of customs clearance.

5.10 Investigations shall, except in special circumstances, be concluded within one year after their initiation, and in no case more than 18 months.

Article 6

Evidence

6.1 All interested parties in an anti-dumping investigation shall be given notice of the information which the authorities require and ample opportunity to present in writing all evidence which they consider relevant in respect of the investigation in question.

6.1.1 Exporters or foreign producers receiving questionnaires used in an anti-dumping investigation shall be given at least thirty days for reply.[46] Due consideration should be given to any request for an extension of the thirty day period and, upon cause shown, such an extension should be granted whenever practicable.

6.1.2 Subject to the requirement to protect confidential information, evidence presented in writing by one interested party shall be made available promptly to other interested parties participating in the investigation.

6.1.3 As soon as an investigation has been initiated, the authorities shall provide the full text of the written application received under paragraph 1 of Article 5 to the known exporters[47] and to the authorities of the exporting country and make it available, upon request, to other interested parties involved. Due regard shall be paid to the requirement for the protection of confidential information as provided for in paragraph 5 below.

---

[46] As a general rule, the time-limit for exporters shall be counted from the date of receipt of the questionnaire, which for this purpose shall be deemed to have been received one week from the day on which it was sent to the respondent or transmitted to the appropriate diplomatic representative of the exporting country or in the case of a separate customs territory Member of the WTO an official representative of the exporting territory.

[47] It being understood that, where the number of exporters involved is particularly high, the full text of the written application should instead be provided only to the authorities of the exporting country or to the relevant trade association.

6.2 Throughout the anti-dumping investigation all interested parties shall have a full opportunity for the defence of their interests. To this end, the authorities shall, on request, provide opportunities for all interested parties to meet those parties with adverse interests, so that opposing views may be presented and rebuttal arguments offered. Provision of such opportunities must take account of the need to preserve confidentiality and of the convenience to the parties, There shall be no obligation on any party to attend a meeting, and failure to do so shall not be prejudicial to that party's case. Interested parties shall also have the right, on justification, to present other information orally.

6.3 Oral information provided under paragraph 2 shall be taken into account by the authorities only insofar as it is subsequently reproduced in writing and made available to other interested parties, as provided for in sub-paragraph 1.2.

6.4 The authorities shall whenever practicable provide timely opportunities for all interested parties to see all information that is relevant to the presentation of their cases, that is not confidential as defined in paragraph 5 and that is used by the authorities in an anti-dumping investigation, and to prepare presentations on the basis of this information.

6.5 Any information which is by nature confidential (for example, because its disclosure would be of significant competitive advantage to a competitor or because its disclosure would have a significantly adverse effect upon a person supplying the information or upon a person from whom he acquired the information) or which is provided on a confidential basis by parties to an investigation shall, upon good cause shown, be treated as such by the authorities. Such information shall not be disclosed without specific permission of the party submitting it.[48]

6.5.1 The authorities shall require interested parties providing confidential information to furnish non-confidential summaries thereof. These summaries shall be in sufficient detail to permit a reasonable understanding of the substance of the information submitted in confidence. In exceptional circumstances, such parties may indicate that such information is not susceptible of summary. In such exceptional circumstances, a statement of the reasons why summarization is not possible must be provided.

6.5.2 If the authorities find that a request for confidentiality is not warranted and if the supplier of the information is either unwilling to make the information public or to authorize its disclosure in

[48] Members are aware that in the territory of certain Members disclosure pursuant to a narrowly-drawn protective order may be required.

generalized or summary form, the authorities may disregard such information unless it can be demonstrated to their satisfaction from appropriate sources that the information is correct.[49]

6.6 Except in circumstances provided for in paragraph 8, the authorities shall during the course of an investigation satisfy themselves as to the accuracy of the information supplied by interested parties upon which their findings are based.

6.7 In order to verify information provided or to obtain further details, the authorities may carry out investigations in other countries as required, provided they obtain the agreement of the firms concerned and provided they notify the representatives of the government of the country in question and unless the latter object to the investigation. The procedures described in Annex I shall apply to verifications carried out in exporting countries. The authorities shall, subject to the requirement to protect confidential information, make the results of any verifications available or provide disclosure thereof pursuant to paragraph 9, to the firms to which they pertain and may make such results available to the applicants.

6.8 In cases in which any interested party refuses access to, or otherwise does not provide, necessary information within a reasonable period or significantly impedes the investigation, preliminary and final determinations, affirmative or negative, may be made on the basis of the facts available. The provisions of Annex II shall be observed in the application of this paragraph.

6.9 The authorities shall, before a final determination is made, inform all interested parties of the essential facts under consideration which form the basis for the decision whether to apply definitive measures. Such disclosure should take place in sufficient time for the parties to defend their interests.

6.10 The authorities shall, as a rule, determine an individual margin of dumping for each known exporter or producer concerned of the product under investigation. In cases where the number of exporters, producers, importers or types of products involved is so large as to make such a determination impracticable, the authorities may limit their examination either to a reasonable number of interested parties or produce by using samples which are statistically valid on the basis of information available to the authorities at the time of the selection, or to the largest percentage of the volume of the exports from the country in question which can reasonably be investigated.

6.10.1 Any selection of exporters, producers, importers or types of products made under this paragraph shall preferably be chosen

---

[49] Members agree that requests for confidentiality should not be arbitrarily rejected.

in consultation with and with the consent of the exporters, producers or importers concerned.

6.10.2 In cases where the authorities have limited their examination, as provided for in this paragraph, they shall nevertheless determine an individual margin of dumping for any exporter or producer not initially selected who submits the necessary information in time for that information to be considered during the course of the investigation, except where the number of exporters or producers is so large that individual examinations would be unduly burdensome to the authorities and prevent the timely completion of the investigation. Voluntary responses shall not be discouraged.

6.11 For the purposes of this Agreement, "interested parties" shall include:

(i) an exporter or foreign producer or the importer of a product subject to investigation, or a trade or business association a majority of the members of which are producers, exporters or importers of such product;

(ii) the government of the exporting country; and

(iii) a producer of the like product in the importing country or a trade and business association a majority of the members of which produce the like product in the improving country.

This list shall not preclude Members from allowing domestic or foreign parties other than those mentioned above to be included as interested parties.

6.12 The authorities shall provide opportunities for industrial users of the product under investigation, and for representative consumer organizations in cases where the product is commonly sold at the retail level, to provide information which is relevant to the investigation regarding dumping, injury and causality.

6.13 The authorities shall take due account of any difficulties experienced by interested parties, in particular small companies, in supplying information requested and provide any assistance practicable.

6.14 The procedures set out above are not intended to prevent the authorities of a Member from proceeding expeditiously with regard to initiating an investigation, reaching preliminary or final determinations, whether affirmative or negative, or from applying provisional or final measures, in accordance with relevant provisions of this Agreement.

Article 7
Provisional Measures

7.1 Provisional measures may be applied only if:

(i) an investigation has been initiated in accordance with the provisions of Article 5, a public notice has been given to that effect and interested parties have been given adequate opportunities to submit information and make comments;

(ii) a preliminary affirmative determination has been made of dumping and consequent injury to a domestic industry; and

(iii) the authorities concerned judge such measures necessary to prevent injury being caused during the investigation.

7.2 Provisional measures may take the form of a provisional duty or, preferably, a security – by cash deposit or bond – equal to the amount of the anti-dumping duty provisionally estimated, being not greater than the provisionally estimated margin of dumping. Withholding of appraisement is an appropriate provisional measure, provided that the normal duty and the estimated amount of the antidumping duty be indicated and as long as the withholding of appraisement is subject to the same conditions as other provisional measures.

7.3 Provisional measures shall not be applied sooner than 60 days from the date of initiation of the investigation.

7.4 The application of provisional measures shall be limited to as short a period as possible, not exceeding four months or, on decision of the authorities concerned, upon request by exporters representing a significant percentage of the trade involved, to a period not exceeding six months. When authorities, in the course of an investigation, examine whether a duty lower than the margin of dumping would be sufficient to remove injury, these periods may be six and nine months, respectively.

7.5 The relevant provisions of Article 9 shall be followed in the application of provisional measures.

Article 8
Price Undertakings

8.1 Proceedings may[50] be suspended or terminated without the imposition of provisional measures or anti-dumping duties upon receipt of satisfactory voluntary undertakings from any exporter to revise its prices or to cease exports to the area in question at dumped prices so that the authorities are satisfied that the injurious effect of the dumping is eliminated. Price increases under such undertakings shall not be higher than necessary to eliminate the margin of dumping. It is desirable that the price increases be less than the

[50] The word "may" shall not be interpreted to allow the simultaneous continuation of proceedings with the implementation of price undertakings except as provided in paragraph 4.

margin of dumping if such increases would be adequate to remove the injury to the domestic industry.

8.2 Price undertakings shall not be sought or accepted from exporters unless the authorities of the importing country have made a preliminary affirmative determination of dumping and injury caused by such dumping.

8.3 Undertakings offered need not be accepted if the authorities consider their acceptance impractical, for example, if the number of actual or potential exporters is too great, or for other reasons, including reasons of general policy. Should the case arise and where practicable, the authorities shall provide to the exporter the reasons which have led them to consider acceptance of an undertaking as inappropriate, and shall, to the extent possible, give the exporter an opportunity to make comments thereon.

8.4 If the undertakings are accepted, the investigation of dumping and injury shall nevertheless be completed if the exporter so desires or the authorities so decide. In such a case, if a negative determination of dumping or injury is made, the undertaking shall automatically lapse except in cases where such a determination is due in large part to the existence of a price undertaking. In such cases the authorities may require that an undertaking be maintained for a reasonable period consistent with the provisions of this Agreement. In the event that an affirmative determination of dumping and injury is made, the undertaking shall continue consistent with its terms and the provisions of this Agreement.

8.5 Price undertakings may be suggested by the authorities of the importing country, but no exporter shall be forced to enter into such an undertaking. The fact that exporters do not offer such undertakings, or do not accept an invitation to do so, shall in no way prejudice the consideration of the case. However, the authorities are free to determine that a threat of injury is more likely to be realized if the dumped imports continue.

8.6 Authorities of an importing country may require any exporter from whom undertakings have been accepted to provide periodically information relevant to the fulfilment of such undertakings, and to permit verification of pertinent data. In case of violation of undertakings, the authorities of the importing country may take, under this Agreement in conformity with its provisions, expeditious actions which may constitute immediate application of provisional measures using the best information available. In such cases definitive duties may be levied in accordance with this Agreement on goods entered for consumption not more than ninety days before the application of such provisional measures, except that any such retroactive assessment shall not apply to imports entered before the violation of the undertaking.

Article 9

Imposition and Collection of Anti-Dumping Duties

9.1 The decision whether or not to impose an anti-dumping duty in cases where all requirements for the imposition have been fulfilled and the decision whether the amount of the anti-dumping duty to be imposed shall be the full margin of dumping or less, are decisions to be made by the authorities of the importing country or customs territory. It is desirable that the imposition be permissive in all countries or customs territories Members, and that the duty be less than the margin, if such lesser duty would be adequate to remove the injury to the domestic industry.

9.2 When an anti-dumping duty is imposed in respect of any product, such anti-dumping duty shall be collected in the appropriate amounts in each case, on a non-discriminatory basis on imports of such product from all sources found to be dumped and causing injury, except as to imports from those sources from which price undertakings under the terms of this Agreement have been accepted. The authorities shall name the supplier or suppliers of the product concerned. If, however, several suppliers from the same country are involved, and it is impracticable to name all these suppliers, the authorities may name the supplying country concerned. If several suppliers from more than one country are involved, the authorities may name either all the suppliers involved, or, if this is impracticable, all the supplying countries involved.

9.3 The amount of the anti-dumping duty shall not exceed the margin of dumping as established under Article 2.

9.3.1 When the amount of the anti-dumping duty is assessed on a retrospective basis, the determination of the final liability for payment of anti-dumping duties shall take place as soon as possible, normally within 12 months, and in no case more than 18 months, after the date on which a request for a final assessment of the amount of anti-dumping duty has been made.[51] Any refund shall be made promptly and normally in not more than 90 days following the determination of final liability made pursuant to this subparagraph. In any case, where a refund is not made within 90 days the authorities shall provide an explanation if so requested.

9.3.2 When the amount of the anti-dumping duty is assessed on a prospective basis, provision shall be made for a prompt refund, upon request, of any duty paid in excess of the margin of dumping. – A refund of any such duty paid in excess of the actual margin

[51] It is understood that the observance of the time-limits mentioned in this sub-paragraph and in sub-paragraph 2 may not be possible in question is subject to judicial review proceedings.

of dumping shall normally take place within 12 months, and in no case more than months, after the date on which a request for a refund, duly supported by evidence, been made by an importer of the product subject to the anti-dumping duty. The refund authorized should normally be made within 90 days of the above-noted decision.

9.3.3 In determining whether and to what extent a reimbursement should be made when the export price is constructed in accordance with paragraph 3 of Article 2, authorities should take account of any change in normal value, any change of costs incurred between importation and resale, and any movement in the resale price which is duly reflected in subsequent selling prices, and should calculate the export price with no deduction for the amount of anti-dumping duties paid when conclusive evidence of the above is provided.

9.4 When the authorities have limited their examination in accordance with the second sentence paragraph 10 of Article 6, any anti-dumping duty applied to imports from exporters or producers not included in the examination shall not exceed:

(a) the weighted average margin of dumping established with respect to the selected exporters or producers or,

(b) where the liability for payment of anti-dumping duties is calculated on the basis of a prospective normal value, the difference between the weighted average normal value of the selected exporters or producers and the export prices of exporters or producers not individually examined

provided that the authorities shall disregard for the purpose of this paragraph any zero and *de minimis* margins and margins established under the circumstances referred to in paragraph 8 of Article 6. The authorities shall apply individual duties or normal values to imports from any exporter or producer not included in the examination who has provided the necessary information during the course of the investigation, as provided for in sub-paragraph 10.2 of Article 6.

9.5 If a product is subject to anti-dumping duties in an importing Member, the authorities shall promptly carry out a review for the purpose of determining individual margins of dumping for any exporters or producers in the exporting country in question who have not exported the product to the importing Member during the period of investigation provided that these exporters or producers can show that they are not related to any of the exporters or producers in the exporting country who are subject to the anti-dumping duties on the product. Such a review shall be initiated and carried out on an accelerated basis, compared to normal duty assessment and review proceedings in the importing country No anti-dumping duties shall be levied on imports from such exporters or producers while the review is being carried out. The authorities may, however, withhold appraisement and/or request guarantees to ensure that, should such a review result in a determination of dumping in respect of such producers or exporters, anti-dumping duties can be levied retroactively to the date of the initiation of the review.

Article 10

Retroactivity

10.1 Provisional measures and anti-dumping duties shall only be applied to products which enter for consumption after the time when the decision taken under paragraph 1 of Article7 and paragraph 1 of Article 9, respectively, enters into force, subject to the exceptions set out in this Article.

10.2 Where a final determination of injury (but not of a threat thereof or of a material retardation of the establishment of an industry) is made or, in the case of a final determination of a threat of injury, where the effect of the dumped imports would, in the absence of the provisional measures, have led to a determination of injury, anti-dumping duties may be levied retroactively for the period for which provisional measures, if any, have been applied.

10.3 If the definitive anti-dumping duty is higher than the provisional duty paid or payable, or the amount estimated for the purpose of the security, the difference shall not be collected. If the definitive duty is lower than the provisional duty paid or payable, or the amount estimated for the purpose of the security, the difference shall be reimbursed or the duty recalculated, as the case may be.

10.4 Except as provided in paragraph 2 above, where a determination of threat of injury or material retardation is made (but no injury has yet occurred) a definitive anti-dumping duty may be imposed only from the date of the determination of threat of injury or material retardation and any cash deposit made during the period of the application of provisional measures shall be refunded and any bonds released in an expeditious manner.

10.5 Where a final determination is negative, any cash deposit made during the period of the application of provisional measures shall be refunded and any bonds released in an expeditious manner.

10.6 A definitive anti-dumping duty may be levied on products which were entered for consumption not more than 90 days prior to the date of application of provisional measures, when the authorities determine for the dumped product in question that:

(i) there is a history of dumping which caused injury or that the importer was. or should have been, aware that the exporter practises dumping and that such dumping would cause injury, and

(ii) the injury is caused by massive dumped imports of a product in a relatively short time which in light of the timing and the volume of the dumped imports and other circumstances (such as a rapid build-up of inventories of the imported product) is likely to seriously undermine the remedial effect of the definitive anti-dumping duty to be applied, provided that the importers concerned have been given an opportunity to comment.

10.7 The authorities may, after initiating an investigation, take such measures as the withholding of appraisement or assessment as may be necessary to collect anti-dumping duties retroactively as provided for in paragraph 6, once they have sufficient evidence that the conditions set forth in that paragraph are satisfied.

10.8 No duties shall be levied retroactively pursuant to paragraph 6, on products entered for consumption prior to the date of initiation of the investigation.

Article 11

Duration and Review of Anti-Dumping Duties and Price Undertakings

11.1 An anti-dumping duty shall remain in force only as long as and to the extent necessary to counteract dumping which is causing injury.

11.2 The authorities shall review the need for the continued imposition of the duty, where warranted, on their own initiative or, provided that a reasonable period of time has elapsed since the imposition of the definitive anti-dumping duty, upon request by any interested party which submits positive information substantiating the need for a review.[52] Interested parties shall have the right to request the authorities to examine whether the continued imposition of the duty is necessary to offset dumping, whether the injury would be likely to continue or recur if the duty were removed or varied, or both. If, as a result of the review under this paragraph, the authorities determine that the anti-dumping duty is no longer warranted, it shall be terminated immediately.

11.3 Notwithstanding the provisions of paragraphs 1 and 2, any definitive anti-dumping duty shall be terminated on a date not later than five years from its imposition (or from that date of the most recent review under paragraph 2

[52] A determination of final liability for payment of anti-dumping duties as provided for in paragraph 3 of Article 9 does not by itself constitute a review within the meaning of this Article.

if that review has covered both dumping and injury, or under this paragraph), unless the authorities determine, in a review initiated before that date on their own initiative or upon a duly substantiated request made by or on behalf of the domestic industry within a reasonable period of time prior to that date, that the expiry of the duty, would be likely to lead to continuation or recurrence of dumping and injury.[53] The duty may remain in force pending the outcome of such a review.

11.4 The provisions of Article 6 regarding evidence and procedure shall apply to any review carried out under this Article. Any such review shall be carried out expeditiously and shall normally be concluded within twelve months of the date of initiation of the review.

11.5 The provisions of this Article shall *mutatis mutandis* apply to price undertakings accepted under Article 8.

Article 12

Public Notice and Explanation of Determinations

12.1 When the authorities are satisfied that there is sufficient evidence to justify the initiation of an anti-dumping-investigation pursuant to Article 5, the Member or Members the products of which are subject to such investigation and other interested parties known to the investigating authorities to have an interest therein shall be notified and a public notice shall be given.

12.1.1 A public notice of the initiation of an investigation shall contain or otherwise make available through a separate report[54] adequate information on the following:

(i) the name of the exporting country or countries and the product involved;

(ii) the date of initiation of the investigation;

(iii) the basis on which dumping is alleged in the application;

(iv) a summary of the factors on which the allegation of injury is based;

(v) the address to which representations by interested parties should be directed;

(vi) the time-limits allowed to interested parties for making their views known.

---

[53] When the amount of the anti-dumping duty is assessed on a retrospective basis, a finding in the most recent assessment proceeding under sub-paragraph 3.1 of Article 9 that no duty is to be levied shall not by itself require the authorities to terminate the definitive duty.

[54] Where authorities provide information and explanations under the provisions of this Article in a separate report, they shall ensure that such report is readily available to the public.

12.2 Public notice shall be given of any preliminary or final determination, whether affirmative or negative, of any decision to accept an undertaking pursuant to Article 8, of the termination of such an undertaking, and of the revocation of a determination. Each such notice shall set forth or otherwise make available through a separate report in sufficient detail the findings and conclusions reached on all issues of fact and law considered material by the investigating authorities. All such notices and reports shall be forwarded to the Member or Members the products of which are subject to such determination or undertaking and to other interested parties known to have an interest therein.

12.2.1 A public notice of the imposition of provisional measures shall set forth or otherwise make available through a separate report sufficiently detailed explanations for the preliminary determinations on dumping and injury and shall refer to the matters of fact and law which have led to arguments being accepted or rejected. Such a notice or report shall, due regard being paid to the requirement for the protection of confidential information, contain in particular:

(i) the names of the suppliers, or when this is impracticable, the supplying countries involved;

(ii) a description of the product which is sufficient for customs purposes;

(iii) the margins of dumping established and a full explanation of the reasons for the methodology used in the establishment and comparison of the export price and the normal value under Article 2;

(iv) considerations relevant to the injury determination as set out in Article 3;

(v) the main reasons leading to the determination.

12.2.2 A public notice of conclusion or suspension of an investigation in the case of an affirmative determination providing for the imposition of a definitive duty or the acceptance of a price undertaking shall contain or otherwise make available through a separate report all relevant information on the matters of fact and law and reasons which have led to the imposition of final measures or the acceptance of a price undertaking, due regard being paid to the requirement for the protection of confidential information. The notice or report shall in particular contain the information described in sub-paragraph 2.1 of Article 12, as well as the reasons for the acceptance or rejection of relevant arguments or claims made by the exporters and importers, and the basis for any decision made under sub-paragraph 10.2 of Article 6.

12.2.3 A public notice of the termination or suspension of an investigation following the acceptance of an undertaking pursuant to Article 8 shall include or otherwise make available through a separate report the non-confidential part of this undertaking.

12.3 The provisions of this Article shall apply *mutatis mutandis* to the initiation and completion of reviews pursuant to Article 11 and to decisions under Article 10 to apply duties retroactively.

Article 13
Judicial Review

Each Member, whose national legislation contains provisions on anti-dumping measures, shall maintain judicial, arbitral or administrative tribunals or procedures for the purpose, *inter alia,* of the prompt review of administrative actions relating to final determinations and reviews of determinations within the meaning of Article 11 of this Agreement. Such tribunals or procedures shall be independent of the authorities responsible for the determination or review in question.

Article 14
Anti-dumping action on behalf of a third country

14.1 An application for anti-dumping action on behalf of a third country shall be made by the authorities of the third country requesting action.

14.2 Such an application shall be supported by price information to show that the imports are being dumped and by detailed information to show that the alleged dumping is causing injury to the domestic industry concerned in the third country. The government of the third country shall afford all assistance to the authorities of the importing country to obtain any further information which the latter may require.

14.3 The authorities of the importing country in considering such an application shall consider the effects of the alleged dumping on the industry concerned as a whole in the third country; that is to say the injury shall not be assessed in relation only to the effect of the alleged dumping on the industry's export to the importing country or even on the industry's total exports.

14.4 The decision whether or not to proceed with a case shall rest with the importing country. If the importing country decides that it is prepared to take action, the initiation of the approach to the Council for Trade in Goods seeking its approval for such action shall rest with the importing country.

Article 15

Developing country Members

It is recognized that special regard must be given by developed country Members to the special situation of developing country Members when considering the application of anti-dumping measures under this Agreement. Possibilities of constructive remedies provided for by this Agreement shall be explored before applying anti-dumping duties where they would affect the essential interests of developing country Members.

PART II

Article 16

Committee on Anti-Dumping Practices

16.1 There shall be established under this Agreement a Committee on Anti-Dumping Practices (hereinafter referred to as the "Committee") composed of representatives from each of the Members. The Committee shall elect its own Chairman and shall meet not less than twice a year and otherwise as envisaged by relevant provisions of this Agreement at the request of any Member. The Committee shall carry out responsibilities as assigned to it under this Agreement or by the Members and it shall afford Members the opportunity of consulting on any matters relating to the operation of the Agreement or the furtherance of its objectives. The WTO Secretariat shall act as the secretariat to the Committee.

16.2 The Committee may set up subsidiary bodies as appropriate.

16.3 In carrying out their functions, the Committee and any subsidiary bodies may consult with and seek information from any source they deem appropriate. However, before the Committee or a subsidiary body seeks such information from a source within the jurisdiction of a Member, it shall inform the Member involved. It shall obtain the consent of the Member and any firm to be consulted.

16.4 Members shall report without delay to the Committee all preliminary or final anti-dumping actions taken. Such report will be available in the WTO Secretariat for inspection by government representatives. The Members shall also submit, on a semi-annual basis, reports of any anti-dumping actions taken within the preceding six months.

16.5 Each Member shall notify the Committee (a) which of its authorities are competent to initiate and conduct investigations referred to in Article 5 and (b) its domestic procedures governing the initiation and conduct of such investigations.

Article 17

Consultation and Dispute Settlement

17.1 Except as otherwise provided herein, the Understanding on Rules and Procedures Governing the Settlement of Disputes is applicable to consultations and the settlement of disputes under this Agreement.

17.2 Each Member shall afford sympathetic consideration to, and shall afford adequate opportunity for consultation regarding representations made by another Member with respect to any matter affecting the operation of this Agreement.

17.3 If any Member considers that any benefit accruing to it, directly or indirectly, under this Agreement is being nullified or impaired, or that the achievement of any objective is being impeded, by another Member or Members, it may, with a view to reaching a mutually satisfactory resolution of the matter, request in writing consultations with the Member or Members in question. Each Member shall afford sympathetic consideration to any request from another Member for consultation.

17.4 If the Member that requested consultations considers that the consultations pursuant to paragraph 3 of Article 17 have failed to achieve a mutually agreed solution and final action has been taken by the administering authorities of the importing Member to levy definitive anti-dumping duties or to accept price undertakings, it may refer the matter to the Dispute Settlement Body (DSB). When a provisional measure has a significant impact and the Member considers the measure was taken contrary to the provisions of paragraph 1 of Article 7 of this Agreement, that Member may also refer such matter to the DSB.

17.5 The DSB shall, at the request of the complaining party, establish a panel to examine the matter based upon:

(a) a written statement of the Member making the request indicating how a benefit accruing to it, directly or indirectly, under this Agreement has been nullified or impaired, or that the achieving of the objectives of the Agreement is being impeded, and

(b) the facts made available in conformity with appropriate domestic procedures to the authorities of the importing Member.

17.6 In examining the matter in paragraph 5:

(i) in its assessment of the facts of the matter, the panel shall determine whether the authorities' establishment of the facts was proper and whether their evaluation of those facts was unbiased and objective. If the establishment of the facts was proper and the evaluation was unbiased and objective, even though the panel might have reached a different conclusion, the evaluation shall not be overturned;

(ii) the panel shall interpret the relevant provisions of the Agreement in accordance with customary rules of interpretation of public international law. Where the panel finds that a relevant provision of the Agreement admits of more than one permissible interpretation, the panel shall find the authorities measure to be in conformity with the Agreement if it rests upon one of those permissible interpretations.

17.7 Confidential information provided to the panel shall not be disclosed without formal authorization from the person, body or authority providing such information. Where such information is requested from the panel but release of such information by the panel is not authorized, a non-confidential summary of the information, authorized by the person, body or authority providing the information, shall be provided.

PART III

Article 18

Final Provisions

18.1 No specific action against dumping of exports from another Member can be taken except in accordance with the provisions of the GATT 1994, as interpreted by this Agreement.[55]

18.2 Reservations may not be entered in respect of any of the provisions of this Agreement without the consent of the other Members.

18.3 Subject to sub-paragraphs 1 and 2, the provisions of this Agreement shall apply to investigations, and reviews of existing measures, initiated pursuant to applications which have been made on or after the date of entry into force for a Member of the Agreement Establishing the WTO .

18.3.1 With respect to the calculation of margins of dumping in refund procedures under Article 9.3, the rules used in the most recent determination or review of dumping shall apply.

18.3.2 For the purposes of paragraph 3 of Article 11, existing anti-dumping measures shall be deemed to be imposed on a date not later than the date. of entry into force for a Member of the Agreement Establishing the WTO except in cases in which the domestic legislation of a Member in force at that date already included a clause of the type provided for in that paragraph.

---

[55] This is not intended to preclude action under other relevant provisions of the GATT 1994, as appropriate.

18.4 (a) Each government accepting or acceding to the MTO shall take all necessary steps, of a general or particular character, to ensure, not later than the date of entry into force of the Agreement Establishing the WTO for it, the conformity of its laws, regulations and administrative procedures with the provisions of this Agreement as they may apply for the Member in question.

(b) Each Member shall inform the Committee of any changes in its laws and regulations relevant to this Agreement and in the administration of such laws and regulations.

18.5 The Committee shall review annually the implementation and operation of this Agreement taking into account the objectives thereof. The Committee shall annually inform the Council for Trade in Goods of developments during the period covered by such reviews.

18.6 The Annexes to this Agreement Constitute an integral part thereof.

ANNEX I

Procedures for On-The-Spot Investigations Pursuant to paragraph 7 of Article 6

1. Upon initiation of an investigation, the authorities of the exporting country and the firms known to be concerned should be informed of the intention to carry out on-the-spot investigations.

2. If in exceptional circumstances it is intended to include non-governmental experts in the investigating team, the firms and the authorities of the exporting country should be so informed. Such non-governmental experts should be subject to effective sanctions for breach of confidentiality requirements.

3. It should be standard practice to obtain explicit agreement of the firms concerned in the exporting country before the visit is finally scheduled.

4. As soon as the agreement of the firms concerned has been obtained the investigating authorities should notify the authorities of the exporting country of the names and addresses of the firms to be visited and the dates agreed.

5. Sufficient advance notice should be given to the firms in question before the visit is made.

6. Visits to explain the questionnaire should only be made at the request of an exporting firm. Such a visit may only be made if the authorities of the importing country notify the representatives of the government of the country in question and unless the latter do not object to the visit.

7. As the main purpose of the on-the-spot investigation is to verify information provided or to obtain further details, it should be carried out

after the response to the questionnaire has been received unless the firm agrees to the contrary and the government of the exporting country is informed by the investigating authorities of the anticipated visit and does not object to it; further, it should be standard practice prior to the visit to advise the firms concerned of the general nature of the information to be verified and of any further information which needs to be provided, though this should not preclude requests to be made on the spot for further details to be provided in the light of information obtained.

8. Enquiries or questions put by the authorities or firms of the exporting countries and essential to a successful on-the-spot investigation should, whenever possible, be answered before the visit is made.

ANNEX II

Best Information Available in Terms of paragraph 8 of Article 6

1. As soon as possible after the initiation of the investigation, the investigating authorities should specify in detail the information required from any interested party, and the way in which that information should be structured by the interested party in its response. The authorities should also ensure that the party is aware that if information is not supplied within a reasonable time, the authorities will be free to make determinations on the basis of the facts available, including those contained in the request for the initiation of the investigation by the domestic industry.

2. The authorities may also request that an interested party provide its response in a particular medium (*e.g.*, computer tape) or computer language. Where such a request is made, the authorities should consider the reasonable ability of the interested party to respond in the preferred medium or computer language, and should not request the company to use for its response a computer system other than that used by the firm. The authority should not maintain a request for a computerized response, if the interested party does not maintain computerized accounts and if presenting the response as requested would result in an unreasonable extra burden on the interested party, *e.g.*, it would entail unreasonable additional cost and trouble. The authorities should not maintain a request for a response in a particular medium or computer language if the interested party does not maintain its computerized accounts in such medium or computer language and if presenting the response as requested would result in an unreasonable extra burden on the interested party, e.g., it would entail unreasonable additional cost and trouble.

3. All information which is verifiable, which is appropriately submitted so that it can be used in the investigation without undue difficulties and which is supplied in a timely fashion, and, where applicable, supplied in a medium or

computer language requested by the authorities, should be taken into account when determinations are made. If a party does not respond in the preferred medium or computer language but the authorities find that the circumstances set out in paragraph 2 have been satisfied, this should not be considered to significantly impede the investigation.

4. Where the authorities do not have the ability to process information if provided in a particular medium (*e.g.*, computer tape) the information should be supplied in the form of written material or any other form acceptable to the authorities.

5. Even though the information provided may not be ideal in all respects, this should not justify the authorities from disregarding it provided the interested party has acted to the best of its ability.

6. If evidence or information is not accepted, the supplying party should be informed forthwith of the reasons thereof and have an opportunity to provide further explanations within a reasonable period, due account being taken of the time-limits of the investigation. If the explanations are considered by the authorities as not being satisfactory, the reasons for rejection of such evidence or information should be given in any published findings.

7. If the authorities have to base their determinations, including those with respect to normal value, on information from a secondary source, including the information supplied in the request for the initiation of the investigation, they should do so with special circumspection. In such cases, the authorities should, where practicable, check the information from other independent sources at their disposal, such as published price lists, official import statistics and customs returns, and from the information obtained from other interested parties during the investigation. It is clear, however, that if an interested party does not co-operate and thus relevant information is being withheld from the authorities, this situation could lead to a result which is less favourable to the party than if the party did co-operate.

AGREEMENT ON IMPLEMENTATION OF ARTICLE VII OF THE GENERAL AGREEMENT ON TARIFFS AND TRADE 1994

General Introductory Commentary

1. The primary basis for customs value under this Agreement is "transaction value" as defined in Article 1. Article 1 is to be read together with Article 8 which provides, *inter alia,* for adjustments to the price actually paid or payable in cases where certain specific elements which are considered to form a part of the value for customs purposes are incurred by the buyer but are not included in the price actually paid or payable for the imported goods. Article

8 also provides for the inclusion in the transaction value of certain considerations which may pass from the buyer to the seller in the form of specified goods or services rather than in the form of money. Articles 2 to 7, inclusive, provide methods of determining the customs value whenever it cannot be determined under the provisions of Article 1.

2. Where the customs value cannot be determined under the provisions of Article 1 there should normally be a process of consultation between the customs administration and importer with a view to arriving at a basis of value under the provisions of Articles 2 or 3. It may occur, for example, that the importer has information about the customs value of identical or similar imported goods which is not immediately available to the customs administration in the port of importation. On the other hand, the customs administration may have information about the customs value of identical or similar imported goods which is not readily available to the importer. A process of consultation between the two parties will enable information to be exchanged, subject to the requirements of commercial confidentiality, with a view to determining a proper basis of value for customs purposes.

3. Articles 5 and 6 provide two bases for determining the customs value where it cannot be determined on the basis of the transaction value of the imported goods or of identical or similar imported goods. Under paragraph 1 of Article 5 the customs value is determined on the basis of the price at which the goods are sold in the condition as imported to an unrelated buyer in the country of importation. The importer also has the right to have goods which are further processed after importation valued under the provisions of Article 5 if he so requests. Under Article 6 the customs value is determined on the basis of the computed value. Both these methods present certain difficulties and because of this the importer is given the right, under the provisions of Article 4, to choose the order of application of the two methods.

4. Article 7 sets out how to determine the customs value in cases where it cannot be determined under the provisions of any of the preceding Articles.

Members,

Having regard to the Multilateral Trade Negotiations,

Desiring to further the objectives of the GATT 1994 and to secure additional benefits for the international trade of developing countries;

Recognizing the importance of the provisions of Article VII of the GATT 1994 and desiring to elaborate rules for their application in order to provide greater uniformity and certainty in their implementation;

Recognizing the need for a fair, uniform and neutral system for the valuation of goods for customs purposes that precludes the use of arbitrary or fictitious customs values;

Recognizing that the basis for valuation of goods for customs purposes should, to the greatest extent possible, be the transaction value of the goods being valued;

Recognizing that customs value should be based on simple and equitable criteria consistent with commercial practices and that valuation procedures should be of general application without distinction between sources of supply;

Recognizing that valuation procedures should not be used to combat dumping;

Hereby agree as follows:

PART I

RULES ON CUSTOMS VALUATION

Article 1

1. The customs value of imported goods shall be the transaction value, that is the price actually paid or payable for the goods when sold for export to the country of importation adjusted in accordance with the provisions of Article 8, provided:

(a) that there are no restrictions as to the disposition or use of the goods by the buyer other than restrictions which:

(i) are imposed or required by law or by the public authorides in the country of importation;

(ii) limit the geographical area in which the goods may be resold; or

(iii) do not substantially affect the value of the goods;

(b) that the sale or price is not subject to some condition or consideration for which a value cannot be determined with respect to the goods being valued;

(c) that no part of the proceeds of any subsequent resale, disposal or use of the goods by the buyer will accrue directly or indirectly to the seller, unless an appropriate adjustment can be made in accordance with the provisions of Article 8; and

(d) that the buyer and seller are not related, or where the buyer and seller are related, that the transaction value is acceptable for customs purposes under the provisions of paragraph 2 of this Article.

2. (a) In determining whether the transaction value is acceptable for the purposes of paragraph 1 of this Article, the fact that the buyer and the seller are related within the meaning of Article 15

shall not in itself be grounds for regarding the transaction value as unacceptable. In such case the circumstances surrounding the sale shall be examined and the transaction value shall be accepted provided that the relationship did not influence the price. If, in the light of information provided by the importer or otherwise, the customs administration has grounds for considering that the relationship influenced the price, it shall communicate its grounds to the importer and he shall be given a reasonable opportunity to respond. If the importer so requests, the communication of the grounds shall be in writing.

(b) In a sale between related persons, the transaction value shall be accepted and the goods valued in accordance with the provisions of paragraph 1 of this Article whenever the importer demonstrates that such value closely approximates to one of the following occurring at or about the same time:

(i) the transaction value in sales to unrelated buyers of identical or similar goods for export to the same country of importation;

(ii) the customs value of identical or similar goods as determined under the provisions of Article 5;

(iii) the customs value of identical or similar goods as determined under the provisions of Article 6;

In applying the foregoing tests, due account shall be taken of demonstrated differences in commercial levels, quantity levels, the elements enumerated in Article 8 and costs incurred by the seller in sales in which he and the buyer are not related that are not incurred by the seller in sales in which he and the buyer are related.

(c) The tests set forth in paragraph 2(b) of this Article are to be used at the initiative of the importer and only for comparison purposes. Substitute values may not be established under the provisions of paragraph 2(b) of this Article.

Article 2

1. (a) If the customs value of the imported goods cannot be determined under the provisions of Article 1, the customs value shall be the transaction value of identical goods sold for export to the same country of importation and exported at or about the same time as the goods being valued.

(b) In applying this Article, the transaction value of identical goods in a sale at the same commercial level and in substantially the same quantity as the goods being valued shall be used to determine the customs value. Where no such sale is found, the transaction value of identical goods sold at a different commercial level and/or in different quantities, adjusted to take account of differences attributable to commercial level and/or to quantity, shall be used, provided that such adjustments can be made on the basis of demonstrated evidence which clearly establishes the reasonableness and accuracy of the adjustment, whether the adjustment leads to an increase or a decrease in the value.

2. Where the costs and charges referred to in paragraph 2 of Article 8 are included in the transaction value, an adjustment shall be made to take account of significant differences in such costs and charges between the imported goods and the identical goods in question arising from differences in distances and modes of transport.

3. If, in applying this Article, more than one transaction value of identical goods is found, the lowest such value shall be used to determine the customs value of the imported goods.

Article 3

1. (a) If the customs value of the imported goods cannot be determined under the provision of Articles 1 and 2, the customs value shall be the transaction value of similar goods sold for export to the same country of importation and exported at or about the same time as the goods being valued.

(b) In applying this Article, the transaction value of similar goods in a sale at the same commercial level and in substantially the same quantity as the goods being valued shall be used to determine the customs value. Where no such sale is found, the transaction value of similar goods sold at a different commercial level and/or in different quantities, adjusted to take account of differences attributable to commercial level and/or to quantity, shall be used, provided that such adjustments can be made on the basis of demonstrated evidence which clearly establishes the reasonableness and accuracy of the adjustment, whether the adjustment leads to an increase or a decrease in the value.

2. Where the costs and charges referred to in paragraph 2 of Article 8 are included in the transaction value, an adjustment shall be made to take account of significant differences in such costs and charges between the imported goods and the similar goods in question arising from differences in distances and modes of transport.

3. If, in applying this Article, more than one transaction value of similar

goods is found, the lowest such value shall be used to determine the customs value of the imported goods.

Article 4

If the customs value of the imported goods cannot be determined under the provisions of Articles 1, 2 and 3 the customs value shall be determined under the provisions of Article 5 or, when the customs value cannot be determined under that Article, under the provisions of Article 6 except that, at the request of the importer, the order of application of Articles 5 and 6 shall be reversed.

Article 5

1. (a) If the imported goods or identical or similar imported goods are sold in the country of importation in the condition as imported, the customs value of the imported goods under the provisions of this Article shall be based on the unit price at which the imported goods or identical or similar imported goods are so sold in the greatest aggregate quantity, at or about the time of the importation of the goods being valued, to persons who are not related to the persons from whom they buy such goods, subject to deductions for the following:

   (i) either the commissions usually paid or agreed to be paid or the additions usually made for profit and general expenses in connection with sales in such country of imported goods of the same class or kind;

   (ii) the usual costs of transport and insurance and associated costs incurred within the country of importation;

   (iii) where appropriate, the costs and charges referred to in paragraph 2 of Article 8; and

   (iv) the customs duties and other national taxes payable in the country of importation by reason of the importation or sale of the goods.

   (b) If neither the imported goods nor identical nor similar imported goods are sold at or about the time of importation of the goods being valued, the customs value shall, subject otherwise to the provisions of paragraph 1 (a) of this Article, be based on the unit price at which the imported goods or identical or similar imported goods are sold in the country of importation in the condition as imported at the earliest date after the importation of the goods being valued but before the expiration of ninety days after such importation.

2. If neither the imported goods nor identical nor similar imported goods are sold in the country of importation in the condition as imported, then, if the importer so requests, the customs value shall be based on the unit price at which the imported goods, after further processing, are sold in the greatest aggregate quantity to persons in the country of importation who are not related to the persons from whom they buy such goods, due allowance being made for the value added by such processing and the deductions provided for in paragraph l (a) of this Article.

Article 6

1. The customs value of imported goods under the provisions of this Article shall be based on a computed value. Computed value shall consist of the sum of:

(a) the cost or value of materials and fabrication or other processing employed in producing the imported goods;

(b) an amount for profit and general expenses equal to that usually reflected in sales of goods of the same class or kind as the goods being valued which are made by producers in the country of exportation for export to the country of importation;

(c) the cost or value of all other expenses necessary to reflect the valuation option chosen by the Member under paragraph 2 of Article 8.

2. No Member may require or compel any person not resident in its own territory to produce for examination, or to allow access to, any account or other record for the purposes of determining a computed value. However, information supplied by the producer of the goods for the purposes of determining the customs value under the provisions of this Article may be verified in another country by the authorities of the country of importation with the agreement of the producer and provided they give sufficient advance notice to the government of the country in question and the latter does not object to the investigation.

Article 7

1. If the customs value of the imported goods cannot be determined under the provisions of Articles 1 to 6, inclusive, the customs value shall be determined using reasonable means consistent with the principles and general provisions of this Agreement and of Article VII of the GATT 1994 and on the basis of data available in the country of importation.

2. No customs value shall be determined under the provisions of this Article on the basis of:

(a) the selling price in the country of importation of goods produced in such country;

(b) a system which provides for the acceptance for customs purposes of the higher of two alternative values;

(c) the price of goods on the domestic market of the country of exportation;

(d) the cost of production other than computed values which have been determined for identical or similar goods in accordance with the provisions of Article 6;

(e) the price of the goods for export to a country other than the country of importation;

(f) minimum customs values; or

(g) arbitrary or fictitious values.

3. If he so requests, the importer shall be informed in writing of the customs value determined under the provisions of this Article and the method used to determine such value.

Article 8

1. In determining the customs value under the provisions of Article 1, there shall be added to the price actually paid or payable for the imported goods:

(a) the following, to the extent that they are incurred by the buyer but are not included in the price actually paid or payable for the goods:

(i) commissions and brokerage, except buying commissions;

(ii) the cost of containers which are treated as being one for customs purposes with the goods in question;

(iii) the cost of packing whether for labour or materials;

(b) the value, apportioned as appropriate, of the following goods and services where supplied directly or indirectly by the buyer free of charge or at reduced cost for use in connection with the production and sale for export of the imported goods, to the extent that such value has not been included in the price actually paid or payable:

(i) materials, components, parts and similar items incorporated in the imported goods;

(ii) tools, dies, moulds and similar items used in the production of the imported goods;

(iii) materials consumed in the production of the imported goods;

(iv) engineering, development, artwork, design work, and plans and sketches undertaken elsewhere than in the country of importation and necessary for the production of the imported goods;

(c) royalties and licence fees related to the goods being valued that the buyer must pay, either directly or indirectly, as a condition of sale of the goods being valued, to the extent that such royalties and fees are not included in the price actually paid or payable;

(d) the value of any part of the proceeds of any subsequent resale, disposal or use of the imported goods that accrues directly or indirectly to the seller.

2. In framing its legislation, each Member shall provide for the inclusion in or the exclusion from the customs value, in whole or in part, of the following:

(a) the cost of transport of the imported goods to the port or place of importation; loading,

(b) unloading and handling charges associated with the transport of the imported goods to the port or place of importation; and

(c) the cost of insurance.

3. Additions to the price actually paid or payable shall be made under this Article only on the basis of objective and quantifiable data.

4. No additions shall be made to the price actually paid or payable in determining the customs value except as provided in this Article.

Article 9

1. Where the conversion of currency is necessary for the determination of the customs value, the rate of exchange to be used shall be that duly published by the competent authorities of the country of importation concerned and shall reflect as effectively as possible, in respect of the period covered by each such document of publication, the current value of such currency in commercial transactions in terms of the currency of the country of importation.

2. The conversion rate to be used shall be that in effect at the time of exportation or the time of importation, as provided by each Member.

Article 10

All information which is by nature confidential or which is provided on a confidential basis for the purposes of customs valuation shall be treated as strictly confidential by the authorities concerned who shall not disclose it without the specific permission of the person or government providing such information, except to the extent that it may be required to be disclosed in the context of judicial proceedings.

Article 11

1. The legislation of each Member shall provide in regard to a determination of customs value for the right of appeal, without penalty, by the importer or any other person liable for the payment of the duty.

2. An initial right of appeal without penalty may be to an authority within the customs administration or to an independent body, but the legislation of each Member shall provide for the right of appeal without penalty to a judicial authority.

3. Notice of the decision on appeal shall be given to the appellant and-the reasons for such decision shall be provided in writing. He shall also be informed of his rights of any further appeal.

Article 12

Laws, regulations, judicial decisions and administrative rulings of general application giving effect to this Agreement shall be published in conformity with Article X of the GATT 1994 by the country of importation concerned.

Article 13

If, in the course of determining the customs value of imported goods, it becomes necessary to delay the final determination of such customs value, the importer shall nevertheless be able to withdraw his goods from customs if, where so required, he provides sufficient guarantee in the form of a surety, a deposit or some other appropriate instrument, covering the ultimate payment of customs duties for which the goods may be liable. The legislation of each Member shall make provisions for such circumstances.

Article 14

The notes at Annex I to this Agreement form an integral part of this Agreement and the Articles of this Agreement are to be read and applied in conjunction with their respective notes. Annexes II and III also form an integral part of this Agreement.

Article 15

1. In this Agreement:

(a) "customs value of imported goods" means the value of goods for the purposes of levying *ad valorem* duties of customs on imported goods;

(b) "country of importation" means country or customs territory of importation; and

(c) "produced" includes grown, manufactured and mined.

2. (a) In this Agreement "identical goods" means goods which are the same in all respects, including physical characteristics, quality and reputation. Minor differences in appearance would not preclude goods otherwise conforming to the defamation from being regarded as identical.

(b) In this Agreement "similar goods" means goods which, although not alike in all respects, have like characteristics and like component materials which enable them to perform the same functions and to be commercially interchangeable. The quality of the goods, their reputation and the existence of a trademark are among the factors to be considered in determining whether goods are similar.

(c) The terms "identical goods" and "similar goods" do not include, as the case may be, goods which incorporate or reflect engineering, development, artwork, design work, and plans and sketches for which no adjustment has been made under paragraph l(b)(iv) of Article 8 because such elements were undertaken in the country of importation.

(d) Goods shall not be regarded as "identical goods" or "similar goods unless they were produced in the same country as the goods being valued.

(e) Goods produced by a different person shall be taken into account only when there are no identical goods or similar goods, as the case may be, produced by the same person as the goods being valued.

3. In this Agreement "goods of the same class or kind" means goods which fall within a group or range of goods produced by a particular industry or industry sector, and includes identical or similar goods.

4. For the purposes of this Agreement, persons shall be deemed to be related only if:

(a) they are officers or directors of one another's businesses;

(b) they are legally recognized partners in business;

(c) they are employer and employee;

(d) any person directly or indirectly owns, controls or holds 5 per cent or more of the outstanding voting stock or shares of both of them;

(e) one of them directly or indirectly controls the other;

(f) both of them are directly or indirectly controlled by a third person;

(g) together they directly or indirectly control a third person; or

(h) they are members of the same family.

5. Persons who are associated in business with one another in that one is the sole agent, sole distributor or sole concessionaire, however described, of the other shall be deemed to be related for the purposes of this Agreement if they fall within the criteria of paragraph 4 of this Article.

Article 16

Upon written request, the importer shall have the right to an explanation in writing from the customs administration of the country of importation as to how the customs value of his imported goods was determined.

Article 17

Nothing in this Agreement shall be construed as restricting or calling into question the rights of customs administrations to satisfy themselves as to the truth or accuracy of any statement, document or declaration presented for customs valuation purposes.

PART II
ADMINISTRATION, CONSULTATIONS AND DISPUTE SETTLEMENT

Article 18

Institutions

There shall be established under this Agreement:

1. A Committee on Customs Valuation (hereinafter referred to as "the Committee") composed of representatives from each of the Members. The Committee shall elect its own Chairman and shall normally meet once a year, or as is otherwise envisaged by the relevant provisions of this Agreement, for the purpose of affording Members the opportunity to consult on matters relating to the administration of the customs valuation system by any Member as it might affect the operation of this Agreement or the furtherance of its objectives and carrying out such other responsibilities as may be assigned to it by the Members. The WTO Secretariat shall act as the secretariat to the Committee.

2. A Technical Committee on Customs Valuation (hereinafter referred to as "the Technical Committee") under the auspices of the Customs Co-operation Council (hereinafter referred to as "the CCC"). which shall carry out the responsibilities described in Annex II to this Agreement and shall operate in accordance with the rules of procedure contained therein.

Article 19

Consultations and Dispute Settlement

1. Except as otherwise provided herein, the Understanding on Rules and Procedures Governing Settlement of Disputes is applicable to consultations and the settlement of disputes under this Agreement.

2. If any Member considers that any benefit accruing to it, directly or indirectly, under this Agreement is being nullified or impaired, or that the achievement of any objective of this Agreement being impeded, as a result of the actions of another Member or of other Members, it may, with a view to reaching a mutually satisfactory solution of this matter, request consultations with the Member or Members in question. Each Member shall afford sympathetic consideration to any request from another Member for consultations.

3. The Technical Committee shall provide, upon request, advice and assistance to Members engaged in consultations.

4. At the request of a party to the dispute, or on its own initiative, a panel established to examine a dispute relating to the provisions of this Agreement may request the Technical Committee to carry out an examination of any questions requiring technical consideration. The panel shall determine the terms of reference of the Technical Committee for the particular dispute and set a time period for receipt of the report of the Technical Committee. The panel shall take into consideration the report of the Technical Committee. In the event that the Technical Committee is unable to reach consensus on a matter referred to it pursuant to this paragraph, the panel should afford the parties to the dispute with an opportunity to present their views on the matter to the panel.

5. Confidential information provided to the panel shall not be disclosed without formal authorization from the person, body or authority providing such information. Where such information is requested from the panel but release of such information by the panel is not authorized, a non-confidential summary of this information, authorized by the person, body or authority providing the information, shall be provided.

PART III

SPECIAL AND DIFFERENTIAL TREATMENT

Article 20

1. Developing country Members, not party to the Agreement (1979) on Implementation of Article VII of the General Agreement on Tariffs and Trade, may delay application of the provisions of this Agreement for a period not exceeding five years from the date of entry into force of the Agreement

Establishing the WTO for such Members. Developing country Members who choose to delay application of this Agreement shall notify the Director-General of the WTO accordingly.

2. In addition to paragraph 1 above, developing country Members, not party to the Agreement (1979) on Implementation of Article VII of the General Agreement on Tariffs and Trade, may delay application of paragraph 2(b)(iii) of Article 1 and Article 6 for a period not exceeding three years following their application of all other provisions of this Agreement. Developing country Members that choose to delay application of the provisions specified in this paragraph shall notify the Director-General of the WTO accordingly.

3. Developed country Members shall furnish, on mutually agreed terms, technical assistance to developing country Members that so request. On this basis developed country Members shall draw up programmes of technical assistance which may include, *inter alia,* training of personnel, assistance in preparing implementation measures, access to sources of information regarding customs valuation methodology, and advice on the application of the provisions of this Agreement.

PART IV

FINAL PROVISIONS

Article 21

Reservations

Reservations may not be entered in respect of any of the provisions of this Agreement without the consent of the other Members.

Article 22

National Legislation

1. Each Member shall ensure, not later than the date of application of the provisions of this Agreement for it, the conformity of its laws, regulations and administrative procedures with the provision of this Agreement.

2. Each Member shall Inform the Committee of any changes in its laws and regulations relevant to this Agreement and in the administration of such laws and regulations.

Article 23

Review

The Committee shall review annually the implementation and operation of this Agreement taking into account the objectives thereof. The Committee shall annually inform the Council for Trade in Goods of developments during the period covered by such reviews.

Article 24
Secretariat

This Agreement shall be serviced by the WTO Secretariat except in regard to those responsibilities specifically assigned to the Technical Committee, which will be serviced by the Secretariat of the CCC.

ANNEX I
INTERPRETATIVE NOTES

General Note

Sequential Application of Valuation Methods

1. Articles 1 to 7, inclusive, define how the customs value of imported goods is to be determined under the provisions of this Agreement. The methods of valuation are set out in a sequential order of application. The primary method for customs valuation is defined in Article 1 and imported goods are to be valued in accordance with the provisions of this Article whenever the conditions prescribed therein are fulfilled.

2. Where the customs value cannot be determined under the provisions of Article 1, it is to be determined by proceeding sequentially through the succeeding Articles to the first such Article under which the customs value can be determined. Except as provided in Article 4, it is only when the customs value cannot be determined under the provisions of a particular Article that the provisions of the next Article in the sequence can be used.

3. If the importer does not request that the order of Articles 5 and 6 be reversed, the normal order of the sequence is to be followed. If the importer does so request but it then proves impossible to determine the customs value under the provisions of Article 6, the customs value is to be determined under the provisions of Article 5, if it can be so determined.

4. Where the customs value cannot be determined under the provisions of Articles 1 to 6, inclusive, it is to be determined under the provisions of Article 7.

Use of Generally Accepted Accounting Principles

1. "Generally accepted accounting principles" refers to the recognized consensus or substantial authoritative support within a country at a particular time as to which economic resources and obligations should be recorded as assets and liabilities, which changes in assets and liabilities should be recorded, how the assets and liabilities and changes in them should be measured, what information should be disclosed and how it should be disclosed, and which financial statements should be prepared. These standards may be broad

guidelines of general application as well as detailed practices and procedures.

2. For the purposes of this Agreement, the customs administration of each Member shall utilize information prepared in a manner consistent with generally accepted accounting principles in the country which is appropriate for the Article in question. For example, the determination of usual profit and general expenses under the provisions of Article 5 would be carried out utilizing information prepared in a manner consistent with generally accepted accounting principles of the country of importation. On the other hand, the determination of usual profit and general expenses under the provisions of Article 6 would be carried out utilizing information prepared in a manner consistent with generally accepted accounting principles of the country of production. As a further example, the determination of an element provided for in paragraph 1 (b)(ii) of Article 8 undertaken in the country of importation would be carried out utilizing information in a manner consistent with the generally accepted accounting principles of that country.

Note to Article 1

Price Actually Paid or Payable

The price actually paid or payable is the total payment made or to be made by the buyer to or for the benefit of the seller for the imported goods. The payment need not necessarily take the form of a transfer of money. Payment may be made by way of letters of credit or negotiable instruments. Payment may be made directly or indirectly. An example of an indirect payment would be the settlement by the buyer, whether in whole or in part, of a debt owed by the seller.

Activities undertaken by the buyer on his own account, other than those for which an adjustment is provided in Article 8, are not considered to be an indirect payment to the seller, even though they might be regarded as of benefit to the seller. The costs of such activities shall not, therefore, be added to the price actually paid or payable in determining the customs value.

The customs value shall not include the following charges or costs, provided that they are distinguished from the price actually paid or payable for the imported goods:

(a) charges for construction, erection, assembly, maintenance or technical assistance, undertaken after importation on imported goods such as industrial plant, machinery or equipment;

(b) the cost of transport after importation;

(c) duties and taxes of the country of importation.

The price actually paid or payable refers to the price for the imported goods. Thus the flow of dividends or other payments from the buyer to the seller that do not relate to the imported goods are not part of the customs value.

Paragraph 1 (a) (iii)

Among restrictions which would not render a price actually paid or payable unacceptable are restrictions which do not substantially affect the value of the goods. An example of such restrictions would be the case where a seller requires a buyer of automobiles not to sell or exhibit them prior to a fixed date which represents the beginning of a model year.

Paragraph 1 (b)

If the sale or price is subject to some condition or consideration for which a value cannot be determined with respect to the goods being valued, the transaction value shall not be acceptable for customs purposes. Some examples of this include:

(a) the seller establishes the price of the imported goods on condition that the buyer will also buy other goods in specified quantities;

(b) the price of the imported goods is dependent upon the price or prices at which the buyer of the imported goods sells other goods to the seller of the imported goods;

(c) the price is established on the basis of a form of payment extraneous to the imported goods, such as where the imported goods are semi-finished goods which have been provided by the seller on condition that he will receive a specified quantity of the finished goods.

However, conditions or considerations relating to the production or marketing of the imported goods shall not result in rejection of the transaction value. For example, the fact that the buyer furnishes the seller with engineering and plans undertaken in the country of importation shall not result in rejection of the transaction value for the purposes of Article 1. Likewise, if the buyer undertakes on his own account, even though by agreement with the seller, activities relating to the marketing of the imported goods, the value of these activities is not part of the customs value nor shall such activities result in rejection of the transaction value.

Paragraph 2

1. Paragraphs 2(a) and 2(b) provide different means of establishing the acceptability of a transaction value.

2. Paragraph 2(a) provides that where the buyer and the seller are related, the circumstances surrounding the sale shall be examined and the transaction value shall be accepted as the customs value provided that the

relationship did not influence the price. It is not intended that there should be an examination of the circumstances in all cases where the buyer and the seller are related. Such examination will only be required where there are doubts about the acceptability of the price. Where the customs administration have no doubts about the acceptability of the price, it should be accepted without requesting further information from the importer. For example, the customs administration may have previously examined the relationship, or it may already have detailed information concerning the buyer and the seller, and may already be satisfied from such examination or information that the relationship did not influence the price.

3. Where the customs administration is unable to accept the transaction value without further inquiry, it should give the importer an opportunity to supply such further detailed information as may be necessary to enable it to examine the circumstances surrounding the sale. In this context, the customs administration should be prepared to examine relevant aspects of the transaction, including the way in which the buyer and seller organize their commercial relations and the way in which the price in question was arrived at, in order to determine whether the relationship influenced the price. Where it can be shown that the buyer and seller, although related under the provisions of Article 15, buy from and sell to each other as if they were not related, this would demonstrate that the price had not been influenced by the relationship. As an example of this, if the price had been settled in a manner consistent with the normal pricing practices of the industry in question or with the way the seller settles prices for sales to buyers who are not related to him, this would demonstrate that the price had not been influenced by the relationship. As a further example, where it is shown that the price is adequate to ensure recovery of all costs plus a profit which is representative of the firms overall profit realized over a representative period of time (*e.g.* on an annual basis) in sales of goods of the same class or kind, this would demonstrate that the price had not been influenced.

4. Paragraph 2(13) provides an opportunity for the importer to demonstrate that the transaction value closely approximates to a "test" value previously accepted by the customs administration and is therefore acceptable under the provisions of Article 1. Where a test under paragraph 2(b) is met, it is not necessary to examine the question of influence under paragraph 2(a). If the customs administration has already sufficient information to be satisfied, without further detailed inquiries, that one of the tests provided in paragraph 2(b) has been met, there is no reason for it to require the importer to demonstrate that the test can be met. In paragraph 2(b) the term "unrelated buyers" means buyers who are not related to the seller in any particular case.

Paragraph 2(b)

A number of factors must be taken into consideration in determining whether one value "closely approximates" to another value. These factors include the nature of the imported goods, the nature of the industry itself, the season in which the goods are imported, and, whether the difference in values is commercially significant. Since these factors may vary from case to case, it would be impossible to apply a uniform standard such as a fixed percentage, in each case. For example, a small difference in value in a case involving one type of goods could be unacceptable while a large difference in a case involving another type of goods might be acceptable in determining whether the transaction value closely approximates to the "test" values set forth in paragraph 2(b) of Article 1.

Note to Article 2

1. In applying Article 2, the customs administration shall, wherever possible, use a sale of identical goods at the same commercial level and in substantially the same quantities as the goods being valued. Where no such sale is found, a sale of identical goods that takes place under any one of the following three conditions may be used:

(a) a sale at the same commercial level but in different quantities;

(b) a sale at a different commercial level but in substantially the same quantities; or

(c) a sale at a different commercial level and in different quantities.

2. Having found a sale under any one of these three conditions adjustments will then be made as the case may be, for:

(a) quantity factors only;

(b) commercial level factors only; or

(c) both commercial level and quantity factors.

3. The expression "and/or" allows the flexibility to use the sales and make the necessary adjustments in any one of the three conditions described above.

4. For the purposes of Article 2, the transaction value of identical imported goods means a customs value, adjusted as provided for in paragraphs 1 (b) and 2 of this Article, which has already beeen accepted under Article 1.

5. A condition for adjustment because of different commercial levels or different quantities is that such adjustment, whether it leads to an increase or a decrease in the value, be made only on the basis of demonstrated evidence that clearly establishes the reasonableness and accuracy of the adjusments, *e.g.* valid price lists containing prices referring to different levels or different

quantities. As an example of this, if the imported goods being valued consist of a shipment of 10 units and the only identical imported goods for which a transaction value exists involved a sale of 500 units, and it is recognized that the seller grants quantity discounts, the required adjustment may be accomplished by resorting to the seller's price list and using that price applicable to a sale of 10 units. This does not require that a sale had to have been made in quantities of 10 as long as the price list has been established as being *bona fide* through sales at other quantities. In the absence of such an objective measure, however, the determination of a customs value under the provisions of Article 2 is not appropriate.

Note to Article 3

1. In applying Article 3, the customs administration shall, wherever possible, use a sale of similar goods at the same commercial level and in substantially the same quantities as the goods being valued. Where no such sale is found, a sale of similar goods that takes place under any one of the following three conditions may be used:

(a) a sale at the same commercial level but in different quantities;

(b) a sale at a different commercial level but in substantially the same quantities: or

(c) a sale at a different commercial level and in different quantities.

2. Having found a sale under any one of these three conditions adjustments will then be made, as the case may be, for:

(a) quantity factors only;

(b) commercial level factors only; or

(c) both commercial level and quantity factors.

3. The expression "and/or" allows the flexibility to use the scales and make the necessary adjustments in any one of the three conditions described above.

4. For the purpose of Article 3, the transaction value of similar imported goods means a customs value, adjusted as provided for in paragraphs 1 (b) and 2 of this Article, which has already been accepted under Article 1.

5. A condition for adjustment because of different commercial levels or different quantities is that such adjustment, whether it leads to an increase or a decrease in the value, be made only on the basis of demonstrated evidence that clearly establishes the reasonableness and accuracy of the adjustment. *e.g.* valid price lists containing prices referring to different levels or different quantities. As an example of this, if the imported goods being valued consist of a shipment of 10 units and the only similar imported goods for which a transaction value exists involved a sale of 500 units, and it is recognized that

the seller grants quantity discounts, the required adjustment may be accomplished by resorting to the seller's price list and using that price applicable to a sale of 10 units. This does not require that a sale had to have been made in quantities of 10 as long as the price list has been established as being *bona fide* through sales at other quantities. In the absence of such an objective measure, however, the determination of a customs value under the provisions of Article 3 is not appropriate.

Note to Article 5

1. The term "unit price at which ... goods are sold in the greatest aggregate quantity" means the price at which the greatest number of units is sold in sales to persons who are not related to the persons from whom they buy such goods at the first commercial level after importation at which such sales take place.

2. As an example of this, goods are sold from a price list which grants favourable unit prices for purchases made in larger quantities.

Sale quantity	*Unit price*	*Number of sales*	*Total quantity sold at each price*
1-10 units	100	10 sales of 5 units 5 sales of 3 units	65
11-25 units	95	5 sales of 11 units	55
over 25 units	90	1 sale of 30 units 1 sale of 50 units	80

The greatest number of units sold at a price is 80; therefore, the unit price in the greatest aggregate quantity is 90.

3. As another example of this, two sales occur. In the first sale 500 units are sold at a price of 95 currency units each. In the second sale 400 units are sold at a price of 90 currency units each. In this example, the greatest number of units sold at a particular price is 500; therefore, the unit price in the greatest aggregate quantity is 95.

4. A third example would be the following situation where various quantities are sold at various prices.

(a) *Sales*

Sale quantity	*Unit price*
40 units	100
30 units	90
15 units	100
50 units	95
25 units	105
35 units	90
5 units	100

(b) *Totals*

Total quantity sold	*Unit price*
65	90
50	95
60	100
25	105

In this example, the greatest number of units sold at a particular price is 65; therefore, the unit price in the greatest aggregate quantity is 90.

5. Any sale in the importing country, as described in paragraph 1 above, to a person who supplies directly or indirectly free of charge or at reduced cost for use in connection with the production and sale for export of the imported goods any of the elements specified in paragraph l(b) of Article 8, should not be taken into account in establishing the unit price for the purposes of Article 5.

6. It should be noted that "profit and general expenses" referred to in paragraph 1 of Article 5 should be taken as a whole. The figure for the purposes of this deduction should be determined on the basis of information supplied by or on behalf of the importer unless his figures are inconsistent with those obtained in sales in the country of importation of imported goods of the same class or kind. Where the importer's figures are inconsistent with such figures, the amount for profit and general expenses may be based upon relevant information other than that supplied by or on behalf of the importer.

7. The "general expenses" include the direct and indirect costs of marketing the goods in question.

8. Local taxes payable by reason of the sale of the goods for which a deduction is not made under the provisions of paragraph l (a) (iv) of Article 5 shall be deducted under the provisions of paragraph l (a) (i) of Article 5.

9. In determining either the commissions or the usual profits and general expenses under the provisions of paragraph 1 of Article 5, the question whether certain goods are "of the same class or kind" as other goods must be determined on a case-by-case basis by reference to the circumstances involved. Sales in the country of importation of the narrowest group or range of imported goods of the same class or kind, which includes the goods being valued, for which the necessary information can be provided, should be examined. For the purposes of Article 5, "goods of the same class or kind" includes goods imported from the same country as the goods being valued as well as goods imported from other countries.

10. For the purposes of paragraph l (b) of Article 5, the "earliest date" shall be the date by which sales of the imported goods or of identical or

similar imported goods are made in sufficient quantity to establish the unit price.

11. Where the method in paragraph 2 of Article 5 is used, deductions made for the value added by further processing shall be based on objective and quantifiable data relating to the cost of such work. Accepted industry formulas, recipes, methods of construction, and other industry practices would form the basis of the calculations.

12. It is recognized that the method of valuation provided for in paragraph 2 of Article 5 would normally not be applicable when, as a result of the further processing, the imported goods lose their identity. However, there can be instances where, although the identity of the imported goods is lost, the value added by the processing can be determined accurately without unreasonable difficulty. On the other hand, there can also be instances where the imported goods maintain their identity but form such a minor element in the goods sold in the country of importation that the use of this valuation method would be unjustified. In view of the above, each situation of this type must be considered on a case-by-case basis.

Note to Article 6

1. As a general rule, customs value is determined under this Agreement on the basis of information readily available in the country of importation. In order to determine a computed value, however, it may be necessary to examine the costs of producing the goods being valued and other information which has to be obtained from outside the country of importation. Furthermore, in most cases the producer of the goods will be outside the jurisdiction of the authorities of the country of importation. The use of the computed value method will generally be limited to those cases where the buyer and seller are related, and the producer is prepared to supply to the authorities of the country of importation the necessary costings and to provide facilities for any subsequent verification which may be necessary.

2. The "cost or value" referred to in paragraph l(a) of Article 6 is to be determined on the basis of information relating to the production of the goods being valued supplied by or on behalf of the producer. It is to be based upon the commercial accounts of the producer, provided that such accounts are consistent with the generally accepted accounting principles applied in the country where the goods are produced.

3. The "cost or value" shall include the cost of elements specified in paragraphs l(a)(ii) and (iii) of Article 8. It shall also include the value, apportioned as appropriate under the provisions of the relevant note to Article 8, of any element specified in paragraph 1 (b) of Article 8 which has been supplied directly or indirectly by the buyer for use in connection with the

production of the imported goods. The value of the elements specified in paragraph 1 (b)(iv) of Article 8 which are undertaken in the country of importation shall be included only to the extent that such elements are charged to the producer. It is to be understood that no cost or value of the elements referred to in this paragraph shall be counted twice in determining the computed value.

4. The "amount for profit and general expenses" referred to in paragraph 1(b) of Article 6 is to be determined on the basis of information supplied by or on behalf of the producer unless his figures are inconsistent with those usually reflected in sales of goods of the same class or kind as the goods being valued which are made by producers in the country of exportation for export to the country of importation.

5. It should be noted in this context that the "amount for profit and general expenses" has to be taken as a whole. It follows that if, in any particular case, the producers profit figure is low and his general expenses are high, his profit and general expenses taken together may nevertheless be consistent with that usually reflected in sales of goods of the same class or kind. Such a situation might occur, for example, if a product were being launched in the country of importation and the producer accepted a nil or low profit to offset high general expenses associated with the launch. Where the producer can demonstrate that he is taking a low profit on his sales of the imported goods because of particular commercial circumstances, his actual profit figures should be taken into account provided that he has valid commercial reasons to justify them and his pricing policy reflects usual pricing policies in the branch of industry concerned. Such a situation might occur, for example, where producers have been forced to lower prices temporarily because of an unforeseeable drop in demand, or where they sell goods to complement a range of goods being produced in the country of importation and accept a low profit to maintain competitivity. Where the producers own figures for profit and general expenses are not consistent with those usually reflected in sales of goods of the same class or kind as the goods being valued which are made by producers in the country of exportation for export to the country of importation, the amount for profit and general expenses may be based upon relevant information other than that supplied by or on behalf of the producer of the goods.

6. Where information other than that supplied by or on behalf of the producer is used for the purposes of determining a computed value, the authorities of the importing country shall inform the importer, if the latter so requests, of the source of such information, the data used and the calculations based upon such data, subject to the provisions of Article 10.

7. The "general expenses" referred to in paragraph 1(b) of Article 6

covers the direct and indirect costs of producing and selling the goods for export which are not included under paragraph l(a) of Article 6.

8. Whether certain goods are "of the same class or kind" as other goods must be determined on a case-by-case basis with reference to the circumstances involved. In determining the usual profits and general expenses under the provisions of Article 6, sales for export to the country of importation of the narrowest group or range of goods, which includes the goods being valued, for which the necessary information can be provided, should be examined. For the purposes of Article 6. "goods of the same class or kind" must be from the same country as the goods being valued.

Note to Article 7

1. Customs values determined under the provisions of Article 7 should, to the greatest extent possible, be based on previously determined customs values.

2. The methods of valuation to be employed under Article 7 should be those laid down in Articles 1 to 6, inclusive, but a reasonable flexibility in the application of such methods would be in conformity with the aims and provisions of Article 7.

3. Some examples of reasonable flexibility are as follows:

(a) *Identical goods* – the requirement that the identical goods should be exported at or about the same time as the goods being valued could be flexibly interpreted; identical imported goods produced in a country other than the country of exportation of the goods being valued could be the basis for customs valuation; customs values of identical imported goods already determined under the provisions of Articles 5 and 6 could be used.

(b) *Similar goods* – the requirement that the similar goods should be exported at or about the same time as the goods being valued could be flexibly interpreted; similar imported goods produced in a country other than the country of exportation of the goods being valued could be the basis for customs valuation; customs values of similar imported goods already determined under the provisions of Articles 5 and 6 could be used.

(c) *Deductive method* – the requirement that the goods shall have been sold in the "condition as imported" in paragraph l(a) of Article 5 could be flexibly interpreted; the "ninety days" requirement could be administered flexibly.

Note to Article 8

Paragraph I (a) (i)

The term "buying commissions" means fees paid by an importer to his agent for the service of representing him abroad in the purchase of the goods being valued.

Paragraph I (b) (ii)

1. There are two factors involved in the apportionment of the elements specified in paragraph 1 of Article 8 to the imported goods – the value of the element itself and the way in which that value is to be apportioned to the imported goods. The apportionment of these elements should be made in a reasonable manner appropriate to the circumstances and in accordance with generally accepted accounting principles.

2. Concerning the value of the element, if the importer acquires the element from a seller not related to him at a given cost, the value of the element is that cost. If the element was produced by the importer or by a person related to him, its value would be the cost of producing it. If the element had been previously used by the importer, regardless of whether it had been acquired or produced by such importer, the original cost of acquisition or production would have to be adjusted downward to reflect its use in order to arrive at the value of the element.

3. Once a value has been determined for the element, it is necessary to apportion that value to the imported goods. Various possibilities exist. For example, the value might be apportioned to the first shipment if the importer wishes to pay duty on the entire value at one time. As another example, the importer may request that the value be apportioned over the number of units produced up to the time of the first shipment. As a further example, he may request that the value be apportioned over the entire anticipated production where contracts or firm commitments exist for that production. The method of apportionment used will depend upon the documentation provided by the importer.

4. As an illustration of the above, an importer provides the producer with a mould to be used in the production of the imported goods and contracts with him to buy 10,000 units. By the time of arrival of the first shipment of 1,000 units, the producer has already produced 4,000 units. The importer may request the customs administration to apportion the value of the mould over 1,000 units, 4,000 units or 10,000 units.

Paragraph 1 (b) (iv)

1. Additions for the elements specified in paragraph 1(b)(iv) of Article 8 should be based on objective and quantifiable data. In order to minimize the

burden for both the importer and customs administration in determining the values to be added, data readily available in the buyers commercial record system should be used in so far as possible.

2. For those elements supplied by the buyer which were purchased or leased by the buyer, the addition would be the cost of the purchase or the lease. No addition shall be made for those elements available in the public domain, other than the cost of obtaining copies of them.

3. The ease with which it may be possible to calculate the values to be added will depend on a particular firms structure and management practice, as well as its accounting methods.

4. For example, it is possible that a firm which imports a variety of products from several countries maintains the records of its design centre outside the country of importation in such a way as to show accurately the costs attributable to a given product. In such cases, a direct adjustment may appropriately be made under the provisions of Article 8.

5. In another case, a firm may carry the cost of the design centre outside the country of importation as a general overhead expense without allocation to specific products. In this instance, an appropriate adjustment could be made under the provisions of Article 8 with respect to the imported goods by apportioning total design centre costs over total production benefiting from the design centre and adding such apportioned cost on a unit basis to imports.

6. Variations in the above circumstances will, of course, require different factors to be considered in determining the proper method of allocation.

7. In cases where the production of the element in question involves a number of countries and over a period of time, the adjustment should be limited to the value actually added to that element outside the country of importation.

Paragraph I (c)

1. The royalties and licence fees referred to in paragraph l(c) of Article 8 may include, among other things, payments in respect to patents, trade marks and copyrights. However, the charges for the right to reproduce the imported goods in the country of importation shall not be added to the price actually paid or payable for the imported goods in determining the customs value.

2. Payments made by the buyer for the right to distribute or resell the imported goods shall not be added to the price actually paid or payable for the imported goods if such payments are not a condition of the sale for export to the country of importation of the imported goods.

Paragraph 3

Where objective and quantifiable data do not exist with regard to the additions required to be made under the provisions of Article 8, the transaction value cannot be determined under the provisions of Article 1. As an illustration of this, a royalty is paid on the basis of the price in a sale in the importing country of a litre of a particular product that was imported by the kilogram and made up into a solution after importation. If the royalty is based partially on the imported goods and partially on other factors which have nothing to do with the imported goods (such as when the imported goods are mixed with domestic ingredients and are no longer separately identifiable, or when the royalty cannot be distinguished from special financial arrangements between the buyer and the seller), it would be inappropriate to attempt to make an addition for the royalty. However, if the amount of this royalty is based only on the imported goods and can be readily quantified, an addition to the price actually paid or payable can be made.

Note to Article 9

For the purposes of Article 9, "time of importation" may include the time of entry for customs purposes.

Note to Article 11

1. Article 11 provides the importer with the right to appeal against a valuation determination made by the customs administration for the goods being valued. Appeal may first be to a higher level in the customs administration, but the importer shall have the right in the final instance to appeal to the judiciary.

2. "Without penalty" means that the importer shall not be subject to a fine or threat of fine merely because he chose to exercise his right of appeal. Payment of normal court costs and lawyers fees shall not be considered to be a fine.

3. However, nothing in Article 11 shall prevent a Member from requiring full payment of assessed customs duties prior to an appeal.

Note to Article 15

Paragraph 4

For the purposes of this Article, the term "persons" includes legal person, where appropriate.

Paragraph 4(e)

For the purposes of this Agreement, one person shall be deemed to control another when the former is legally or operationally in a position to exercise restraint or direction over the latter.

ANNEX II

TECHNICAL COMMITTEE ON CUSTOMS VALUATION

1. In accordance with Article 18 of this Agreement, the Technical Committee shall be established under the auspices of the CCC with a view, at the technical level, towards uniformity in interpretation and application of this Agreement.

2. The responsibilities of the Technical Committee shall include the following:

(a) to examine specific technical problems arising in the day-to-day administration of the customs valuation system of Members and to give advisory opinions on appropriate solutions based upon the facts presented;

(b) to study, as requested, valuation law procedures and practices as they relate to this Agreement and to prepare reports on the results of such studies;

(c) to prepare and circulate annual reports on the technical aspects of the operation and status of this Agreement;

(d) to furnish such information and advice on any matters concerning the valuation of imported goods for customs purposes as may be requested by any Member or the Committee. Such information and advice may take the form of advisory opinions, commentaries or explanatory notes;

(e) to facilitate, as requested, technical assistance to Members with a view to furthering the international acceptance of this Agreement;

(f) to carry out an examination of a matter referred to it by a panel under Article 19 of this Agreement; and

(g) to exercise such other responsibilities as the Committee may assign to it.

General

3. The Technical Committee shall attempt to conclude its work on specific matters, especially those referred to it by Members, the Committee or a panel, in a reasonably short period of time. As provided in paragraph 4 of Article 19, a panel shall set a specific time period for receipt of a report of the Technical Committee and the Technical Committee shall provide its report within that period.

4. The Technical Committee shall be assisted as appropriate in its activities by the Secretariat of the CCC.

Representation

5. Each Member shall have the right to be represented on the Technical Committee. Each Member may nominate one delegate and one or more alternates to be its representatives on the Technical Committee. Such a Member so represented on the Technical Committee is hereinafter referred to as a member of the Technical Committee, Representatives of members of the Technical Committee may be assisted by advisers. The WTO Secretariat may also attend such meetings with observer status.

6. Members of the CCC who are not Members of the WTO· may be represented at meetings Of the Technical Committee by one delegate and one or more alternates. Such representatives shall attend meetings of the Technical Committee as observers.

7. Subject to the approval of the Chairman of the Technical Committee, the Secretary-General of the CCC (hereinafter referred to as "the Secretary-General") may invite representatives of governments which are neither Members of the MTO nor members of the CCC and representatives of international governmental and trade organizations to attend meetings of the Technical Committee as observers.

8. Nominations of delegates, alternates and advisers to meetings of the Technical Committee shall be made to the Secretary-General.

Technical Committee Meetings

9. The Technical Committee shall meet as necessary but at least two times a year. The date of each meeting shall be fixed by the Technical Committee at its preceding session. The date of the meeting may be varied either at the request of any member of the Technical Committee concurred in by a simple majority of the members of the Technical Committee or, in cases requiring urgent attention, at the request of the Chairman. Notwithstanding the provisions in sentence of this paragraph, the Technical Committee shall meet as necessary to consider matters referred to it by a panel under the provisions of Article 19 of this Agreement.

10. The meetings of the Technical Committee shall be held at the headquarters of the CCC unless otherwise decided.

11. The Secretary-General shall inform all members of the Technical Committee and those included under paragraphs 6 and 7 at least thirty days in advance, except in urgent cases, of the opening date of each session of the Technical Committee.

Agenda

12. A provisional agenda for each session shall be drawn up by the Secretary-General and circulated to the members of the Technical Committee and to those included under paragraphs 6 and 7 at least thirty days in advance of the session, except in urgent cases. This agenda shall comprise all items whose inclusion has been approved by the Technical Committee during its preceding session, all items included by the Chairman on his own initiative, and all items whose inclusion has been requested by the Secretary-General, by the Committee or by any member of the Technical Committee.

13. The Technical Committee shall determine its agenda at the opening of each session. During the session the agenda may be altered at any time by the Technical Committee.

Officers and Conduct of Business

14. The Technical Committee shall elect from among the delegates of its members a Chairman and one or more Vice-Chairmen. The Chairman and Vice-Chairmen shall each hold office for a period of one year. The retiring Chairman and Vice-Chairmen are eligible for re-election. A Chairman or Vice-Chairman who ceases to represent a member of the Technical Committee shall automatically lose his mandate.

15. If the Chairman is absent from any meeting or part thereof, a Vice-Chairman shall preside. In that event, the latter shall have the same powers and duties as the Chairman.

16. The Chairman of the meeting shall participate in the proceedings of the Technical Committee as such and not as the representative of a member of the Technical Committee.

17. In addition to exercising the powers conferred upon him elsewhere by these rules, the Chairman shall declare the opening and closing of each meeting, direct the discussion, accord the right to speak, and, pursuant to these rules, have control of the proceedings. The Chairman may also call a speaker to order if his remarks are not relevant.

18. During discussion of any matter a delegation may raise a point of order. In this event, the Chairman shall immediately state his ruling. If this ruling is challenged, the Chairman shall submit it to the meeting for decision and it shall stand unless overruled.

19. The Secretary-General, or officers of the Secretariat designated by him, shall perform the secretarial work of meetings of the Technical Committee.

Quorum and voting

20. Representatives of a simple majority of the members of the Technical Committee shall constitute a quorum.

21. Each member of the Technical Committee shall have one vote. A decision of the Technical Committee shall be taken by a majority comprising at least two-thirds of the members present. Regardless of the outcome of the vote on a particular matter, the Technical Committee shall be free to make a full report to the Committee and to the CCC on that matter indicating the different views expressed in the relevant discussions. Notwithstanding the above provisions of this paragraph, on matters referred to it by a panel, the Technical Committee shall take decisions by consensus. Where no agreement is reached in the Technical Committee on the question referred to it by a panel, the Technical Committee shall provide a report detailing the facts of the matter and indicating the views of the members.

Languages and Records

22. The official languages of the Technical Committee shall be English, French and Spanish. Speeches or statements made in any of these three languages shall be immediately translated into the other official languages unless all delegations agree to dispense with translation. Speeches or statements made in any other language shall be translated into English, French and Spanish, subject to the same conditions, but in that event the delegation concerned shall provide the translation into English, French or Spanish. Only English, French and Spanish shall be used for the official documents of the Technical Committee. Memoranda and correspondence for the consideration of the Technical Committee must be presented in one of the official languages.

23. The Technical Committee shall draw up a report of all its sessions and, if the Chairman considers it necessary, minutes or summary records of its meetings. The Chairman or his designee shall report on the work of the Technical Committee at each meeting of the Committee and at each meeting of the CCC.

ANNEX III

1. The five-year delay in the application of the provisions of the Agreement by developing country Members provided for in paragraph 1 of Article 20 may, in practice, be insufficient for certain developing country Members. In such cases a developing country Member may request before the end of the period referred to in paragraph 1 of Article 20 an extension of such period, it being understood that the Members will give sympathetic consideration to such a request in cases where the developing country Member in question can show good cause.

2. Developing countries which currently value goods on the basis of officially established minimum values may wish to make a reservation to enable them to retain such values on a limited and transitional basis under such terms and conditions as may be agreed to by the Members.

3. Developing countries which consider that the reversal of the sequential order at the request of the importer provided for in Article 4 of the Agreement may give rise to real difficulties for them may wish to make a reservation to Article 4 in the following terms:

> "The Government of .... reserves the right to provide that the relevant provision of Article 4 of the Agreement shall apply only when the customs authorities agree to the request to reverse the order of Articles 5 and 6."

If developing countries make such a reservation, the Members shall consent to it under Article 21 of the Agreement.

4. Developing countries may wish to make a reservation with respect to paragraph 2 of Article 5 of the Agreement in the following terms:

> "The Government of .... reserves the right to provide that paragraph 2 of Article 5 of the Agreement shall be applied in accordance with the provisions of the relevant note thereto whether or not the importer so requests."

If developing countries make such a reservation, the Members shall consent to it under Article 21 of the Agreement.

5.. Certain developing country Members have expressed concern that there may be problems in the implementation of Article 1 of the Agreement insofar as it relates to importations into their countries by sole agents, sole distributors and sole concessionaires. If such problems arise in practice in developing country Members applying the Agreement, a study of this question shall be made, at the request of such Members, with a view to finding appropriate solutions.

6. Article 17 recognizes that in applying the Agreement, customs administrations may need to make enquiries concerning the truth or accuracy of any statement, document or declaration presented to them for customs valuation purposes. The Article thus acknowledges that enquiries may be made which are, for example, aimed at verifying that the elements of value declared or presented to customs in connection with a determination of customs value are complete and correct. Members, subject to their national laws and procedures, have the right to expect the full co-operation of importers in these enquiries.

7. The price actually paid or payable includes all payments actually made or to be made as a condition of sale of the imported goods, by the buyer to the seller, or by the buyer to a third party to satisfy an obligation of the seller.

AGREEMENT ON PRESHIPMENT INSPECTION

Members,

Noting that Ministers on 20 September 1986 agreed that "the Uruguay Round of Multilateral Trade Negotiations shall aim to bring about further liberalization and expansion of world trade, strengthen the role of GATT and increase the responsiveness of the GATT system to the evolving international economic environment";

Noting that a number of developing country Members have recourse to preshipment inspection;

Recognizing the need of developing countries to do so for as long and insofar as it is necessary to verify the quality, quantity or price of imported goods;

Mindful that such programmes must be carried out without giving rise to unnecessary delays or unequal treatment;

Noting that this inspection is by definition carried out on the territory of exporter Members;

Recognizing the need to establish an agreed international framework of rights and obligations of both user Members and exporter Members;

Recognizing that the principles and obligations of the GATT 1994 apply to those activities of preshipment inspection entities that are mandated by governments that are Members of the WTO·

Recognizing that it is desirable to provide transparency of the operation of preshipment inspection entities and of laws and regulations relating to preshipment inspection;

Desiring to provide for the speedy, effective and equitable resolution of disputes between exporters and preshipment inspection entities arising under this Agreement;

Hereby agree as follows:

Article I

Coverage – Definitions

1. This Agreement shall apply to all preshipment inspection activities carried out on the territory of Members, whether such activities are contracted or mandated by the government, or any government body, of a Member (hereinafter referred to as "user Member").

2. Preshipment inspection activities are all activities relating to the verification of the quality, the quantity, the price, including currency exchange rate and financial terms, and/or the customs classification of goods to be exported to the territory of the user Member.

3. The term "preshipment inspection entity" is any entity con-tracted or mandated by a Member to carry out preshipment inspection activities.[56]

Article 2

Obligations of User Members

Non-discrimination

1. User Members shall ensure that preshipment inspection activities are carried out in a non-discriminatory manner, that the procedures and criteria employed in the conduct of these activities are objective and are applied on an equal basis to all exporters affected by such activities. They shall ensure uniform performance of inspection by all the inspectors of the preshipment inspection entities contracted or mandated by them.

Governmental Requirements

2. User Members shall ensure that in the course of preshipment inspection activities relating to their laws, regulations and requirements, the provisions of Article III:4 of the GATT 1994 are respected to the extent that these are relevant.

Site of Inspection

3. User Members shall ensure that all preshipment inspection activities, including the issuance of a Clean Report of Findings or a note of non-issuance, are performed in the customs territory from which the goods are exported or, if the inspection cannot be carried out in that customs territory given the complex nature of the products involved, or if both parties agree, in the customs territory in which the goods are manufactured.

Standards

4. User Members shall ensure that quantity and quality inspections are performed in accordance with the standards defined by the seller and the buyer in the purchase agreement and that, in the absence of such standards, relevant international standards[57] apply.

---

[56] It is understood that this provision does not obligate Members to allow government entities of other Members to conduct preshipment inspection activities on their territory.

[57] An international standard is a standard adopted by a governmental or non-governmental body whose membership is open to all Members, one of whose recognized activities is in the field of standardization.

Transparency

5. User Members shall ensure that preshipment inspection activities are conducted in a transparent manner.

6. User Members shall ensure that, when initially contacted by exporters, preshipment inspection entities provide to the exporters a list of all the information which is necessary for the exporters to comply with inspection requirements. The preshipment inspection entities shall provide the actual information when so requested by exporters. This information shall include a reference to the laws and regulations of the user Members relating to preshipment inspection activities, and shall also include the procedures and criteria used for inspection and for price and currency exchange rate verification purposes, the exporters' rights *vis-a-vis* the inspection entities, and the appeals procedures set up under paragraph 21 of this Article. Additional procedural requirements or changes in existing procedures shall not be applied to a shipment unless the exporter concerned is informed of these changes at the time the inspection date is arranged. However, in emergency situations of the types addressed by Articles XX and XXI of the GATT 1994, such additional requirements or changes may be applied to a shipment before the exporter has been informed. This assistance shall not, however, relieve exporters from their obligations in respect of compliance with the import regulations of the user Members.

7. User Members shall ensure that the information referred to in paragraph 6 of this Article is made available to exporters in a convenient manner, and that the preshipment inspection offices maintained by preshipment inspection entities serve as information points where this information is available.

8. User Members shall publish promptly all applicable laws and regulations relating to preshipment inspection activities in such a manner as to enable other governments and traders to become acquainted with them.

Protection of Confidential Business Information

9. User Members shall ensure that preshipment inspection entities treat all information received in the course of the preshipment inspection as business confidential to the extent that such information is not already published, generally available to third parties, or otherwise in the public domain. User Members shall ensure that preshipment inspection entities maintain procedures to this end.

10. User Members shall provide information to Members on request on the measures they are taking to give effect to paragraph 9 of this Article. The provisions of this paragraph shall not require any Member to disclose confidential information the disclosure of which would jeopardize the effectiveness of the

preshipment inspection programmes or would prejudice the legitimate commercial interest of particular enterprises, public or private.

11. User Members shall ensure that preshipment inspection entities do not divulge confidential business information to any third party, except that preshipment inspection entities may share this information with the government entities that have contracted or mandated them. User Members shall ensure that confidential business information which they receive from preshipment inspection entities contracted or mandated by them is adequately safeguarded. Preshipment inspection entities shall share confidential business information with the governments contracting or mandating them only to the extent that such information is customarily required for letters of credit or other forms of payment or for customs, import licensing or exchange control purposes.

12. User Members shall ensure that preshipment inspection entities do not request exporters to provide information regarding:

(a) manufacturing data related to patented, licensed or undisclosed processes, or to processes for which a patent is pending;

(b) unpublished technical data other than data necessary to demonstrate compliance with technical regulations or standards;

(c) internal pricing, including manufacturing costs;

(d) profit levels;

(e) the terms of contracts between exporters and their suppliers unless it is not otherwise possible for the entity to conduct the inspection in question. In such cases, the entity shall only request the information necessary for this purpose.

13. The information referred to in paragraph 12 of this Article, which preshipment inspection entities shall not otherwise request, may be released voluntarily by the exporter to illustrate a specific case.

Conflicts of Interest

14. User Members shall ensure that preshipment inspection entities, bearing in mind also the provisions on protection of confidential business information in paragraphs 9-13 of this Article, maintain procedures to avoid conflicts of interest:

(a) between preshipment inspection entities and any related entities of the preshipment inspection entities in question, including any entities in which the latter have a financial or commercial interest or any entities which have a financial interest in the preshipment inspection entities in question, and whose shipments the preshipment inspection entities are to inspect;

(b) between preshipment inspection entities and any other entities, including other entities subject to preshipment inspection, with the exception of the government entities contracting or mandating the inspections;

(c) with divisions of preshipment inspection entities engaged in activities other than those required to carry out the inspection process.

Delays

15. User Members shall ensure that preshipment inspection entities avoid unreasonable delays in inspection of shipments. User Members shall ensure that, once a preshipment inspection entity and an exporter agree on an inspection date, the preshipment inspection entity conducts the inspection on that date unless it is rescheduled on a mutually-agreed basis between the exporter and the preshipment inspection entity, or the preshipment inspection entity is prevented from doing so by the exporter or by *force majeure*.[58]

16. User Members shall ensure that, following receipt of the final documents and completion of the inspection, preshipment inspection entities, within five working days, either issue a Clean Report of Findings or provide a detailed written explanation specifying the reasons for non-issuance. User Members shall ensure that, in the latter case, preshipment inspection entities give exporters the opportunity to present their views in writing and, if exporters so request, arrange for re-inspection at the earliest mutually convenient date.

17. User Members shall ensure that, whenever so requested by the exporters, preshipment inspection entities undertake, prior to the date of physical inspection, a preliminary verification of price and, where applicable, of currency exchange rate, on the basis of the contract between exporter and importer, the *pro forma* invoice and, where applicable, the application for import authorization. User Members shall ensure that a price or currency exchange rate that has been accepted by a preshipment inspection entity on the basis of such preliminary verification is not withdrawn, providing the goods conform to the import documentation and/or import licence. They shall ensure that, after a preliminary verification has taken place, preshipment inspection entities immediately inform exporters in writing either of their acceptance or of their detailed reasons for non-acceptance of the price and/or currency exchange rate.

18. User Members shall ensure that, in order to avoid delays in payment, preshipment inspection entities send to exporters or to designated representatives of the exporters a Clean Report of Findings as expeditiously as possible.

19. User Members shall ensure that, in the event of a clerical error in the

[58] It is understood that for the purposes of this Agreement, *force majeure* shall mean "irresistible compulsion or coercion, unforeseeable course of events excusing from fulfilment of contract".

Clean Report of Findings, preshipment inspection entities correct the error and forward the corrected information to the appropriate parties as expeditiously as possible.

Price Verification

20. User Members shall ensure that, in order to prevent over-and under-invoicing and fraud, preshipment inspection entities conduct price verification[59] according to the following guidelines:

(a) preshipment inspection entities shall only reject a contract price agreed between an exporter and an importer if they can demonstrate that their findings of an unsatisfactory price are based on a verification process which is in conformity with the criteria set out in (b)-(c) below;

(b) the preshipment inspection entity shall base its price comparison for the verification of the export price on the price(s) of identical or similar goods offered for export from the same country of exportation at or about the same time, under competitive and comparable conditions of sale, in conformity with customary commercial practices and net of any applicable standard discounts. Such comparison shall be based on the following:

- only prices providing a valid basis of comparison shall be used, taking into account the relevant economic factors pertaining to the country of importation and a country or countries used for price comparison;
- the preshipment inspection entity shall not rely upon the price of goods offered for export to different countries of importation to arbitrarily impose the lowest price upon the shipment;
- the preshipment inspection entity shall take into account the specific elements listed in paragraph 20(c) of this Article;
- at any stage in the process described above, the preshipment inspection entity shall provide the exporter with an opportunity to explain his price;

(c) when conducting price verification, preshipment inspection entities shall make appropriate allowances for the terms of the sales contract and generally applicable adjusting factors pertaining to the transaction; these factors shall include but not be limited to the commercial level and quantity of the sale, delivery periods

---

[59] The obligations of user Members with respect to the services of preshipment inspection entities in connection with customs valuation shall be the obligations which they have accepted in the GATT 1994 and the other World Trade Organisation included in Annex IA of the Agreement Establishing the World Trade Organisation .

and conditions, price escalation clauses, quality specifications, special design features, special shipping or packing specifications, order size, spot sales, seasonal influences, licence or other intellectual property fees, and services rendered as part of the contract if these are not customarily invoiced separately; they shall also include certain elements relating to the exporters price, such as the contractual relationship between the exporter and importer;

(d) the verification of transportation charges shall relate only to the agreed price of the mode of transport in the country of exportation as indicated in the sales contract;

(e) the following shall not be used for price verification purposes:

(i) the selling price in the country of importation of goods produced in such country;

(ii) the price of goods for export from a country other than the country of exportation;

(iii) the cost of production;

(iv) arbitrary or fictitious prices or values.

Appeals Procedures

21. User Members shall ensure that preshipment inspection entities establish procedures to receive, consider and render decisions concerning grievances raised by exporters, and that information concerning such procedures is made available to exporters in accordance with the provisions of paragraphs 6-7 of this Article. User Members shall ensure that the procedures are developed and maintained in accordance with the following guidelines:

(a) preshipment inspection entities shall designate one or more officials who shall be available during normal business hours in each city or port in which they maintain a preshipment inspection administrative office to receive, consider and render decisions on exporters' appeals or grievances;

(b) exporters shall provide in writing to the designated official(s) the facts concerning the specific transaction in question, the nature of the grievance and a suggested solution:

(c) the designated official(s) shall afford sympathetic consideration to exporters grievances and shall render a decision as soon as possible after receipt of the documentation referred to in (b) above.

Derogation

22. By derogation to the provisions of Article 2, user Members shall provide that, with the exception of part shipments, shipments whose value is less than a minimum value applicable to such shipments as defined by the user Member shall not be inspected, except in exceptional circumstances. This minimum value shall form part of the information furnished to exporters under the provisions of paragraph 6 of this Article.

Article 3

Obligations of Exporter Members

Non-discrimination

1. Exporter Members shall ensure that their laws and regulations relating to preshipment inspection activities are applied in a non-discriminatory manner.

Transparency

2. Exporter Members shall publish promptly all applicable laws and regulations relating to preshipment inspection activities in such a manner as to enable other governments and traders to become acquainted with them.

Technical Assistance

3. Exporter Members shall offer to provide to user Members, if requested, technical assistance directed towards the achievement of the objectives of this Agreement on mutually agreed terms.[60]

Article 4

Independent Review Procedures

Members shall encourage preshipment inspection entities and exporters mutually to resolve their disputes. However, two working days after submission of the grievance in accordance with the provisions of paragraph 21 of Article 2, either party may refer the dispute to independent review. Members shall take such reasonable measures as may be available to them to ensure that the following procedures are established and maintained to this end:

(a) these procedures shall be administered by an independent entity constituted jointly by an organization representing preshipment inspection entities and an organization representing exporters for the purposes of this Agreement;

(b) the independent entity referred to in sub-paragraph (a) of this Article shall establish a list of experts as follows:

---

[60] It is understood that such technical assistance may be given on a bilateral, plurilateral or multilateral basis.

(i) a section of members nominated by an organization representing preshipment inspection entities;

(ii) a section of members nominated by an organization representing exporters;

(iii) a section of independent trade experts, nominated by the independent entity referred to in sub-paragraph (a) of this Article.

The geographical distribution of the experts on this list shows such as to enable any disputes raised under these procedures and dealt with immediately. This list shall be drawn up within two months of the entry into force of the Agreement Establishing the WTO and shall be updated annually. The list shall be publicly available. It shall be notified to the WTO Secretariat and circulated to all Members;

(c) an exporter or preshipment inspection entity wishing to raise a dispute shall contact the independent entity referred to in sub-paragraph (a) of this Article and request the formation of a panel. The independent entity shall be responsible for establishing a panel. This panel shall consist of three members. The members of the panel shall be chosen so as to avoid unnecessary costs and delays. The first member shall be chosen from section (i) of the above list by the preshipment inspection entity concerned, provided that this member is not affiliated to that entity. The second member shall be chosen from section (ii) of the above list by the exporter concerned, provided that this member is not affiliated to that exporter. The third member shall be chosen from section (iii) of the above list by the independent entity referred to in sub-paragraph (a) of this Article. No objections shall be made to any independent trade expert drawn from section (iii) of the above list;

(d) the independent trade expert drawn from section (iii) of the above list shall serve as the chairman of the panel. He shall take the necessary decisions to ensure an expeditious settlement of the dispute by the panel, for instance, whether the facts of the case require the panellists to meet and, if so, where such a meeting shall take place, taking into account the site of the inspection in question;

(e) if the parties to the dispute so agree, one independent trade expert could be selected from section (iii) of the above list by the independent entity referred to in sub-paragraph (a) of this Article to review the dispute in question. This expert shall take the necessary decisions to ensure an expeditious settlement of the dispute, for instance taking into account the site of the inspection in question;

(f) the object of the review shall be to establish whether, in the course of the inspection in dispute, the parties to the dispute have complied with the provisions of this Agreement. The procedures shall be expeditious and provide the opportunity for both parties to present their views in person or in writing;

(g) decisions by a three-member panel shall be taken by majority vote. The decision on the dispute shall be rendered within eight working days of the request for independent review and be communicated to the parties to the dispute. This time-limit could be extended upon agreement by the parties to the dispute. The panel or independent trade expert shall apportion the costs, based on the merits of the case;

(h) the decision of the panel shall be binding upon the preshipment inspection entity and the exporter which are parties to the dispute.

Article 5
Notification

Members shall submit to the WTO Secretariat copies of their laws and regulations by which they put this Agreement into force, as well as copies of any other laws and regulations relating to preshipment inspection when the Agreement comes into force for the Member concerned. No changes in the laws and regulations relating to preshipment inspection shall be enforced before such changes have been officially published. They shall be notified to the WTO Secretariat immediately after their publication. The WTO Secretariat shall inform the Members of the availability of this information.

Article 6
Review

At the end of the second year from the entry into force of the Agreement Establishing the WTO and every three years thereafter, the Ministerial Conference shall review the provisions, implementation and operation of this Agreement, taking into account the objectives thereof and experience gained in its operation. As a result of such review, the Ministerial Conference may amend the provisions of the Agreement.

Article 7
Consultation

Members shall consult with other Members upon request with respect to any matter affecting the operation of this Agreement. In such cases, the provisions of Article XI of the GATT 1994, as elaborated and applied by the Understanding on Rules and Procedures Governing the Settlement of Disputes, are applicable to this Agreement.

Article 8
Dispute Settlement

Any disputes among Members regarding the operation of this Agreement shall be subject to the provisions of Article XXIII of the GATT 1994, as elaborated and applied by the Understanding on Rules and Procedures Governing the Settlement of Disputes.

Article 9
Final Provisions

1. Members shall take the necessary measures for the implementation of the present Agreement.

2. Members shall ensure that their laws and regulations shall not be contrary to the provisions of this Agreement.

AGREEMENT ON RULES OF ORIGIN

Members,

Noting that Ministers on 20 September 1986 agreed that "the Uruguay Round of Multilateral Trade Negotiations shall aim to bring about further liberalization and expansion of world trade, strengthen the role of the GATT and increase the responsiveness of the GATT system to the invoking international economic environment";

Desiring to further the objectives of the GATT 1994;

Recognizing that clear and predictable rules of origin and their application facilitate the flow of international trade;

Desiring to ensure that rules of origin themselves do not create unnecessary obstacles to trade;

Desiring to ensure that rules of origin do not nullify or impair the rights of Members under the GATT 1994;

Recognizing that it is desirable to provide transparency of laws, regulations, and practices regarding rules of origin;

Desiring to ensure that rules of origin are prepared and applied in an impartial, transparent, predictable, consistent and neutral manner;

Recognizing the availability of a consultation mechanism and procedures for the speedy, effective and equitable resolution of disputes arising under this Agreement;

Desiring to harmonize and clarify rules of origin;

Hereby agree as follows:

PART I
DEFINITIONS AND COVERAGE

Article 1
Rules of Origin

1. For the purposes of Parts I to IV of this Agreement, rules of origin shall be defined as those laws, regulations and administrative determinations of general application applied by any Member to determine the country of origin of goods provided such rules of origin are not related to contractual or autonomous trade regimes leading to the granting of tariff preferences going beyond the application of Article I:1 of the GATT 1994.

2. Rules of origin referred to in paragraph 1 shall include all rules of origin used in non-preferential commercial policy instruments, such as in the application of: most-favoured-nation treatment under Articles I, II, III, XI and XIII of the GATT 1994; anti-dumping and countervailing duties under Article VI of the GATT 1994; safeguard measures under Article XIX of the GATT 1994; origin marking requirements under Article IX of the GATT 1994; and any discriminatory quantitative restrictions or tariff quotas. They shall also include rules of origin used for government procurement and trade statistics.[61]

PART II
DISCIPLINES AFTER THE TRANSITION PERIOD

Article 2
Disciplines During the Transition Period

Until the work programme for the harmonization of rules of origin set out in Part IV below is completed, Members shall ensure that :

(a) when they issue administrative determinations of general application, the requirements to be fulfilled are clearly defined. In particular:

– in cases where the criterion of change of tariff classification is applied, such a rule of origin, and any exceptions to the rule,

---

[61] It is understood that this provision is without prejudice to those determinations made for purposes of defining "domestic industry" or like "products of domestic industry" or similar terms wherever they apply.

must clearly specify the subheadings or headings within the tariff nomenclature that are addressed by the rule;

- in cases where the *ad valorem* percentage criterion is applied, the method for calculating this percentage shall also be indicated in the rules of origin;
- in cases where the criterion of manufacturing or processing operation is prescribed, the operation that confers origin on the good concerned shall be precisely specified;

(b) notwithstanding the measure or instrument of commercial policy to which they are linked, their rules of origin are not used as instruments to pursue trade objectives directly or indirectly;

(c) rules of origin shall not themselves create restrictive, distorting, or disruptive effects on international trade. They shall not pose unduly strict requirements or require the fulfilment of a certain condition not related to manufacturing or processing, as a prerequisite for the determination of the country of origin. However, costs not directly related to manufacturing or processing may be included for the purposes of the application of an *ad valorem* percentage criterion consistent with sub-paragraph (a) above;

(d) the rules of origin that they apply to imports and exports are not more stringent than the rules of origin they apply to determine whether or not a good is domestic and shall not discriminate between other Members, irrespective of the affiliation of the manufacturers of the good concerned;[62]

(e) their rules of origin are administered in a consistent, uniform, impartial and reasonable manner;

(f) their rules of origin are based on a positive standard. Rules of origin that state what does not confer origin (negative standard) are permissible as part of a clarification of a positive standard or in individual cases where a positive determination of origin is not necessary;

(g) their laws, regulations, judicial and administrative rulings of general application relating to rules of origin are published as if they were subject to, and in accordance with, the provisions of Article X:1 of the GATT 1994;

(h) upon the request of an exporter, importer or any person with a justifiable cause, assessments of the origin they would accord to a

[62] With respect to rules of origin applied for the purposes of government procurement, this provision shall not create obligations additional to those already assumed by Members under the GATT 1994.

good are issued as soon as possible but no later than 150 days[63] after a request for such an assessment provided that all necessary elements have been submitted. Requests for such assessments shall be accepted before trade in the good concerned begins and may be accepted at any later point in time. Such assessments shall remain valid for three years provided that the facts and conditions, including the rules of origin, under which they have been made remain comparable. Provided that the parties concerned are informed in advance, such assessments will no longer be valid when a decision contrary to the assessment is made in a review as referred to in sub-paragraph (j) below. Such assessments shall be made publicly available subject to the provisions of sub-paragraph (k) below;

(i) when introducing changes to their rules of origin or new rules of origin, they shall not apply such changes retroactively as defined in, and without prejudice to, their laws or regulations;

(j) any administrative action which they take in relation to the determination of origin is reviewable promptly by judicial, arbitral or administrative tribunals or procedures, independent of the authority issuing the determination, which can effect the modification or reversal of the determination;

(k) all information that is by nature confidential or that is provided on a confidential basis for the purpose of the application of rules of origin is treated as strictly confidential by the authorities concerned, which shall not disclose it without the specific permission of the person or government providing such information, except to the extent that it may be required to be disclosed in the context of judicial proceedings.

Article 3

Disciplines after the Transition Period

Taking into account the aim of all Members to achieve as a result of the harmonization work programme set out in Part IV below, the establishment of harmonized rules of origin, the Members shall ensure, upon the implementation of the results of the harmonization work programme that :

(a) they apply rules of origin equally for all purposes as set out in Article 1 above;

(b) under their rules of origin, the country to be determined as the

[63] In respect of requests made during the first year from entry into force of the Agreement Establishing the WTO Members shall only be required to issue these assessments as soon as possible.

origin of a particular good is either the country where the good has been wholly obtained or, when more than one country is concerned in the production of the good, the country where the last substantial transformation has been carried out;

(c) the rules of origin that they apply to imports and exports are not more stringent than the rules of origin they apply to determine whether or not a good is domestic and shall not discriminate between other Members, irrespective of the affiliation of the manufacturers of the good concerned;

(d) the rules of origin are administered in a consistent, uniform, impartial and reasonable manner;

(e) their laws, regulations judicial and administrative rulings of general application relating to rules of origin are published as if they were subject to, and in accordance with, the provisions of Article X:1 of the GATT 1994;

(f) upon the request of an exporter, importer or any person with a justifiable cause, assessments of the origin they would accord to a good are issued as soon as possible but no later than 150 days after a request for such an assessment provided that all necessary elements have been submitted. Requests for such assessments shall be accepted before trade in the good concerned begins and may be accepted at any later point in time. Such assessments shall remain valid for three years provided that the facts and conditions, including the rules of origin, under which they have been made remain comparable. Provided that the parties concerned are informed in advance, such assessments will no longer be valid when a decision contrary to the assessment is made in a review as referred to in sub-paragraph (h) below. Such assessments shall be made publicly available subject to the provisions of sub-paragraph (i) below;

(g) when introducing changes to their rules of origin or new rules of origin, they shall not apply such changes retroactively as defined in, and without prejudice to, their laws or regulations;

(h) any administrative action which they take in relation to the determination of origin is reviewable promptly by judicial, arbitral or administrative tribunals or procedures, independent of the authority issuing the determination, which can effect the modification or reversal of the determination;

(i) all information which is by nature confidential or which is provided on a confidential basis for the purpose of the application of rules of origin is treated as strictly confidential by the authorities concerned, which shall not disclose it without the specific permission of the person or government providing such information, except to the extent that it may be required to be disclosed in the context of judicial proceedings.

PART III
PROCEDURAL ARRANGEMENTS ON NOTIFICATION, REVIEW, CONSULTATION AND DISPUTE SETTLEMENT

Article 4
Institutions

There shall be established under this Agreement:

1. a Committee on Rules of Origin (hereinafter referred to as "the Committee") composed of the representatives from each of the Members. The Committee shall elect its own Chairman and shall meet as necessary, but not less than once a year, for the purpose of affording Members the opportunity to consult on matters relating to the operation of Parts I, II, III and IV of the Agreement or the furtherance of the objectives set out in these Parts and to carry out such other responsibilities assigned to it under this Agreement or by the Council for Trade in Goods. Where appropriate, the Committee shall request information and advice from the Technical Committee (referred to in paragraph 2 below) on matters related to this Agreement. The Committee may also request such other work from the Technical Committee as it considers appropriate for the furtherance of the above-mentioned objectives of this Agreement. The WTO Secretariat shall act as the Secretariat to the Committee;

2. a Technical Committee on Rules of Origin (hereinafter referred to as "the Technical Committee") under the auspices of the Customs Co-operation Council (CCC) as set out in Annex I of this Agreement. The Technical Committee shall carry out the technical work called for in Part IV and prescribed in Annex I of this Agreement. Where appropriate, the Technical Committee shall request information and advice from the Committee on matters related to this Agreement. The Technical Committee may also request such other work from the Committee as it considers appropriate for the furtherance of the above-mentioned objectives of the Agreement. The CCC secretariat shall act as the Secretariat to the Technical Committee.

Article 5
Information and Procedures for Modification and Introduction of New Rules of Origin

1. Upon entry into force of the Agreement Establishing the WTO, each

Member shall provide to the WTO Secretariat within 90 days its rules of origin, judicial decisions, and administrative rulings of general application relating to rules of origin in effect on the date of entry into force of the Agreement Establishing the WTO. If by inadvertence a rule of origin has not been provided, the Member concerned shall provide it immediately after this fact becomes known. Lists of information received and available with the MTO Secretariat shall be circulated to the Members by the WTO Secretariat.

2. During the period referred to in Article 2 above, Members introducing modifications, other than *de minimis* modifications, to their rules of origin or introducing new rules of origin, which, for the purpose of this Article, shall include any rule of origin referred to in paragraph 1 above and not provided to the WTO Secretariat, shall publish a notice to that effect at least 60 days before the entry into force of the modified or new rule in such a manner as to enable interested parties to become acquainted with the intention to modify a rule of origin or to introduce a new rule of origin, unless exceptional circumstances arise or threaten to arise for a Member. In these exceptional cases, the Member shall publish the modified or new rule as soon as possible.

Article 6

Review

1. The Committee shall review annually the implementation and operation of Parts I1 and III of this Agreement having regard to its objectives. The Committee shall annually inform the Council for Trade in Goods of developments during the period covered by such reviews.

2. The Committee shall review the provisions of Parts I, II and III above and propose amendments as necessary to reflect the results of the harmonization work programme.

3. The Committee, in cooperation with the Technical Committee, shall set up a mechanism to consider and propose amendments to the results of the harmonization work programme, taking into account the objectives and principles set out in Article 9. This may include instances where the rules need to be made more operational or need to be updated to take into account new production processes as affected by any technological change.

Article 7

Consultation

The provisions of Article XXII of the GATT 1994, as elaborated and applied by the Understanding on Rules and Procedures Governing the Settlement of Disputes, are applicable to this Agreement.

Article 8
Dispute Settlement

The provisions of Article XXIII of the GATT 1994, as elaborated and applied by the Understanding on Rules and Procedures Governing the Settlement of Disputes, are applicable to this Agreement.

PART IV
HARMONIZATION OF RULES OF ORIGIN
Article 9

Objectives and Principles

1. With the objectives of harmonizing rules of origin and, *inter alia,* providing more certainty in the conduct of world trade, the Ministerial Conference shall undertake the work programme set out below in conjunction with the CCC, on the basis of the following principles :

(a) rules of origin should be applied equally for all purposes as set out in Article 1 above:

(b) rules of origin should provide for the country to be determined as the origin of a particular good to be either the country where the good has been wholly obtained or, when more than one country is concerned in the production of the good, the country where the last substantial transformation has been carried out;

(c) rules of origin should be objective, understandable and predictable;

(d) notwithstanding the measure or instrument to which they may be linked, rules of origin should not be used as instruments to pursue trade objectives directly or indirectly. They should not themselves create restrictive, distorting or disruptive effects on international trade. They should not pose unduly strict requirements or require the fulfilment of a certain condition not relating to manufacturing or processing as a prerequisite for the determination of the country of origin. However, costs not directly related to manufacturing or processing may be included for purposes of the application of an *ad valorem* percentage criterion;

(e) rules of origin should be administrable in a consistent, uniform, impartial and reasonable manner;

(f) rules of origin should be coherent;

(g) rules of origin should be based on a positive standard. Negative standards may be used to clarify a positive standard.

Work Programme

2. (a) The work programme shall be initiated as soon after the entry into force of the Agreement Establishing the WTO as possible and will be completed within three years of initiation.

(b) The Committee and the Technical Committee provided for in Article 4 of this Agreement shall be the appropriate bodies to conduct this work.

(c) To provide for detailed input by the CCC, the Committee shall request the Technical Committee to provide its interpretations and opinions resulting from the work described below on the basis of the principles listed in paragraph 1 of this Article. To ensure timely completion of the work programme for harmonization, such work shall be conducted on a product sector basis, as re-presented by various chapters or sections of the Harmonized System (HS) nomenclature.

(i) *Wholly Obtained and Minimal Operations or Processes*

The Technical Committee shall develop harmonized definitions of :

- the goods that are to be considered as being wholly obtained in one country. This work shall be as detailed as possible;
- minimal operations or processes that do not by themselves confer origin to a good.

The results of this work shall be submitted to the Committee within three months of receipt of the request from the Committee.

(ii) *Substantial Transformation – Change in Tariff Classification*

- The Technical Committee shall consider and elaborate upon, on the basis of the criterion of substantial transformation, the use of change in tariff subheading or heading when developing rules of origin for particular products or a product sector and, if appropriate, the minimum change within the nomenclature that meets this criterion.
- The Technical Committee shall divide the above work on a product basis taking into account the chapters or sections of the HS nomenclature, so as to submit results of its work to the Committee at least on a quarterly basis. The Technical Committee shall complete the above work within one year and three months from receipt of the request of the Committee.

(iii) *Substantial Transformation –Supplementary Criteria*

Upon completion of the work under (ii) for each product sector or individual product category where the exclusive use of the HS nomenclature does not allow for the expression of substantial transformation, the Technical Committee:

– shall consider and elaborate upon, on the basis of the criterion of substantial transformation, the use, in a supplementary or exclusive manner, of other requirements, including *ad valorem* percentages[64] and/or manufacturing or processing operations[65], when developing rules of origin for particular products or a product sector;

— may provide explanations for its proposals;

– shall divide the above work on a product basis taking into account the chapters or sections of the HS nomenclature, so as to submit results of its work to the Committee at least on a quarterly basis. The Technical Committee shall complete the above work within two years and three months of receipt of the request from the Committee.

Rôle of the Committee

3. On the basis of the principles listed in paragraph 1 of this Article:

(a) the Committee shall consider the interpretations and opinions of the Technical Committee periodically in accordance with the time-frames provided in (i), (ii) and (iii) above with a view to endorsing such interpretations and opinions. The Committee may request the Technical Committee to refine or elaborate its work and/or to develop new approaches. To assist the Technical Committee, the Committee should provide its reasons for requests for additional work and, as appropriate, suggest alternative approaches;

(b) upon completion of all the work identified in (i), (ii) and (iii) above, the Committee shall consider the results in terms of their overall coherence.

Results of the Harmonization Work Programme and Subsequent Work

4. The Ministerial Conference shall establish the results of the harmonization work programme in annex as an integral part of this Agreement.[66]

[64] If the *ad valorem* criterion is prescribed, the method for calculating this percentage shall also be indicated in the rules of origin.

[65] If the criterion of manufacturing or processing operation is prescribed, the operation that confers origin on the product concerned shall be precisely specified.

[66] At the same time, consideration shall be given to arrangements concerning the settlement of disputes relating to customs classification.

The Ministerial Conference shall establish a time for the entry into force of this annex.

ANNEX I

Technical Committee on Rules of Origin

Responsibilities

1. The on-going responsibilities of the Technical Committee shall include the following :

(a) at the request of any member of the technical Committee, to examine specific technical problems arising in the day-to-day administration of the rules of origin of Members and to give advisory opinions on appropriate solutions based upon the facts presented;

(b) to furnish information and advice on any matters concerning the origin determination of goods as may be requested by any Member or the Committee;

(c) to prepare and circulate periodic reports on the technical aspects of the operation and status of this Agreement; and

(d) to review annually the technical aspects of the implementa'.. and operation of Parts II and III of this Agreement.

2. The Technical Committee shall exercise such other responsi-bilities as the Committee may request of it.

3. The Technical Committee shall attempt to conclude its work on specific matters, especially those referred to it by Members or the Committee, in a reasonably short period of time.

Representation

4. Each Member shall have the right to be represented on the Technical Committee. Each Member may nominate one delegate and one or more alternates to be its representatives on the Technical Committee. Such a Member so represented on the Technical Committee is hereinafter referred to as a "member" of the Technical Committee. Representatives of members of the Technical Committee may be assisted by advisers at meetings of the Technical Committee. The WTO Secretariat may also attend such meetings with observer status.

5. Members of the CCC who are not WTO Members may be represented at meetings of the Technical Committee by one delegate and one or more alternates. Such representatives shall attend meetings of the Technical Committee as observers.

6. Subject to the approval of the Chairman of the Technical Committee, the Secretary-General of the CCC (hereinafter referred to as "the Secretary-General") may invite representatives of governments which are neither WTO Members nor members of the CCC and representatives of international governmental and trade organizations to attend meetings of the Technical Committee as observers.

7. Nominations of delegates, alternates and advisers to meetings of the technical Committee shall be made to the Secretary-General.

Meetings

8. The Technical Committee shall meet as necessary, but not less than once a year.

Procedures

9. The Technical Committee shall elect its own Chairman and shall establish its own procedures.

ANNEX II

Common Declaration with Regard to Preferential Rules of Origin

1. Recognizing that some Members apply preferential rules of origin, distinct from non-preferential rules of origin, the Members hereby agree as follows.

2. For the purposes of this Common Declaration, preferential rules of origin shall be defined as those laws, regulations and administrative determinations of general application applied by any Member to determine whether goods qualify for preferential treatment under contractual or autonomous trade regimes leading to the granting of tariff preferences going beyond the application of Article I : 1 of the GATT 1994.

3. The Members agree to ensure that:

(a) when they issue administrative determinations of general application, the requirements to be fulfilled, are clearly defined. In particular:

- in cases where the criterion of change of tariff classification is applied, such a preferential rule of origin, and any exceptions to the rule, must clearly specify the sub-headings or headings within the tariff nomenclature that are addressed by the rule;
- in cases where the *ad valorem* percentage criterion is applied, the method for calculating this percentage shall also be indicated in the preferential rules of origin;
- in cases where the criterion of manufacturing or processing operation is prescribed, the operation that confers preferential origin shall be precisely specified;

(b) their preferential rules of origin are based on a positive standard. Preferential rules of origin that state what does not confer preferential origin (negative standard) are permissible as part of a clarification of a positive standard or in individual cases where a positive determination of preferential origin is not necessary;

(c) their laws regulations, judicial and administrative rulings of general application relating to preferential rules of origin are published as if they were subject to, and in accordance with, the provisions of Article X:1 of the GATT 1994:

(d) upon request of an exporter, importer or any person with a justifiable cause, assessments of the preferential origin they would accord to a good are issued as soon as possible but no later than 150 days[67] after a request for such an assessment provided that all necessary elements have been submitted. Requests for such assessments shall be accepted before trade in the good concerned begins and may be accepted at any later point in time. Such assessments shall remain valid for three years provided that the facts and conditions, including the preferential rules of origin, under which they have been made remain comparable. Provided that the parties concerned are informed in advance, such assessments will no longer be valid when a decision contrary to the assessment is made in a review as referred to in sub-paragraph (f) below. Such assessments shall be made publicly available subject to the provisions of sub-paragraph (g) below;

(e) when introducing changes to their preferential rules of origin or new preferential rules of origin, they shall not apply such changes retroactively as defined in, and without prejudice to, their laws or regulations;

(f) any administrative action which they take in relation to the determination of preferential origin is reviewable promptly by judicial arbitral or administrative tribunals or procedures, independent of the authority issuing the determination, which can effect the modification or reversal of the determination;

(g) all information that is by nature confidential or that is provided on a confidential basis for the purpose of the application of preferential rules of origin is treated as strictly confidential by the authorities concerned, which shall not disclose it without the specific permission of the person or government providing such information, except

[67] In respect of requests made during the first year from entry into force of the Agreement Establishing the WTO Members shall only be required to issue these assessments as soon as possible.

to the extent that it may be required to be disclosed in the context of judicial proceedings.

4. The Members agree to provide to the WTO Secretariat promptly their preferential rules of origin, including a listing of the preferential arrangements to which they apply, judicial decisions, and administrative rulings of general application relating to their preferential rules of origin in effect on the date of entry into force of this Common Declaration. Furthermore, Members agree to provide any modifications to their preferential rules of origin or new preferential rules of origin as soon as possible to the WTO Secretariat. Lists of information received and available with the WTO Secretariat shall be circulated to the Members by the WTO Secretariat.

AGREEMENT ON IMPORT LICENSING PROCEDURES

Members,

Having regard to the Multilateral Trade Negotiations; *Desiring* to further the objectives of the GATT 1994;

Taking into account the particular trade, development and financial needs of developing country Members;

Recognizing the usefulness of automatic import licensing for certain purposes and that such licensing should not be used to restrict trade;

Recognizing that import licensing may be employed to administer measures such as those adopted pursuant to the relevant provisions of the GATT 1994;

Recognizing the provisions of the GATT 1994 as they apply to import licensing procedures;

Desiring to ensure that import licensing procedures are not utilized in a manner contrary to the principles and obligations of the GATT 1994;

Recognizing that the flow of international trade could be impeded by the inappropriate use import licensing procedures;

Convinced that import licensing, particularly non-automatic import licensing, should be implemented in a transparent and predictable manner;

Recognizing that non-automatic licensing procedures should be no more administratively burdensome than absolutely necessary to administer the relevant measure;

Desiring to simplify, and bring transparency to, the administrative procedures and practices used in international trade, and to ensure the fair and equitable application and administration of such procedures and practices;

Desiring to provide for a consultative mechanism and the speedy, effective and equitable resolution of disputes arising under this Agreement;

Hereby agree as follows :

Article 1

General Provisions

1. For the purpose of this Agreement, import licensing is defined as administrative procedures[68] used for the operation of import licensing regimes requiring the submission of an application or other documentation (other than that required for customs purposes) to the relevant administrative body as a prior condition for importation into the customs territory of the importing Member.

Members shall ensure that the administrative procedures used to implement import licensing regimes are in conformity with the relevant provisions of the GATT 1994 including its annexes and protocols, as interpreted by this Agreement, with a view to preventing trade distortions that may arise from an inappropriate operation of those procedures, taking into account the economic development purposes and financial and trade needs of developing country Members.[69]

3. The rules for import licensing procedures shall be neutral in application and administered in a fair and equitable manner.

4. (a) The rules and all information concerning procedures for the submission of applications, including the eligibility of persons, firms and institutions to make such applications, the administrative body(ies) to be approached, and the lists of products subject to the licensing requirement shall be published in the sources notified to the Committee established under Article 4, in such a manner as to enable governments[70] and traders to become acquainted with them. Such publication shall take place, whenever practicable, twenty-one days prior to the effective date or the requirement but in all events not later than such effective date. Any exception, derogations or changes in or from the rules concerning licensing procedures or the list of products subject to import licensing shall also be published in the same manner and within the same time periods as specified above. Copies of these publications shall also be made available to the WTO Secretariat.

(b) Members who wish to make comments in writing shall be provided the opportunity to discuss these comments upon request. The concerned

---

68 Those procedures referred to as "licensing" as well as other similar administrative procedures.

69 Nothing in this Agreement shall be taken as implying that the basis scope or duration of a measure being implemented by a licensing procedure is subject to question under this Agreement.

70 For the purpose of this Agreement, the term "governments" is deemed to include the competent authorities of the European Communities.

Member shall give due consideration to these comments and results of discussion.

5. Application forms and, where applicable, renewal forms shall be as simple as possible. Such documents and information as are considered strictly necessary for the proper functioning of the licensing regime may be required on application.

6. Application procedures and, where applicable, renewal procedures shall be as simple as possible. Applicants shall be allowed a reasonable period for the submission of licence applications. Where there is a closing date, this period should be at least twenty-one days with provision for extension in circumstances where insufficient applications have been received within this period. Applicants shall have to approach only one administrative body in connection with an application. Where it is strictly indispensable to approach more than one administrative body, applicants shall not need to approach more than three administrative bodies.

7. Application shall be refused for minor documentation errors which do not alter basic data contained therein. No penalty greater than necessary to serve merely as a warning shall be imposed in respect of any omission or mistake in documentation or procedures which is obviously made without fraudulent intent or gross negligence.

8. Licensed imports shall not be refused for minor variations in value, quantity or weight from the amount designated on the licence due to differences occurring during shipment, differences incidental to bulk loading and other minor differences consistent with normal commercial practice.

9. The foreign exchange necessary to pay for licensed imports shall be made available to licence holders on the same basis as to importers of goods not requiring import licences.

10. With regard to security exceptions, the provisions of Article XXI of the GATT 1994 apply.

11. The provisions of this Agreement shall not require any Member to disclose confidential information which would impede law enforcement or otherwise be contrary to the public interest or would prejudice the legitimate commercial interests of particular enterprises, public or private.

Article 2

Automatic Import Licensing[71]

1. Automatic import licensing is defined as import licensing where

[71] Those import licensing procedures requiring a security which have no restrictive effects on imports are to be considered as falling within the scope of paragraphs 1 and 2 of this Article.

approval of the application is granted in all cases, and in accordance with the requirements of paragraph 2(a) of this Article.

2. The following provisions,[72] in addition to those in paragraphs 1 to 11 of Article 1 and paragraph 1 of the present Article, shall apply to automatic import licensing procedures:

(a) automatic licensing procedures shall not be administered in such a manner as to have restricting effects on imports subject to automatic licensing. Automatic licensing procedures shall be deemed to have trade restricting effects unless, *inter alia:*

(i) any person, firm or institution which fulfils the legal requirements of the importing Member for engaging in import operations involving products subject to automatic licensing is equally eligible to apply for and to obtain import licences;

(ii) applications for licences may be submitted on any working day prior to the customs clearance of the goods;

(iii) applications for licences when submitted in appropriate and complete form are approved immediately on receipt, to the extent administratively feasible, but within a maximum of ten working days;

(b) Members recognize that automatic import licensing may be necessary whenever other appropriate procedures are not available. Automatic import licensing may be maintained as long as the circumstances which gave rise to its introduction prevail and as long as its underlying administrative purposes cannot be achieved in a more appropriate way.

Article 3

Non-automatic Import Licensing

1. The following processions, in addition to those in paragraphs 1 to 11 of Article 1, shall apply to non-automatic import licensing procedures. Non-automatic import licensing procedures are defined as import licensing not falling within the definition contained in paragraph 1 of Article 2.

2. Non-automatic licensing shall not have trade restrictive or distortive effects on imports additional to those caused by the imposition of the restriction. Non-automatic licensing procedures shall correspond in scope and duration

---

[72] A developing country Member, other than a developing country Member which was a Party to the Agreement on Import Licensing Procedures 1979, which has specific difficulties with the requirements of sub-paragraphs (a)(ii) and (a)(iii) may, upon notification to the Committee referred to in Article 4, delay the application of these sub-paragraphs by not more than two years from the date of entry into force of the Agreement Establishing the WTO for such Member.

to the measure they are used to implement, and shall be no more administratively burdensome than absolutely necessary to administer the measure.

3. In the case of licensing requirements for purposes other than the implementation of quantitative restrictions, Members shall publish sufficient information for other Members and traders to know the basis for granting and/or allocating licences.

4. Where a Member provides the possibility for persons, firms or institutions to request exceptions or derogations from a licensing requirement, it shall include this fact in the information published under paragraph 4 of Article 1 as well as information on how to make such a request and, to the extent possible, an indication of the circumstances under which requests would be considered.

5. (a) Members shall provide, upon the request of any Member having an interest in the trade in the product concerned, all relevant information concerning:

(i) the administration of the restrictions;

(ii) the import licences granted over a recent period;

(iii) the distribution of such licences among supplying countries;

(iv) where practicable, import statistics (*i e* value and/or volume) with respect to the products subject to import licensing. Developing country Members would not be expected to take additional administrative or financial burdens on this account;

(b) Members administering quotas by means of licensing shall publish the overall amount of quotas to be applied by quantity and/or value, the opening and closing dates of quotas, and any change thereof, within the time periods specified in paragraph 4 of Article 1 and in such a manner as to enable governments and traders to become acquainted with them;

(c) in the case of quotas allocated among supplying countries, the Member applying the restrictions shall promptly inform all other Members having an interest in supplying the product concerned of the shares in the quota currently allocated, by quantity or value, to the various supplying countries and shall publish this information within the time periods specified in paragraph 4 of Article 1 and in such a manner as to enable governments and traders to become acquainted with them;

(d) where situations arise which make it necessary to provide for an early opening date of quotas, the information referred to in paragraph 4 of Article 1 should be published within the time periods specified in paragraph 4 of Article 1 and in such a manner as to enable governments and traders to become acquainted with them;

(e) any person, firm or institution which fulfils the legal and administrative requirements of the importing Member shall be equally eligible to apply and to be considered for a licence. If the licence application is not approved, the applicant shall, on request, be given the reason therefor and shall have a right of appeal or review in accordance with the domestic legislation or procedures of the importing Member;

(f) the period for processing applications shall, except when not possible for reasons outside the control of the Member, not be longer than thirty days if applications are considered as and when received, *i.e.* on a first-come first-served basis, and no longer than sixty days if all applications ate considered simultaneously. In the latter case, the period for processing applications shall be considered to begin on the day following the closing date of the announced application period;

(g) the period of licence validity shall be of reasonable duration and not be so short as to preclude imports. The period of licence validity shall not preclude imports from distant sources, except in special cases where imports are necessary to meet unforeseen short-term requirements;

(h) when administering quotas, Members shall not prevent importation from being effected in accordance with the issued licences, and shall not discourage the full utilization of quotas;

(i) when issuing licences, Members shall take into account the desirability of issuing licences for products in economic quantities;

(j) in allocating licences, the Member should consider the import performance of the applicant. In this regard, consideration should be given as to whether licences issued to applicants in the past have been fully utilized during a recent representative period. In cases where licences have not been fully utilized, the Member shall examine the reasons for this and take these reasons into consideration when allocating new licences. Consideration shall also be given to ensuring a reasonable distribution of licences to new importers, taking into account the desirability of issuing licences for products in economic quantities. In this regard special consideration should be given to those importers importing products originating in developing country Members and, in particular, the least-developed country Members;

(k) in the case of quotas administered through licence which are not allocated among supplying countries, licence holders[73] shall be free to choose the sources of imports. In the case of quotas allocated among supplying countries, the licence shall clearly stipulate the country or countries;

(l) in applying paragraph 8 of Article 1, compensating adjustments may be made in future licence allocations where imports exceeded a previous licence level.

Article 4
Institutions

There shall be established under this Agreement a Committee on Import Licensing composed of representatives from each of the Members (referred to in this Agreement as "the Committee"). The Committee shall elect its own Chairman and Vice-Chairman and shall meet as necessary for the purpose of affording Members the opportunity of consulting on any matters relating to the operation of this Agreement or the furtherance of its objectives.

Article 5
Notification

1. Members which institute licensing procedures or changes in these procedures shall notify the Committee of such within sixty days of publication.

2. Notifications of the institution of import licensing procedures shall include the following information:

(a) list of products subject to licensing procedures;

(b) contact point for information on eligibility;

(c) administrative body(ies) for submission of applications;

(d) date and name of publication where licensing procedures are published;

(e) indication of whether the licensing procedure is automatic or non-automatic according to definitions contained in Articles 2 and 3;

(f) in the case of automatic import licensing procedures, their administrative purpose;

(g) in the case of non-automatic import licensing procedures, indication of the measure being implemented through the licensing procedure; and

(h) expected duration of the licensing procedure if this can be estimated

---

[73] Sometimes referred to as "quota holders".

with some probability, and if not, reason why this information cannot be provided.

3. Notifications of changes in import licensing procedures shall indicate the elements mentioned above, if changes in such occur.

4. Members shall notify the Committee of the publication(s) in which the information required in paragraph 4 of Article 1 will be published.

5. Any interested Member which considers that another Member has not notified the institution of a licensing procedure or changes therein in accordance with the provisions of paragraphs 1 to 3 of this Article may bring the matter to the attention of such other Member. If notification is not made promptly thereafter, such Member may itself notify the licensing procedure or changes therein, including all relevant and available information.

Article 6
Consultation and Dispute Settlement

Consultations and the settlement of disputes with respect to any matter affecting the operation of this Agreement shall be subject to the provisions of Articles XXII and XXIII of the GATT 1994, as elaborated and applied by the Understanding on Rules and Procedures Governing the Settlement of Disputes.

Article 7
Review

1. The Committee shall review as necessary, but at least once every two years, the implementation and operation of this Agreement, taking into account the objectives thereof, and the rights and obligations contained therein.

2. As a basis for the Committee review, the WTO Secretariat shall prepare a factual report based on information provided under Article 5, responses to the annual questionnaire on import licensing procedures[74] and other relevant reliable information which is available to it. This report shall provide a synopsis of the aforementioned information, in particular indicating any changes or developments during the period under review, and including any other information as agreed by the Committee.

3. Members undertake to complete the annual questionnaire on import licensing procedures promptly and in full.

4. The Committee shall inform the Council for Trade in Goods of developments during the period covered by such reviews.

---

[74] Originally circulated as GATT, 1947 document L/3515 of 23 March 1971.

Article 8
Final Provisions

Reservations

1. Reservations may not be entered in respect of any of the provisions of this Agreement without the consent of the other Members.

Domestic Legislation

2. (a) Each Member shall ensure, not later than the date of entry into force of the Agreement Establishing the WTO for it, the conformity of its laws, regulations and administrative procedures with the provisions of this Agreement.

   (b) Each Member shall inform the Committee of any changes in its laws and regulations relevant to this Agreement and in the administration of such laws and regulations.

AGREEMENT ON SUBSIDIES AND COUNTERVAILING MEASURES

PART I : GENERAL

Article I
Definition of a Subsidy

1.1 For the purpose of this Agreement, a subsidy shall be deemed to exist if :

(a) (1) there is a financial contribution by a government or any public body within the territory of a Member (hereinafter referred to as "government"), *i.e.*, where:

(i) Government practice involves a direct transfer of funds (*e.g.*, grants, loans, and equity infusion), potential direct transfers of funds or liabilities (*e.g.*, loan guarantees);

(ii) government revenue that is otherwise due, is foregone or not collected (*e.g.*, fiscal incentives such as tax credits[75];

(iii) a government provides goods or services other than general infrastructure, or purchases goods;

(iv) a government makes payments to a funding mechanism, or entrusts or directs a private body to carry out one or more of

---

[75] In accordance with the provisions of Article XVI of the GATT 1994 (Note to Article XVI) and the provisions of Annexes I through III of this Agreement, the exemption of an exported producted from duties or taxes borne by the like product when destined for domestic consumption, or the remission of such duties or taxes in amount not in excess of those which have accrued, shall not be deemed to be a subsidy.

the type of functions illustrated in (i) to (iii) above which would normally be vested in the government and the practice, in no real sense, differs from practices normally followed by governments;

or

(a) (2) there is any form of income or price support in the sense of Article XVI of the GATT 1994;

and

(b) a benefit is thereby conferred.

1.2 A subsidy as defined in paragraph 1 above shall be subject to the provisions of Part II or shall be subject to the provisions of Part III or V of this Agreement only if such a subsidy is specific in accordance with the provisions of Article 2 below.

Article 2

Specificity

2.1 In order to determine whether a subsidy. as defined in paragraph 1 of Article 1 above is specific to an enterprise or industry or group of enterprises or industries (hereinafter referred to as "certain enterprises") within the jurisdiction of the granting authority, the following principles shall apply :

(a) Where the granting authority, or the legislation pursuant to which the granting authority operates, explicitly limits access to a subsidy to certain enterprises, such subsidy shall be specific.

(b) Where the granting authority, or the legislation pursuant to which the granting authority operates, establishes objective criteria or conditions[76] governing the eligibility for, and the amount of, a subsidy, specificity shall not exist, provided that the eligibility is automatic and that such criteria and conditions are strictly adhered to. The criteria or conditions must be clearly spelled out in law, regulation, or other official document, so as to be capable of verification.

(c) If, notwithstanding any appearance of non-specificity resulting from the application of the principles laid down in subparagraphs (a) and (b) above, there are reasons to believe that the subsidy may in fact be specific, other factors may be considered. Such factors are: use of a subsidy programme by a limited number of

[76] Objective criteria or conditions, as used herein, mean criteria or conditions which are neutral, which do not favour certain enterprises over others, and which are economic in nature and horizontal in application such as number of employees or size of enterprise.

certain enterprises, predominant use by certain enterprises, the granting of disproportionately large amounts of subsidy to certain enterprises, and the manner in which discretion has been exercised by the granting authority in the decision to grant a subsidy.[77] In applying this subparagraph, account shall be taken of the extent of diversification of economic activities within the jurisdiction of the granting authority, as well as of the length of time during which the subsidy programme has been in operation.

2.2 A subsidy which is limited to certain enterprises located within a designated geographical region within the jurisdiction of the granting authority will be specific. It is understood that the setting or change of generally applicable tax rates by all levels of government entitled to do so shall not be deemed to be a specific subsidy for the purposes of this Agreement.

2.3 Any subsidy falling under the provisions of Article 3 shall be deemed to be specific.

2.4 Any determination of specificity under the provisions of this Article shall be clearly substantiated on the basis of positive evidence.

PART II: PROHIBITED SUBSIDIES

Article 3
Prohibition

3.1 Except as provided in the Agreement on Agriculture, the following subsidies, within the meaning of Article 1 above, shall be prohibited :

(a) subsidies contingent, in law or in fact[78], whether solely or as one of several other conditions, upon export performance, including those illustrated in Annex I;[79]

(b) subsidies contingent, whether solely or as one of several other conditions, upon the use of domestic over imported goods.

3.2 Members shall not grant nor maintain subsidies referred to in paragraph 1.

---

[77] In this regard, information on the frequency with which applications for a subsidy are refused or approved and the reasons for such decisions shall, in particular, be considered.

[78] This standard is met when the facts demonstrate that the granting of a subsidy, without having been made legally contingent upon export performance, is in fact tied to actual or anticipated exportation or export earnings. The mere fact that a subsidy is accorded to enterprises which export shall not for that reason alone be considered to be an export subsidy within the meaning of this provision.

[79] Measures referred to in Annex I as not constituting export subsidies shall not be prohibited under this or any other provision of this Agreement.

Article 4
Remedies

4.1 Whenever a Member has reason to believe that a prohibited subsidy is being granted or maintained by another Member, such Member may request consultations with such other Member.

4.2 A request for consultations under paragraph 1 above shall include a statement of available evidence with regard to the existence and nature of the subsidy in question.

4.3 Upon request for consultations under paragraph 1 above, the Member believed to be granting or maintaining the subsidy in question shall enter into such consultations as quickly as possible. The purpose of the consultations shall be to clarify the facts of the situation and to arrive at a mutually acceptable solution.

4.4 If no mutually acceptable solution has been reached within thirty days[80] of the request for consultations, any Member party to such consultations may refer the matter to the Dispute Settlement Body[81] (the DSB) for the immediate establishment of a Panel, unless the DSB decides by consensus not to establish a panel.

4.5 Upon its establishment, the Panel may request the assistance of the Permanent Group of Experts (hereinafter referred to as "PGE") with regard to whether the measure in question is a prohibited subsidy. If so requested, the PGE shall immediately review the evidence with regard to the existence and nature of the measure in question and shall provide an opportunity for the Member granting or maintaining the measure to demonstrate that the measure in question is not a prohibited subsidy. The PGE shall report its conclusions to the Panel within a time limit determined by the Panel. The PGE's conclusions on the issue of whether or not the measure in question is a prohibited subsidy shall be accepted by the Panel without modification.

4.6 The Panel, established pursuant to paragraph 4 above, shall submit its final report to the Members party to the dispute. The report shall be circulated to all Members within ninety days of the date of the composition and the establishment of the Panel's terms of reference.

4.7 If the measure in question is found to be a prohibited subsidy, the Panel shall recommend that the subsidizing Member withdraw the subsidy without delay. In this regard, the Panel shall specify in its recommendation the time period within which the measure must be withdrawn.

---

[80] Any time periods mentioned in this Article may be extended by mutual agreement.

[81] As established in the Agreement Establishing the WTO and hereinafter referred to as the DSB.

4.8 Within thirty days of the issuance of the Panel's report to all Members, the report shall be adopted by the DSB unless one of the parties to the dispute formally notifies the DSB of its decision to appeal or the DSB decides by consensus not to adopt the report.

4.9 Where a panel report is appealed, the Appellate Body shall issue its decision within thirty days from the date when the party to the dispute formally notifies its intention to appeal. When the Appellate Body considers that it cannot provide its report within thirty days, it shall inform the DSB in writing of the reasons for the delay together with an estimate of the period within which it will submit its report. In no case shall the proceedings exceed sixty days. The appellate report shall be adopted by the DSB and unconditionally accepted by the parties to the dispute unless the DSB decides by consensus not to adopt the appellate report within twenty days following its issuance to the Members.[82]

4.10 In the event the recommendation of the DSB is not followed within the time period specified by the Panel, which shall commence from the date of adoption of the Panel's report or the Appellate Body's report, the DSB shall grant authorization to the complaining Member to take appropriate[83] countermeasures, unless the DSB decides by consensus to reject the request.

4.11 In the event a party to the dispute requests arbitration under paragraph 22.6 of the Understanding on Rules and Procedures Governing the Settlement of Disputes (the DSU), the arbitrator shall determine whether the countermeasures are appropriate.[84]

4.12 For purposes of disputes conducted pursuant to this Article, except for time periods specifically prescribed in this Article, time periods applicable under the DSU for the conduct of such disputes shall be half the time prescribed therein.

PART III: ACTIONABLE SUBSIDIES

Article 5

Trade Effects

5.1 No Member should cause, through the use of any subsidy referred to in paragraphs 1 and 2 of Article 1 above, adverse effects to the interests of other Members, *i.e*,:

---

[82] If a meeting of the DSB is not scheduled during this period, such a meeting of the DSB shall be held for this purpose.

[83] This expression is not meant to allow countermeasures that are disproportionate in light of the fact that the subsidies dealt with under these provisions are prohibited.

[84] This expression is not meant to allow countermeasures that are disproportionate in light of the fact that the subsidies dealt with under these provisions are prohibited.

(a) injury to the domestic industry of another Member;[85]

(b) nullification or impairment of benefits accruing directly or indirectly to other Members under the GATT 1994 in particular the benefits of concessions bound under Article II of the GATT 1994;[86]

(c) serious prejudice to the interests of another Member.[87]

This Article does not apply to subsidies maintained on agricultural products as provided in Article 13 of the Agreement on Agriculture.

Article 6
Serious Prejudice

6.1 Serious prejudice in the sense of Article 5(c) shall be deemed to exist in the case of:

(a) the total ad *valorem* subsidization[88] of a product exceeding 5 per' cent;[89]

(b) subsidies to cover operating losses sustained by an industry;

(c) subsidies to cover operating losses sustained by an enterprise, other than one-time measures which are non-recurrent and cannot be repeated for that enterprise and which are given merely to provide time for the development of long-term solutions and to avoid acute social problems;

(d) direct forgiveness of debt, *i.e.*, forgiveness of government-held debt, and grants to cover debt repayment.[90]

6.2 Notwithstanding the provisions of paragraph 1 above, serious prejudice shall not be found if the subsidizing Member demonstrates that the subsidy in question has not resulted in any of the effects enumerated in paragraph 3 below.

---

[85] Injury to the domestic industry is used here in the same sense as it is used in Part V of this Agreement.

[86] Nullification or impairment is used in the Agreement in the same sense as it is used in the relevant provisons of the GATT 1994, and the existence of such nullification or impairment shall be established in accordance with the practice of application of these provisions.

[87] Serious prejudice to the interests of another Member is used in this Agreement in the same sense as it is used in Article XVI:1 of the GATT 1994, and includes threat of serious prejudice.

[88] The total *ad valorem* subsidization shall be calculated in accordance with the provisions of Annex IV.

[89] Since it is anticipated that civil aircraft will be subject to specific multilateral rules, the threshold in this sub-paragraph does not apply to civil aircraft

[90] Members recognize that, where royalty-based financing for a civil aircraft programme is not being fully repaid due to the level of actual sales falling below the level of forecast sales, this does not in itself constitute serious prejudice for the purposes of this sub-paragraph.

6.3 Serious prejudice in the sense of Article 5(c) may arise in any case where one or several of the following apply:

(a) the effect of the subsidy is to displace or impede the imports of like product into the market of the subsidizing Member;

(b) the effect of the subsidy is to displace or impede the exports of like product of another Member from a third country market;

(c) the effect of the subsidy is a significant price undercutting by the subsidized products as compared with the price of a like product of another Member in the same market or significant price suppression, price depression or lost sales in the same market;

(d) the effect of the subsidy is an increase in the world market share of the subsidizing Member in a particular subsidized primary product or commodity[91] as compared to the average share it had during the previous period of 3 years and this increase must follow a consistent trend over a period when subsidies have been granted.

6.4 For the purpose of paragraph 3(b) above, displacing or impeding exports shall include any case in which, subject to the provisions of paragraph 7 below, it has been demonstrated to the Committee that there has been a change in relative shares of the market to the disadvantage of the non-subsidized like product (over an appropriately representative period of, in normal circumstances, at least one year, sufficient to demonstrate clear trends in the development of the market for the product concerned). "Change in relative shares of the market" shall include any of the following situations: (i) there is an increase in the market Share of the subsidized product; (ii) the market share of the subsidized product remains constant in circumstances in which, in the absence of the subsidy, it would have declined: (iii) the market share of the subsidized product declines, but at a slower rate than would have been the case in the absence of the subsidy.

6.5 For the purpose of paragraph 3(c) above, price undercutting shall include any case in which it has been demonstrated to the Committee through comparing prices of the subsidized product with prices of non-subsidized like products supplied to the same market. The comparison shall be made at the same level of trade and at comparable times, due account being taken of any other factor affecting price comparability. However, if such a direct comparison is not possible, the existence of price undercutting may be demonstrated on the basis of export unit values.

6.6 Each Member, in the market of which serious prejudice is alleged to have arisen, shall, subject to the provisions of paragraph 3 of Annex V, make

[91] Unless other multilaterally agreed specific rules apply to the trade in the product or commodity in question.

available to the parties to a dispute and to the Committee all relevant information that can be obtained as to the changes in market shares of the disputing parties as well as concerning prices of the products involved.

6.7 Displacement or impedance resulting in serious prejudice shall not arise under paragraph 3 above where any of the following circumstances exist[92] during the relevant period :

(a) prohibition or restriction on exports of the like product from the complaining Member or on imports from the complaining Member into the third market concerned;

(b) decision by an importing government operating a monopoly of trade or state trading in the product concerned to shift, for non-commercial reasons, imports from the complaining Member to another country or countries;

(c) natural disasters, strikes, transport disruptions or other *force majeure* substantially affecting production, qualities, quantities or prices of the product available for exports from the complaining Member;

(d) existence of arrangements limiting exports from the complaining Member;

(e) voluntary decrease in the availability for export of the product concerned from the complaining Member (including, *inter alia,* a situation where firms in the complaining Member have been autonomously reallocating exports of this product to new markets);

(f) failure to conform to standards and other regulatory requirements in the importing country.

6.8 In the absence of circumstances referred to in paragraph 7 above the existence of serious prejudice should be determined on the basis of the information submitted in accordance with the provisions of Annex V.

6.9 This Article does not apply to subsidies maintained on agricultural products as provided in Article 13 of the Agreement on Agriculture.

Article 7
Remedies

7.1 Except as provided in Article 13 of the Agreement on Agriculture, whenever a Member has reason to believe that any subsidy referred to in Article 1, granted or maintained by another Member, results in injury to its domestic industry, nullification or impairment or serious prejudice, such Member may request consultations with such other Member.

---

[92] The fact that certain circumstances are referred to in this paragraph does not, in itself, confer upon them any legal status in terms of either the GATT 1994 or this Agreement. These circumstances must not be isolated, sporadic or otherwise insignificant.

7.2 A request for consultations under paragraph 1 above shall include a statement of available evidence with regard to (a) the existence and nature of the subsidy in question, and (b) the injury caused to the domestic industry, or the nullification or impairment, or serious prejudice[93] caused to the interests of the Member requesting consultations.

7.3 Upon request for consultations under paragraph 1 above, the Member believed to be granting or maintaining the subsidy practice in question shall enter into such consultations as quickly as possible. The purpose of the consultations shall be to clarify the facts of the situation and to arrive at a mutually acceptable solution.

7.4 If consultations do not result in a mutually acceptable solution within sixty days[94]. any Member party to such consultations may refer the matter to the Dispute Settlement Body for the establishment of a Panel, unless the DSB decides by consensus not to establish a panel. The composition of the Panel and its terms of reference shall be established within fifteen days from the date when it is established.

7.5 The Panel, established pursuant to paragraph 4 above, shall review the matter and shall submit its final report to the Members party to the dispute. The report shall be circulated to all Members within 120 days of the date of the composition and establishment of the Panel's terms of reference.

7.6 Within thirty days of the issuance of the Panel's report to all Members, the report shall be adopted by the DSB[95] unless one of the parties to the dispute formally notifies the DSB of its decision to appeal or the DSB decides by consensus not to adopt the report.

7.7 Where a panel report is appealed, the Appellate Body shall issue its decision within sixty days from the date when the party to the dispute formally notifies its intention to appeal. When the Appellate Body considers that it cannot provide its report within sixty days, it shall inform the DSB in writing of the reasons for the delay together with an estimate of the period within which it will submit its report. In no case shall the proceedings exceed ninety days. The appellate report shall be adopted by the DSB and unconditionally accepted by the parties to the dispute unless the DSB decides by consensus not to adopt the appellate report within twenty days following its issuance to the Members.[96]

---

[93] In the event that the request relates to a subsidy deemed to result in serious prejudice in terms of Article 6.1 above, the available evidence of serious prejudice may be limited to the available evidence as to whether the conditions of Article 6.1 have been met or not.

[94] Any time periods mentioned in this Article may be extended by mutual agreement.

[95] If a meeting of the DSB is not scheduled during this period, such a meeting of the DSB shall be held for this purpose.

[96] If a meeting of the DSB is not scheduled during this period, such a meeting of the DSB shall be held for this purpose.

7.8 Where a panel report or an Appellate Body report is adopted, in which it is determined that any subsidy has resulted in adverse effects to the interests of another Member within the meaning of Article 5 of this Agreement, the Member granting or maintaining such subsidy shall take appropriate steps to remove the adverse effects or shall withdraw the subsidy.

7.9 In the event the Member has not taken appropriate steps to remove the adverse effects of the subsidy or withdraw the subsidy within six months from the date when the DSB adopts the panel repor or the Appellate Body report, and in the absence of agreement on compensation, the DSB shall grant authorization to the complaining Member to take countermeasures, commensurate with the degree and nature of the adverse effects determined to exist, unless the DSB decides by consensus to reject the request.

7.10 In the event that a party to the dispute requests arbitration under paragraph 22.6 of the DSU, the arbitrator shall determine whether the countermeasures are commensurate with the degree and nature of the adverse effects determined to exist.

PART IV

NON-ACTIONABLE SUBSIDIES

Article 8

Identification of Non-Actionable Subsidies

8.1 The following subsidies shall be considered as non-actionable:

(a) subsidies which are not specific, within the meaning of paragraph 1 of Article 2 above;

(b) subsidies which are specific within the meaning of Article 2 above but which meet all of the conditions provided for in paragraphs 2(a) or 2(b) below.

8.2 Notwithstanding the provisions of Parts III and V of this Agreement, the following subsidies shall be non-actionable[97]:

(a) assistance for research activities conducted by firms or by higher

---

[97] It is recognized that government assistance for various purposes is widely provided by Members and the mere fact that such assistance may not qualify for non-actionable treatment under the provisions of this Article does not in itself restrict the ability of Members to provide such assistance.

education or research establishments on a contract basis with firms if: [98, 99, 100]

the assistance covers not more than 75 per cent of the costs of industrial research[101] or 50 per cent of the costs of pre-competitive development activity;[102] and provided that such assistance is limited exclusively to:

(i) personnel costs (researchers, technicians and other supporting staff employed exclusively in the research activity);

(ii) costs of instruments, equipment, land and buildings used exclusively and permanently (except when disposed of on a commercial basis) for the research activity;

(iii) costs of consultancy and equivalent services used exclusively for the research activity, including bought-in research, technical knowledge, patents, etc.;

(iv) additional overhead costs incurred directly as a result of the research activity;

(v) other running costs (such as those of materials, supplies and the like), incurred directly as a result of the research activity.

---

[98] Since it is anticipated that civil aircraft will be subject to specific multilateral rules, the provisions of this sub-paragraph do not apply to that product. Not later than 18 months after the date of entry into force of the Agreement Establishing the **WTO** the Committee shall review the operation of the provisions of this sub-paragraph with a view to making all necessary modifications to improve the operation of these provisions. In its consideration of possible modifications, the Committee shall carefully review the definitions of the categories set forth in this sub-paragraph in the light of the experience of Members in the operation of research programmes and the work in other relevant international institutions. The provisions of this Agreement do not apply to fundamental research activities independently conducted by higher education or research establishments. The term "fundamental research" means an enlargement of general scientific and technical knowledge not linked to industrial or commercial objectives.

[99] In the case of programmes which span "industrial research" and "pre-competitive development activity", the allowable level of non-actionable assistance shall not exceed the simple average of the allowable levels of non-actionable assistance applicable to the above two categories, calculated on the basis of all eligible costs as set forth in items (i)-(v) of this subparagraph.

[100] The allowable levels of non-actionable assistance referred to in this sub-paragraph shall be established by reference to the total eligible costs incurred over the duration of an individual project.

[101] The term "industrial research" means planned search or critical investigation aimed at discovery of new knowledge, with the objective that such knowledge may be useful in developing new products, processes or services, or in bringing about a significant improvement to existing products, processes or services.

[102] The term "pre-competitive development activity" means the translation of industrial research findings into a plan, blueprint or design for new modified or improved products, processes or services whether intended for sale or use, including the creation of a first prototype which would not be capable of commercial use. It may further include the conceptual formulation and design of products, processes or services alternatives and initial demonstration or pilot projects, provided that these same projects cannot be converted or used for industrial application or commercial exploitation. It does not include routine or periodic alterations to existing products, production lines, manufacturing processes, services, and other on-going operations even though those alterations may represent improvements.

(b) assistance to disadvantaged regions within the territory of a Member given pursuant to a general framework of regional development[103] and non-specific (within the meaning of paragraph 1 of Article 2 above) within eligible regions provided that :

(i) each disadvantaged region must be a clearly designated contiguous geographical area with a definable economic and administrative identity;

(ii) the region is considered as disadvantaged on the basis of neutral and objective criteria[104], indicating that the region's difficulties arise out of more than temporary circumstances; such criteria must be clearly spelled out in law, regulation, or other official document, so as to be capable of verification;

(iii) the criteria shall include a measurement of economic development which shall be based on at least one of the following factors:

– one of either income per capita or household income per capita, or GDP per capita, which must not be above 85 per cent of the average for the territory concerned;

– unemployment rate, which must be at least 110 per cent of the average for the territory concerned;

as measured over a three-year period: such measure-ment, however, may be a composite one and may include other factors.

(c) assistance to promote adaptation of existing facilities[105] to new environmental requirements imposed by law and/or regulations which result in greater constraints and financial burden on firms, provided that the assistance:

(i) is a one-time non-recurring measure;and

---

103 A "general framework of regional development" means that regional subsidy programmes are part of an internally consistent and generally applicable regional development policy and that regional development subsidies are not granted in isolated geographical points having no, or virtually no influence on the development of a region.

104 "Neutral and objective criteria" means criteria which do not favour certain regions beyond what is appropriate for the elimmation or reduction of regional disparities within the framework of the regional development policy. In this regard, regional subsidy programmes shall include ceilings on the amount of assistance which can be granted to each subsidized project. Such ceilings must be differentiated according to the different levels of development of assisted regions and must be expressed in terms of investment costs or cost of job creation. Within such ceilings, the distribution of assistance shall be sufficiently broad and even to avoid the predominant use of a subsidy by, or the granting of disproportionately large amounts of subsidy to certain enterprises as provided for in Article 2 of this Agreement.

105 The term "existing facilities" means facilities having been in operation for at least two years at the time when new environmental requirements are imposed.

(ii) is limited to 20 per cent of the cost of adaptation; and
(iii) does not cover the cost of replacing and operating the assisted investment, which must be fully borne by firms; and
(iv) is directly linked to and proportionate to a firm's planned reduction of nuisances and pollution, and does not cover any manufacturing cost savings which may be achieved; and
(v) is available to all firms which can adopt the new equipment and/or production processes.

8.3 A subsidy programme for which the provisions of paragraph 2 above are invoked shall be notified in advance of its implementation to the Committee in accordance with the provisions of Part VII of this Agreement. Any such notification shall be sufficiently precise to enable other Members to evaluate the consistency of the programme with the conditions and criteria provided for in the relevant provisions of paragraph 2 above. Members shall also provide the Committee with yearly updating of such notifications, in particular by supplying information on global expenditure for each programme, and about any modification of the programme since the previous update. Other Members shall have the right to request information about individual cases of subsidization under a notified programme.[106]

8.4 Upon request of a Member, the **WTO** Secretariat shall review a notification made pursuant to paragraph 3 above and, where necessary, may require additional information from the subsidizing Member concerning the notified programme under review. The Secretariat shall report its finding to the Committee. The Committee shall then, upon request, promptly review the findings of the Secretariat (or, if a review by the Secretariat has not been requested, the notification itself), with a view to determining whether the conditions and criteria laid down in paragraph 2 above have not been met. The procedure provided for in this paragraph shall be completed at the latest at the first regular meeting of the Committee following the notification of a subsidy programme, provided that at least two months have elapsed between such notification and the regular meeting of the Committee. The review procedure described in this paragraph shall also apply, upon request, to substantial modifications of a programme notified in the yearly updates referred to in paragraph 3 above.

8.5 Upon the request of a Member, the determination by the Committee referred to in paragraph 4 above, or a failure by the Committee to make such a determination, as well as the violation, in individual cases, of the conditions set out in a notified programme, shall be submitted to binding arbitration.

---

[106] It is recognized that nothing in this notification provision requires the provision of confidential information, including confidential business information.

The arbitration body shall present its conclusions to the Members within 120 days from the date when the matter was referred to the arbitration body. Except as otherwise provided in this paragraph, the DSU shall apply to arbitrations conducted under this paragraph.

Article 9

Consultations and Authorized Remedies

9.1 If, in the course of implementation of a programme referred to in paragraph 2 of Article 8 above, notwithstanding the fact that the programrmme is consistent with the criteria laid down in paragraph 2 of Article 8, a Member has reasons to believe that this programme has resulted in serious adverse effects to the domestic industry of that Member, such as to cause damage which would be difficult to repair, such Member may request consultations with the Member granting the subsidy.

9.2 Upon request for consultations under paragraph 1 above, the Member maintaining the subsidy programme in question shall enter into such consultations as quickly as possible. The purpose of the consultations shall be to clarify the facts of the situation and to arrive at a mutually acceptable solution.

9.3 If no mutually acceptable solution has been reached in consultations under paragraph 2 within 60 days of the request for such consultations, the requesting Member may refer the matter to the Committee

9.4 Where a matter is referred to the Committee, the Committee shall immediately review the facts involved and the evidence of the effects referred to in paragraph 1 above. If the Committee determines that such effects exist, it may recommend to the subsidizing Member to modify this programme in such a way as to remove these effects. The Committee shall present its conclusions within 120 days from the date when the matter is referred to it under this provision. In the event the recommendation is not followed within 6 months, the Committee shall authorize the requesting Member to take appropriate countermeasures commensurate with the nature and degree of the effects determined to exist.

PART V : COUNTERVAILING MEASURES

Article 10

Application of Article VI of the GATT 1994[107]

Members shall take all necessary steps to ensure that the imposition of a

---

[107] The provisions of Parts II or I11 may be invoked in parallel with the provisions of Part V of this Agreement; however, with regard to the effects of a particular subsidy in the domestic market of the importing country, only one form of relief (either a countervailing duty, if

countervailing duty[108] on any product of the territory of any Member imported into the territory of another Member is in accordance with the provisions of Article VI of the GATT 1994 and the terms of this Agreement. Countervailing duties may only be imposed pursuant to investigations initiated[109] and conducted in accordance with the provisions of this Agreement and the Agreement on Agriculture.

Article 11

Initiation and Subsequent Investigation

11.1 Except as provided in paragraph 6 of Article 11, an investigation to determine the existence, degree and effect of any alleged subsidy shall be initiated upon a written application by or on behalf of the domestic industry.

11.2 An application under paragraph 1 shall include sufficient evidence of the existence of (a) a subsidy and, if possible, its amount, (b) injury within the meaning of Article VI of the GATT 1994 as interpreted by this Agreement, and (c) a causal link between the subsidized imports and the alleged injury. Simple assertion, unsubstantiated by relevant evidence, cannot be considered sufficient to meet the requirements of this paragraph. The application shall contain such information as is reasonably available to the applicant on the following :

(i) identity of the applicant and a description of the volume and value of the domestic production of the like product by the applicant. Where a written application is made on behalf of the domestic industry, the application shall identify the industry on behalf of which the application is made by a list of all known domestic producers of the like product (or associations of domestic producers of the like product) and, to the extent

---

other requirements of Part V are met, or a countermeasure under Articles 4 or 7 of this Agreement) shall be available. The provisions of Parts III and V shall not be invoked regarding measures considered non-actionable in accordance with the provisions of Part IV of this Agreement. However, measures referred to in Article 8.1(a) above may be investigated in order to determine whether or not they are specific within the meaning of Article 2 above. In addition, in the case of a subsidy referred to in paragraph 2 of Article 8 conferred pursuant to a programme which has not been notified in accordance with paragraph 3 of Article 8, the provisions of Parts III or V may be invoked, but such subsidy shall be treated as non-actionable if it is found to conform to the standards set forth in paragraph 2 of Article 8.

[108] The term "countervailing duty" shall be understood to mean a special duty levied for the purpose of off-setting any subsidy bestowed directly or indirectly upon the manufacture, production or export of any merchandise, as provided for in Article VI:3 of the GATT 1994.

[109] The term "initiated as used hereinafter means procedural action by which a Member formally commences an investigation as provided in Article 11.

possible, a description of the volume and value of domestic production of the like product accounted for by such producers;

(ii) a complete description of the allegedly subsidized product, the names of the country or countries of origin or export in question, the identity of each known exporter or foreign producer and a list of known persons importing the product in question;

(iii) evidence with regard to the existence, amount and nature of the subsidy in question;

(iv) evidence that alleged material injury to a domestic industry is caused by subsidized imports through the effects of the subsidies; this evidence includes information on the evolution of the volume of the allegedly subsidized imports, the effect of these imports on prices of the like product in the domestic market and the consequent impact of the imports on the domestic industry, as demonstrated by relevant factors and indices having a bearing on the state of the domestic industry, such as those listed in paragraphs 2 and 4 of Article 15.

11.3 The authorities shall review the accuracy and adequacy of the evidence provided in the application to determine whether the evidence is sufficient to justify the opening of an investigation.

11.4 An investigation shall not be initiated pursuant to paragraph 1 unless the authorities have determined, on the basis of an examination of the degree of support for, or opposition to, the application expressed[110] by domestic producers of the like product, that the application has been made by or on behalf of the domestic industry.[111] The application shall be considered to have been made "by or on behalf of the domestic industry" if it is supported by those domestic producers whose collective output constitutes more than 50 per cent of the total production of the like product produced by that portion of the domestic industry expressing either support for or opposition to the application. However, no investigation shall be initiated when domestic producers expressly supporting the application account for less than 25 per cent of total production of the like product produced by the domestic industry.

11.5 The authorities shall avoid, unless a decision has been made to

[110] In the case of fragmented industries involving an exceptionally large number of producers, authorities may determine support and opposition by using statistically valid sampling techniques.

[111] Members are aware that in the territory of certain Members, employees of domestic producers of the like product or representatives of those employees, may make or support an application for an investigation under paragraph 1.

initiate an investigation, any publicizing of the application for the initiation of an investigation.

11.6 If in special circumstances, the authorities concerned decide to initiate an investigation without having received a written application by or on behalf of a domestic industry for the initiation of such investigation, they shall proceed only if they have sufficient evidence of the existence of a subsidy, injury and causal link, as described in paragraph 2, to justify the initiation of an investigation.

11.7 The evidence of both subsidy and injury shall be considered simultaneously (a) in the decision whether or not to initiate an investigation and (b) thereafter during the course of the investigation, starting on a date not later than the earliest date on which in accordance with the provisions of this Agreement provisional measures may be applied.

11.8 In cases where products are not imported directly from the country of origin but are exported to the country of importation from an intermediate country, the provisions of this Agreement shall be fully applicable and the transaction or transactions shall, for the purposes of this Agreement, be regarded as having taken place between the country of origin and the country of importation.

11.9 An application under paragraph 1 shall be rejected and an investigation shall be terminated promptly as soon as the authorities concerned are satisfied that there is not sufficient evidence of either subsidization or of injury to justify proceeding with the case. There shall be immediate termination in cases where the amount of a subsidy is *de minimis,* or where the volume of subsidized imports, actual or potential, or the injury, is negligible. For the purpose of this paragraph, the amount of the subsidy shall be considered to be *de minimis* if the subsidy is less than 1 per cent *ad valorem.*

11.10 An investigation shall not hinder the procedures of customs clearance.

11.11 Investigations shall, except in special circumstances, be concluded within one year after their initiation, and in no case more than 18 months.

Article 12

Evidence

12.1 Interested Members and all interested parties in a countervailing duty investigation shall be given notice of the information which the authorities require and ample opportunity to present in writing all evidence which they consider relevant in respect of the investigation in question.

12.1.1 Exporters, foreign producers or interested Members receiving questionnaires used in a countervailing duty investigation shall be given at least thirty days for reply.[112] Due consideration should be given to any request for an extension of the thirty day period and, upon cause shown, such an extension should be granted whenever practicable.

12.1.2 Subject to the requirement to protect confidential information, evidence presented in writing by one interested Member or interested party shall be made available promptly to other interested Members or interested parties participating in the investigation.

12.1.3 As soon as an investigation has been initiated, the authorities shall provide the full text of the written application received under paragraph 1 of Article 11 to the known exporters[113] and to the authorities of the exporting country and make it available, upon request, to other interested parties involved. Due regard shall be paid to the protection of confidential information as provided for in paragraph 4 below.

12.2 Interested Members and interested parties also shall have the right, upon justification, to present information orally. Where such information is provided orally, the interested parties subsequently shall be required to reduce such submissions to writing. Any decision of the investigating authorities can only be based on such information and arguments as were on the written record of this authority and which were available to interested Members and interested parties participating in the investigation, due account having been given to the need to protect confidential information.

12.3 The authorities shall whenever practicable provide timely opportunities for all interested Members and interested parties to see all information that is relevant to the presentation of their cases, that is not confidential as defined in paragraph 4 and that is used by the authorities in a countervailing duty investigation, and to prepare presentations on the basis of this information.

12.4 Any information which is by nature confidential (for example, because its disclosure would be of significant competitive advantage to a competitor or because its disclosure would have a significantly adverse effect

---

[112] As a general rule, the time limit for exporters shall be counted from the date of receipt of the questionnaire, which for this purpose shall be deemed to have been received one week from the day on which it was sent to the respondent or transmitted to the appropriate diplomatic representatives of the exporting country or in the case of a separate customs territory Member of the WTO, an official representative of the exporting territory.

[113] It being understood that where the number of exporters involved is particularly high, the full text of the application should instead be provided only to the authorities of the exporting country or to the relevant trade association who then should forward copies to the exporters concerned.

upon a person supplying the information or upon a person from whom the supplier acquired the information), or which is provided on a confidential basis by parties to an investigation shall, upon good cause shown, be treated as such by the authorities. Such information shall not be disclosed without specific permission of the party submitting it.[114]

12.4.1 The authorities. shall require interested Members or interested parties providing confidential information to furnish non-confidential summaries thereof. These summaries shall be in sufficient detail to permit a reasonable understanding of the substance of the information submitted in confidence. In exceptional circumstances, such Members or parties may indicate that such information is not susceptible of summary. In such exceptional circumstances, a statement of the reasons why summarization is not possible must be provided.

12.4.2 If the authorities find that a request for confidentiality is not warranted and if the supplier of the information is either unwilling to make the information public or to authorize its disclosure in generalized or summary form, the authorities may disregard such information unless it can be demonstrated to their satisfaction from appropriate sources that the information is correct.[115]

12.5 Except in circumstances provided for in paragraph 7, the authorities shall during the course of an investigation satisfy themselves as to the accuracy of the information supplied by interested parties or interested Members upon which their findings are based.

12.6 The investigating authorities may carry out investigations in the territory of other Members as required, provided that they have notified in good time the Member in question and unless the latter objects to the investigation. Further, the investigating authorities may carry out investigations on the premises of a firm and may examine the records of a firm if (a) the firm so agrees and (b) the Member in question is notified and does not object. The procedures set forth in Annex VI to this Agreement shall apply to investigations on the premises of a firm. The authorities shall, subject to the requirement to protect confidential information, make the results of any verifications available or provide disclosure thereof pursuant to paragraph 8, to the firms to which they pertain and may make such results available to the applicants.

---

[114] Members are aware that in the territory of certain Members disclosure pursuant to a narrowly-drawn protective order may be required.

[115] Members agree that requests for confidentiality should not be arbitrarily rejected. Members further agree that the investigating authority may request the waiving of confidentiality only regarding information relevant to the proceedings.

12.7 In cases in which any interested party or Member refuses access to, or otherwise does not provide, necessary information within a reasonable period or significantly impedes the investigation, preliminary and final determinations, affirmative or negative, may be made on the basis of the facts available.

12.8 The authorities shall, before a final determination is made, inform all interested Members or interested parties of the essential facts under consideration which form the basis for the decision whether to apply definitive measures. Such disclosure should take place in sufficient time for the parties to defend their interests.

12.9 For the purposes of this Agreement, "interested parties" shall include:

(i) an exporter or foreign producer or the importer of a product subject to investigation, or a trade or business association a majority of the members of which are producers, exporters or importers of such product; and

(ii) a producer of the like product in the importing country or a trade and business association a majority of the members of which produce the like product in the importing country.

This list shall not preclude Members from allowing domestic or foreign parties other than those mentioned above to be included as interested parties.

12.10 The authorities shall provide opportunities for industrial users of the product under investigation, and for representative consumer organizations in cases where the product is commonly sold at the retail level, to provide information which is relevant to the investigation regarding subsidization, injury and causality.

12.11 The authorities shall take due account of any difficulties experienced by interested parties, in particular small companies, in supplying information requested and provide any assistance practicable.

12.12 The procedures set out above are not intended to prevent the authorities of a Member from proceeding expeditiously with regard to initiating an investigation, reaching preliminary or final determinations, whether affirmative or negative, or from applying provisional or final measures, in accordance with relevant provisions of this Agreement.

Article 13
Consultations

13.1 As soon as possible after an application under Article 11 is accepted, and in any event before the initiation of any investigation, Members the products of which may be subject to such investigation shall be invited for consultations with the aim of clarifying the situation as to the matters referred to in Article 11:1 above and arriving at a mutually agreed solution.

13.2 Furthermore, throughout the period of investigation, Members the products of which are the subject of the investigation shall be afforded a reasonable opportunity to continue consultations, with a view to clarifying the factual situation and to arriving at a mutually agreed solution.[116]

13.3 Without prejudice to the obligation to afford reasonable opportunity for consultation, these provisions regarding consultations are not intended to prevent the authorities of a Member from proceeding expeditiously with regard to initiating the investigation, reaching preliminary or final determinations, whether affirmative or negative, or from applying provisional or final measures, in accordance with the provisions of this Agreement.

13.4 The Member which intends to initiate any investigation or is conducting such an investigation shall permit, upon request, the Member or Members the products of which are subject to such investigation access to non-confidential evidence including the non-confidential summary of confidential data being used for initiating or conducting the investigation.

Article 14

Calculation of the Amount of a Subsidy in Terms of the Benefit to the Recipient

For the purpose of Part V of this Agreement, any method used by the investigating authority to calculate the benefit to the recipient conferred pursuant to paragraph 1 of Article 1 above shall be provided for in the national legislation or implementing regulations of the Member concerned and its application to each particular case shall be transparent and adequately explained. Furthermore any such method shall be consistent with the following guidelines:

(a) Government provision of equity capital shall not he considered as conferring a benefit, unless the investment decision can be regarded as inconsistent with the usual investment practice (including for the provision of risk capital) of private investors in the territory of that Member;

(b) A loan by a government shall not be considered as conferring a benefit, unless there is a difference between the amount that the firm receiving the loan pays on the government loan and a comparable commercial loan which the firm could actually obtain

---

[116] It is particularly important, in accordance with the provisions of this paragraph, that no affirmative determination whether preliminary or final be made without reasonable opportunity for consultations having been given. Such consultations may establish the basis for proceeding under the provisions of Parts II, III and X of this Agreement.

on the market. In this case the benefit shall be the difference between these two amounts;

(c) A loan guarantee by a government shall not be considered as conferring a benefit, unless there is a difference between the amount that the firm receiving the guarantee pays on a loan guaranteed by the government and the amount that the firm would pay for a comparable commercial loan absent the government guarantee. In this case the benefit shall be the difference between these two amounts adjusted for any differences in fees;

(d) The provision of goods or services or purchase of goods by a government shall not be considered as conferring a benefit unless the provision is made for less than adequate remuneration, or the purchase is made for more than adequate remuneration. The adequacy of remuneration shall be determined in relation to prevailing market conditions for the good or service in question in the country of provision or purchase (including price, quality, availability, marketability, transportation and other conditions of purchase or sale).

Article 15

Determination of Injury[117]

15.1 A determination of injury for purposes of Article VI of the GATT 1994 shall be based on positive evidence and involve an objective examination of both (a) the volume of the subsidized imports and the effect of the subsidized imports on prices in the domestic market for like products[118] and (b) the consequent impact of these imports on the domestic producers of such products.

15.2 With regard to the volume of the subsidized imports, the investigating authorities shall consider whether there has been a significant increase in subsidized imports, either in absolute terms or relative to production or consumption in the importing Member. With regard to the effect of the subsidized imports on prices, the investigating authorities shall consider whether there has been a significant price undercutting by the subsidized imports as compared with the price of a like product of the importing Member, or

---

117 Under this Agreement the term "injury shall, unless otherwise specified, be taken to mean material injury to a domestic industry, threat of material injury to a domestic industry or material retardation of the establishment of such an industry and shall be interpreted in accordance with the provisions of this Article.

118 Throughout this Agreement the term "like product" ("produit similaire") shall be interpreted to mean a product which is identical, *i.e.*, alike in all respects to the product under consideration, or in the absence of such a product, another product which although not alike in all respects, has characteristics closely resembling those of the product under consideration.

whether the effect of such imports is otherwise to depress prices to a significant degree or to prevent price increases, which otherwise would have occurred, to a significant degree. No one or several of these factors can necessarily give decisive guidance.

15.3 Where imports of a product from more than one country are simultaneously subject to countervailing duty investigations, the investigating authorities may cumulatively assess effects of such imports only if they determine that (1) the amount of subsidization established in relation to the imports from each country is more than *de minimis* as defined in paragraph 9 of Article 11 and that the volume of imports from each country is not negligible and (2) a cumulative assessment of the effects of the imports is appropriate in light of the conditions of competition between imported products and the conditions of competition between the imported products and the like domestic product.

15.4 The examination of the impact of the subsidized imports on the domestic industry shall include an evaluation of all relevant economic factors and indices having a bearing on the state of the industry, including actual and potential decline in output, sales, market share, profits, productivity, return on investments, or utilization of capacity; factors affecting domestic prices; actual and potential negative effects on cash flow, inventories, employment, wages, growth, ability to raise capital or investments and, in the case of agriculture, whether there has been an increased burden on Government support programmes. This list is not exhaustive, nor can one or several of these factors necessarily give decisive guidance.

15.5 It must be demonstrated that the subsidized imports are, through the effects[119] of subsidies, causing injury within the meaning of this Agreement. The demonstration of a causal relationship between the subsidized imports and the injury to the domestic industry shall be based on an examination of all relevant evidence before the authorities. The authorities shall also examine any known factors other than the subsidized imports which at the same time are injuring the domestic industry, and the injuries caused by these other factors must not be attributed to the subsidized imports. Factors which may be relevant in this respect include, *inter alia,* the volumes and prices of non-subsidized imports of the product in question, contraction in demand or changes in the patterns of consumption, trade restrictive practices of and competition between the foreign and domestic producers, developments in technology and the export performance and productivity of the domestic industry.

15.6 The effect of the subsidized imports shall be assessed in relation to

---

[119] As set forth in paragraphs 2 and 4 of this Article.

the domestic production of the like product when available data permit the separate identification of that production on the basis of such criteria as the production process, producers'sales and profits. If such separate identification of that production is not possible, the effects of the subsidized imports shall be assessed by the examination of the production of the narrowest group or range of products, which includes the like product, for which the necessary information can be provided.

15.7 A determination of a threat of material injury shall be based on facts and not merely on allegation, conjecture or remote possibility. The change in circumstances which would create a situation in which the subsidy would cause injury must be clearly foreseen and imminent. In making a determination regarding the existence of a threat of material injury, the investigating authorities should consider, *inter alia,* such factors as:

(i) nature of the subsidy or subsidies in question and the trade effects likely to arise therefrom;

(ii) a significant rate of increase of subsidized imports into the domestic market indicating the likelihood of substantially increased importations;

(iii) sufficient freely disposable or an imminent, substantial increase in capacity of the exporter indicating the likelihood of substantially increased subsidized exports to the importing country's market, taking into account the availability of other export markets to absorb any additional exports;

(iv) whether imports are entering at prices that will have a significant depressing or suppressing effect on domestic prices, and would likely increase demand for further imports;

(v) inventories of the product being investigated.

No one of these factors by itself can necessarily give decisive guidance but the totality of the factors considered must lead to the conclusion that further subsidized exports are imminent and that, unless protective action is taken, material injury would occur.

15.8 With respect to cases where injury is threatened by subsidized imports, the application of countervailing measures shall be considered and decided with special care.

Article 16

Definition of Domestic Industry

16.1 For the purposes of this Agreement, the term "domestic industry" shall, except as provided in paragraph 2 below, be interpreted as referring to the domestic producers as a whole of the like products or to those of them whose collective output of the products constitutes a major proportion of the total domestic production of those products, except that when producers are related[120] to the exporters or importers or are themselves importers of the allegedly subsidized product or a like product from other countries, the term "domestic industry" may be interpreted as referring to the rest of the producers.

16.2 In exceptional circumstances, the territory of a Member may, for the production in question, be divided into two or more competitive markets and the producers within each market may be regarded as a separate industry if (a) the producers within such market sell all or almost all of their production of the product in question in that market, and (b) the demand in that market is not to any substantial degree supplied by producers of the product in question located elsewhere in the territory. In such circumstances, injury may be found to exist even where a major portion of the total domestic industry is not injured, provided there is a concentration of subsidized imports into such an isolated market and provided further that the subsidized imports are causing injury to the producers of all or almost all of the production within such market.

16.3 When the domestic industry has been interpreted as referring to the producers in a certain area, *i.e.* a market as defined in paragraph 2 above, countervailing duties shall be levied only on the products in question consigned for final consumption to that area. When the constitutional law of the importing Member does not permit the levying of countervailing duties on such a basis, the importing Member may levy the countervailing duties without limitation only if (a) the exporters shall have been given an opportunity to cease exporting at subsidized prices to the area concerned or otherwise give assurances pursuant to Article 18 of this Agreement, and adequate assurances in this regard have not been promptly given, and (b) such duties cannot be levied only on products of specific producers which supply the area in question.

16.4 Where two or more countries have reached under the provisions of paragraph 8(a) of Article XXIV of the GATT 1994 such a level of integration that they have the characteristics of a single, unified market, the industry in the entire area of integration shall be taken to be the domestic industry referred to in paragraphs 1 and 2 above.

---

[120] For the purpose of this paragraph, producers shall be deemed to be related to exporters or importers only if (a) one of them directly or indirectly controls the other; or (b) both of them are directly or indirectly controlled by a third person; or (c) together they directly or indirectly control a third person, provided that there are grounds for believing or suspecting that the effect of the relationship is such as to cause the producer concerned to behave differently, from non-related producers. For the purpose of this paragraph. one shall be deemed to control another when the former is legally or operationally in a position to exercise restraint or direction over the latter.

16.5 The provisions of paragraph 6 of Article 15 shall be applicable to this Article.

Article 17
Provisional Measures

17.1, Provisional measures may be applied only if:

(a) an investigation has been initiated in accordance with the provisions of Article 11, a public notice has been given to that effect and interested Members and interested parties have been given adequate opportunities to submit information and make comments;

(b) a preliminary affirmative determination has been made that a subsidy exists and that there is material injury or threat thereof to a domestic industry caused by subsidized imports; and

(c) the authorities concerned judge such measures necessary to prevent injury being caused during the investigation.

17.2 Provisional measures may take the form of provisional countervailing duties guaranteed by cash deposits or bonds equal to the amount of the provisionally calculated amount of subsidization.

17.3 Provisional measures shall not be applied sooner than 60 days from the date of initiation of the investigation.

17.4 The application of provisional measures shall be limited to as short a period as possible, not exceeding four months.

17.5 The relevant provisions of Article 19 shall be followed in the application of provisional measures.

Article 18
Undertakings

18.1 Proceedings may[121] be suspended or terminated without the imposition of provisional measures or countervailing duties upon receipt of satisfactory voluntary undertakings under which:

(i) the government of the exporting country agrees to eliminate or limit the subsidy or take other measures concerning its effects; or

(ii) the exporter agrees to revise its prices so that the investigating authorities are satisfied that the injurious effect of the subsidy is eliminated. Price increases under such undertakings shall

---

121 The word 'may' shall not be interpreted to allow the simultaneous continuation of proceedings with the implementation of undertakings, except as provided in paragraph 4 of this Article.

not be higher than necessary to eliminate the amount of the subsidy. It is desirable that the price increases be less than the amount of the subsidy if such increases would be adequate to remove the injury to the domestic industry.

18.2 Undertakings shall not be sought or accepted unless the authorities of the importing country have made a preliminary affirmative determination of subsidization and injury caused by such subsidization and, in case of undertakings from exporters, have obtained the consent of the exporting Member.

18.3 Undertakings offered need not be accepted if the authorities of the importing Member consider their acceptance impractical, for example if the number of actual or potential exporters is too great, or for other reasons, including reasons of general policy. Should the case arise and where practicable, the authorities shall provide to the exporter the reasons which have led them to consider acceptance of an undertaking as inappropriate, and shall, to the extent possible, give the exporter an opportunity to make comments thereon.

18.4 If the undertakings are accepted, the investigation of subsidization and injury shall nevertheless be completed if the exporting Member so desires or the importing Member so decides. In such a case, if a negative determination of subsidization or injury or threat thereof is made, the undertaking shall automatically lapse, except in cases where such a determination is due in large part to the existence of an undertaking. In such cases the authorities concerned may require that an undertaking be maintained for a reasonable period consistent with the provisions of this Agreement. In the event that an affirmative determination of subsidization and injury is made, the undertaking shall continue consistent with its terms and the provisions of this Agreement.

18.5 Price undertakings may be suggested by the authorities of the importing Member, but no exporter shall be forced to enter into such an undertaking. The fact that governments or exporters do not offer such undertakings, or do not accept an invitation to do so, shall in no way prejudice the consideration of the case. However, the authorities are free to determine that a threat of injury is more likely to be realized if the subsidized imports continue.

18.6 Authorities of an importing Member may require any government or exporter from whom undertakings have been accepted to provide periodically information relevant to the fulfilment of such undertakings, and to permit verification of pertinent data. In case of violation of undertakings, the authorities of the importing Member may take, under this Agreement in conformity with its provisions, expeditious actions which may constitute immediate application of provisional measures using the best information available. In such cases definitive duties may be levied in accordance with this Agreement on goods entered for consumption not more than ninety days before the application of such provisional measures, except that any such retroactive assessment shall not apply to imports entered before the violation of the undertaking.

Article 19
Imposition and Collection of Countervailing Duties

19.1 If, after reasonable efforts have been made to complete consultations, a Member makes a final determination of the existence and amount of the subsidy and that, through the effects of the subsidy, the subsidized imports are causing injury, it may impose a countervailing duty in accordance with the provisions of this section unless the subsidy or subsidies are withdrawn.

19.2 The decision whether or not to impose a countervailing duty in cases where all requirements for the imposition have been fulfilled and the decision whether the amount of the countervailing duty to be imposed shall be the full amount of the subsidy or less, are decisions to be made by the authorities of the importing Member. It is desirable that the imposition should be permissive in the territory of all Members, that the duty should be less than the total amount of the subsidy if such lesser duty would be adequate to remove the injury to the domestic industry, and that procedures should be established which would allow the authorities concerned to take due account of representations made by domestic interested parties[122] whose interests might be adversely affected by the imposition of a countervailing duty.

19.3 When a countervailing duty is imposed in respect of any product, such countervailing duty shall be levied, in the appropriate amounts in each case, on a non-discriminatory basis on imports of such product from all sources found to be subsidized and causing injury, except as to imports from those sources which have renounced any subsidies in question or from which undertakings under the terms of this Agreement have been accepted. Any exporter whose exports are subject to a definitive countervailing duty but who was not actually investigated for reasons other than a refusal to co-operate, shall be entitled to an expedited review in order that the investigating authorities promptly establish an individual countervailing duty rate for that exporter.

19.4 No countervailing duty shall be levied[123] on any imported product in excess of the amount of the subsidy found to exist, calculated in terms of subsidization per unit of the subsidized and exported product.

---

[122] For the purpose of this paragraph the term "domestic interested parties" shall include consumers and industrial users of the imported product subject to investigation.

[123] As used in this Agreement "levy" shall mean the definitive or final legal assessment or collection of a duty or tax.

Article 20

Retroactivity

20.1 Provisional measures and countervailing duties shall only be applied to products which enter for consumption after the time when the decision under paragraph 1 of Article 17 and paragraph 1 of Article 19, respectively, enters into force, subject to the exceptions set out below.

20.2 Where a final determination of injury (but not of a threat thereof or of a material retardation of the establishment of an industry) is made or, in the case of a final determination of a threat of injury, where the effect of the subsidized imports would, in the absence of the provisional measures, have led to a determination of injury, countervailing duties may be levied retroactively for the period for which provisional measures, if any, have been applied.

20.3 If the definitive countervailing duty is higher than the amount guaranteed by the cash deposit or bond, the difference shall not be collected. If the definitive duty is less than the amount by the cash deposit or bond, the excess amount shall be reimbursed or the bond released in an expeditious manner.

20.4 Except as provided in paragraph 2 above, where a determination of threat of injury or material retardation is made (but no injury has yet occurred) a definitive countervailing duty may be imposed only from the date of the determination of threat of injury or material retardation and any cash deposit made during the period of the application of provisional measures shall be refunded and any bonds released in an expeditious manner.

20.5 Where a final determination is negative, any cash deposit made during the period of the application of provisional measure shall be refunded and any bonds released in an expeditious manner.

20.6 In critical circumstances where for the subsidized product in question the authorities find that injury which is difficult to repair is caused by massive imports in a relatively short period of a product benefiting from subsidies paid or bestowed inconsistently with the provisions of the GATT 1994 and of this Agreement and where it is deemed necessary, in order to preclude the recurrence of such injury, to assess countervailing duties retroactively on those imports, the definitive countervailing duties may be assessed on imports which were entered for consumption not more than ninety days prior to the date of application of provisional measures.

Article 21

Duration and Review of Countervailing Duties and Undertakings

21.1 A countervailing duty shall remain in force only as long as and to the extent necessary to counteract subsidization which is causing injury.

21.2 The authorities shall review the need for the continued imposition of the duty, where warranted, on their own initiative or, provided that a reasonable period of time has elapsed since the imposition of the definitive countervailing duty, upon request by any interested party which submits positive information substantiating the need for a review. Interested parties shall have the right to request the authorities to examine whether the continued imposition of the duty is necessary to offset subsidization, whether the injury would be likely to continue or recur if the duty were removed or varied, or both. If, as a result of the review under this paragraph, the authorities determine that the countervailing duty is no longer warranted, it shall be terminated immediately.

21.3 Notwithstanding the provisions of paragraphs 1 and 2, any definitive countervailing duty shall be terminated on a date not later than five years from its imposition (or from the date of the most recent review under paragraph 2 if that review has covered both subsidization and injury, or under this paragraph), unless the authorities determine, in a review initiated before that date on their own initiative or upon a duly substantiated request made by or on behalf of the domestic industry within a reasonable period of time prior to that date, that the expiry of the duty would be likely to lead to continuation or recurrence of subsidization and injury.[124] The duty may remain in force pending the outcome of such a review.

21.4 The provisions of Article 12 regarding evidence and procedure shall apply to any review carried out under this Article. Any such review shall be carried out expeditiously and shall normally be concluded within twelve months of the date of initiation of the review.

21.5 The provisions of this Article shall *mutatis mutandis* apply to undertakings accepted under Article 18

Article 22

Public Notice and Explanation of Determinations

22.1 When the authorities are satisfied that there is sufficient evidence to justify the initiation of an investigation pursuant to Article 11, the Member or Members, the products of which are subject to such investigation and other interested parties known to the investigating authorities to have an interest therein shall be notified and a public notice shall be given.

22.2 A public notice of the initiation of an investigation shall contain or

124 When the amount of the countervailing duty is assessed on a retrospective basis, a finding in the most recent assessment proceeding that no duty is to be levied shall not by itself require the authorities to terminate the definitive duty.

otherwise make available through a separate report[125] adequate information on the following: (i) the name of the exporting country or countries and the product involved; (ii) the date of initiation of the investigation; (iii) a description of the subsidy practice or practices to be investigated; (iv) a summary of the factors on which the allegation of injury is based; (v) the address to which representations by interested parties should be directed; and (vi) the time-limits allowed to interested parties for making their views known.

22.3 Public notice shall be given of any preliminary or final determination, whether affirmative or negative, of any decision to accept an undertaking pursuant to Article 18, of the termination of such an undertaking, and of the revocation of a determination. Each such notice shall set forth or otherwise make available through a separate report in sufficient detail the findings and conclusions reached on all issues of fact and law considered material by the investigating authorities. All such notices and reports shall be forwarded to the Member or Members the products of which are subject to such determination or undertaking and to other interested parties known to have an interest therein.

22.4 A public notice of the imposition of provisional measures shall set forth or otherwise make available through a separate report sufficiently detailed explanations for the preliminary determinations on the existence of a subsidy and injury and shall refer to the matters of fact and law which have led to arguments being accepted or rejected. Such a notice or report shall, due regard being paid to the requirement for the protection of confidential information, contain in particular: (i) the names of the suppliers or when this is impracticable, the supplying countries involved; (ii) a description of the product which is sufficient for customs purposes; (iii) the amount of subsidy established and the basis on which the existence of a subsidy has been determined; (iv) considerations relevant to the injury determinations as set out in Article 15; (v) the main reasons leading to thc determination.

22.5 A public notice of conclusion or suspension of an investigation in the case of an affirmative determination providing for the imposition of a definitive duty or the acceptance of an undertaking shall contain or otherwise make available through a separate report all relevant information on the matters of fact and law and reasons which have led to the imposition of final measures or the acceptance of an undertaking, due regard being paid to the requirement for the protection of confidential information. The notice or report shall in particular contain the information described in paragraph 4 above as well as the reasons for the acceptance or rejection of relevant arguments or claims made by the exporters and importers.

[125] Where authorities provide information and explanations under the provisions of this Article in a separate report, they shall ensure that such report is readily available to the public.

22.6 A public notice of the termination or suspension of an investigation following the acceptance of an undertaking pursuant to Article 18 shall include or otherwise make available through a separate report the non-confidential part of this undertaking.

22.7 The provisions of this Article shall apply *mutatis mutandis* to the initiation and completion of reviews pursuant to Article 21 and to decisions under Article 20 to apply duties retroactively.

Article 23
Judicial Review

Each Member, whose national legislation contains provisions on countervailing duty measures, shall maintain judicial, arbitral or administrative tribunals or procedures for the purpose, *inter alia,* of the prompt review of administrative actions relating to final determinations and reviews of determinations within the meaning of Article 21 of this Agreement. Such tribunals or procedures shall be independent of the authorities responsible for the determination or review in question, and shall provide all interested parties who participated in the administrative proceeding and are directly and individually affected by the administrative actions with access to review.

PART VI : INSTITUTIONS

Article 24
Committee on Subsidies and Countervailing Measures and other Subsidiary Bodies

24.1 There shall be established under this Agreement a Committee on Subsidies and Countervailing Measures composed of representatives from each of the Members. The Committee shall elect its own Chairman and shall meet not less than twice a year and otherwise as envisaged by relevant provisions of this Agreement at the request of any Member. The Committee shall carry out responsibilities as assigned to it under this Agreement or by the Members and it shall afford Members the opportunity of consulting on any matter relating to the operation of the Agreement or the furtherance of its objectives. The WTO Secretariat shall act as the secretariat to the Committee.

24.2 The Committee may set up subsidiary bodies as appropriate.

24.3 The Committee shall establish a Permanent Group of Experts composed of five independent persons, highly qualified in the fields of subsidies and trade relations. The experts will be elected by the Committee and one of them will serve in rotation every year. The Committee may request the Group of Experts to prepare a proposed conclusion on the existence of a prohibited subsidy, as provided for in paragraph 5 of Article 4 above. The Committee may also seek an advisory opinion on the existence and nature of any subsidy.

24.4 The Group of Experts may be consulted by any Member and give advisory opinions on the nature of any subsidy proposed to be introduced or currently maintained by that Member. Such advisory opinions will be confidential and may not be invoked in proceedings under Article 7 of this Agreement.

24.5 In carrying out their functions, the Committee and any subsidiary bodies may consult with and seek information from any source they deem appropriate. However, before the Committee or a subsidiary body seeks such information from a source within the jurisdiction of a Member, it shall inform the Member involved.

PART VII : NOTIFICATION AND SURVEILLANCE

Article 25

Notifications

25.1 Members agree that without prejudice to the provisions of paragraph 1 of Article XVI of the GATT 1994. their notifications of subsidies shall be submitted not later than June 30 of each year and shall conform to the provisions of paragraphs 2 through 6 below.

25.2 Members shall notify any subsidy as defined in paragraphs 1 and 2 of Article 1 above, granted or maintained within their territory.

25.3 The content of notifications should be sufficiently specific to enable other Members to evaluate the trade effects and to understand the operation of notified subsidy programmes. In this connection and without prejudice to the contents and form of the questionnaire on subsidies[126], Members shall ensure that their notifications contain the following information:

(i) form of' a subsidy (*i.e.* grant, loan, tax concession, etc.);

(ii) subsidy per unit or. in cases where it is not possible, the total amount or the annual amount budgeted for that subsidy (indicating, possible, the average subsidy per unit in the previous year);

(iii) policy objective and/or purpose of a subsidy;

(iv) duration of a subsidy and/or any other time-limits attached to it;

(v) statistical data permitting an assessment of the trade effects of a subsidy.

---

[126] The Committe shall establish a Working Party to review the contents and form of the questionnaire as contained in BISD. 9S/193-194.

25.4 Where specific points in paragraph 3 above have not been addressed in a notification, an explanation shall be provided in the notification itself.

25.5 If subsidies are granted to specific products or sectors, the notifications should be organized by product or sectors.

25.6 Members which consider that there are not measures or schemes in their countries requiring notification under paragraph 1 of Article XVI of the GATT 1994 and this Agreement shall so inform the **WTO** Secretariat in writing.

25.7 Members recognize that notification of a measure does not prejudge either its legal status under the GATT 1994 and this Agreement, the effects under this Agreement, or the nature of the measure itself.

25.8 Any Member may, at any time, make a written request for information on the nature and extent of any subsidy granted or maintained by another Member (including any subsidy referred to in Part IV above), or for explanation of the reasons for which a specific measure has been considered as not notifiable.

25.9 Members so requested shall provide such information as quickly as possible and in a comprehensive manner, and shall be ready, upon request, to provide additional information to the requesting Member. In particular they shall provide sufficient details to enable the other Member to assess their compliance with the terms of this Agreement. Any Member which considers that such information has not been provided may bring the matter to the attention of the Committee.

25.10 Any interested Member which considers that any practice of another Member having the effects of a subsidy has not been notified in accordance with the provisions of paragraph 1 of Article XVI of the GATT 1994 and this Article may bring the matter to the attention of such other Member. If the alleged subsidy is not thereafter notified promptly, such Member may itself bring the alleged subsidy in question to the notice of the Committee.

25.11 Members shall report without delay to the Committee all preliminary or final actions taken with respect to countervailing duties. Such reports will be available in the MTO Secretariat for inspection by government representatives. The Members shall also submit, on a semi-annual basis, reports on any countervailing duty actions taken within the preceding six months.

25.12 Each Member shall notify the Committee (a) which of its authorities are competent to initiate and conduct investigations referred to in Article 11 and (b) its domestic procedures governing the initiation and conduct of such investigations.

Article 26

Surveillance

26.1 The Committee shall examine new and full notifications submitted under paragraph 1 of Article XVI of the GATT 1994 and paragraph 1 of Article 25 of this Agreement at special sessions held every third year. Notifications submitted in the intervening years updating notifications shall be examined at each regular meeting of the Committee.

26.2 The Committee shall examine reports submitted under paragraph 1 of Article 25 above, at each regular meeting of the Committee. The semi-annual reports shall be submitted on an agreed standard form.

PART VIII : DEVELOPING COUNTRY MEMBERS

Article 27

Special and Differential Treatment for Developing Country Members

27.1 Members recognize that subsidies may play an important role in economic development programmes of developing country Members.

27.2 The prohibition of paragraph l(a) of Article 3 shall not apply to:

(a) developing country Members referred to in Annex VII.

(b) other developing country Members for eight years from the date of entry into force of the Agreement Establishing the **WTO** subject to compliance with the provisions in paragraph 3 below.

27.2b The prohibition of paragraph l(b) of Article 3 shall not apply to developing countries for a period of five years, and shall not apply to least developed countries for a period of eight years, from the date of entry into force of the Agreement Establishing the **WTO**

27.3 Any developing country Member referred to in paragraph 2(b) above shall phase out its export subsidies within the eight year period, preferably in a progressive manner. However, a developing country Member shall not increase the level of its export subsidies[127], and shall eliminate them within a period shorter than that provided for in this provision when the use of such export subsidies is inconsistent with its development needs. If a developing country Member deems it necessary to apply such subsidies beyond the eight year period, it shall not later than one year before the expiry of this period enter into consultation with the Committee, which will determine whether an extension of this period is justified, after examining all the relevant economic, financial and development needs of the Member in question. If the Committee

---

[127] For countries not granting export subsidies as of the day of entry into force of the Agreement establishing the **WTO**. this provision shall apply on the basis of the level of export subsidies granted in 1986.

determines that the extension is justified, the developing country Member concerned shall hold annual consultations with the Committee to determine the necessity of maintaining the subsidies. If no such determination is made by the Committee, the developing country Member shall phase out the remaining export subsidies within two years from the end of the last authorized period.

27.4 A developing country Member that has reached export competitiveness in any given product shall phase out its export subsidies for such product(s), over a period of two years. However, for a country which is referred to in Annex VII and which has reached export competitiveness in one or more products, export subsidies on such products shall be gradually phased out over a period of 8 years.

27.5 Export competitiveness in a product exists if a country's exports of that product have reached a share of at least 3.25 per cent in world trade of that product for two consecutive calendar years. Export competitiveness shall exist either (a) on the basis of notification by the country having reached export competitiveness, or (b) on the basis of a computation undertaken by the **WTO** Secretariat at the request of any Member. For the purpose of this paragraph a product is defined as a section heading of the Harmonized System Nomenclature. Members agree that the Committee shall review the operation of this provision 5 years from the date of the entry into force of the Agreement Establishing the WTO.

27.6 Provisions of Article 4 shall not apply to a developing country Member in the case of export subsidies which are in conformity with the provisions of paragraphs 2 through 4 above. The relevant provisions in such a case shall be those of Article 7.

27.7 There shall be no presumption in terms of paragraph 1 of Article 6 that a subsidy granted by a developing country Member results in serious prejudice, as defined in this Agreement. Such serious prejudice where applicable under the terms of paragraph 8 below, shall be demonstrated by positive evidence, in accordance with the provisions of paragraphs 3 through 8 of Article 6.

27.8 Regarding actionable subsidies other than those referred to in paragraph 1 of Article 6, action may not be authorized or taken under Article 7 of this Agreement unless nullification or impairment of tariff concessions or other obligations under the GATT 1994 is found to exist as a result of such a subsidy, in such a way as to displace or impede imports of like products into the market of the subsidizing country or unless injury to domestic industry in the im-porting market of a Member occurs in terms of Article 15 of this Agreement.

27.9 Any countervailing duty investigation of a product originating in a developing Member shall be terminated as soon as the authorities concerned determine that:

(a) the overall level of subsidies granted upon the product in question does not exceed 2 per cent of its value/calculated on a per unit basis; or

(b) the volume of the subsidized imports represents less than 4 per cent of the total imports for the like product in the importing Member, unless imports from developing country Members whose individual shares of total import represent less than 4 per cent collectively account for more than 9 per cent of the total imports for the like product in the importing country.

27.10 For those Members within the scope of paragraph 2(b) of Article 27 which have eliminated export subsidies prior to the expiry of the period of 8 years from the entry into force of the Agreement Establishing the WTO and those in Annex VII, the number in paragraph 9(a) shall be 3 per cent rather than 2 per cent. This provision shall apply from the date that this elimination of export subsidies is notified to the Committee for so long as export subsidies are not granted by the notifying Member. This provision shall expire 8 years from the date of entry into force of the Agreement Establishing the WTO

27.11 The provisions of paragraphs 9 and 10 shall govern any determination of *de minimis* under paragraph 3 of Article 15 of this Agreement.

27.12 The provisions of Part III of this Agreement shall not be applicable to direct forgiveness of debts, subsidies to cover social costs, in whatever form, including relinquishment of government revenue and other transfer of liabilities when such subsidies are granted within and directly linked to a privatization programme of a developing country Member provided that both such programme and the subsidies involved are granted for a limited period and notified to the Committee and that the programme results in eventual privatization of the enterprise concerned.

27.13 The Committee shall, upon request by an interested Member, undertake a review of a specific export subsidy practice of a developing country Member to examine whether the practice is in conformity with its development needs.

27.14 The Committee shall, upon request by an interested developing country Member, undertake a review of a specific countervailing measure to examine whether it is consistent with the provisions of paragraphs 9 and 10 above as applicable to the developing country Member in question.

PART IX : TRANSITIONAL ARRANGEMENTS

Article 28

Existing Programmes

28.1 Subsidy programmes that have been established within the territory of any Member before the date on which such a Member signed the Agreement Establishing the WTO and which are inconsistent with the provisions of this Agreement shall be:

(i) notified to the Committee not later than 90 days after the entry into force of the Agreement Establishing the **WTO** for such Member;

(ii) "brought into conformity with the provisions of this Agreement within 3 years of the date of entry into force of the Agreement Establishing the **WTO** for such Member and until then shall not be subject to Part II of this Agreement.

28.2 No Member shall extend the scope of any such programme, nor shall such a programme be renewed upon its expiration.

Article 29

Transformation into a Market Economy

29.1 Members in the process of transformation from a centrally-planned into a market, free enterprise economy, may apply programmes and measures necessary for such a transformation.

29.2 For such Members, subsidy programmes falling within the scope of Article 3, and notified according to paragraph 3 below, shall be phased out or brought into conformity with Article 3 within a period of 7 years from the date of entry into force of the Agreement Establishing the WTO. In such a case, Article 4 shall not apply. In addition during the same period:

- Subsidy programmes falling within the scope of paragraph l(d) of Article 6 shall not be actionable under Article 7;
- With respect to other actionable subsidies, provisions of paragraph 8 of Article 27 shall apply.

29.3 Subsidy programmes falling within the scope of Article 3 shall be notified to the Committee by the earliest practicable date after entry into force of the Agreement Establishing the **WTO** Further notifications of such subsidies may be made up to two years after entry into force of the Agreement Establishing the **WTO**.

29.4. In exceptional circumstances Members may be given departures from their notified programmes and measures and their time-frame by the Committee if such departures are deemed necessary, for the process of transformation.

PART X : DISPUTE SETTLEMENT

Article 30

The provisions of Articles XXII and XXIII of the GATT 1994 as elaborated and applied by the Understanding on Rules and Procedures Governing the Settlement of Disputes shall apply to consultations and the settlement of disputes under this Agreement, except as otherwise specifically provided herein.

PART XI : FINAL PROVISIONS

Article 31

Provisional Application

The provisions of paragraph 1 of Article 6, and the provisions of Article 8 and Article 9 shall apply for a period of 5 years, beginning with the date of entry into force of the Agreement Establishing the **WTO** Not later than 180 days before the end of this period, the Committee shall review the operation of those provisions, with a view to determining whether to extend their application, either as presently drafted or in a modified form, for a further period.

Article 32

Other Final Provisions

32.1 No specific action against a subsidy of another Member can be taken except in accordance with the provisions of the GATT 1994, as interpreted by this Agreement.[128]

32.2 Reservations may not be entered in respect of any of the provisions of this Agreement without the consent of the other Members.

32.3 Subject to sub-paragraph 1, the provisions of this Agreement shall apply to investigations, and reviews of existing measures, initiated pursuant to applications which have been made on or after the date of entry into force for a Member of the Agreement Establishing the **WTO** .

32.3.1 For the purposes of paragraph 3 of Article 21, existing countervailing measures shall be deemed to be imposed on a date not later than the date of entry into force for a Member of the Agreement Establishing the **WTO**, except in cases in which the domestic legislation of a Member in force at that date already included a clause of the type provided for in that paragraph.

32.4 (a) Each government accepting or acceding to the **WTO** shall take

---

[128] This paragraph is not intended to preclude action under other relevant provisions of the GATT 1994, where appropriate.

all necessary steps, of a general or particular character, to ensure, not later than the date of entry into force of the Agreement Establishing the WTO for it, the conformity of its laws, regulations and administrative procedures with the provisions of this Agreement as they may apply to the Member in question.

(b) Each Member shall inform the Committee of any changes in its laws and regulations relevant to this Agreement and in the administration of such laws and regulations.

32.5 The Committee shall review annually the implementation and operation of this Agreement taking into account the objectives thereof. The Committee shall annually inform the Council for Trade in Goods of developments during the period covered by such reviews.

32.6 The Annexes to this Agreement constitute an integral part thereof.

ANNEX I

Illustrative List of Export Subsidies

(a) The provision by governments of direct subsidies to a firm or an industry contingent upon export performance.

(b) Currency retention schemes or any similar practices which involve a bonus on exports.

(c) Internal transport and freight charges on export shipments, provided or mandated by governments, on terms more favourable than for domestic shipments

(d) The provision by governments or their agencies either directly or indirectly through government-mandated schemes, of imported or domestic products or services for use in the production of exported goods, on terms or conditions more favourable than for provision of like or directly competitive products or services for use in the production of goods for domestic consumption, if (in the case of products) such terms or conditions are more favourable than those commercially available[129] on world markets to their exporters.

(e) The full or partial exemption, remission, or deferral specifically related to exports, of direct taxes[130] or social welfare charges paid

---

[129] The term 'commercially available ' means that the choice between domestic and imported products is unrestricted and depends only on commercial considerations.

[130] For the purpose of this Agreement:

The term 'direct taxes' shall mean taxes on wages, profits, interests, rents, royalties, and all other forms of income, and taxes on the ownership of real property;

The term 'import charges' shall mean tariffs, duties, and other fiscal charges not elsewhere enumerated in this note that are levied on imports;

–Contd.

or payable by industrial or commercial enterprises.[131]

(f) The allowance of special deductions directly related to exports or export performance, over and above those granted in respect to production for domestic consumption, in the calculation of the base on which direct taxes are charged.

(g) The exemption or remission in respect of the production and distribution of exported products, of indirect taxes[130] in excess of those levied in respect of the production and distribution of like products when sold for domestic consumption.

(h) The exemption, remission or deferral of prior stage cumulative indirect taxes[130] on goods or services used in the production of exported products in excess of the exemption, remission or deferral of like prior stage cumulative indirect taxes on goods or services used in the production of like products when sold for domestic consumption; provided, however, that prior stage cumulative indirect taxes may be exempted, remitted or deferred on exported products even when not exempted, remitted or deferred on like products when sold for domestic consumption, if the prior stage cumulative indirect taxes are levied on inputs that are consumed in the production of the exported product (making normal allowance for

---

The term 'indirect taxes' shall mean sales, excise, turnover, value added, franchise, stamp, transfer, inventory and equipment taxes, border taxes and all taxes other than direct taxes and import charges;

'Prior stage' indirect taxes are those levied on goods or services used directly or indirectly in making the product;

'Cumulative ' indirect taxes are multi-staged taxes levied where there is no mechanism for subsequent crediting of the tax if the goods or services subject to tax at one stage of production are used in a succeeding stage of production;

'Remission' of taxes includes the refund or rebate of taxes;

'Remission or drawback' includes the full or partial exemption or deferral of import charges.

[131] The Members recognize that deferral need not amount to an export subsidy where, for example, appropriate interest charges are collected. The Members reaffirm the principle that prices for goods in transactions between exporting enterprises and foreign buyers under their or under the same control should for tax purposes be the prices which would be charged between independent enterprises acting at arm's length. Any Member may draw the attention of another Member to administrative or other practices which may contravene this principle and which result in a significant saving of direct taxes in export transactions. In such circumstances the Members shall normally attempt to resolve their differences using the facilities of existing bilateral tax treaties or other specific international mechanisms, without prejudice to the rights and obligations of Members under the GATT 1994, including the right of consultation created in the preceding sentence.

Paragraph (e) is not intended to limit a Member from taking measures to avoid the double taxation of foreign source income earned by its enterprises or the enterprises of another Member.

waste).[132] This item shall be interpreted in accordance with the guidelines on consumption of inputs in the production process contained in Annex II.

(i) The remission or drawback of import charges[131] in excess of those levied on imported inputs that are consumed in the production of the exported product (making normal allowance for waste); provided, however, that in particular cases a firm may use a quantity of home market inputs equal to, and having the same quality and characteristics as, the imported inputs as a substitute for them in order to benefit from this provision if the import and the corresponding export operations both occur within a reasonable time period, not to exceed two years. This item shall be interpreted in accordance with the guidelines on consumption of inputs in the production process contained in Annex II and the guidelines in the determination of substitution drawback systems as export subsidies contained in Annex III.

(j) The provision by governments (or special institutions controlled by governments) of export credit guarantee or insurance programmes, of insurance or guarantee programmes against increases in the cost of exported products or of exchange risk programmes, at premium rates which are inadequate to cover the long-term operating costs and losses of the programmes.

(k) The grant by governments (or special institutions controlled by and/or acting under the authority of governments) of export credits at rates below those which they actually have to pay for the funds so employed (or would have to pay if they borrowed on international capital market in order to obtain funds of the same maturity and other credit terms and denominated in the same currency as the export credit), or the payment by them of all or part of the costs incurred by exporters or financial institutions in obtaining credits, in so far as they are used to secure a material advantage in the field of export credit terms.

Provided, however, that if a Member is a party to an international undertaking on official export credits to which at least twelve original Members to this Agreement are parties as of 1 January, 1979 (or a successor undertaking which has been adopted by those original Members), or if in practice a Member applies the interest

[132] Paragraph (h) does not apply to value-added tax systems and border-tax adjustment in lieu thereof; the problem of the excessive remission of value-added taxes is exclusively covered by paragraph (g).

rates provisions of the relevant undertaking, an export credit practice which is in conformity with those provisions shall not be considered an export subsidy prohibited by this Agreement.

(l) Any other charge on the public account constituting an export subsidy in the sense of Article XVI of the GATT 1994.

ANNEX II

Guidelines on Consumption of inputs in the Production Process[133]

I

1. Indirect tax rebate schemes can allow for exemption, remission or deferral of prior stage cumulative indirect taxes levied on inputs that are consumed in the production of the exported product (making normal allowance for waste). Similarly, drawback schemes can allow for the remission or drawback of import charges levied on inputs that are consumed in the production of the exported product (making normal allowance for waste).

2. The Illustrative List of Export Subsidies in Annex I of this Agreement makes reference to the term "inputs that are consumed in the production of the exported product" in paragraphs (h) and (i). Pursuant to paragraph (h), indirect tax rebate schemes can constitute an export subsidy to the extent that they result in exemption, remission or deferral of prior stage cumulative indirect taxes in excess of the amount of such taxes actually levied on inputs that are consumed in the production of the exported product. Pursuant to paragraph (i), drawback schemes can constitute an export subsidy to the extent that they result in a remission or drawback of import charges in excess of those actually levied on inputs that are consumed in the production of the exported product. Both paragraphs stipulate that normal allowance for waste must be made in findings regarding consumption of inputs in the production of exported product. Paragraph (i) also provides for substitution, where appropriate.

II

In examining whether inputs are consumed in the production of the exported product, as part of a countervailing duty investigation pursuant to this Agreement, investigating authorities should proceed on the following basis :

1. Where it is alleged that an indirect tax rebate scheme, or a drawback scheme, conveys a subsidy by reason of over-rebate or excess drawback of

[133] Inputs consumed in the production process are inputs physically incorporated, energy, fuels and oil used in the production process and catalysts which are consumed in the course of their use to obtain the exported product.

indirect taxes or import charges on inputs consumed in the production of the exported product, the investigating authorities should first determine whether the government of the exporting country has in place and applies a system or procedure to confirm which inputs are consumed in the production of the exported product and in what amounts. Where such a system or procedure is determined to be applied, the investigating authorities should then examine the system or procedure to see whether it is reasonable, effective for the purpose intended, and based on generally accepted commercial practices in the country of export. The investigating authorities may deem it necessary to carry out, in accordance with paragraph 6 of Article 12 of this Agreement certain practical tests in order to verify information or to satisfy themselves that the system or procedure is being effectively applied.

2. Where there is no such system or procedure, where it is not reasonable, or where it is instituted and considered reasonable but is found not to be applied or not to be applied effectively, a further examination by the exporting country based on the actual inputs involved would need to be carried out in the context of determining whether an excess payment occurred. if the importing country deemed it necessary, a further examination would be carried out in accordance with paragraph 1 above.

3. Investigating authorities should treat inputs as physically incorporated if such inputs are used in the production process and are physically present in the product exported. The Members note that an input need not be present in the final product in the same form in which it entered the production process.

4. In determining the amount of a particular input that is consumed in the production of the exported product, a "normal allowance for waste" should be taken into account, and such waste should be treated as consumed in the production of the exported product. The term "waste" refers to that portion of a given input which does not serve an independent function in the production process, is not consumed in the production of the exported product (for reasons such as inefficiencies) and is not recovered, used nor sold by the same manufacturer.

The investigating authority's determination of whether the claimed allowance for waste is "normal" should take into account the production process, the average experience of the industry in the country of export, and other technical factors, as appropriate. The investigating authority should bear in mind that an important question is whether the authorities in the exporting country have reasonably calculated the amount of waste, when such an amount is intended to be included in the tax or duty rebate or remission.

ANNEX III

Guidelines in the Determination of Substitution Drawback Systems as Export Subsidies

I

Drawback systems can allow for the refund or drawback of import charges on inputs which are consumed in the production process of another product and where the export of this latter product contains domestic inputs having the same quality and characteristics as those substituted for the imported inputs. Pursuant to paragraph (i) of the Illustrative List of Export Subsidies in Annex I of this Agreement substitution drawback systems can constitute an export subsidy to the extent that they result in an excess drawback of the import charges levied initially on the imported inputs for which drawback is being claimed.

II

In examining any substitution drawback system as part of a countervailing duty investigation pursuant to this Agreement, investigating authorities should proceed on the following basis:

1. Paragraph (i) of the Illustrative List stipulates that home market inputs may be substituted for imported inputs in the production of a product for export provided such inputs are equal in quantity to, and have the same quality and characteristics as, the imported inputs being substituted. The existence of a verification system or procedure is important because it enables the government of the exporting country to ensure and demonstrate that the quantity of inputs for which drawback is claimed does not exceed the quantity of similar products exported, in whatever form, and that there is not drawback of import charges in excess of those originally levied on the imported inputs in question.

2. Where it is alleged that a substitution drawback system conveys a subsidy, the investigating authorities should first proceed to determine whether the government of the exporting country has in place and applies a verification system or procedure. Where such a system or procedure is determined to be applied, the investigating authorities should then examine the verification procedures to see whether they are reasonable, effective for the purpose intended, and based on generally accepted commercial practices in the country of export. To the extent that the procedures are determined to meet this test

and are effectively applied, no subsidy should be presumed to exist. It may be deemed necessary by the investigating authorities to carry out, in accordance with paragraph 6 of Article 12 of this Agreement, certain practical tests in order to verify information or to satisfy themselves that the verification procedures are being effectively applied.

3. Where there are no verification procedures, where they are not reasonable, or where such procedures are instituted and considered reasonable but are found not to be actually applied or not applied effectively, there may be a subsidy. In such cases a further examination by the exporting country based on the actual transactions involved would need to be carried out to determine whether an excess payment occurred. If the importing country deemed it necessary a further examination would be carried out in accordance with paragraph 2 above.

4. The existence of a substitution drawback provision under which exporters are allowed to select particular import shipments on which drawback is claimed should not of itself be considered to convey a subsidy.

5. An excess drawback of import charges in the sense of paragraph (i) would be deemed to exist where governments paid interest on any monies refunded under their drawback schemes, to the extent of the interest actually paid or payable.

ANNEX IV

Calculation of the Total *Ad Valorem* Subsidization (paragraph I(a) of Article 6)[134]

1. Any calculation of the amount of a subsidy for the purpose of paragraph 1 of Article 6 above shall be done in terms of the cost to the granting government.

2. Except as provided in paragraphs 3-5, in determining whether the overall rate of subsidization exceeds 5 per cent of the value of the product, the value of the product shall be calculated as the total value of the recipient firm's[135] sales in the most recent twelve-month period, for which sales data is available, preceding the period in which the subsidy is granted.[136]

3. Where the subsidy is tied to the production or sale of a given product,

---

[134] An understanding among Members should be developed, as necessary, on matters which are not specified in this Annex or which need further clarification for the purposes of paragraph l(a) of Article 6.

[135] The recipient firm is a firm in the subsidizing country.

[136] In the case of tax-related subsidies the value of the product shall be calculated as the total value of the recipient firm's sales in the fiscal year in which the tax-related measure was earned.

the value of the product shall be calculated as the total value of the recipient firm's sales of that product in the most recent twelve-month period, for which sales data is available, preceding the period in which the subsidy is granted.

4. Where the recipient firm is in a start-up situation, the overall rate of subsidization shall not exceed 15 per cent of the total funds invested. For purposes of this paragrapha start-up period will not extend beyond the first year of production.[137]

5. Where the recipient firm is located in an inflationary economy country, the value of the product shall be calculated as the recipient firm's total sales (or sales of the relevant product, if the subsidy is tied) in the preceding calendar year indexed by the rate of inflation experienced in the twelve months preceding the month in which the subsidy is to be given.

6. In determining the overall rate of subsidization in a given year, subsidies given under different programmes and by different authorities in the territory of a Member shall be aggregated.

7. Subsidies granted prior to the entry into force of the Agreement Establishing the **WTO** the benefits of which are allocated to future production, shall be included in the overall rate of subsidization.

8. Subsidies which are non-actionable under relevant provisions of this Agreement shall not be included in the calculation of the amount of a subsidy for the purpose of paragraph 1 of Article 6 above.

ANNEX V

Procedures for Developing Information Concerning Serious Prejudice

1. Every Member shall co-operate in the development of evidence to be examined by the Committee or its subsidiary bodies in procedures under Article 7 above, paragraphs 4 through 6. The parties to the dispute and any third-country Member concerned shall notify the Committee, as soon as the provisions of paragraph 4 of Article 7 have been invoked, the organization responsible for administration of this provision within its territory and the procedures to be used to comply with requests for information.

2. In cases where matters are referred to in the Committee under paragraph 4 of Article 7, the Committee shall upon request, initiate the procedure to

---

[137] Start-up situations include instances where financial commitments for product development or construction of facilities manufacture products benefiting from the subsidy have been made, even though production has not begun.

obtain such information from the government of the subsidizing Member as necessary to establish the existence and amount of subsidizations, the value of total sales of the subsidized firms, as well as information necessary to analyze the adverse effects caused by the subsidized product.[138] This process may include where appropriate, presentation of questions to the government of the subsidizing country and of the complaining country to collect information, as well as to clarify and obtain elaboration of information available to the parties to a dispute through the notification procedures set forth in Part VII above.[139]

3. In the case of effects in third-country markets, a Member party to a dispute may collect information, including through the use of questions to the government of the third-country, necessary to analyze adverse effects, which is not otherwise reasonably available from the complaining Member or the subsidizing Member. This requirement should be administered in such a way as not to impose an unreasonable burden on the third-country Member. In particular, such a Member is not expected to make a market or price analysis specially for that purpose. The information to be supplied is that which is already available or can be readily obtained by this Member (*e.g.*, most recent statistics which have already been gathered by relevant statistical services but which have not yet been published, customs data concerning imports and declared values of the products concerned, etc.). However, if a Member party to a dispute undertakes a detailed market analysis at its own expense, the task of the person or firm conducting such an analysis shall be facilitated by the authorities of the third-country Member and such a person or firm shall be given access to all information which is not normally maintained confidential by the government.

4. The Committee shall designate a representative to serve the function of facilitating the information-gathering process. The sole purpose of the representative shall be to ensure the timely development of the information necessary to facilitate expeditious subsequent multilateral review of the dispute. In particular, the representative may suggest ways to most efficiently solicit necessary information as well as encourage the co-operation of the parties.

5. The information-gathering process outlined in paragraphs 2-4 above shall be completed within 60 days of the date on which the matter has been referred to the Committee under paragraph 4 of Article 7 above. The information obtained during this process shall be submitted to the Committee or to a panel established by the Committee in accordance with the provisions of Part

[138] In cases where the existence of serious prejudice has to be demonstrated.

[139] The information gathering process by the Committee shall take into account the need to protect information which is by nature confidential or which is provided on a confidential basis by any Member involved in this process.

X above. This information should include, *inter alia,* data concerning the amount of the subsidy in question (and, where appropriate, the value of total sales of the subsidized firms), prices of the subsidized product, prices of the non-subsidized product, prices of other suppliers to the market, changes' in the supply of the subsidized product to the market in question and changes in market shares. It should also include rebuttal evidence, as well as such supplemental information as the Committee or the panel deems relevant in the course of reaching its conclusions.

6. If the subsidizing and/or third-country Member fail to co-operate in the information-gathering process, the complaining Member will present its case of serious prejudice, based on evidence available to it, together with facts and circumstances of the non co-operation of the subsidizing and/or third-country Member. Where information is unavailable due to non co-operation by the subsidizing and/or third country Member, the Committee or the panel may complete the record as necessary relying on best information otherwise available.

7. In making its determination, the Committee or the panel should draw adverse inferences from instances of non-cooperation by any party involved in the information-gathering process.

8. In making a determination to use either best information available or adverse inferences, the Committee or the panel shall consider the advice of the Committee representative nominated under paragraph 4 above as to the reasonableness of any requests for information and the efforts made by parties to comply with these requests in a co-operative and timely manner.

9. Nothing in the information-gathering process shall limit the ability of the Committee or the panel to seek such additional information it deems essential to a proper resolution to the dispute, and which was not adequately sought or developed during that process. However, ordinarily the panel should not request additional information to complete the record where the information would support a particular party's position and the absence of that information in the record is the result of unreasonable non-cooperation by that party in the information-gathering process.

ANNEX VI

Procedures for On-The-Spot Investigations Pursuant to Paragraph 6 of Article 12

(a) Upon initiation of an investigation, the authorities of the exporting country and the firms known to be concerned should be informed of the intention to carry out on-the-spot investigations.

(b) If in exceptional circumstances it is intended to include non-governmental experts in the investigating team, the firms and the authorities of the exporting country should be so informed. Such non-governmental experts should be subject to effective sanctions for breach of confidentiality requirements.

(c) It should be standard practice to obtain explicit agreement of the firms concerned in the exporting country before the visit is finally scheduled.

(d) As soon as the agreement of the firms concerned has been obtained the investigating authorities should notify the authorities of the exporting country of the names and addresses of the firms to be visited and the dates agreed.

(e) Sufficient advance notice should be given to the firms in question before the visit is made.

(f) Visits to explain the questionnaire should only be made at the request of an exporting firm. In case of such a request the investigating authorities may place themselves at the disposal of the firm; such a visit may only be made, provided the authorities of the importing country notify the representatives of the government of the country in question and unless the latter do not object to the visit.

(g) As the main purpose of the on-the-spot investigation is to verify information provided or to obtain further details, it should be carried out after the response to the questionnaire has been received unless the firm agrees to the contrary and the government of the exporting country is informed by the investigating authorities of the anticipated visit and does not object to it; further, it should be standard practice prior to the visit to advise the firms concerned of the general nature of the information to be verified and of any further information which needs to be provided, though this should not preclude requests to be made on the spot for further details to be provided in the light of information obtained.

(h) Enquiries or questions put by the authorities or firms of the exporting countries and essential to a successful on-the-spot investigation should, whenever possible, be answered before the visit is made.

ANNEX VII

Developing Country Members Referred to in Paragraph 2(a) of Article 27

The developing country Member not subject to the provisions of paragraph l(a) of Article 3 under the terms of paragraph 2(a) of Article 27 are:

(a) Least-developed countries designated as such by the United Nations that are Members of the WTO.

(b) Each of the following developing country Members shall be subject to the provisions which are applicable to other developing country Members according to paragraph 2(b) of Article 27 when GNP *per capita* has reached $1,000 per annum: Bolivia, Cameroon, Congo, Côte d'Ivoire, Dominican Republic, Egypt, Ghana, Guatemala, Guyana, India, Indonesia, Kenya, Morocco, Nicaragua, Nigeria, Pakistan, Philippines, Senegal, Sri Lanka and Zimbabwe.

NOTE: The inclusion of countries in the list in (b) is based on the most recent data from the World Bank on GNP *per capita.*

AGREEMENT ON SAFEGUARDS

Members.

Having in mind the overall objective of the Members to improve and strengthen the international trading system based on the GATT 1994;

Recognizing the need to clarify and reinforce the disciplines of the GATT 1994, and specifically those of its Article XIX (Emergency Action on Imports of Particular Products), to re-establish multilateral control over safeguards and eliminate measures that escape such control;

Recognizing the importance of structural adjustment and the need to enhance rather than limit competition in international markets; and

Recognizing further that, for these purposes, a comprehensive agreement, applicable to all Members and based on the basic principles of the GATT 1994, is called for;

Hereby *agree as* follows:

SECTION I
General

1. This Agreement establishes rules for the application of safeguard measures which shall be understood to mean those measures provided for in Article XIX of the GATT 1994.

SECTION II
Conditions

2. A Member[140] may apply a safeguard measure to a product only if that

[140] A customs union may apply a safeguard measure as a single unit or on behalf of a member state. When a customs union applies a safeguard measure as a single unit, all the requirements for the determination of serious injury or threat thereof under this Agreement shall be based on the conditions existing in the customs union as a whole. When a safeguard measure is applied on behalf of a member state, all the requirements for the determination of serious *–Contd.*

Member has determined, pursuant to the provisions set out below, that such product is being imported into its territory in such increased quantities, absolute or relative to domestic production, and under such conditions as to cause or threaten to cause serious injury to the domestic industry that produces like or directly competitive products.

3. (a) A Member may apply a safeguard measure only following an investigation by the competent authorities of that Member pursuant to procedures previously established and made public in consonance with Article X of the GATT 1994. This investigation shall include reasonable public notice to all interested parties and public hearings or other appropriate means in which importers, exporters and other interested parties could present evidence and their views, including the opportunity to respond to the presentations of other parties and to submit their views, *inter alia, as* to whether or not the application of a safeguard measure would be in the public interest. The competent authorities shall publish a report setting forth their findings and reasoned conclusions reached on all pertinent issues of fact and law.

(b) Any information which is by nature confidential or which is provided on a confidential basis shall, upon cause being shown, be treated as such by the competent auth-orities. Such information shall not be disclosed without permission of the party submitting it. Parties providing confidential information may be requested to furnish non-confidential summaries thereof or, if such parties indicate that such infonnation cannot be summarized, the reasons why a summary cannot be provided. However, if the competent authorities find that a request for confidentiality is not warranted and if the party concerned is either unwilling to make the information public or to authorize its disclosure in generalized or summary form, the authorities would be free to disregard such information unless it can be demonstrated to their satisfaction from appropriate sources that the information is correct.

4. In critical circumstances where delay would cause damage which it would be difficult to repair, a provisional safeguard measure may be taken pursuant to a preliminary determination that there is clear evidence that increased imports have caused or are threatening to cause serious injury. The duration of the provisional measure shall not exceed 200 days, during which period the pertinent requirements of this Section and Section VII shall be

---

injury or threat thereof shall be based on the conditions existing in that member state and the measure shall be limited to that member state. Nothing in this Agreement prejudges the interpretation of the relationship between Article XIX and Article XXIV:8 of GATT 1994.

met. Such measures should take the form of tariff increases to be promptly refunded if the subsequent investigation referred to in paragraph 7 below does not determine that increased imports have caused or threatened to cause serious injury to a domestic industry. The duration of any such provisional measure shall be counted as a part of the initial period and any extension referred to in paragraphs 10, 11 and 12 below.

5. Safeguard measures shall be applied to a product being imported irrespective of its source.

6. For the purposes of this Agreement:

(a) serious injury shall be understood to mean a significant overall impairment in the position of a domestic industry;

(b) threat of serious injury shall be understood to mean serious injury that is clearly imminent, in accordance with the provisions of paragraph 7 below. A determination of the existence of a threat of serious injury shall be based on facts and not merely on allegation, conjecture or remote possibility; and

(c) in determining injury or threat thereof, a domestic industry shall be understood to mean the producers as a whole of the like or directly competitive products operating within the territory of a Member, or those whose collective output of the like or directly competitive products constitutes a major proportion of the total domestic production of those products.

7. (a) In the investigation to determine whether increased imports have caused or are threatening to cause serious injury to a domestic industry under the terms of this Agreement, the competent authorities shall evaluate all relevant factors of an objective and quantifiable nature having a bearing on the situation of that industry, in particular, the rate and amount of the increase in imports of the product concerned in absolute and relative terms, the share of the domestic market taken by increased imports, changes in the level of sales, production, productivity, capacity utilization, profits and losses, and employment.

(b) The determination referred to in sub-paragraph 7(a) shall not be made unless this investigation demonstrates, on the basis of objective evidence, the existence of the causal link between increased imports of the product concerned and serious injury or threat thereof. When factors other than increased imports are causing injury to the domestic industry at the same time, such injury shall not be attributed to increased imports.

(c) The competent authorities shall publish promptly, in accordance with the provisions of paragraph 3 above, a detailed analysis of the case under investigation as well as a demonstration of the relevance of the factors examined.

8. Safeguard measures shall be applied only to the extent as may be necessary to prevent or remedy serious injury and to facilitate adjustment. If a quantitative restriction is used, such a measure shall not reduce the quantity of imports below the level of a recent period which shall be the average of imports in the last three representative years for which statistics are available, unless clear justification is given that a different level is necessary to prevent or remedy serious injury. Members should choose measures most suitable for the achievement of these objectives.

9. (a) In cases in which a quota is allocated among supplying countries, the Member applying the restrictions may seek agreement with respect to the allocation of shares in the quota with all other Members having a substantial interest in supplying the product concerned. In cases in which this method is not reasonably practicable, the Member concerned shall allot to Members having a substantial interest in supplying the product shares based upon the proportions, supplied by such Members during a previous representative period, of the total quantity or value of imports of the product, due account being taken of any special factors which may have affected or may be affecting the trade in the product.

(b) A Member may depart from the provisions in (a) above provided that consultations under paragraph 27 are conducted under the auspices of the Committee on Safeguards established in paragraph 36 of this Agreement and that clear demonstration is provided to the Committee that (i) imports from certain Members have increased in disproportionate percentage in relation to the total increase of imports of the product concerned in the representative period, (ii) the reasons for the departure from the provisions in (a) above are justified, and (iii) the conditions of such departure are equitable to all suppliers of the product concerned. The duration of any such measure shall not be extended beyond the initial period under paragraph 10 below. The departure referred to above shall not be permitted in the case of threat of serious injury.

10. Safeguard measures shall be applied only for a period of time as may be necessary to prevent or remedy serious injury and to facilitate adjustment. The period shall not exceed four years, unless it is extended under paragraph 11 below.

11. The period mentioned in paragraph 10 above may be extended provided that the competent authorities of the importing Member have determined, in conformity with the procedures set out in this Section, that the safeguard measure continues to be necessary to prevent or remedy serious injury; that there is evidence that the industry is adjusting; and provided that the pertinent provisions of Sections III and VII below are observed.

12. The total period of application of a safeguard measure including the period of application of any provisional measure, the period of initial application and any extension thereof, shall not exceed eight years.

13. In order to facilitate adjustment, if the expected duration of a safeguard measure as notified under the provisions of paragraph 25 is over one year, it shall be progressively liberalized at regular intervals during the period of application. If the duration of the measure exceeds three years, the Member applying such a measure shall review the situation not later than the mid-term of the measure and, if appropriate, withdraw it or increase the pace of liberalization. A measure extended under paragraph 11 above shall not be more restrictive than it was at the end of the initial period, and should continue to be liberalized.

14. No safeguard measure shall be applied again to the import of a product which has been subject to such a measure, taken after the date of entry into force of the Agreement Establishing the **WTO** for a period of time equal to that during which such measure had been previously applied, provided that the period of non-application is at least two years.

15. Not withstanding the provisions of paragraph 14 above, a safeguard measure with a duration of 180 days or less may be applied again to the import of a product if:

(a) at least one year has elapsed since the date of introduction of a safeguard measure on the import of that product; and

(b) such a safeguard measure has not been applied on the same product more than twice in the five-year period immediately preceding the date of introduction of the measure.

SECTION III

Level of concessions and other obligations

16. A Member proposing to apply a safeguard measure or seeking an extension of a safeguard measure shall endearour to maintain a substantially equivalent level of concessions and other obligations to that existing between it and the exporting Members which would be affected by such a measure under the GATT 1994, in accordance with the provisions of paragraph 27 below. To achieve this objective, the Members concerned may agree on any adequate means of trade compensation for the adverse effects of the measure on their trade.

17. If no agreement is reached within 30 days in the consultations under paragraph 27 below, then the affected exporting Members are free, not later than 90 days after the measure is applied, to suspend, upon the expiration of 30 days from the day on which written notice of such suspension is received by the Council for Trade in Goods, the application of substantially equivalent concessions or other obligations under the GATT 1994, to the trade of the Member applying the safeguard measure, the suspension of which the Council for Trade in Goods does not disapprove.

18. The right of suspension referred to in paragraph 17 above shall not be exercised for the first three years that a safeguard measure is in effect, provided that the safeguard measure has been taken as a result of an absolute increase in imports and that such a measure conforms to the provisions of this Agreement

SECTION IV

Developing country members

19. Safeguard measures shall not be applied against a product originating in a developing country Member as long as its share of imports of the product concerned in the importing Member does not exceed 3 per cent, provided that, developing country Members with less than 3 per cent import share collectively account for not more than 9 per cent of total imports of the product concerned.[141]

20. A developing country Member shall have the right to extend the period of application of a safeguard measure for a period of up to two years beyond the maximum period provided for in paragraph 12 above. Notwithstanding the provisions of paragraph 14 above, a developing country Member shall have the right to apply a safeguard measure again to the import of a product which has been subject to such a measure, taken after the date of entry into force of the Agreement Establishing the WTO, after a period of time equal to half that during which such a measure has been previously applied, provided that the period of non-application is at least two years.

SECTION V

Pre-existing Article XIX measures

21. Members shall terminate all safeguard measures taken pursuant to Article XIX of the GATT 1947 that were in existence at the date of entry into force of the Agreement Establishing the WTO not later than eight years after

[141] A Member shall immediately notify an action taken under paragraph 19 to the Committee on Safeguards.

the date on which they were first applied or five years after the date of entry into force of the Agreement Establishing the WTO, whichever comes later.

SECTION VI

Prohibition and elimination of certain measures

22. (a) A Member shall not take or seek any emergency action on imports of particular products as set forth in Article XIX of the GATT 1994 unless such action conforms with the provisions of that Article applied in accordance with this Agreement.

(b) Furthermore, a Member shall not seek, take or maintain any voluntary export restraints, orderly marketing arrangements or any other similar measures on the export or the import side.[142, 143] These include actions taken by a single Member as well as actions under agreements, arrangements and understandings entered into by two or more Members. Any such measure in effect at the time of entry into force of the Agreement Establishing the WTO shall be brought into conformity with this Agreement or phased out in accordance with paragraph 23 below.

(c) This Agreement does not apply to measures sought, taken or maintained by a Member pursuant to provisions of the GATT 1994 other than Article XIX, and Multilateral Trade Agreements in Annex IA other than this Agreement, or pursuant to protocols and agreements or arrangements concluded within the flamework of the GATT 1994.

23. The phasing out of measures referred to in paragraph 22 (b) above shall be carried out according to timetables to be presented to the Committee on Safeguards by the Members concerned not later than 180 days after the date of entry into force of the Agreement Establishing the WTO. These timetables shall provide for all measures referred to in paragraph 22 above to be phased out or brought into conformity with this Agreement within a period not exceeding four years after the date of entry into force of the Agreement Establishing the WTO subject to not more than one specific measure per importing Member[144], the duration of which shall not extend beyond December

---

[142] An import quota applied as a safeguard measure in conformity with the relevant provisions of the GATT 1994 and this Agreement may, by mutual agreement, be administered by the exporting Member.

[143] Examples of similar measures include export moderation, export price or import price monitoring systems, export or import surveillance, compulsory import cartels and discretionary export or import licensing schemes, any of which afford protection.

[144] The only such exception to which the European Communities is entitled is indicated in the Annex to this Agreement.

31, 1999. Any such exception must be mutually agreed between the Members directly concerned and notified to the Committee on Safeguards for its review and acceptance within 90 days of the coming into force of the Agreement Establishing the WTO The Annex to this Agreement indicates a measure which has been agreed as falling under this exception.

24. Members shall not encourage or support the adoption or maintenance by public and private enterprises of non-governmental measures equivalent to those referred to in paragraph 22 above.

SECTION VII

Notification and consultation

25. A Member shall immediately notify the Committee on Safeguards upon:

(a) initiating an investigatory process relating to serious injury or threat thereof and the reasons for it;

(b) making a finding of serious injury or threat thereof caused by increased imports; and

(c) taking a decision to apply or extend a safeguard measure.

26. In making the notifications referred to in sub-paragraphs 25(b) and (c) above, the Member proposing to apply or extend a safeguard measure shall provide the Committee on Safeguards with all pertinent information, which shall include evidence of serious injury or threat thereof caused by increased imports, precise description of the product involved and the proposed measure, proposed date of introduction, expected duration and timetable for progressive liberalization. In the case of an extension of a measure, evidence that the industry concerned is adjusting shall also be provided. The Council for Trade in Goods or the Committee on Safeguards may request such additional information as they may consider necessary from the Member proposing to apply or extend the measure.

27. A Member proposing to apply or extend a safeguard measure shall provide adequate opportunity for prior consultations with those Members having a substantial interest as exporters of the product concerned, with a view to, *inter alia,* reviewing the information provided under paragraph 26 above, exchanging views on the measure and reaching an understanding on ways to achieve the objective set out in Paragraph 16 above.

28. A Member shall make a notification before taking a provisional safeguard measure referred to in paragraph 4 above. Consultations shall be initiated immediately after the measure is taken.

29. The results of the consultations referred to in this Section, as well as the results of mid-term reviews referred to in paragraph 13, any form of

compensation referred to in paragraph 16, and proposed suspensions of concessions and other obligations referred to in paragraph 17, shall be notified immediately to the Council for Trade in Goods by the Members concerned.

30. Members shall notify promptly the Committee on Safeguards of their laws, regulations and administrative procedures relating to safeguard measures as well as any modifications made to them.

31. Members maintaining measures described in paragraphs 21 and 22 above which exist at the date on which the Agreement Establishing the WTO enters into force shall notify such measures to the Committee on Safeguards, not later than 60 days after the entry into force of the Agreement Establishing the **WTO**

32. Any Member may notify the Committee on Safeguards of all laws, regulations, administrative procedures and any measures or actions dealt with in this Agreement that have not been notified by other Members that are required by this Agreement to make such notifications.

33. Any Member may notify the Committee on Safeguards of any non-governmental measures referred to in paragraph 24 above.

34. All notifications to the Council for Trade in Goods referred to in this Agreement shall normally be made through the Committee on Safeguards.

35. The provisions on notification in this Agreement shall not require any Member to disclose confidential information the disclosure of which would impede law enforcement or otherwise be contrary to the public interest or would prejudice the legitimate commercial interests of particular enterprises, public or private.

SECTION VIII
Surveillance

36. There shall be a Committee on Safeguards under the authority of the Council for Trade in Goods, which shall be open to the participation of any Member indicating its wish to serve on it. The Committee will have the following functions:

(a) to monitor, and report annually to the Council for Trade in Goods on the general implementation of this Agreement and make recommendations towards its improvement;

(b) to find, upon request of an affected Member, whether or not the procedural requirements of this Agreement have been complied with in connection with a safeguard measure, and report its findings to the Council for Trade in Goods;

(c) to assist Members, if they so request, in their consultations under the provisions of this Agreement;

(d) to examine measures covered by paragraphs 21 and 22, monitor the phase-out of such measures and report as appropriate to the Council for Trade in Goods;

(e) to review, at the request of the Member taking a safeguard measure, whether proposals to suspend concessions or other obligations are "substantially equivalent", and report as appropriate to the Council for Trade in Goods;

(f) to 'receive and review all notifications provided for in this Agreement and report as appropriate to the Council for Trade in Goods; and

(g) to perform any other function connected with this Agreement that the Council for Trade in Goods may determine.

37. To assist the Committee in carrying out its surveillance function, the WTO Secretariat shall prepare annually a factual report on the operation of the Agreement based on notifications and other reliable information available to it.

SECTION IX
Dispute settlement

38. The provisions of Articles XXII and XXIII of the GATT 1994 as elaborated and applied by the Understanding on Rules and Procedures Governing the Settlement of Disputes shall apply to consultations and the settlement of disputes arising under this Agreement.

ANNEX
Exception Referred to in Paragraph 23

Members concerned	Product	Termination
EC/Japan	Passenger cars, off road vehicles, light commercial vehicles, light trucks (up to 5 tonnes), and the same vehicles in wholly knocked-down form (CKD sets).	31 December, 1999

GENERAL AGREEMENT ON TRADE IN SERVICES

PREAMBLE

GENERAL AGREEMENT ON TRADE IN SERVICES

Members,

Recognizing the growing importance of trade in services for the growth and development of the world economy;

Wishing to establish a multilateral framework of principles and rules for trade in services with a view to the expansion of such trade under conditions of transparency and progressive liberalization and as a means of promoting the economic growth of all trading partners and the development of developing countries;

Desiring the early achievement of progressively higher levels of liberalization of trade in services through successive rounds of multilateral negotiations aimed at promoting the interests of all participants on a mutually advantageous basis and at securing an overall balance of rights and obligations, while giving due respect to national policy objectives;

Recognizing the right of Members to regulate, and to introduce new regulations, on the supply of services within their territories in order to meet national policy objectives and, given asymmetries existing with respect to the degree of development of services regulations in different countries, the particular need of developing countries to exercise this right;

Desiring to facilitate the increasing participation of developing countries in trade in services and the expansion of their service exports including, *inter alia,* through the strengthening of their domestic services capacity' and its efficiency and competitiveness;

Taking particular account of the serious difficulty of the least developed countries in view of their special economic situation and their development, trade and financial needs;

Hereby *agree* as follows :

PART I : SCOPE AND DEFINITION

Article I

Scope and Definition

This Agreement applies to measures by Members affecting trade in services.

For the purposes of this Agreement, trade in services is defined as the supply of a service:

(a) from the territory of one Member into the territory of any other Member;

(b) in the territory of one Member to the service consumer of any other Member;

(c) by a service supplier of one Member, through commercial presence in the territory of any other Member;

(d) by a service supplier of one Member, through presence of natural persons of a Member in the territory of any other Member.

For the purposes of this Agreement:

(a) "measures by Members" means measures taken by:

(i) central, regional or local governments and authorities; and

(ii) non-governmental bodies in the exercise of powers delegated by central, regional or local governments or authorities;

In fulfilling its obligations and commitments under the Agreement, each Member shall take such reasonable measures as may be available to it to ensure their observance by regional and local governments and authorities and non-governmental bodies within its territory.

(b) "services" includes any service in any sector except services supplied in the exercise of governmental authority.

(c) A service supplied in the exercise of governmental authority means any service which is supplied neither on a commercial basis, nor in competition with one or more service suppliers.

PART II : GENERAL OBLIGATIONS AND DISCIPLINES

Article II
Most-Favoured-Nation Treatment

1. With respect to any measure covered by this Agreement, each Member shall accord immediately and unconditionally to services and service suppliers of any other Member, treatment no less favourable than that it accords to like services and service suppliers of any other country.

2. A Member may maintain a measure inconsistent with paragraph 1 provided that such a measure is listed in, and meets the conditions of, the Annex on Article II Exemptions.

3. The provisions of this Agreement shall not be so construed as to prevent any Member from conferring or according advantages to adjacent countries in order to facilitate exchanges limited to contiguous frontier zones of services that are both locally produced and consumed.

Article III
Transparency

1. Each Member shall publish promptly and, except in emergency situations, at the latest by the time of their entry into force, all relevant measures of general application, which pertain to or affect the operation of this Agreement. International agreements pertaining to or affecting trade in services to which a Member is a signatory shall also be published.

2. Where publication as referred to in paragraph 1 is not practicable, such information shall be made otherwise publicly available.

3. Each Member shall promptly and at least annually inform the Council for Trade in Services of the introduction of any new, or any changes to existing, laws, regulations or administrative guidelines which significantly affect trade in services covered by its specific commitments under this Agreement.

4. Each Member shall respond promptly to all requests for specific information, by any other Member, on any of its measures of general application or international agreements within the meaning of paragraph 1. Each Member shall also establish one or more enquiry points to provide specific information to other Members, upon request, on all such matters as well as those subject to the notification requirement in paragraph 3. Such enquiry points shall be established within two years from the entry into force of the Agreement

Establishing the WTO. Appropriate flexibility with respect to the time-limit within which such enquiry points are to be established may be agreed upon for individual developing countries. Enquiry points need not be depositories of laws and regulations.

5. Any Member may notify to the Council for Trade in Services any measure, taken by any other Member, which it considers affects the operation of this Agreement.

Article III bis

Disclosure of Confidential Information

Nothing in this Agreement shall require any Member to provide confidential information, the disclosure of which would impede law enforcement, or otherwise be contrary to the public interest, or which would prejudice legitimate commercial interests of particular enterprises, public or private.

Article IV

Increasing Participation of Developing Countries

1. The increasing participation of developing countries in world trade shall be facilitated through negotiated specific commitments, by different Members pursuant to Parts III and IV of this Agreement, relating to :

(a) the strengthening of their domestic services capacity and its efficiency and competitiveness *inter alia* through access to technology on a commercial basis;

(b) the improvement of their access to distribution channels and information networks; and

(c) the liberalization of market access in sectors and modes of supply of export interest to them.

2. Developed country Members, and to the extent possible other Members, shall establish contact points within two years from the entry into force of the Agreement Establishing the **WTO** to facilitate the access of developing countries' service suppliers to information, related to their respective markets, concerning:

(a) commercial and technical aspects of the supply of services;

(b) registration, recognition and obtaining of professional qualifications; and

(c) the availability of services technology.

3. Special priority shall be given to the least developed countries in the implementation of paragraphs 1 and 2 above. Particular account shall be taken of the serious difficulty of the least developed countries in accepting negotiated specific commitments in view of their special economic situation and their development, trade and financial needs.

Article V

Economic Integration

1. This Agreement shall not prevent any of its Members from being a party to or entering into an agreement liberalizing trade in services between or among the parties to such an agreement, provided that such an agreement:

(a) has substantial sectoral coverage[145], and

(b) provides for the absence or elimination of substantially all discrimination, in the sense of Article XVII, between or among the parties, in the sectors covered under sub-paragraph (a), through :

(i) elimination of existing discriminatory measures, and/or

(ii) prohibition of new or more discriminatory measures,

either at the entry into force of that agreement or on the basis of a reasonable time-frame, except for measures permitted under Articles XI, XII, XIV and XIV bis.

2. In evaluating whether the conditions under paragraph 1 (b) are met, consideration may be given to the relationship of the agreement to a wider process of economic integration or trade liberalization among the countries concerned.

3. (a) Where developing countries are parties to an agreement of the type referred to in paragraph 1, flexibility shall be provided for regarding the conditions set out in paragraph 1, in particular sub-paragraph (b), in accordance with the level of development of the countries concerned, both overall and in individual sectors and sub-sectors.

(b) Notwithstanding paragraph 6 below, in the case of an agreement of the type referred to in paragraph 1 involving only developing countries, more favourable treatment may be granted to juridical persons owned or controlled by natural persons of the parties to such an agreement.

4. Any agreement referred to in paragraph 1 shall be designed to facilitate trade between the parties to the agreement and shall not in respect of any Member outside the agreement raise the overall level of barriers to trade in services within the respective sectors or sub-sectors compared to the level applicable prior to such an agreement.

5. If, in the conclusion, enlargement or any significant modification of

---

[145] This condition is understood in terms of number of sectors, volume of trade affected and modes of supply. In order to meet this condition, agreements should not provide for the *a priori* exclusion of any mode of supply.

any agreement under paragraph 1, a Member intends to withdraw or modify a specific commitment inconsistently with the terms and conditions set out in its schedule, it shall provide at least 90 days advance notice of such modification or withdrawal and the procedure set forth in paragraphs 2-4 of Article XXI shall apply.

6. A service supplier of any other Member that is a juridical person constituted under the laws of a party to an agreement referred to in paragraph 1 shall be entitled to treatment granted under such agreement, provided that it engages in substantivebusiness operations in the territory of the parties to such agreement.

7. (a) Members which are parties to any agreement referred to in paragraph 1 shall promptly notify any such agreement and any enlargement or any significant modification thereto the Council for Trade in Services. They shall also make available to the Council such relevant information as may be requested by it. The Council may establish a working party to examine such an agreement or enlargement or modification thereto and to report to the Council on its consistency with this Article.

(b) Members which are parties to any agreement referred to in paragraph 1 which is implemented on the basis of a time-frame shall report periodically to the Council for Trade in Services on its implementation. The Council may establish a working party to examine such reports if it deems it necessary.

(c) Based on the reports of the working parties referred to in paragraphs (a) and (b), the Council may make recommendations to the parties as it deems appropriate.

8. A Member which is a party to any agreement referred to in paragraph 1 may not seek compensation for trade benefits that may accrue to any other Member from such agreement.

Article V bis

Labour Markets Integration Agreements

This Agreement shall not prevent any of its Members from being a party to an agreement establishing full integration[146] of the labour markets between or among the parties to such an agreement, provided that such an agreement:

(a) exempts citizens of parties to the agreement from requirements concerning residency and work permits;

146 Typically, such integration provides citizens of the parties concerned with a right of free entry to the employment markets of the parties and includes measures concerning conditions of pay, other conditions of employment and social benefits.

(b) is notified to the Council for Trade in Services.

Article VI

Domestic Regulation

1. In sectors where specific commitments are undertaken, each Member shall ensure that all measures of general application affecting trade in services are administered in a reasonable, objective and impartial manner.

2. (a) Each Member shall maintain or institute as soon as practicable judicial, arbitral or administrative tribunals or procedures which provide, at the request of an affected service supplier, for the prompt review of, and where justified appropriate remedies for administrative decisions affecting trade in services. Where such procedures are not independent of the agency entrusted with the administrative decision concerned, the Member shall ensure that they do in fact provide for an objective and impartial review.

(b) The provisions of sub-paragraph (a) shall not be construed to require a Member to institute such tribunals or procedures where this would be inconsistent with its constitutional structure or the nature of its legal system.

3. Where authorization is required for the supply of a service on which a specific commitment has been made, the competent authorities of a Member shall, within a reasonable period of time after the submission of an application considered complete under domestic laws and regulations, inform the applicant of the decision concerning the application. At the request of the applicant, the competent authorities of the Member shall provide, without undue delay, information concerning the status of the application.

4. With a view to ensuring that measures relating to qualification requirements and procedures, technical standards and licensing requirements do not constitute unnecessary barriers to trade in services, the Council for Trade in Services shall, through appropriate bodies it may establish, develop any necessary disciplines. Such disciplines shall aim to ensure that such requirements are, *inter alia:*

(a) based on objective and transparent criteria, such as competence and the ability to supply the service;

(b) not more burdensome than necessary to ensure the quality of the service;

(c) in the case of licensing procedures, not in themselves a restriction on the supply of the service.

5. (a) In sectors in which a Member has undertaken specific commitments, pending the entry into force of disciplines developed

in these sectors pursuant to paragraph 4, the Member shall not apply licensing and qualification requirements and technical standards that nullify, or impair such specific commitments in a manner which:

(i) does not comply with the criteria outlined in sub-paragraphs 4(a), (b) or (c); and

(ii) could not reasonably have been expected of that Member at the time the specific commitments in those sectors were made.

(b) In determining whether a Member is in conformity with the obligation under paragraph 5(a) above, account shall be taken of international standards of relevant international organizations[147] applied by that Member.

6. In sectors where specific commitments regarding professional services are undertaken, each Member shall provide for adequate procedures to verify the competence of professionals of any other Member.

Article VII

Recognition

1. For the purposes of the fulfilment, in whole or m part, of its standards or criteria for the authorization, licensing or certification of services suppliers, and subject to the requirements of paragraph 3 below, a Member may recognize the education or experience obtained, requirements met, or licenses or certifications granted in a particular country. Such recognition, which may be achieved through harmonization or otherwise, may be based upon an agreement or arrangement with the country concerned or may be accorded autonomously.

2. A Member that is a party to an agreement or arrangement referred to in-paragraph 1, whether existing or future, shall afford adequate opportunity for other interested Members to negotiate their accession to such an agreement or arrangement or to negotiate comparable ones with it. Where a Member accords recognition autonomously, it shall afford adequate opportunity for any other Member to demonstrate that education, experience, licenses, or certifications obtained or requirements met in its territory should be recognized.

3. A Member shall not accord recognition in a manner which would constitute a means of discrimination between countries in the application of its standards or criteria for the authorization, licensing or certification of services suppliers, or a disguised restriction on trade in services.

---

[147] The term "relevant international organizations" refers to international bodies whose membership is open to the relevant bodies of at least all Members of the WTO.

4. Each Member shall:

(a) within 12 months from the date on which the Agreement Establishing the WTO takes effect for it, inform the Council for Trade in Services of its existing recognition measures and state whether such measures are based on agreements or arrangements of the type referred to in paragraph 1;

(b) promptly inform the Council for Trade in Services as far in advance as possible of the opening of negotiations on an agreement or arrangement referred to in paragraph 1 in order to provide adequate opportunity to any other Member to indicate their interest in participating in the negotiations before they enter a substantive phase;

(c) promptly inform the Council for Trade in Services when it adopts new recognition measures or significantly modifies existing ones and state whether the measures are based on an agreement or arrangement referred to in paragraph 1.

5. Wherever appropriate, recognition should be based on multilaterally agreed criteria. In appropriate cases, Members shall work in co-operation with relevant intergovernmental and non-governmental organizations towards the establishment and adoption of common international standards and criteria for recognition and common international standards for the practice of relevant services trades and professions.

Article VIII

Monopolies and Exclusive Service Suppliers

1. Each Member shall ensure that any monopoly supplier of a service in its territory does not, in the supply of the monopoly service in the relevant market, act in a manner inconsistent with that Member's obligations under Article II and specific commitments.

2. Where a Member's monopoly supplier competes, either directly or through an affiliated company, in the supply of a service outside the scope of its monopoly rights and which is subject to that Member's specific commitments, the Member shall ensure that such a supplier does not abuse its monopoly position to act in its territory in a manner inconsistent with such commitments

3. The Council for Trade in Services may, at the request of a Member which has a reason to believe that a monopoly supplier of a service of any other Member is acting in a manner inconsistent with paragraph 1 or 2 above, request the Member establishing, maintaining or authorizing such supplier to provide specific information concerning the relevant operations.

4. If, after the entry into force of the Agreement Establishing the WTO

a Member grants monopoly rights regarding the supply of a service covered by its specific commitments, that Member shall make such notification to the Council for Trade in Services no later than three months before the intended implementation of the grant of monopoly rights and the provisions of paragraphs 2, 3 and 4 of Article XXI shall apply.

5. The provisions of this Article shall also apply to cases of exclusive service suppliers, where a Member, formally or in effect, (a) authorizes or establishes a small number of service suppliers and (b) substantially prevents competition among those suppliers in its territory.

Article IX
Business Practices

1. Members recognize that certain business practices of service suppliers, other than those falling under Article VIII, may restrain competition and thereby restrict trade in services.

2. Each Member shall, at the request of any other Member, enter into consultations with a view to eliminating practices referred to in paragraph 1. The Member addressed shall accord full and sympathetic consideration to such a request and shall cooperate through the supply of publicly available non-confidential information of relevance to the matter in question. The Member addressed shall also provide other information available to the requesting Member, subject to its domestic law and to the conclusion of satisfactory agreement concerning the safeguarding of its confidentiality by the requesting Member.

Article X
Emergency Safeguards Measures

1. There shall be multilateral negotiations on the question of emergency safeguard measures based on the principle of non-discrimination. The results of such negotiations shall enter into effect on a date not later than three years from the entry into force of the Agreement Establishing the WTO.

2. In the period before the entry into effect of the results of the negotiations referred to in paragraph 1, any Member may, notwithstanding the provisions of paragraph 1 of Article XXI, notify the Council on Trade in Services of its intention to modify or withdraw a specific commitment after a period of one year from the date on which the commitment enters into force; provided that the Member shows cause to the Council that the modification or withdrawal cannot await the lapse of the three-year period provided for in paragraph 1 of Article XXI.

3. The provisions of paragraph 2 shall cease to apply three years after the entry into force of the Agreement Establishing the WTO.

Article XI
Payments and Transfers

1. Except under the circumstances envisaged in Article XII, a Member shall not apply restrictions on international transfers and payments for current transactions relating to its specific commitments.

2. Nothing in this Agreement shall affect the rights and obligations of the members of the International Monetary Fund under the Articles of Agreement of the Fund, including the use of exchange actions which are in conformity with the Articles of Agreement, provided that a Member shall not impose restrictions on any capital transactions inconsistently with its specific commitments regarding such transactions, except under Article XII or at the request of the Fund.

Article XII
Restrictions to Safeguard the Balance of Payments

1. In the event of serious balance-of-payments and external financial difficulties or threat thereof, a Member may adopt or maintain restrictions on trade in services on which it has undertaken specific commitments, including on payments or transfers for transactions related to such commitments. It is recognized that particular pressures on the balance of payments of a Member in the process of economic development or economic transition may necessitate the use of restrictions to ensure, *inter alia*, the maintenance of a level of financial reserves adequate for the implementation of its programme of economic development or economic transition.

2. The restrictions referred to in paragraph 1 above :

(a) shall not discriminate among Members;

(b) shall be consistent with the Articles of Agreement of the International Monetary Fund;

(c) shall avoid unnecessary damage to the commercial, economic and financial interests of any other Member;

(d) shall not exceed those necessary to deal with the circumstances described in paragraph 1;

(e) shall be temporary and be phased out progressively as the situation specified in paragraph 1 improves.

3. In determining the incidence of such restrictions, Members may give priority to the supply of services which are more essential to their economic or development programmes. However, such restrictions shall not be adopted or maintained for the purpose of protecting a particular service sector.

4. Any restrictions adopted or maintained under paragraph 1 of this

Article, or any changes therein, shall be promptly notified to the General Council.

5. (a) Members applying the provisions of this Article shall consult promptly with the Committee on Balance-of-Payments Restrictions on restrictions adopted under this Article.

(b) The Ministerial Conference shall establish procedures[148] for periodic consultations with the objective of enabling such recommendations to be made to the Member concerned as it may deem appropriate.

(c) Such consultations shall assess the balance-of-payment situation of the Member concerned and the restrictions adopted or maintained under this Article, taking into account, *inter alia*, such factors as:

(i) the nature and extent of the balance-of-payments and the external financial difficulties;

(ii) the external economic and trading environment of the consulting Member;

(iii) alterative corrective measures which may be available.

(d) The consultations shall address the compliance of any restrictions with paragraph 2, in particular the progressive phase out of restrictions in accordance with paragraph 2(e).

(e) In such consultations, all findings of statistical and other facts presented by the International Monetary Fund relating to foreign exchange, monetary reserves and balance of payments shall be accepted and conclusions shall be based on the assessment by the Fund of the balance-of-payments and the extemal financial situation of the consulting Member.

6. If a Member which is not a member of the International Monetary Fund wishes to apply the provisions of this Article, the Ministerial Conference shall establish review and any other procedures necessary.

Article XIII

Government Procurement

1. Articles II, XVI and XVII shall not apply to laws, regulations or requirements governing the procurement by governmental agencies of services purchased for governmental purposes and not with a view to commercial resale or with a view to use in the supply of services for commercial sale.

---

[148] It is understood that the procedures under paragraph 5 shall be the same as the GATT 1994 procedures.

2. There shall be multilateral negotiations on government procurement in services under this Agreement within two years from the entry into force of the Agreement Establishing the WTO.

Article XIV
General Exceptions

Subject to the requirement that such measures are not applied in a manner which would constitute a means of arbitrary or unjustifiable discrimination between countries where like conditions prevail, or a disguised restriction on trade in services, nothing in this Agreement shall be construed to prevent the adoption or enforcement by any Member of measures :

(a) necessary to protect public morals or to maintain public order;[149]

(b) necessary to protect human, animal or plant life or health;

(c) necessary to secure compliance with laws or regulations which are not inconsistent with the provisions of this Agreement including those relating to :

(i) the prevention of deceptive and fraudulent practices or to deal with the effects of a default on services contracts;

(ii) the protection of the privacy of individuals in relation to the processing and dissemination of personal data and the protection of confidentiality of individual records and accounts;

(iii) safety;

(d) inconsistent with Article XVII, provided that the difference in treatment is aimed at ensuring the equitable or effective[150]

---

[149] The public order exception may be invoked only where a genuine and sufficiently serious threat is posed to one of the fundamental interests of society.

[150] Measure that are aimed at ensuring the equitable or effective imposition or collection of direct taxes include measures taken by a Member under its taxation system which:
- apply to non-resident service suppliers in recognition of the fact that the tax obligation of non-residents is determined with respect to taxable items sourced or located in the Member's territory; or
- apply to non-residents in order to ensure the imposition or collection of taxes in the Member's territory; or
- apply to non-residents or residents in order to prevent the avoidance or evasion of taxes, including compliance measures; or
- apply to consumers of services supplied in or from the territory of another Member in order to ensure the imposition or collection of taxes on such consumers derived from sources in the Member's territory; or
- distinguish service suplliers subject to tax on worldwide taxable items from other service suppliers, .in recognition of the difference in the nature of the tax base between them; or
- determine, allocate or apportion income, profit, gain, loss, deduction or credit of resident persons or branches, or between related persons or branches of the same person, in order to safeguard the Member's tax base.

Tax terms or concepts in Article XIV(d) and in this footnote are determined according to tax definitions and concepts or equivalent or similar definitions and concepts, under the domestic law of the Member taking the measure.

imposition or collection of direct taxes[151] in respect of services or service suppliers of other Members;

(e) inconsistent with Article II, provided that the difference in treatment is the result of an agreement on the avoidance of double taxation or provisions on the avoidance of double taxation in any other international agreement or arrangement by which the Member is bound.

Article XIV bis
Security Exceptions

1. Nothing in this Agreement shall be construed:

(a) to require any Member to furnish any information, the disclosure of which it considers contrary to its essential security interests; or

(b) to prevent any Member from taking any action which it considers necessary for the protection of its essential security interests:

(i) relating to the supply of services as carried out directly or indirectly for the purpose of provisioning a military establishment;

(ii) relating to fissionable and fusionable materials or the materials from which they are derived;

(iii) taken in time of war or other emergency in international relations; or

(c) to prevent any Member from taking any action in pursuance of its obligations under the United Nations Charter for the maintenance of international peace and security.

2. The Council for Trade in Services shall be informed to the fullest extent possible of measures taken under paragraphs 1 (b) and (c) and of their termination.

Article XV
Subsidies

1. Members recognize that, in certain circumstances, subsidies may have distortive effects on trade in services. Members shall enter into negotiations with a view to developing the necessary multilateral disciplines to avoid such

[151] For the purpose of this Agreement "direct taxes" comprise all taxes on total income, on total capital or on elements of income or of capital, including taxes on gains from the alienation of property, taxes on estates, inheritances and gifts, and taxes on the total amounts of wages or salaries paid by enterprises, as well as taxes on capital appreciation.

trade distortive effects.[152] The negotiations shall also address the appropriateness of countervailing procedures. Such negotiations shall recognize the role of subsidies in relation to the development programmes of developing countries and take into account the needs of Members, particularly developing country Members, for flexibility in this area. For the purpose of such negotiations, Members shall exchange information concerning all subsidies related to trade in services that they provide to their domestic service suppliers.

2. Any Member which considers that it is adversely affected by a subsidy of another Member may request consultations with that Member on such matters. Such requests shall be accorded sympathetic consideration.

PART III : SPECIFIC COMMITMENTS

Article XVI
Market Access

1. With respect to market access through the modes of supply identified in Article 1, each Member shall accord services and service suppliers of any other Member treatment no less favourable than that provided for under the terms, limitations and conditions agreed and specified in its schedule.[153]

2. In sectors where market access commitments are undertaken, the measures which a Member shall not maintain or adopt either on the basis of a regional sub-division or on the basis of its entire territory, unless otherwise specified in its schedule, are defined as:

(a) limitations on the number of service suppliers whether in the form of numerical quotas, monopolies, exclusive service suppliers or the requirements of an economic needs test;

(b) limitations on the total value of service transactions or assets in the form of numerical quotas or the requirement of an economic needs test;

(c) limitations on the total number of service operations or on the total quantity of service output expressed in terms of designated numerical units in the form of quotas or the requirement of an economic needs test;[154]

---

152 A future work programme shall determine how and in what time-frame negotiations on the multilateral disciplines will be conducted.

153 If a Member undertakes a market access commitment in relation to the supply of a service through the mode of supply referred to in paragraph 2(a) of Article I and if the cross-border movement of capital is an essential part of the service itself, that Member is thereby committed to allow such movement of capital. If a Member undertakes a market access commitment in relation to the supply of a service through the mode of supply referred to in paragraph 2(c) of Article 1, it is thereby committed to allow related transfers of capital into its territory.

154 Sub-paragraph 2(c) does not cover measures of a Member which limit inputs for the supply of services.

(d) limitations on the total number of natural persons that may be employed in a particular service sector or that a service supplier may employ and who are necessary for, and directly related to, the supply of a specific service in the form of numerical quotas or the requirement of an economic needs test;

(e) measures which restrict or require specific types of legal entity or joint venture through which a service supplier may supply a service; and

(f) limitations on the participation of foreign capital in terms of maximum percentage limit on foreign shareholding or the total value of individual or aggregate foreign investment.

Article XVII
National Treatment

1. In the sectors inscribed in its schedule, and subject to any conditions and qualifications set out therein, each Member shall accord to services and service suppliers of any other Member, in respect of all measures affecting the supply of services, treatment no less favourable than that it accords to its own like services and service suppliers.[155]

2. A Member may meet the requirement of paragraph 1 by according to services and service suppliers of any other Member, either formally identical treatment or formally different treatment to that it accords to its own like services and service suppliers.

3. Formally identical or formally different treatment shall be considered to be less favourable if it modifies the conditions of competition in favour of services or service suppliers of the Member compared to like services or service suppliers of any other Member.

Article XVIII
Additional Commitments

Members may negotiate commitments with respect to measures affecting trade in services not subject to scheduling under Articles XVI or XVII, including those regarding qualifications, standards or licensing matters. Such commitments shall be inscribed in a Member's schedule.

---

[155] Specific commitments assumed under this Article shall not be construed to require any Member to compensate for any inherent competitive disadvantages which result from the foreign character of the relevant services or service suppliers.

PART IV : PROGRESSIVE LIBERALIZATION

Article XIX

Negotiation of Specific Commitments

1. In pursuance of the objectives of this Agreement, Members shall enter into successive rounds of negotiations, beginning not later than five years from the date of entry into force of the Agreement Establishing the WTO and periodically thereafter, with a view to achieving a progressively higher level of liberalization. Such negotiations shall be directed to the reduction or elimination of the adverse effects on trade in services of measures as a means of providing effective market access. The process shall take place with a view to promoting the interests of all participants on a mutually advantageous basis and to securing an overall balance of rights and obligations.

2. The process of liberalization shall take place with due respect for national policy objectives and the level of development of individual Members, both overall and in individual sectors. There shall be appropriate flexibility for individual developing countries for opening fewer sectors, liberalization fewer types of transactions, progressively extending market access in line with their development situation and, when making access to their markets available to foreign service suppliers, attaching to it conditions aimed at achieving the objectives referred to in Article IV.

3. For each round, negotiating guidelines and procedures shall be established. For the purposes of establishing such guidelines, the Council for Trade in Services shall carry out an assessment of trade in services in overall terms and on a sectoral basis with reference to the objectives of the Agreement including those set out in paragraph 1 of Article IV. Negotiating guidelines shall establish modalities for the treatment of liberalization undertaken autonomously by Members since previous negotiators, as well as for the special treatment of the least-developed countries under the provisions of paragraph 3 of Article IV.

4. The process of progressive liberalization shall be advanced in each such round through bilateral, plurilateral or multilateral negotiations directed towards increasing the general level of specific commitments undertaken by Members under this Agreement.

Article XX

Schedules of Specific Commitments

1. Each Member shall set out in a schedule the specific commitments it undertakes under Part III of this Agreement. With respect to sectors where such commitments are undertaken each schedule shall specify :

(a) terms, limitations and conditions on market access;

(b) conditions and qualifications on national treatment;

(c) undertaking relating to additional commitment;

(d) where appropriate the time-frame for implementation of such commitments; and

(e) date of entry into force of such commitments.

2. Measures inconsistent with both Articles XVI and XVII shall be inscribed in the column relating to Article XVI. In this case the inscription will be considered to provide a condition or qualification to Article XVII as well.

3. Schedules of specific commitments shall be annexed to this Agreement and form an integral part thereof.

Article XXI
Modification of Schedules

1. (a) A Member (hereafter in this Article referred to as the "modifying Member") may modify or withdraw any commitment in its schedule, at any time after three years have elapsed from the date on which that commitment entered into force, in accordance with the provisions of this Article.

(b) A modifying Member shall notify its intent to modify or withdraw a commitment pursuant to this Article to the Council for Trade in Services no later than three months before the intended date of implementation of the modification or withdrawal.

2. (a) At the request of any Member whose benefits under this Agreement may be affected (hereafter "an affected Member") by a proposed modification or withdrawal notified under paragraph 1 (b), the modifying Member shall enter into negotiations with a view to reaching agreement on any necessary compensatory adjustment. In such negotiations and agreement, the Members concerned shall endeavour to maintain a general level of mutually advantageous commitments not less favourable to trade than that provided for in schedules of specific commitments prior to such negotiations.

(b) Compensatory adjustments shall be made on a most-favoured-nation basis.

3. (a) If agreement is not reached between the modifying Member and any affected Member before the end of the period provided for negotiations, such affected Member may refer the matter to arbitration. Any affected Member that wishes to enforce a right that it may have to compensation must participate in the arbitration.

(b) If no affected Member has requested arbitration, the modifying Member shall be free to implement the proposed modification or withdrawal.

4. (a) The modifying Member may not modify or withdraw its commitment until it has made compensatory adjustments in conformity with the findings of the arbitration.

(b) If the modifying Member implements its proposed modification or withdrawal and does not comply with the findings of the arbitration, any affected Member that participated in the arbitration may modify or withdraw substantially equivalent benefits in conformity with those findings. Notwithstanding Article II, such a modification or withdrawal may be implemented solely with respect to the modifying Member.

5. The Council for Trade in Services shall establish procedures for rectification or modification of schedules of commitments. Any Member which has modified or withdrawn scheduled commitmeres under this Article shall modify its schedule according to such procedures.

PART V : INSTITUTIONAL PROVISIONS

Article XXII
Consultation

1. Each Member shall accord sympathetic consideration to, and shall afford adequate opportunity for, consultation, regarding such representations as may be made by any other Member with respect to any matter affecting the operation of this Agreement. The Understanding on Rules and Procedures Governing the Settlement of Disputes shall apply to such consultations.

2. The Council for Trade in Services or the Dispute Settlement Body (DSB) may, at the request of a Member, consult with any Member or Members in respect of any matter for which it has not been possible to find a satisfactory solution through consultation under paragraph 1.

3. A Member may not invoke Article XVII, either under this Article or Article XXIII with respect to a measure of another Member that fails within the scope of an international agreement between them relating to the avoidance of double taxation. In case of disagreement between Members as to whether a measure falls within the scope of such an agreement between them, it shall be open to either Member to bring this matter before the Council for Trade in Services.[156] The Council shall refer the matter to arbitration. The decision of the arbitrator shall be final and binding on the Members.

[156] With respect to agreements on the avoidance of double taxation which exist at the time of entry into force of the Agreement Establishing the WTO such a matter may be brought before the Council for Trade in Services only with the consent of both parties to the agreement.

Article XXIII

Dispute Settlement and Enforcement

1. If any Member should consider that any other Member fails to carry out its obligations or specific commitments under this Agreement, it may with a view to reaching a mutually satisfactory resolution of the matter, have recourse to the Understanding on Rules and Procedures Governing the Settlement of Disputes.

2. If the DSB considers that the circumstances are serious enough to justify such action. it may authorize a Member or Members to suspend the application to any other Member or Members of such obligations and specific commitments in accordance with Section 22 (Compensation and the Suspension of Concessions) of the Understanding on Rules and Procedures Governing the Settlement of Disputes.

3. If any Member considers that any benefit it could reasonably have expected to accrue to it a specific commitment of another Member under Part III of this Agreement is being nullified or impaired as a result of the application of any measure which does not conflict with the provisions of this Agreement, it may have recourse to the Understanding on Rules and Procedures Governing the Settlement of Disputes. If the measure is determined by the DSB to have nullified or impaired such a benefit, the Member affected shall be entitled to a mutually satisfactory adjustment on the basis of paragraph 2 of Article XXI, which may include the modification or withdrawal of the measure. In the event an agreement cannot be reached between the Members concerned, Section 22 (Compensation and the Suspension of Concessions) of the Understanding on Rules and Procedures Governing the Settlement of Disputes shall apply.

Article XXIV

Council for Trade in Services

1. The Council for Trade in Services shall carry out such functions as may be assigned to it to facilitate the operation of this Agreement and further its objectives. The Council may establish such subsidiary bodies as it considers appropriate for the effective discharge of its functions.

2. The Council and, unless the Council decides otherwise, its subsidiary bodies shall be open to participation by representatives of all Members.

3. The Chairman of the Council shall be elected by the Members. The Council shall establish its own rules of procedure.

Article XXV

Technical Cooperation

1. Service suppliers of Members which are in need of such assistance

shall have access to the services of contact points referred to in paragraph 2 of Article IV.

2. Technical assistance to developing countries shall be provided at the multilateral level by the WTO Secretariat and shall be decided upon by the Council for Trade in Services.

Article XXVI

Relationship with Other International Organizations

The General Council shall make appropriate arrangements for consultation and cooperation with the United Nations and its specialized agencies as well as with other intergovernmental organizations concerned with services.

PART VI : FINAL PROVISIONS

Article XXVII

Denial of Benefits

A Member may deny the benefits of this Agreement:

(a) to the supply of a service, if it establishes that the service is supplied from the territory of a non-Member, or in the territory of a Member to which the denying Member does not apply this Agreement;

(b) in the case of the supply of a maritime transport service, if it establishes that the service is supplied:

(i) by a vessel registered under the laws of a non-Member or of a Member to which the denying Member does not apply this Agreement, and

(ii) by a person which operates and/or uses the vessel in whole or in part but which is of a non-Member or of a Member to which the denying Membe does not apply this Agreement;

(c) to a service supplier that is a juridical person, if it establishes that it is not a service supplier of another Member, or that it is a service supplier of a Member to which the denying Member does not apply this Agreement.

Article XXVIII

Definitions

For the 'purpose of this Agreement :

(a) "measure" means any measure by a Member, whether in the form of a law, regulation, rule, procedure, decision, administrative action, or any other form;

(b) "supply of a service" includes the production, distribution, marketing, sale and delivery of a service;

(c) "measures by Members affecting trade in services" include measures in respect of :

(i) the purchase, payment or use of a service,

(ii) the access to and use of, in connection with the supply of a service, services which are required by those Members to be offered to the public generally;

(iii) the presence, including commercial presence, of persons of a Member for the supply of a service in the territory of another Member;

(d) commercial presence means any type of business or professional establishment, including through –

(i) the constitution, acquisition or maintenance of a juridical person, or

(ii) the creation or maintenance of a branch or a representative office, within the territory of a Member for the purpose of supplying a service.

(e) 'sector" of a service means :

(i) with reference to a specific commitment, one or more, or all, sub-sectors of that service, as specified in a Member's schedule.

(ii) otherwise, the whole of that service sector, including all of its sub-sectors;

(f) "service of another Member" means a service which is supplied :

(i) from or in the territory of that other Member, or in the case of maritime transport, by a vessel registered under the laws of that other Member, or by a person of that other Member which supplies the service through the operation of a vessel and/or its use in whole or in part, or

(ii) in the case of the supply of a service through commercial presence or through the presence of natural persons, by a service supplier of that other Member;

(g) "service supplier" means any person that supplies a service;[157]

---

[157] Where the service is not supplied directly by a juridical person but through other forms of commercial presence such as a branch or a representative office, the service supplier (*i.e.* the juridical person) shall, nonetheless, through such presence be accorded the treatment provided for service suppliers under the Agreement. Such treatment shall be extended to the presence through which the service is supplied and need not be extended to any other parts of the supplier located outside the territory where the service is supplied.

(h) "monopoly supplier of a service" means any person, public or private, which in the relevant market of the territory of a Member is authorized or established formally or in effect by that Member as the sole supplier of that service;

(i) "service consumer" means any person that receives or uses a service;

(j) "person' means either a natural person or a juridical person;

(k) "natural person of another Member" means a natural person who resides in the territory of that other Member or any other Member, and who under the law of that other Member :

(i) is a national of that other Member, or

(ii) has the right of permanent residence in that other Member, in the case of a Member which

1. does not have nationals, or

2. accords substantially the same treatment to its permanent residents as it does to its nationals in respect of measures affecting trade in services, as notified in its acceptance or accession to this Agreement, provided that no Member is obligated to accord to such permanent residents treatment more favourable than would be accorded by that other Member to such permanent residents. Such notification include the assurance to assume, with respect to those permanent residents, in accordance with its laws and regulations, the same responsibilities that other Member bears with respect to its nationals.

(l) "juridical person" means any legal entity duly constituted or otherwise organized under applicable law, whether for profit or otherwise, and whether privately-owned or governmentally-owned, including any corporation, trust,' partnership, joint venture, sole proprietorship or association;

(m) "juridical 'person of another Member" means a juridical person which is either

(i) constituted or otherwise organized under the law of that other Member, and is engaged in substantive business operations in the territory of that Member or any other Member; or

(ii) in the case of the supply of a service through commercial presence, owned or controlled by

1. natural persons of that Member, or

2. juridical persons of that other Member identified under subparagraph (i);

(n) A juridical person is

(i) "owned" by persons of a Member if more than 50 per cent of the equity interest in it is beneficially owned by persons of that Member;

(ii) "controlled' by persons of a Member, if such persons have the power to name a majority of its directors or otherwise to legally direct its actions;

(iii) "affiliated" with another person when it controls, or is controlled by, that other person; or when it and the other person are both controlled by the same person.

Article XXIX

ANNEXES

ANNEX ON ARTICLE II EXEMPTIONS

Scope

1. This Annex specifies the conditions under which a Member, at the entry into force of this Agreement, is exempted from its obligations under paragraph 1 of Article II.

2. Any new exemptions applied for after the entry into force of the Agreement Establishing the WTO shall be dealt with under paragraph 3 of Article IX of that Agreement.

Review

3. The Council for Trade in Services shall review all exemptions granted for a period of more than 5 years. The first such review shall take place no more than 5 years after the entry into force of the Agreement Establishing the WTO.

4. The Council for Trade in Services in a review shall :

(a) examine whether the conditions which created the need for the exemption still prevail; and

(b) determine the date of any further review.

Termination

5. The exemption of a Member from its obligations under paragraph 1 of Article II of the Agreement with respect to a particular measure terminates on the date provided for in the exemption.

6. In principle, such exemptions should not exceed the period of 10 years.

In any event, they shall be subject to negotiation in subsequent trade liberalizing rounds.

7. A Member shall notify the Council for Trade in Services at the termination of the exemption period that the inconsistent measure has been brought into conformity with paragraph 1 of Article II of the Agreement.

ANNEX ON MOVEMENT OF NATURAL PERSONS SUPPLYING SERVICES UNDER THE AGREEMENT

1. The Annex applies to measures affecting natural persons who are service suppliers of a Member, and to natural persons of a Member who are employed by a service supplier of a Member, in respect of the supply of a service for which specific commitments relating to entry and temporary stay of such natural persons have been undertaken.

2. The Agreement shall not apply to measures affecting natural persons seeking access to the employment market of a Member, nor shall it apply to measures regarding citizenship, residence or employment on a permanent basis.

3. In accordance with Parts III and IV of the Agreement, Members may negotiate specific commitments applying to the movement of all categories of natural persons supplying services under the Agreement. Natural persons covered by a specific commitment shall be allowed to supply the service in accordance with the terms of that commitment.

4. The Agreement shall not prevent a Member from applying measures to regulate the entry of natural persons into, or their temporary stay in, its territory, including those necessary to protect the integrity of, and to ensure the orderly movement of natural persons across, its borders, provided that such measures are not applied in such a manner as to nullify or impair the benefits accruing to any Member under the terms of a specific commitment.[158]

ANNEX ON FINANCIAL SERVICES

1. *Scope and Definition*

1.1 This annex applied to measures affecting the supply of financial services. Reference to the supply of a financial service in the Annex shall mean the supply of a service as defined in paragraph 2 of Article I of this Agreement.

1.2 For the purposes of paragraph 3(b) of Article I of the Agreement,

---

[158] *Interpretative Note:* The sole fact of requiring a visa for natural persons of certain Members and not for those of others shall not be regarded as nullifying or impairing benefits under a specific commitment.

"Service supplied in the exercise of governmental authority" means the following :

1.2.1 activities conducted by a central bank or monetary authority or by any other public entity in pursuit of monetary or exchange rate policies;

1.2.2 activities conducted by a central bank or monetary authority or by any other public entity in pursuit of monetary or exchange rate policies;

1.2.3 other activities conducted by a public entity for the account or with the guarantee or using the financial resources of the Government.

1.3 For the purposes of paragraph 3(b) Article I of Agreement, if a Member allows any of the activities referred to in paragraph 1.2.2 or 1.2.3 to be conducted by its financial service suppliers in competition with a public entity or a financial service supplier, "services" shall include such activities.

1.4 Article I : 3 (c) of the Agreement shall not apply to services covered by this Annex.

2. *Domestic Regulation*

2.1 Notwithstanding any other provisions of the Agreement, a Member shall not be prevented from taking measures for prudential reasons, including for the protection of investors, depositors, policy holders or persons to whom a fiduciary duty is owed by a financial service supplier, or to ensure the integrity and stability of the financial system. Where such measures do not conform with the provision of the Agreement, they shall not be used as a means of avoiding the Member's commitments or obligations under the Agreement.

2.2 Nothing in the Agreement shall be construed to require a Member to disclose information relating to the affairs and accounts of individual customers or any confidential or proprietary information in the possession of public entities.

3. *Recognition*

3.1 A Member may recognize prudential measures of any other country in determining how the Member's measures relating to financial services shall be applied. Such recognition, which may be achieved through harmonization or otherwise, may be based upon an agreement or arrangement with the country concerned or may be accorded autonomously.

3.2 A Member that is party to such an agreement or arrangement referred to in paragraph 3.1 whether future or existing, shall afford adequate opportunity for other interested Members to negotiate their accession to such agreements or arrangement, or to negotiate comparable ones with it, under circumstances in which there would be equivalent regulation, oversight, implementation of such regulation, and, if appropriate, procedures concerning the sharing of information between the parties to the agreement or arrangement. Where a Member accords recognition autonomously, it shall afford adequate opportunity for any other Member to demonstrate that such circumstances exist.

3.3 Where a Member is contemplating according recognition to prudential measures of any other country, paragraph 4 (b) of Article VII of the Agreement shall not apply.

4. *Dispute Settlement*

4.1 Panels for disputes' on prudential issues and other financial matters shall have the necessary expertise relevant to the specific financial service under dispute.

5. *Definitions*

For the purposes of this Annex:

5.1 A financial service is any service of a financial nature offered by a financial service supplier of a Member. Financial services include all insurance and insurance-related services, and all banking and other financial' services (excluding insurance). Financial services include the following activities:

Insurance and insurance-related services

(a) Direct insurance (including co-insurance):

   (i) life

   (ii) non-life

(b) Reinsurance and retrocession;

(c) Insurance intermediation, such as brokerage and agency;

(d) Services auxiliary to insurance, such as consultancy, actuarial, risk assessment and claim settlement services.

Banking and other financial services (excluding insurance)

(e) Acceptance of deposits and other repayable funds from the public;

(f) Lending of all types, including consumer credit, mortgage, credit, factoring and financing of commercial transaction

(g) Financial leasing ;

(h) All payment and money transmission services, including credit, charge and debit cards, travellers cheques and bankers drafts;

(i) Guarantees and commitments;

(j) Trading for own account or for account of customers, whether on an exchange, in an over-the-counter market or otherwise, the following:

(i) money market instruments (including cheques, bills, certificates of deposits);

(ii) foreign exchange;

(iii) derivative products including, but not limited to, futures and options;

(iv) exchage rate and interest rate instruments, including products such as swaps, forward rate agreements;

(v) transferable securities;

(vi) other negotiable instruments and financial assets, including bullion.

(k) Participation in issues of all kinds of securities, including underwriting and placement as agent (whether publicly or privately) and provision of services related to such issues;

(l) Money broking;

(m) Asset management, such as cash or portfolio management, all forms of collective investment management, pension fund management, custodial, depository and trust services;

(n) Settlement and clearing services for financial assets, including securities, derivative products, and other negotiable instruments;

(o) Provision and transfer of financial information, and financial data processing and related software by suppliers of other financial services;

(p) Advisory, intermediation and other auxiliary financial services on all the activities listed in sub-paragraphs (e) to (o), including credit reference and analysis, investment and portfolio research and advice, advice on acquisitions and on corporate restructuring and strategy.

5.2 A financial service supplier means any natural or juridical person of a Member wishing to supply or supplying financial services but the term "financial service supplier" does not include a public entity.

5.3 "Public entity" means :

5.3.1 a government, a central bank or a monetary authority, of a Member, or an entity owned or controlled by a Member, that is principally engaged in carrying out governmental functions or activities for governmental purposes, not including an entity principally engaged in supplying financial services on commercial terms; or

5.3.2 a private entity, performing functions normally performed by a central bank or monetany authority, when exercising those functions.

5.4 "Agreement", means the Articles of the General Agreement on Trade in Services, this Sectoral Annex on Financial Services and the schedule of each Party with respect to financial services.

SECOND ANNEX ON FINANCIAL SERVICES

1. Notwithstanding Article II of the General Agreement on Trade in Services and paragraphs 1 and 2 of the Annex on Article II Exemptions, a Member may, during a period of 60 days beginning four months after the date of entry into force of the Agreement Establishing the WTO, list in that Annex measures relating to Financial Services which are inconsistent with paragraph 1 of Article II of the Agreement.

2. Notwithstanding Article XXI of the General Agreement on Trade in Services, a Member may, during a period of 60 days beginning four months after the date of entry into force of the Agreement Establishing the WTO, improve, modify or withdraw all or part of the commitments on Financial Services inscribed in its schedule.

3. The Council for Trade in Services shall establish any procedures necessary for the application of paragraphs 1 and 2.

ANNEX ON TELECOMMUNICATIONS

1. *Objectives*

1.1 Recognizing the specificities of the telecommunications services sector and, in particular, its dual role as a distinct sector of economic activity and as the underlying transport means for other economic activities, the Members have agreed to the following Annex with the objective of elaborating upon the provisions of the Agreement with respect to measures affecting access to and use of public telecommunications transport networks and services. Accordingly, this Annex provides notes and supplementary provisions to the Agreement.

2. *Scope*

2.1 This Annex shall apply to all measures of a Member that affect access to and use of public telecommunications transport networks and services.[159]

2.2 This Annex shall not apply to measures affecting the cable or broadcast distribution of radio or television programming.

2.3 Nothing in this Annex. shall be construed:

2.3.1 to require a Member to authorize a service supplier of any other Member to establish, construct, acquire, lease, operate, or supply telecommunications transport networks or services, other than as provided for in its schedule; or

2.3.2 to require a Member (or to require a Member to oblige service suppliers under its jurisdiction) to establish, construct, acquire, lease, operate or supply telecommunications transport networks or services not offered to the public generally.

3. *Definitions*

For the purposes of this Annex:

3. 1 *Telecommunications* means the transmission and reception of signals by any electromagnetic means

3.2 *Public telecommunications transport service* means any telecommunications transport service required, explicitly or in effect, by a Member to be offered to the public generally. Such services may include, *inter alia*, telegraph, telephone, telex, and data transmission typically involving the real-time transmission of customer-supplied information between two or more points without any end-to-end change in the form or content of the customer's information.

3.3 *Public telecommunications transport network* means the public telecommumcations infrastructure which permits telecommunications between and among defined network termination points.

3.4 *Intra-corporate communications* means telecommunications through which a company communicates within the company or with or among its subsidiaries, branches and, subject to a Member's domestic laws and regulations, affiliates. For these purposes, "subsidiaries", "branches" and, where applicable, "affiliates" shall be as defined by each Party Member. ....

....

[159] This paragraph is understood to mean that each Member shall ensure that the obligations of this Annex are applied with respect to suppliers of public telecommunications transport networks and services by whatever measures are necessary.

6.2 Members shall encourage and support telecommunications cooperation among developing countries at the international, regional and sub-regional levels.

6.3 In co-operation with relevant international organizations, Members shall make available, where practicable, to developing countries information with respect to telecommunications services and developments in telecommunications and information technology to assist in strengthening theft domestic telecommunications services sector.

6.4 Members shall give special consideration to opportunities for the least developed countries to encourage foreign suppliers of telecommunications services to assist in the transfer of technology, training and other activities that support the development of their telecommunications infrastructure and expansion of their telecommunications services trade.

7. *Relation to International Organizations and Agreements*

7.1 Members recognize the importance of international standards for global compatibility and inter-operability of telecommunication networks and services and undertake to promote such standards through the work of relevant international bodies, including the International Telecommunication Union and the International Organization for Standardization.

7.2 Members recognize the role played by inter-governmental and non-governmental organizations and agreements in ensuring the efficient operation of domestic and global telecommunications services, in particular the International Telecommunication Union. Members shall make appropriate arrangements, where relevant, for consultation with such organizations on matters arising from the implementation of this Annex.

ANNEX ON AIR TRANSPORT SERVICES

1. This Annex applies to measures affecting trade in air transport services, whether scheduled or non-scheduled, and ancillary services. It is confirmed that any specific commitment made or obligation assumed under this Agreement shall not reduce or affect a Member's obligations under bilateral or multilateral agreements that are in effect at the entry into force of the Agreement Establishing the WTO.

2. The Agreement, including its dispute settlement procedures, shall not apply to measures affecting:

(a) traffic rights, however granted; or

(b) services directly related to the exercise of traffic rights,

except as provided in paragraph 3 of this Annex.

3. The Agreement shall apply to measures affecting:

(a) aircraft repair and maintenance services;

(b) the selling and marketing of air transport services;

(c) computer reservation system (CRS) services.

4, The dispute settlement procedures of the Agreement may be invoked only where obligations or commitments have been assumed by the concerned Members and where dispute settlement procedures in bilateral and other multilateral arrangements have been exhausted.

5. The Council for Trade in Services shall review periodically, and at least every five years, developments in the air transport sector and the operation of this Annex with a view to considering the possible further application of the Agreement in this sector.

6. Definitions:

(a) *"aircraft repair and maintenance services"* mean such activities when undertaken on an aircraft or a part thereof while it is withdrawn from service and do not include so-called line maintenance.

(b) *"selling and marketing of air transport services"* mean opportunities for the air carrier concerned to sell and market freely its air transport services including all aspects of marketing such as market research, advertising and distribution. These activities do not include the pricing of air transport services nor the applicable conditions.

(c) *"computer reservation system (CRS) services"* mean services provided by computeiised systems that contain information about air carriers' schedules, availability, fares and fare rules, through which reservations can be made or tickets may be issued.

(d) *"traffic rights"* mean the right for scheduled and non-scheduled services to operate and/or to carry passengers, cargo and mail for remuneration or hire from, to, within, or over the territory of a Member, including points to be served, routes to be operated, types of traffic to be carried, capacity to be provided, tariffs to be charged and their conditions, and criteria for designation of airlines, including such criteria as number, ownership, and control.

ANNEX ON NEGOTIATIONS ON BASIC TELECOMMUNICATIONS

1. Notwithstanding paragraph 1 of Article II of the GATS and paragraph 2 of the Annex on Article II Exemptions, Article II and the Annex on Article II Exemptions, including the requirement to list in the Annex any measure inconsistent with most-favoured-nation treatment that a Member will maintain, shall enter into force for basic telecommunications only on :

(a) the date of implementation of the results of the negotiations mandated by the Ministerial Decision on Negotiations on Basic Telecommunications; or

(b) should the negotiations not succeed, on the date of the final report of the Negotiating Group on Basic Telecommunications.

2. Paragraph 1 above shall not apply to any specific commitment on basic telecommunications which is inscribed in a Member's schedule.

3. References to the dates cited under paragraphs 1 (a) and (b) above are contained in paragraph 5 of the Ministerial Decision on Negotiations on Basic Telecommunications.

AGREEMENT ON TRADE-RELATED ASPECTS OF INTELLECTUAL PROPERTY RIGHTS, INCLUDING TRADE IN COUNTERFEIT GOODS

TABLE OF CONTENTS

AGREEMENT ON TRADE-RELATED ASPECTS OF INTELLECTUAL PROPERTY RIGHTS, INCLUDING TRADE IN COUNTERFEIT GOODS

Members,

Desiring to reduce distortions and impediments to international trade, and taking into account the need to promote effective and adequate protection of intellectual property rights, and to ensure that measures and procedures to enforce intellectual property rights do not themselves become barriers to legitimate trade;

Recognizing, to this end, the need for new rules and disciplines concerning:

(a) the applicability of the basic principles of the GATT 1994 and of relevant international intellectual property agreements or conventions;

(b) the provision of adequate standards and principles concerning the availability, scope and use of trade-related intellectual property, rights;

(c) the provision of effective and appropriate means for the enforcement of trade-related intellectual property rights, taking into account differences in national legal systems;

(d) the provision of effective and expeditious procedures for the. multilateral prevention and settlement of disputes between governments; and

(e) transitional arrangements aiming at the fullest participation in the results of the negotiations;

Recognizing the need for a multilateral framework of principles, rules and disciplines dealing with international trade in counterfeit goods;

Recognizing that intellectual property rights are private rights;

Recognizing the underlying public policy objectives of national systems for the protection of intellectual property, including developmental and technological objectives;

Recognizing also the special needs of the least-developed country Members in respect of maximum flexibility in the domestic implementation of laws and regulations in order to enable them to create a sound and viable technological base;

Emphasizing the importance of reducing tensions by reaching strengthened commitments to resolve disputes on trade-related intellectual property issues through multilateral procedures;

Desiring to establish a mutually supportive relationship between the MTO and the World Intellectal Property Organization (WIPO) as well as other relevant international organisations;

Hereby agree as follows:

PART I

GENERAL PROVISIONS AND BASIC PRINCIPLES

Article 1

Nature and Scope of Obligations

1. Members shall give effect to the provisions of this Agreement. Members may, but shall not be obliged to, implement in their domestic law more extensive protection than is required by this Agreement, provided that such protection does not contravene the provisions of this Agreement. Members shall be free to determine the appropriate method of implementing the provisions of this Agreement within their own legal system and practice.

2. For the purposes of this Agreement, the term "intellectual property" refers to all categories of intellectual property that are the subject of Sections 1 to 7 of Part II.

3. Members shall accord the treatment provided for in this Agreement to the nationals of other Members.[160] In respect of the relevant intellectual property right, the nationals of other Members shall be understood as those natural or legal persons that would meet the criteria for eligibility for protection provided for in the Paris Convention (1967), the Berne Convention (1971), the Rome Convention and the Treaty on Intellectual Property in Respect of Integrated Circuits, were all Members of the WTO members of those conventions.[161] Any Member availing itself of the possibilities provided in paragraph 3 of Article 5 or paragraph 2 of Article 6 of the Rome Convention shall make a notification as foreseen in those provisions to the Council for Trade-Related Aspects of Intellectual Property Rights.

---

160 When 'nationals' are referred to in this Agreement, they shall be deemed, in the case of a separate customs territory Member of the WTO to mean persons, natural or legal, who are domiciled or who have a real and effective industrial or commercial establishment in that customs territory.

161 In this Agreement, "Paris Convention" refers to the Paris Convention for the Protection of Industrial Propen'y; "Paris Convention" (1967) refers to the Stockholm Act of this Convention of 14 July 1967. "Berne Convention" refers to the Berne Convention for the Protection of Literary and Artistic Works; "Berne Convention (1971)" refers to the Paris Act of this Convention of 24 July 1971. "Rome Convention" refers to the International Convention for the Protection of Performers, Producers of Phonograms and Broadcasting Organisations, adopted at Rome on 26 October 1961. "Treaty on Intellectual Property in Respect of Integrated Circuits" (IPIC Treaty) refers to the Treaty on Intellectual Property in Respect of Integrated Circuits, adopted at Washington on 26 May, 1989.

Article 2

Intellectual Property Conventions

1. In respect of Parts II, III and IV of this Agreement, Members shall comply with Articles 1-12 and 19 of the Paris Convention (1967).

2. Nothing in Parts I to IV of this Agreement shall derogate from existing obligations that Members may have to each other under the Paris Convention, the Berne Convention, the Rome Convention and the Treaty on Intellectual Property in Respect of Integrated Circuits.

Article 3

National Treatment

1. Each Member shall accord to the nationals of other Members treatment no less favourable than that it accords to its own nationals with regard to the protection[162] of intellectual property, subject to the exceptions already provided in, respectively, the Paris Convention (1967), the Berne Convention (1971), the Rome Convention and the Treaty on Intellectual Property in Respect of Integrated Circuits. In respect of performers, producers of phonograms and broadcasting organizations, this obligation only applies in respect of the rights provided under this Agreement. Any Member availing itself of the possibilities provided in Article 6 of the Berne Convention and paragraph 1 (b) of Article 16 of the Rome Convention shall make a notification as foreseen in those provisions to the Council for Trade-Related Aspects of Intellectual Property Rights.

2. Members may avail themselves of the exceptions permitted under paragraph 1 above in relation to judicial and administrative procedures, including the designation of an address for service or the appointment of an agent within the jurisdiction of a Member, only where such exceptions are necessary to secure compliance with laws and regulations which are not inconsistent with the provisions of this Agreement and where such practices are not applied in a manner which would constitute a disguised restriction on trade.

Article 4

Most-Favoured-Nation Treatment

With regard to the protection of intellectual property, any advantage, favour, privilege or immunity granted by a Member to the nationals of any

[162] For the purposes of Articles 3 and 4 of this Agreement, protection shall include matters affecting the availability, acquisition, scope, maintenance and enforcement of intellectual property rights as well as those matters affecting the use of intellectual property rights specifically addressed in this Agreement.

other country shall be accorded immediately and unconditionally to the nationals of all other Members. Exempted from this obligation are any advantage, favour, privilege or immunity accorded by a Member:

(a) deriving from international agreements on judicial assistance and law enforcement of a general nature and not particularly confined to the protection of intellectual properly;

(b) granted in accordance with the provisions of the Berne Convention (1971) or the Rome Convention authorizing that the treatment accorded be a function not of national treatment but of the treatment accorded in another country;

(c) in respect of the rights of performers, producers of phonograms and broadcasting organizations not provided under this Agreement;

(d) deriving from international agreements related to the protection of intellectual property which entered into force prior to the entry into force of the Agreement Establishing the WTO, provided that such agreements are notified to the Council for Trade-Related Aspects of Intellectual Property Rights and do not constitute an arbitrary or unjustifiable discrimination against nationals of other Members.

Article 5
Multilateral Agreements on Acquisition or Maintenance of Protection

The obligations under Articles 3 and 4 above do not apply to procedures provided in multilateral agreements concluded under the auspices of the World Intellectual Property Organization relating to the acquisition or maintenance of intellectual property rights.

Article 6
Exhaustion

For the purposes of dispute settlement under this Agreement, subject to the provisions of Articles 3 and 4 above nothing in this Agreement shall be used to address the issue of the exhaustion of intellectual property rights.

Article 7
Objectives

The protection and enforcement of intellectual property rights should contribute to the promotion of technological innovation and to the transfer and dissemination of technology, to the mutual advantage of producers and users of technological knowledge and in a manner conducive to social and economic welfare, and to a balance of rights and obligations.

Article 8
Principles

1. Members may, in formulating or amending their national laws and regulations, adopt measures necessary to protect public health and nutrition, and to promote the public interest in Sectors of vital importance to their-socio-economic and technological development, provided that such measures are consistent with the provisions of this Agreement.

2. Appropriate measures, provided that they are consistent with the provisions of this Agreement, may be needed to prevent the abuse of intellectual property rights by right holders or the resort to practices which unreasonably restrain trade or adversely affect the international transfer of technology.

PART II

STANDARDS CONCERNING THE AVAILABILITY, SCOPE. AND USE OF INTELLECTUAL PROPERTY RIGHTS

SECTION I : COPYRIGHT AND RELATED RIGHTS

Article 9
Relation to Berne Convention

1 . Members shall comply with Articles 1-21 and the Appendix of the Berne Convention (1971). However, Members shali not have rights or obligations under this Agreement in respect of the rights conferred under Article 6 *bis* of that Convention or of the rights derived therefrom.

2. Copyright protection shall extend to expressions and not to idea, procedures, methods of operation or mathematical concepts as such.

Article 10
Computer Programs and Compilations of Data

1. Computer programs, whether in source or object code, shall be protected as literary works under the Berne Convention (1971).

2. Compilations of data or other material, whether in machine readable or other form, which by reason of the selection or arrangement of their contents constitute intellectual creations shall be protected as such. Such protection, which shall not extend to the data or material itself, shall be without prejudice to any copyright subsisting in the data or material itself.

Article 11
Rental Rights

In respect of at least computer programs and cinematographic works, a Member shall provide authors and their successors in title the right to authorize or to prohibit the commercial rental to the public of originals or rental copies of their copyright works. A Member shall be excepted from this obligation in respect of cinematographic works unless such rental has led to widespread copying of such works which is materially impairing the exclusive right of reproduction conferred in that Member on authors and their successors in title. In respect of computer programs, this obligation does not apply to rentals where the program itself is not the essential object of the rental.

Article 12
Term of Protection

Whenever the term of protection of a work, other than a photographic work or a work of applied art, is calculated on a basis other than the life of a natural person, such term shall be no less than fifty years from the end of the calendar year of authorized publication, or, failing such authorised publication within fifty years from the making of the work, fifty years from the end of the calendar year of making.

Article 13
Limitations and Exceptions

Members shall confine limitations or exceptions to exclusive rights to certain special cases which do not conflict with a normal exploitation of the work and do not unreasonably prejudice the legitimate interests of the right holder.

Article 14
Protection of Performers, Producers of Phonograms (Sound Recordings) and Broadcasting Organizations

1. In respect of a fixation of their performance on a phonogram, performers shall have the possibility of preventing the following acts when undertaken without their authorization: the fixation of their unfixed performance and the reproduction of such fixation. Performers shall also have the possibility of preventing the following acts when undertaken without their authorization: the broadcasting by wireless means and the communication to the public of their live performance.

2. Producers of phonograms shall enjoy the right to authorize or prohibit the direct or indirect reproduction of their phonograms.

3. Broadcasting organizations shall have the right to prohibit the following acts when undertaken without their authorization: the fixation, the reproduction of fixations, and the rebroadcasting by wireless means of broadcasts, as well as the communication to the public of television broadcasts of the same. Where Members do not grant such rights to broadcasting organizations, they

shall provide owners of copyright in the subject matter of broadcasts with the possibility of preventing the above acts, subject to the provisions of the Berne Convention (1971).

4. The provisions of Article 11 in respect of computer programs shall apply *mutatis mutandis* to producers of phonograms and any other right holders in phonograms as determined in domestic law. If, on the date of the Ministerial Meeting concluding the Uruguay Round of Multilateral Trade Negotiations, a Member has in force a system of equitable remuneration of right holders in respect of the rental of phonograms, it may maintain such system provided that the commercial rental of phonograms is not giving rise to the material impairment of the exclusive rights of reproduction of right holders.

5. The term of the protection available under this Agreement to performers and producers of phonograms shall last at least until the end of a period of fifty years computed from the end of the calendar year in which the fixation was made or the performance took place. The term of protection granted pursuant to paragraph 3 above shall last for at least twenty years from the end of the calendar year in which the broadcast took place.

6. Any Member may, in relation to the rights conferred under paragraphs 1-3 above, provide for conditions, limitations, exceptions and reservations to the extent permitted by the Rome Convention. However, the provisions of Article 18 of the Berne Convention (1971) shall also apply, *mutatis mutandis*, to the rights of performers and producers of phonograms in phonograms.

SECTION 2: TRADEMARKS

Article 15

Protectable Subject Matter

1. Any sign, or any combination of signs, capable of distinguishing the goods or services of one undertaking from those of other undertakings, shall be capable of constituting a trademark. Such signs, in particular words including personal names, letters, numerals, figurative elements and combinations of colours as well as any combination of such signs, shall be eligible for registration as trademarks. Where signs are not inherently capable of distinguishing the relevant goods or services, Members may make registrability depend on distinctiveness acquired through use. Members may require, as a condition of registration, that signs be visually perceptible.

2. Paragraph 1 above shall not be understood to prevent a Member from denying registration of a trademark on other grounds, provided that they do not derogate from the provisions of the Paris Convention (1967).

3. Members may make registrability depend on use. However, actual use

of a trademark shall not be a condition for filing an application for registration. An application shall not be refused solely on the ground that intended use has not taken place before the expiry of a period of three years from the date of application.

4. The nature of the goods or services to which a trademark is to be applied shall in no case form an obstacle to registration of the trademark

5. Members shall publish each trademark either before it is registered or promptly after it is registered and shall afford a reasonable opportunity for petitions to cancel the registration. In addition, Members may afford an opportunity for the registration of a trademark to be opposed.

Article 16

Rights Conferred

1. The owner of a registered trademark shall have the exclusive right to prevent all third parties not having his consent from using in the course of trade identical or similar signs for goods or services which are identical or similar to those in respect of which the trademark is registered where such use would result in a likelihood of confusion. In case of the use of an identical sign for identical goods or services, a likelihood of confusion shall be presumed. The rights described above shall not prejudice any existing prior rights, nor shall they affect the possibility of Members making rights available on the basis of use.

2. Article *6 bis* of the Paris Convention (1967) shall apply, *mutatis mutandis,* to services. In determining whether a trademark is well-known, account shall be taken of the knowledge of the trademark in the relevant sector of the public, including knowledge in that Member obtained as a result of the promotion of the trademark.

3. Article *6 bis* of the Paris Convention (1967) shall apply, *mutatis mutandis,* to goods or services which are not similar to those in respect of which a trademark is registered, provided that use of that trademark in relation to those goods or services would indicate a connection between those goods or services and the owner of the registered trademark and provided that the interests of the owner of the registered trademark are likely to be damaged by such use.

Article 17

Exceptions

Members may provide limited exceptions to the rights conferred by a trademark, such as fair use of descriptive terms, provided that such exceptions take account of the legitimate interests of the owner of the trademark and of third parties.

Article 18

Term of Protection

Initial registration, and each renewal of registration, of a trademark shall be for a term of no less than seven years. The registration of a trademark shall be renewable indefinitely.

Article 19

Requirement of Use

1. If use is required to maintain a registration, the registration may be cancelled only after an uninterrupted period of at least three years of non-use, unless valid reasons based on the existence of obstacles to such use are shown by the trademark owner. Circumstances arising independently of the will of the owner of the trademark which constitute an obstacle to the use of the trademark, such as import restrictions on or other government requirements for goods or services protected by the trademark, shall be recognized as valid reasons for non-use.

2. When subject to the control of its owner, use of a trademark by another person shall be recognized as use of the trademark for the purpose of maintaining the registration.

Article 20

Other Requirements

The use of a trademark in the course of trade shall not be unjustifiably encumbered by special requirements, such as use with another trademark, use in a special form or use in a manner detrimental to its capability to distinguish the goods or services of one undertaking from those of other undertakings. This will not preclude a requirement prescribing the use of the trademark identifying the undertaking producing the goods or services along with, but without linking it to, the trademark distinguishing the specific goods or services in question of that undertaking.

Article 21

Licensing and Assignment

Members may determine conditions on the licensing and assignment of trademarks, it being understood that the compulsory licensing of trademarks shall not be permitted and that the owner of a registered trademark shall have the right to assign his trademark with or without the transfer of the business to which the trademark belongs.

SECTION 3 : GEOGRAPHICAL INDICATIONS

Article 22

Protection of Geographical Indications

1. Geographical indications are, for the purposes of this Agreement, indications which identify a good as originating in the territory of a Member, or a region or locality in that territory, where a given quality, reputation or other characteristic of the good is essentially attributable to its geographical origin.

2. In respect of geographical indications, Members shall provide the legal means for interested parties to prevent:

(a) the use of any means in the designation or presentation of a good that indicates or suggests that the good in question originates in a geographical area other than the true place of origin in a manner which misleads the public as to the geographical origin of the good;

(b) any use which constitutes an act of unfair competition within the meaning of Article *10 bis* of the Paris Convention (1967).

3. A Member shall, *ex officio* if its legislation so permits or at the request of an interested party, refuse or invalidate the registration of a trademark which contains or consists of a geographical indication with respect to goods not originating in the territory indicated, if use of the indication in the trademark for such goods in that Member is of such a nature as to mislead the public as to the true place of origin.

4. The provisions of the preceding paragraphs of this Article shall apply to a geographical indication which, although literally true as to the territory, region or locality in which the goods originate, falsely represents to the public that the goods originate in another territory.

Article 23

Additional Protection for Geographical Indications for Wines and Spirits

1. Each Member shall provide the legal means for interested parties to prevent use of a geographical indication identifying wines for wines not originating in the place indicated by the geographical indication in question or identifying spirits for spirits not originating in the place indicated by the geographical indication in question, even where the true origin of the goods is indicated or the geographical indication is used in translation or accompanied by expressions such as "kind", "type", "style" "imitation" or the like.[163]

---

[163] Notwithstanding the first sentence of Article 42, Members may, with respect to these obligations, instead provide for enforcement by administrative action.

2. The registration of a trademark for wines which contains or consists of a geographical indication identifying wines or for spirits which contains or consists of a geographical indication identifying spirits shall be refused or invalidated, *ex officio* if domestic legislation so permits or at the request of an interested party, with respect to such wines or spirits not having this origin.

3. In the case of homonymous geographical indications for wines, protection shall be accorded to each indication, subject to the provisions of paragraph 4 of Article 22 above. Each Member shall determine the practical conditions under which the homonymous indications in question will be differentiated from each other, taking into account the need to ensure equitable treatment of the producers concerned and that consumers are not misled.

4. In order to facilitate the protection of geographical indications for wines. negotiations shall be undertaken in the Council for Trade-Related Aspects of Intellectual Property Rights concerning the establishment of a multilateral system of notification and registration of geographical indications for wines eligible for protection in those Members participating in the system.

Article 24
International Negotiations; Exceptions

1. Members agree to enter into negotiations aimed at increasing the protection of individual geographical indications under Article 23. The provisions of paragraphs 4-8 below shall not be used by a Member to refuse to conduct negotiations or to conclude bilateral or multilateral agreements. In the context of such negotiations, Members shall be willing to consider the continued applicability of these provisions to individual geographical indications whose use was the subject of such negotiations.

2. The Council for Trade-Related Aspects of Intellectual Property Rights shall keep under review the application of the provisions of this Section; the first such review shall take place within two years of the entry into force of the Agreement Establishing the **WTO**. Any matter affecting the compliance with the obligations under these provisions may be drawn to the attention of the Council, which, at the request of a Member, shall consult with any Member or Members in respect of such matter in respect of which it has not been possible to find a satisfactory solution through bilateral or plurilateral consultations between the Members concerned. The Council shall take such action as may be agreed to facilitate the operation and further the objectives of this Section.

3. In implementing this Section, a Member shall not diminish the protection of geographical indications that existed in that Member immediately prior to the date of entry into force of the Agreement Establishing the WTO

available for any inventions, whether products or processes, in all fields of technology, provided that they are new, involve an inventive step and are capable of industrial application.[164] Subject to paragraph 4 of Article 65, paragraph 8 of Article 70 and paragraph 3 of this Article, patents shall be available and patent rights enjoyable without discrimination as to the place of invention, the field of technology and whether products are imported or locally produced.

2. Members may exclude from patentability inventions, the prevention within their territory of the commercial exploitation of which is necessary to protect *ordre public* or morality, including to protect human, animal or plant life or health or to avoid serious prejudice to the environment, provided that such exclusion is not made merely because the exploitation is prohibited by domestic law.

3. Members may also exclude from patentability :

(a) diagnostic, therapeutic and surgical methods for the treatment of humans or animals;

(b) plants and animals other than micro-organisms. and essentially biological processes for the production of plants or animals other than non-biological and micro-biological processes. However, Members shall provide for the protection of plant varieties either by patents or by an effective *sui generis* system or by any combination thereof. The provisions of this sub-paragraph shall be reviewed four years after the entry into force of the Agreement Establishing the WTO.

Article 28

Rights Conferred

1. A patent shall confer on its owner the following exclusive rights:

(a) where the subject matter of a patent is a product, to prevent third parties not having his consent from the acts of: making, using, offering for sale, selling, or importing[165] for these purposes that product;

(b) where the subject matter of a patent is a process, to prevent third parties not having his consent from the act of using the process, and from the acts of: using, offering for sale, selling, or importing

---

[164] For the purposes of this Article, the terms "inventive step" and "capable of industrial application" may be deemed by a Member to be synonymous with the terms "non-obvious" and "useful" respectively.

[165] This right, like all other rights conferred under this Agreement in respect of the use, sale, importation or other distribution of goods, is subject to the provisions of Article 6 above.

for these purposes at least the product obtained directly by that process.

2. Patent owners shall also have the right to assign, or transfer by succession, the patent and to conclude licensing contracts.

Article 29

Conditions on Patent Applicants

1. Members Shall require that an applicant for a patent shall disclose the invention in a manner sufficiently clear and complete for the invention to be carried out by a person skilled in the art and may require the applicant to indicate the best mode for carrying out the invention known to the inventor at the filing date or, where priority is claimed, at the priority date of the application.

2. Members may require an applicant for a patent to provide information concerning his corresponding foreign applications and grants.

Article 30

Exceptions to Rights Conferred

1. Members may provide limited exceptions to the exclusive rights conferred by a patent, provided that such exceptions do not unreasonably conflict with a normal exploitation of the patent and do not unreasonably prejudice the legitimate interests of the patent owner, taking account of the legitimate interests of third parties.

Article 31

Other Use Without Authorization of the Right Holder

Where the law of a Member allows for other use[166] of the subject matter of a patent without the authorization of the right holder, including use by the government or third parties authorized by the government, the following provisions shall be respected:

(a) authorization of such use shall be considered on its individual merits;

(b) such use may only be permitted if, prior to such use, the proposed user has made efforts to obtain authorization from the right holder on reasonable commercial terms and conditions and that such efforts have not been successful within a reasonable period of time. This requirement may be waived by a Member in the case of a national emergency or other circumstances of extreme

166 "Other use" refers to use other than that allowed under Article 30.

urgency or in cases of public non-commercial use. In situations of national emergency or other circumstances of extreme urgency, the right holder shall, nevertheless, be notified as soon as reasonably practicable. In the case of public non-commercial use, where the government or contractor, without making a patent search, knows or has demonstrable grounds to know that a valid patent is or will be used by or for the government, the right holder shall be informed promptly;

(c) the scope and duration of such use shall be limited to the purpose for which it was authorized, and in the case of semi-conductor technology shall only be for public non-commercial use or to remedy a practice determined after judicial or administrative process to be anti-competitive.

(d) such use shall be non-exclusive;

(e) such use shall be non-assignable, except with that part of the enterprise or goodwill which enjoys such use;

(f) any such use shall be authorized predominantly for the supply of the domestic market of the Member authorizing such use;

(g) authorization for such use shall be liable, subject to adequate protection of the legitimate interests of the persons so authorized, to be terminated if and when the circumstances which led to it cease to exist and are unlikely to recur. The competent authority shall have the authority to review, upon motivated request, the continued existence of these circumstances;

(h) the right holder shall be paid adequate remuneration in the circumstances of each case, taking into account the economic value of the authorization;

(i) the legal validity of any decision relating to the authorization of such use shall be subject to judicial review or other independent review by a distinct higher authority in that Member;

(j) any decision relating to the remuneration provided in respect of such use shall be subject to judicial review or other independent review by a distinct higher authority in that Member;

(k) Members are not obliged to apply the conditions set forth sub-paragraphs (b) and (f) above where such use is permitted to remedy a practice determined after judicial or administrative process to be anti-competitive. The need to correct anti-competitive practices may be taken into account in determining the amount of remuneration in such cases. Competent authorities shall have the authority to refuse termination of authorization if and when the conditions which led to such authorization are likely to recur;

(l) where such use is authorized to permit the exploitation of a patent ("the second patent") which cannot be exploited without infringing another patent ("the first patent"); the following additional conditions shall apply:

(i) the invention claimed in the second patent shall involve an important technical advance of considerable economic significance in relation to the invention claimed in the first patent;

(ii) the owner of the first patent shall be entitled to a cross-licence on reasonable terms to use the invention claimed in the second patents; and

(iii) the use authorized in respect of the first patent shall be non-assignable except with the assignment of the second patent.

Article 32

Revocation/Forfeiture

An opportunity for judicial review of any decision to revoke or forfeit a patent shall be available.

Article 33

Term of Protection

The term of protection available shall not end before the expiration of a period of twenty years counted from the filing date.[167]

Article 34

Process Patents: Burden of Proof

1. For the purposes of civil proceedings in respect of the infringement of the rights of the owner referred to in paragraph l(b) of Article 28 above, if the subject matter of a patent is a process for obtaining a product, the judicial authorities shall have the authority to order the defendant to prove that the process to obtain an identical product is different from the patented process. Therefore, Members shall provide, in at least one of the following circumstances, that any identical product when produced without the consent of the patent owner shall, in the absence of proof to the contrary, be deemed to have been obtained by the patented process:

(a) if the product obtained by the patented process is new;

[167] It is understood that those Members which do not have a system of original grant may provide that the term of protection shall be computed from the filing date in the system of original grant.

(b) if there is a substantial likelihood that the identical product was made by the process and the owner of the patent has been unable through reasonable efforts to determine the process actually used.

2. Any Member shall be free to provide that the burden of proof indicated in paragraph 1 shall be on the alleged infringer only if the condition referred to in sub-paragraph (a) is fulfilled or only if the condition referred to in sub-paragraph (b) is fulfilled.

3. In the adduction of proof to the contrary the legitimate interests of the defendant in protecting his manufacturing and bussiness secrets shall be taken into account.

SECTION 6 : LAYOUT-DESIGNS (TOPOGRAPHIES) OF INTEGRATED CIRCUITS

Article 35
Relation to IPIC Treaty

Members agree to provide protection to the layout-designs (topographies) of integrated circuits (hereinafter referred to as "layout-designs") in accordance with Articles 2-7 (other than paragraph 3 of Article 6), Article 12 and paragraph 3 of Article 16 of the Treaty on Intellectual Property in Respect of Integrated Circuits and, in addition, to comply with the following provisions.

Article 36
Scope of the Protection

Subject to the provisions of paragraph 1 of Article 37 below, Members shall consider unlawful the following acts if performed without the authorization of the right holder:[168] importing, selling, or otherwise distributing for commercial purposes a protected layout-design, an integrated circuit in which a protected layout-design is incorporated, or an article incorporating such an integrated circuit only insofar as it continues to contain an unlawfully reproduced layout-design.

Article 37
Acts not Requiring the Authorization of the Right Holder

1. Notwithstanding Article 36 above, no Member shall consider unlawful the performance of any of the acts referred to in that Article in respect of an integrated circuit incorporating an unlawfully reproduced layout-design or any article incorporating such an integrated circuit where the person performing

[168] The term "right holder" in this Section shall be understood as having the same meaning as the term "holder of the right" in the IPIC Treaty.

or ordering such acts did not know and had no reasonable ground to know, when acquiring the integrated circuit or article incorporating such an integrated circuit, that it incorporated an unlawfully reproduced layout-design. Members shall provide that, after the time that such person has received sufficient notice that the layout-design was unlawfully reproduced, he may perform any of the acts with respect to the stock on hand or ordered before such time, but shall be liable to pay to the right holder a sum equivalent to a reasonable royalty such as would be payable under a freely negotiated licence in respect of such a layout-design.

2. The conditions set out in sub-paragraphs (a)-(k) of Article 31 above shall apply *mutatis mutandis* in the event of any non-voluntary licensing of a layout-design or of its use by or for the government without the authorization of the right holder.

Article 38

Term of Protection

1. In Members requiring registration as a condition of protection, the term of protection of layout-designs shall not end before the expiration of a period of ten years counted from the date of filing an application for registration or from the first commercial exploitation wherever in the world it occurs.

2. In Members not requiring registration as a condition for protection, layout-designs shall be protected for a term of no less than ten years from the date of the first commercial exploitation wherever in the world it occurs.

3. Notwithstanding paragraphs 1 and 2 above, a Member may provide that protection shall lapse fifteen years after the creation of the layout-design.

SECTION 7: PROTECTION OF UNDISCLOSED INFORMATION

Article 39

1. In the course of ensuring effective protection against unfair competition as provided in Article 10 *bis* of the Paris Convention (1967), Members shall protect undisclosed information in accordance with paragraph 2 below and data submitted to governments or governmental agencies in accordance with paragraph 3 below.

2. Natural and legal persons shall have the possibility of preventing information lawfully within their control from being disclosed to, acquired by, or used by others without their consent in a manner contrary to honest commercial practices[169] so long as such information:

[169] For the purpose of this provision, "a manner contrary to honest commercial practices" shall mean at least practices such as breach of contract, breach of confidence and inducement to breach, and includes the acquisition of undisclosed information by third parties who knew, or were grossly negligent in failing to know, that such practices were involved in the acquisition.

- is secret in the sense that it is not, as a body or in the precise configuration and assembly of its components, generally known among or readily accessible to persons within the circles that normally deal with the kind of information in question;
- has commercial value because it is secret; and
- has been subject to reasonable steps under the circumstances, by the person lawfully in control of the information, to keep it secret.

3. Members, when requiring, as a condition of approving the marketing of pharmaceutical or of agricultural chemical products which utilize new chemical entities, the submission of undisclosed test or other data, the origination of which involves a considerable effort, shall protect such data against unfair commercial use. In addition, Members shall protect such data against disclosure, except where necessary to protect the public, or unless steps are taken to ensure that the data are protected against unfair commercial use.

SECTION 8 : CONTROL OF ANTI-COMPETITIVE PRACTICES IN CONTRACTUAL LICENCES

Article 40

1. Members agree that some licensing practices or conditions pertaining to intellectual property rights which restrain competition may have adverse effects on trade and may impede the transfer and dissemination of technology.

2. Nothing in this Agreement shall prevent Members from specifying in their national legislation licensing practices or conditions that may in particular cases constitute an abuse of intellectual property rights having an adverse effect on competition in the relevant market. As provided above, a Member may adopt, consistently with the other provisions of this Agreement, appropriate measures to prevent or control such practices, which may include for example exclusive grantback conditions, conditions preventing challenges to validity and coercive package licensing, in the light of the relevant laws and regulations of that Member.

3. Each Member shall enter, upon request, into consultations with any other Member which has cause to believe that an intellectual property right owner that is a national or domiciliary of the Member to which the request for consultations has been addressed is undertaking practices in violation of the requesting Member's laws and regulations on the subject matter of this Section, and which wishes to secure compliance with such legislation, without prejudice to any action under the law and to the full freedom of an ultimate decision of either Member. The Member addressed shall accord full and sympathetic consideration to, and shall afford adequate opportunity for, consultations with the requesting Member, and shall co-operate through

supply of publicly available non-confidential information of relevance to the matter in question and of other information available to the Member, subject to domestic law and to the conclusion of mutually satisfactory agreements concerning the safeguarding of its confidentiality by the requesting Member.

4. A Member whose nationals or domiciliaries are subject to proceedings in another Member concerning alleged violation of that other Member's laws and regulations on the subject matter of this Section shall, upon request, be granted an opportunity for consultations by the other Member under the same conditions as those foreseen in paragraph 3 above.

PART III

ENFORCEMEET OF INTELLECTUAL PROPERTY RIGHTS

SECTION 1: GENERAL OBLIGATIONS

Article 41

1. Members shall ensure that enforcement procedures as specified in this Part are available under their national laws so as to permit effective action against any act of infringement of intellectual property rights covered by this Agreement, including expeditious remedies to prevent infringements and remedies which constitute a deterrent to further infringements. These procedures shall be applied in such a manner as to avoid the creation of barriers to legitimate trade and to provide for safeguards against their abuse.

2. Procedures concerning the enforcement of intellectual property rights shall be fair and equitable. They shall not be unnecessarily complicated or costly, or entail unreasonable time-limits or unwarranted delays.

3. Decisions on the merits of a case shall preferably be in writing and reasoned. They shall be made available at least to the parties to the proceeding without undue delay. Decisions on the merits of a case shall be based only on evidence in respect of which parties were offered the opportunity to be heard.

4. Parties to a proceeding shall have an opportunity for review by a judicial authority of final administrative decisions and, subject to jurisdictional provisions in national laws concerning the importance of a case, of at least the legal aspects of initial judicial decisions on the merits of a case. However, there shall be no obligation to provide an opportunity for review of acquittals in criminal cases.

5. It is understood that this Part does not create any obligation to put in place a judicial system for the enforcement of intellectual property rights distinct from that for the enforcement of laws in general, nor does it affect the capacity of Members to enforce their laws in general. Nothing in this Part creates any obligation with respect to the distribution of resources as between

enforcement of intellectual property rights and the enforcement of laws in general.

SECTION 2 : CIVIL AND ADMINISTRATIVE PROCEDURES AND REMEDIES

Artide 42

Fair and Equitable Procedures

Members shall make available to right holders[170] civil judicial procedures concerning the enforcement of any intellectual property right covered by this Agreement. Defendants shall have the right to written notice which is timely and contains sufficient detail, including the basis of the claims. Parties shall be allowed to be represented by independent legal counsel, and procedures shall not impose overly burdensome requirements concerning mandatory personal appearances. All parties to such procedures shall be duly entitled to substantiate their claims and to present all relevant evidence. The procedure shall provide a means to identify and protect confidential information, unless this would be contrary to existing constitutional requirements.

Article 43

Evidence of Proof

1. The judicial authorities shall have the authority, where a party has presented reasonably available evidence sufficient to support its claims and has specified evidence relevant to substantiation of its claims which lies in the control of the opposing party, to order that this evidence be produced by the opposing party, subject in appropriate cases to conditions which ensure the protection of confidential information.

2. In cases in which a party to a proceeding voluntarily and without good reason refuses access to, or otherwise does not provide necessary information within a reasonable period, or significantly impedes a procedure relating to an enforcement action, a Member may accord judicial authorities the authority to make preliminary and final determinations, affirmative or negative, on the basis of the information presented to them, including the complaint or the allegation presented by the party adversely affected by the denial of access to information, subject to providing the parties an opportunity to be heard on the allegations or evidence.

Article 44

Injunctions

1. The judicial authorities shall have the authority to order a party to

[170] For the purpose of this Part, the term "right holder" includes federations and associations having legal standing to assert such rights.

desist from an infringement, *inter alia* to prevent the entry into the channels of commerce in their jurisdiction of imported goods that involve the infringement of an intellectual property right, immediately after customs clearance of such goods. Members are not obliged to accord such authority in respect of protected subject matter acquired or ordered by a person prior to knowing or having reasonable grounds to know that dealing in such subject matter would entail the infringement of an intellectual property right.

2. Notwithstanding the other provisions of this Part and provided that the provisions of Part II specifically addressing use by governments, or by third parties authorized by a government, without the authorization of the right holder are complied with, Members may limit the remedies available against such use to payment of remuneration in accordance with sub-paragraph (h) of Article 31 above. In other cases, the remedies under this Part shall apply or, where these remedies are inconsistent with national law, declaratory judgments and adequate compensation shall be available.

Article 45

Damages

1. The judicial authorities shall have the authority to order the infringer to pay the right holder damages adequate to compensate for the injury the right holder has suffered because of an infringement of his intellectual property right by an infringer who knew or had reasonable grounds to know that he was engaged in infringing activity.

2. The judicial authorities shall also have the authority to order the infringer to pay the right holder expenses, which may include appropriate attorney's fees. In appropriate cases, Members may authorize the judicial authorities to order recovery of profits and/or payment of pre-established damages even where the infringer did not know or had no reasonable grounds to know that he was engaged in infringing activity.

Article 46

Other Remedies

In order to create an effective deterrent to infringement, the judicial authorities shall have the authority to order that goods that they have found to be infringing be, without compensation of any sort, disposed of outside the channels of commerce in such a manner as to avoid any harm caused to the right holder, or, unless this would be contrary to existing constitutional requirements, destroyed. The judicial authorities shall also have the authority to order that materials and implements the predominant use of which has been in the creation of the infringing goods be, without compensation of any son, disposed of outside the channels of commerce in such a manner as to minimize the risks of further infringements. In considering such requests, the need for proportionality between the seriousness of the infringement and the remedies ordered as well as the interests of third parties shall be taken into account. In regard to counterfeit trademark goods, the simple removal of the trademark unlawfully affixed shall not be sufficient, other than in exceptional cases, to permit release of the goods into the channels of commerce.

Article 47

Right of Information

Members may provide that the judicial authorities shall have the authority, unless this would be out of proportion to the seriousness of the infringement, to order the infringer to inform the right holder of the identity of third persons involved in the production and distribution of the infringing goods or services and of their channels of distribution.

Article 48

Indemnification of the Defendant

1. The judicial authorities shall have the authority to order a party at whose request measures were taken and who has abused enforcement procedures to provide to a party wrongfully enjoined or restrained adequate compensation for the injury suffered because of such abuse. The judicial authorities shall also have the authority to order the applicant to pay the defendant expenses, which may include appropriate attorney's fees.

2. In respect of the administration of any law pertaining to the protection or enforcement of intellectual property rights, Members shall only exempt both public authorities and officials from liability to appropriate remedial measures where actions are taken or intended in good faith in the course of the administration of such laws.

Article 49

Administrative Procedures

To the extent that any civil remedy can be ordered as a result of administrative procedures on the merits of a case, such procedures shall conform to principles equivalent in substance to those set forth in this Section.

SECTION 3 : PROVISIONAL MEASURES

Article 50

1. The judicial authorities shall have the authority to order prompt and effective provisional measures:

(a) to prevent an infringement of any intellectual property right from occurring, and in particular to prevent the entry into the channels of commerce in their jurisdiction of goods, including imported goods immediately after customs clearance;

(b) to preserve relevant evidence in regard to the alleged infringement.

2. The judicial authorities shall have the authority to adopt provisional measures *inaudita altera parte* where appropriate, in particular where any delay is likely to cause irreparable harm to the right holder, or where there is a demonstrable risk of evidence being destroyed.

3. The judicial authorities shall have the authority to require the applicant to provide any reasonably available evidence in order to satisfy themselves with a sufficient degree of certainty that the applicant is the right holder and that his right is being infringed or that such infringement is imminent, and to order the applicant to provide a security or equivalent assurance sufficient to protect the defendant and to prevent abuse.

4. Where provisional measures have been adopted *inaudita altera parte,* the parties affected shall be given notice, without delay after the execution of the measures at the latest. A review, including a right to be heard, shall take place upon request of the defendant with a view to deciding, within a reasonable period after the notification of the measures, whether these measures shall be modified, revoked or confirmed.

5. The applicant may be required to supply other information necessary for the identification of the goods concerned by the authority that will execute the provisional measures.

6. Without prejudice to paragraph 4 above, provisional measures taken on the basis of paragraphs 1 and 2 above shall, upon request by the defendant, be revoked or otherwise cease to have effect, if proceedings leading to a decision on the merits of the case are not initiated within a reasonable period, to be determined by the judicial authority ordering the measures where national law so permits or, in the absence of such a determination, not to exceed twenty working days or thirty-one calendar days, whichever is the longer.

7. Where the provisional measures are revoked or where they lapse due to any act or omission by the applicant, or where it is subsequently found that there has been no infringement or threat of infringement of an intellectual property right, the judicial authorities shall have the authority to order the applicant, upon request of the defendant, to provide the defendant appropriate compensation for any injury caused by these measures.

8. To the extent that any provisional measure can be ordered as a result of administrative procedures, such procedures shall conform to principles equivalent in substance to those set forth in this Section.

SECTION 4: SPECIAL REQUIREMENTS RELATED TO BORDER MEASURES[171]

Article 51

Suspension of Release by Customs Authorities

Members shall, in conformity with the provisions set out below, adopt procedures[172] to enable a right holder, who has valid grounds for suspecting that the importation of counterfeit trademark or pirated copyright goods[173] may take place, to lodge an application in writing with competent authorities, administrative or judicial, for the suspension by the customs authorities of the release into free circulation of such goods. Members may enable such an application to be made in respect of goods which involve other infringements of intellectual property rights, provided that the requirements of this Section are met. Members may also provide for corresponding procedures concerning the suspension by the customs authorities of the release of infringing goods destined for exportation from their territories.

Article 52

Application

Any right holder initiating the procedures under Article 51 above shall be required to provide adequate evidence to satisfy the competent authorities that, under the laws of the country of importation, there is *prima facie* an infringement of his intellectual property right and to supply a sufficiently detailed description of the goods to make them readily recognizable by the customs authorities. The competent authorities shall inform the applicant within a reasonable period whether they have accepted the application and,

---

[171] Where a Member has dismantled substantially all controls over movement of goods across its border with another Member with which it forms part of a customs union, it shall not be required to apply the provisions of this Section at that border.

[172] It is understood that there shall be no obligation to apply such procedures to imports of goods put on the market in another country by or with the consent of the right holder, or to goods in transit.

[173] For the purposes of this Agreement:

- counterfeit trademark goods shall mean any goods, including packaging, bearing without authorization a trademark which is identical to the trademark validly registered in respect of such goods, or which cannot be distinguished in its essential aspects from such a trademark, and which thereby infringes the rights of the owner of the trademark in question under the law of the country of importation;
- pirated copyright goods shall mean any goods which are copies made without the consent of the right holder or person duly authorized by him in the country of production and which are made directly or indirectly from an article where the making of that copy would have constituted an infringement of a copyright or a related right under the law of the country of importation.

where determined by the competent authorities, the period for which the customs authorities will take action.

Artide 53

Security or Equivalent Assurance

1. The competent authorities shall have the authority to require an applicant to provide a security or equivalent assurance sufficient to protect the defendant and the competent authorities and to prevent abuse. Such security or equivalent assurance shall not unreasonably deter recourse to these procedures.

2. Where pursuant to an application under this Section the release of goods involving industrial designs, patents, layout-designs or undisclosed information into free circulation has been suspended by customs authorities on the basis of a decision other than by a judicial or other independent authority, and the period provided for in Article 55 has expired without the granting of provisional relief by the duly empowered authority, and provided that all other conditions for importation have been complied with, the owner, importer, or consignee of such goods shall be entitled to their release on the posting of a security in an amount sufficient to protect the right holder for any infringement. Payment of such security shall not prejudice any other remedy available to the right holder, it being understood that the security shall be released if the right holder fails to pursue his right of action within a reasonable period of time.

Article 54

Notice of Suspension

The importer and the applicant shall be promptly notified of the suspension of the release of goods according to Article 51 above.

Article 55

Duration of Suspension

If, within a period not exceeding ten working days after the applicant has been served notice of the suspension, the customs authorities have not been informed that proceedings leading to a decision on the merits of the case have been initiated by a party other than the defendant, or that the duly empowered authority has taken provisional measures prolonging the suspension of the release of the goods, the goods shall be released, provided that all other conditions for importation or exportation have been complied with; in appropriate cases, this time-limit may be extended by another ten working days. If proceedings leading to a decision on the merits of the case have been initiated, a review, including a right to be heard, shall take place upon request of the defendant with a view to deciding, within a reasonable period, whether these measures shall be modified, revoked or confirmed. Notwithstanding the above, where the suspension of the release of goods is carried out or continued in accordance with a provisional judicial measure, the provisions of Article 50, paragraph 6 above shall apply.

Article 56

Indemnification of the Importer and of the Owner of the Goods

Relevant authorities shall have the authority to order the applicant to pay the importer, the consignee and the owner of the goods appropriate compensation for any injury caused to them through the wrongful detention of goods or through the detention of goods released pursuant to Article 55 above.

Article 57

Right of Inspection and Information

Without prejudice to the protection of confidential information, Members shall provide the competent authorities the authority to give the right holder sufficient opportunity to have any product detained by the customs authorities inspected in order to substantiate his claims. The competent authorities shall also have authority to give the importer an equivalent opportunity to have any such product inspected. Where a positive determination has been made on the merits of a case, Members may provide the competent authorities the authority to inform the right holder of the names and addresses of the consignor, the importer and the consignee and of the quantity of the goods in question.

Article 58

***Ex-Officio* Action**

Where Members require competent authorities to act upon their own initiative and to suspend the release of goods in respect of which they have acquired *prima facie* evidence that an intellectual property right is being infringed:.

(a) the competent authorities may at any time seek from the right holder any information that may assist them to exercise these powers;

(b) the importer and the right holder shall be promptly notified of the suspension. Where the importer has lodged an appeal against the suspension with the competent authorities, the suspension shall be subject to the conditions, *mutatis mutandis*, set out at Article 55 above;

(c) Members shall only exempt both public authorities and officials from liability to appropriate remedial measures where actions are taken or intended in good faith.

Article 59

Remedies

Without prejudice to other rights of action open to the right holder and subject to the right of the defendant to seek review by a judicial authority, competent authorities shall have the authority to order the destruction or disposal of infringing goods in accordance with the principles set out in Article 46 above. In regard to counterfeit trademark goods, the authorities shall not allow the re-exportation of the infringing goods in an unaltered state or subject them to a different customs procedure, other than in exceptional circumstances.

Article 60

***De Minimis* Imports**

Members may exclude from the application of the above provisions small quantities of goods of a non-commercial nature contained in travellers' personal luggage, or sent in small consignments.

SECTION 5 : CRIMINAL PROCEDURES

Article 61

Members shall provide for criminal procedures and penalties to be applied at least in cases of wilful trademark counterfeiting or copyright piracy on a commercial scale. Remedies available shall include imprisonment and/or monetary fines sufficient to provide a deterrent, consistently with the level of penalties applied for crimes of a corresponding gravity. In appropriate cases, remedies available shall also include the seizure, forfeiture and destruction of the infringing goods and of any materials and implements the predominant use of which has been in the commission of the offence. Members may provide for criminal procedures and penalties to be applied in other cases of infringement of intellectual property rights, in particular where they are committed wilfully and on a commercial scale.

PART IV

ACQUISITION AND MAINTENANCE OF INTELLECTUAL PROPERTY RIGHTS AND RELATED INTER-PARTES PROCEDURES

Article 62

1. Members may require, as a condition of the acquisition or maintenance of the intellectual property rights provided for under Sections 2-6 of Part II of this Agreement, compliance with reasonable procedures and formalities.

Such procedures and formalities shall be consistent with the provisions of this Agreement.

2. Where the acquisition of an intellectual property right is subject to the right being granted or registered, Members shall ensure that the procedures for grant or registration, subject to compliance with the substantive conditions for acquisition of the right, permit the granting or registration of the right within a reasonable period of time so as to avoid unwarranted curtailment of the period of protection.

3. Article 4 of the Paris Convention (1967) shall apply *mutatis mutandis* to service marks.

4. Procedures concerning the acquisition or maintenance of intellectual property rights and, where the national law provides for such procedures, administrative revocation and *inter partes* procedures such as opposition, revocation and cancellation, shall be governed by the general principles set out in paragraphs 2 and 3 of Article 41.

5. Final administrative decisions in any of the procedures referred to under paragraph 4 above shall be subject to review by a judicial or quasi-judicial authority. However, there shall be no obligation to provide an opportunity for such review of decisions in cases of unsuccessful opposition or administrative revocation, provided that the grounds for such procedures can be the subject of invalidation procedures.

PART V

DISPUTE PREVENTION AND SETTLEMENT

Article 63

Transparency

1. Laws and regulations, and final judicial decisions and administrative rulings of general application, made effective by any Member pertaining to the subject matter of this Agreement (the availability, scope, acquisition, enforcement and prevention of the abuse of intellectual property rights) shall be published, or where such publication is not practicable made publicly available, in a national language, in such a manner as to enable governments and right holders to become acquainted with them. Agreements concerning the subject matter of this Agreement which are in force between the government or a governmental agency of any Member and the government or a governmental agency of any other Member shall also be published.

2. Members shall notify the laws and regulations referred to in paragraph 1 above to the Council for Trade-Related Aspects of Intelleclual Property Rights in order to assist that Council in its review of the operation of this Agreement. The Council shall attempt to minimize the burden on Members in carrying out this obligation and may decide to waive the obligation to notify

such laws and regulations directly to the Council if consultations with the World Intellectual Property Organization on the establishment of a common register containing these laws and regulations are successful. The Council shall also consider in this connection any action, required regarding notifications pursuant to the obligations under this Agreement stemming from the provisions of Article *6ter* of the Paris Convention (1967).

3. Each Member shall be prepared to supply, in response to a written request from another Member, information of the sort referred to in paragraph 1 above. A Member, having reason to believe that a specific judicial decision or administrative ruling or bilateral agreement in the area of intellectual property rights affects its rights under this Agreement, may also request in writing to be given access to or be informed in sufficient detail of such specific judicial decisions or administrative rulings or bilateral agreements.

4. Nothing in paragraphs 1 to 3 above shall require Members to disclose confidential information which would impede law enforcement or otherwise be contrary to the public interest or would prejudice the legitimate commercial interests of particular enterprises, public or private.

Article 64
Dispute Settlement

1. The provisions of Articles XXII and XXIII of the General Agreement on Tariffs and Trade 1994 as elaborated and applied by the Understanding on Rules and Procedures Governing the Settlement of Disputes shall apply to consultations and the settlement of disputes under this Agreement except as otherwise specifically provided herein.

2. Sub-paragraphs XXIII: 1(b) and XXIII: l(c) of the General Agreement on Tariffs and Trade 1994 shall not apply to the settlement of disputes under this Agreement for a pericd of five years from the entry into force of the Agreement establishing the **World Trade Organisation**

3. During the time period referred to in paragraph 2, the (TRIPs) Council shall examine the scope and modalities for Article XXIII: l(b) and Article XXIII: l(c) – type complaints made pursuant to this Agreement, and submit its recommendations to the Ministerial Conference for approval. Any decision of the Ministerial Conference to approve such recommendations or to extend the period in paragraph 2 shall be made only by consensus, and approved recommendations shall be effective for all Members without further formal acceptance process.

PART VI
TRANSITIONAL ARRANGEMENTS

Article 65
Transitional Arrangements

1. Subject to the provisions of paragraphs 2, 3 and 4 below, no Member

shall be obliged to apply the provisions of this Agreement before the expiry of a general period of one year following the date of entry into force of the Agreement Establishing the WTO.

2. Any developing country Member is entitled to delay for a further period of four years the date of application, as deftned in paragraph 1 above, of the provisions of this Agreement other than Articles 3, 4 and 5 of Part I.

3. Any other Member which is in the process of transformation from a centrally-planned into a market, free-enterprise economy and which is undertaking structural reform of its intellectual property system and facing special problems in the preparation and implementation of intellectual property laws, may also benefit from a period of delay as foreseen in paragraph 2 above.

4. To the extent that a developing country Member is obliged by this Agreement to extend product patent protection to areas of technology not so protectable in its territory on the general date of application of this Agreement for that Member, as defined in paragraph 2 above, it may delay the application of the provisions on product patents of Section 5 of Part II of this Agreement to such areas of technology for an additional period of five years.

5. Any Member availing itself of a transitional period under paragraphs 1, 2, 3 or 4 above shall ensure that any changes in its domestic laws, regulations and practice made during that period do not result in a lesser degree of consistency with the provisions of this Agreement.

Article 66

Least-Developed Country Members

1. In view of their special needs and requirements, their economic, financial and administrative constraints, and their need for flexibility to create a viable technological base, least-developed country Members shall not be required to apply the provisions of this Agreement, other than Articles 3, 4 and 5, for a period of 10 years from the date of application as defined under paragraph 1 of Article 65 above. The Council shall, upon duly motivated request by a least-developed country Member, accord extensions of this period.

2. Developed country Members shall provide incentives to enterprises and institutions in their territories for the purpose of promoting and encouraging technology transfer to least-developed country Members in order to enable them to create a sound and viable technological base.

Article 67

Technical Cooperation

In order to facilitate the implementation of this Agreement, developed country Members shall provide, on request and on mutually agreed terms and conditions, technical and financial cooperation in favour of developing and least-developed country Members. Such cooperation shall include assistance in the preparation of domestic legislation on the protection and enforcement of intellectual property rights as well as on the prevention of their abuse, and shall include support regarding the establishment or reinforcement of domestic offices and agencies relevant to these matters, including the training of personnel.

PART VII
INSTITUTIONAL ARRANGEMENTS; FINAL PROVISIONS

Article 68
Council for Trade-Related Aspects of Intellectual Property Rights

The Council for Trade-Related Aspects of Intellectual Property Rights shall monitor the operation of this Agreement and, in particular, Members' compliance with their obligations hereunder, and shall afford Members the opportunity of consulting on matters relating to the trade-related aspects of intellectual property rights. It shall carry out such other responsibilities as assigned to it by the Members, and it shall, in particular, provide any assistance requested by them in the context of dispute settlement procedures. In carrying out its functions, the Council may consult with and seek information from any source it deems appropriate. In consultation with the World Intellectual Property Organization, the Council shall seek to establish, within one year of its first meeting, appropriate arrangements for cooperation with bodies of that Organization.

Article 69
International Cooperation

Members agree to cooperate with each other with a view to eliminating international trade in goods infringing intellectual property rights. For this purpose, they shall establish and notify contact points in their national administrations and be ready to exchange information on trade in infringing goods. They shall, in particular, promote the exchange of information and cooperation between customs authorities with regard to trade in counterfeit trademark goods and pirated. copyright goods.

Article 70
Protection of Existing Subject Matter

1. This Agreement does not give rise to obligations in respect of acts which occurred before the date of application of the Agreement for the Member in question.

2. Except as otherwise provided for in this Agreement, this Agreement

gives rise to obligations in respect of all subject matter existing at the date of application of this Agreement for the Member in question, and which is protected in that Member on the said date, or which meets or comes subsequently to meet the criteria for protection under the terms of this Agreement. In respect of this paragraph and paragraphs 3 and 4 below, copyright obligations with respect to existing works shall be solely determined under Article 18 of the Berne Convention (1971), and obligations with respect to the rights of producers of phonograms and performers in existing phonograms shall be determined solely under Article 18 of the Berne Convention (1971) as made applicable under paragraph 6 of Article 14 of this Agreement.

3. There shall be no obligation to restore protection to subject matter which on the date of application of this Agreement for the Member in question has fallen into the public domain.

4. In respect of any acts in respect of specific objects embodying protected subject matter which become infringing under the terms of legislation in conformity with this Agreement, and which were commenced, or in respect of which a significant investment was made, before the date of acceptance of the Agreement Establishing the WTO by that Member, any Member may provide for a limitation of the remedies available to the right holder as to the continued performance of such acts after the date of application of the Agreement for that Member. In such cases the Member shall, however, at least provide for the payment of equitable remuneration.

5. A Member is not obliged to apply the provisions of Article 11 and of paragraph 4 of Article 14 with respect to originals or copies purchased prior to the date of application of this Agreement for that Member.

6. Members shall not be required to apply Article 31, or the requirement in paragraph 1 of Article 27 that patent rights shall be enjoyable without discrimination as to the field of technololy, to use without the authorization of the right holder where authorization for such use was granted by the government before the date this Agreement became known.

7. In the case of intellectual property rights for which protection is conditional upon registration, applications for protection which are pending on the date of application of this Agreement for the Member in question shall be permitted to be amended to claim any enhanced protection provided under the provisions of this Agreement. Such amendments shall not include new matter.

8. Where a Member does not make available as of the date of entry into force of the Agreement Establishing the WTO patent protection for pharmaceutical and agricultural chemical products commensurate with its obligations under Article 27, that Member shall:

(i) notwithstanding the provisions of Part VI above, provide as from the date of entry into force of the Agreement Establishing the WTO a means by which applications for patents for such inventions can be filed;

(ii) apply to these applications, as of the date of application of this Agreement, the criteria for patentability as laid down in this Agreement as if those criteria were being applied on the date of filing in that Member or, where priority is available and claimed, the priority date of the application;

(iii) provide patent protection in accordance with this Agreement as from the grant of the patent and for the remainder of the patent term, counted from the filing date in accordance with Article 33 of this Agreement, for those of these applications that meet the criteria for protection refered to in sub-paragraph (ii) above.

9. Where a product is the subject of a patent application in a Member in accordance with paragraph 8(i) above, exclusive marketing rights shall be granted. notwithstanding the provisions of Part VI above, for a period of five years after obtaining market approval in that Member or until a product patent is granted or rejected in that Member, whichever period is shorter, provided that, subsequent to the entry into force of the Agreement Establishing the WTO a patent application has been filed and a patent granted for that product in another Member and marketing approval obtained in such other Member.

Article 71

Review and Amendment

1. The Council for Trade-Related Aspects of Intellectual Property Rights shall review the implementation of this Agreement after the expiration of the transitional period referred to in paragraph 2 of Article 65 above. The Council shall, having regard to the experience gained in its implementation, review it two years after that date, and at identical intervals thereafter. The Council may also undertake reviews in the light of any relevant new developments which might warrant modification or amendment of this Agreement.

2. Amendments merely serving the purpose of adjusting to higher levels of protection of intellectual property rights achieved, and in force, in other multilateral agreements and accepted under those agreements by all Members of the WTO may be referred to the Ministerial Conference for action in accordance with Article X, paragraph 6, of the Agreement Establishing the WTO on the basis of a consensus proposal from the Council for Trade-Related Aspects of Intellectual Property Rights.

Article 72

Reservations

Reservations may not be entered in respect of any of the provisions of this Agreement without the consent of the other Members.

Article 73

Security Exceptions

Nothing in this Agreement shall be construed:

(a) to require any Member to furnish any information the disclosure of which it considers contrary to its essential security interests; or

(b) to prevent any Member from taking any action which it considers necessary for the protection of its essential security interests :

(i) relating to fissionable materials or the materials from which they are derived;

(ii) relating to the traffic in arms, ammunition and implements of war and to such traffic in other goods and materials as is carried on directly or indirectly for the purpose of supplying a military establishment;

(iii) taken in time of war or other emergency in international relations; or

(c) to prevent any Member from taking any action in pursuance of its obligations under the United Nations Charter for the maintenance of international peace and security.

UNDERSTANDING ON RULE AND PROCEDURES GOVERNING THE SETTLEMENT OF DISPUTES

1. *Coverage and Application*

1.1 The rules and procedures of this Understanding shall apply to disputes brought pursuant to the consultation and dispute settlement rules and procedures of the agreements listed in Appendix 1 to this Understanding, hereinafter referred to as the "covered agreements". The rules and procedures of this Understanding shall also apply to consultations and the settlement of disputes between Members concerning their rights and obligations under the provisions of the Agreement Establishing the **World Trade Organisation** (WTO) and of this Understanding taken in isolation or in combination with any other covered agreement.

1.2 These rules and procedures shall apply subject to such special or additional rules and procedures on dispute settlement contained in the covered agreements as are identified in Appendix 2 to this Understanding. To the extent that there is a difference between the rules and procedures of this Understanding and the special or additional rules and procedures set forth in Appendix 2, the special or additional rules and procedures in Appendix 2 shall prevail. In disputes involving rules and procedures under more than one covered Agreement, if there is a conflict between special or additional rules and procedures of such Agreements under review, and where the parties to the dispute cannot agree on rules and procedures within twenty days of the establishment of the panel, the Chairman of the Dispute Settlement Body, in consultation with the parties to the dispute, shall determine the rules and procedures to be followed within ten days after a request by either Member. The Chairman of the Dispute Settlement Body shall be guided by the principle that special or additional rules and procedures should be used where possible, and the rules and procedures set out in this Understanding should be used to the extent necessary to avoid conflict.

2. *Administration*

2.1 The Dispute Settlement Body (DSB) established pursuant to the Agreement Establishing the WTO shall administer these rules and procedures and, except as otherwise provided in a covered agreement, the consultation and dispute settlement provisions of the covered agreements. Accordingly, the DSB shall have the authority to establish panels, adopt panel and Appellate Body reports, maintain surveillance of implementation of rulings and recommendations, and authorize suspension of concessions and other obligations under the covered agreements. With respect to disputes arising under covered agreements contained in Annex 4 to the WTO Agreement, the term "Member" as used herein shall refer only to those Members that are parties to the relevant Annex 4 Agreements. Where the DSB administers the dispute settlement provisions of a covered agreement contained in Annex 4, only those Members that are parties to that agreement may participate in decisions or actions taken by the DSB with respect to that dispute.

2.2 The DSB shall inform the relevant WTO councils and committees of any developments in disputes related to provisions of the respective covered agreements.

2.3 The DSB shall meet as often as necessary to carry out its functions within the time-flames provided in this Understanding.

2.4 Where the rules and procedures of this Understanding provide for the DSB to take a decision, it shall do so by consensus.[174]

---

[174] The Dispute Settlement Body shall be deemed to have decided by consensus on a matter submitted for its consideration, if no Member, present at the meeting of the Dispute Settlement Body when the decision is taken, formally objects to the proposed decision.

3. *General Provisions*

3.1 The members of the WTO (hereinafter referred to as "Members") affirm their adherence to the principles for the management of disputes heretofore applied under Articles XXII and XXIII of the GATT 1947, as further elaborated and modified herein.

3.2 The dispute settlement system of the **WTO** is a central element in providing security and predictability to the multilateral trading system. The Members of the WTO recognize that it serves to preserve the rights and obligations of Members under the covered agreements, and to clarify the existing provisions of those agreements in accordance with customary rules of interpretation of public international law. Recommendations and rulings of the DSB cannot add to or diminish the rights and obligations provided in the covered agreements.

3.3 The prompt settlement of situations in which a Member considers that any benefits accruing to it directly or indirectly under the covered agreements are being impaired by measures taken by another Member is essential to the effective functioning of the **WTO** and the maintenance of a proper balance between the rights and obligations of Members.

3.4 Recommendations or rulings made by the DSB shall be aimed at achieving a satisfactory settlement of the matter in accordance with the rights and obligations under this Understanding and under the covered agreements.

3.5 All solutions to matters formally raised under the consultation and dispute settlement rules and procedures of the covered agreements, including arbitration awards, shall be consistent with those agreements and shall not nullify or impair benefits accruing to any Member under those agreements, nor impede the attainment of any objective of those agreements.

3.6 Mutually agreed solutions to matters formally raised under the consultation and dispute settlement provisions of the covered agreements shall be notified to the DSB and the relevant councils and committees, where any Member may raise any point relating thereto.

3.7 Before bringing a case, a Member shall exercise its judgement as to whether action under these procedures would be fruitful. The aim of the dispute settlement mechanism is to secure a positive solution to a dispute. A solution mutually acceptable to the parties to a dispute and consistent with the covered agreements is clearly to be preferred. In the absence of a mutually agreed solution, the first objective of the dispute settlement mechanism is usually to secure the withdrawal of the measures concerned if these are found to be inconsistent with the provisions of any of the covered agreements. The provision of compensation should be resorted to only if the immediate withdrawal of the measure is impracticable and as a temporary measure pending the withdrawal of the measure which is inconsistent with a covered agreement. The last resort which this Understanding provides to the Member invoking the dispute settlement procedures is the possibility of suspending the application of concessions or other obligations under the covered agreements on a discriminatory basis *vis-a-vis* the other Member, subject to authorization by the DSB of such measures.

3.8 In cases where there is an infringement of the obligations assumed under a covered agreement, the action is considered *prima facie* to constitute a case of nullification or impairment. This means that there is normally a presumption that a breach of the rules has an adverse impact on other Members parties to that covered agreement, and in such cases, it shall be up to the Member against whom the complaint has been brought to rebut the charge.

3.9 The provisions of this Understanding are without prejudice to the rights of Members to seek authoritative interpretation of provisions of a covered agreement through decision making under the Agreement Establishing the **WTO** or a covered agreement.

3.10 It is understood that requests for conciliation and the use of the dispute settlement procedures should not be intended or considered as contentious acts and that, if disputes arise, all Members will engage in these procedures in good faith in an effort to resolve the disputes. It is also understood that complaints and counter-complaints in regard to distinct matters should not be linked.

3.11 This Understanding shall be applied only with respect to new requests for consultations under the consultation provisions of the covered agreements made on or after the date of entry into force of this Understanding. With respect to disputes for which the request for consultations was made under the GATT 1947 or under any other predecessor agreement to the covered agreements before the date of entry into force of this Understanding, the relevant dispute settlement rules and procedures in effect immediately prior to the date of entry into force of this Understanding shall continue to apply.[175]

3.12 Notwithstanding paragraph 3.11 above, if a complaint based on any of the Agreements covered by this Understanding is brought by a developing country Member against a developed country Member, the complaining party shall have the rights to invoke, as an alternative to the provisions contained in paragraphs 4, 5, 6 and 12 of this Understanding, the corresponding provisions of the Decision of CONTRACTING PARTIES of 5 April 1966 (BISD 14S/18), except that where the Panel considers that the time frame provided for in

[175] This paragraph shall also be applied to disputes on which panel reports have not been adopted or fully implemented.

paragraph 7 of that decision is insufficient to provide its report and with the agreement of the complaining party, that time frame may be extended. To the extent that there is a difference between the rules and procedures of those paragraphs and the corresponding rules and procedures of the Decision, the latter shall prevail.

4. *Consultations*

4.1 The Members affirm their resolve to strengthen and improve the effectiveness of the consultation procedures employed by Members.

4.2 Each Member undertakes to accord sympathetic consideration to and afford adequate opportunity for consultation regarding any representations made by another Member concerning measures affecting the operation of the covered agreements taken within the territory of the former.[176]

4.3 If a request for consultations is made pursuant to a covered agreement, the Member to the request is made shall, unless otherwise mutually agreed, reply to the request within ten days after its receipt and shall enter into consultations in good faith within a period of no more than thirty days from the date of the request, with a view to reaching a mutually satisfactory solution. If the Member does not respond within ten days, or does not enter into consultations within a period of no more than thirty days, or a period otherwise mutually agreed, from the date of the request, then the Member that requested the holding of consultations may proceed directly to request the establishment of a panel.

4.4 All such requests for consultations shall be notified to the DSB and the relevant Councils and Committees by the Member which requests consultations. Any request for consultations shall be submitted in writing and shall give the reasons for the request, including identification of the measures at issue and an indication of the legal basis for the complaint.

4.5 In the course of consultations in accordance with the provisions of a covered agreement, before resorting to further action under this Understanding, Members should attempt to obtain satisfactory adjustment of the matter.

4.6 Consultations shall be confidential, and without prejudice to the rights of either Member in any further proceedings.

4.7 If the consultations fail to settle a dispute within sixty days after the request for consultations, the complaining party may request the establishment of a panel. The complaining party may request a panel during the sixty-day

[176] Where the provisions of any other covered agreement concerning measures taken by regional or local governments or authorities within the territory of a Member contain provisions different from the provisions of this paragraph, the provisions of such other covered agreement shall prevail.

period if the consulting parties jointly consider that consultations have failed to settle the dispute.

4.8 In cases of urgency, including those which concern perishable goods, Members shall enter into consultations within a period of no more than ten days from the date of the request. If the consultations have failed to settle the dispute within a period of twenty days after the request, the complaining party may request the establishment of a panel.

4.9 In cases of urgency, including those which concern perishable goods, the parties to the dispute, panels and the appellate body shall make every effort to accelerate the proceedings to the greatest extent possible.

4.10 During consultations Members should give special attention to the particular problems and interests of developing country Members.

4.11 Whenever a Member other than the consulting Members considers that it has a substantial trade interest in consultations being held pursuant to Article XXII: 1 of the GATT, Article XXII: 1 of the GATS Agreement or the corresponding provisions in other covered agreements,[177] such Member may notify the consulting Members and the DSB, within ten days of the circulation of the request for consultations under said Article, of its desire to be joined in the consultations. Such Member shall be joined in the consultations, provided that the Member to which the request for consultations was addressed agrees that the claim of substantial interest is well-founded. In that event they shall so inform the DSB. If the request to be joined in the consultations is not accepted, the applicant Member shall be free to request consultations under Article XXII: 1 Or XXIII: 1 of the GATT, Article XXII: 1 or XXIII: 1 of the GATS -Agreement or the corresponding provisions in other covered agreements.

5. *Good Offices, Conciliation and Mediation*

5.1 Good offices, conciliation and mediation are procedures that are undertaken voluntarily if the parties to the dispute so agree.

5.2 Proceedings involving good offices conciliation and mediation and in particular positions taken by the parties to the dispute during these proceedings,

---

[177] The corresponding consultations provisions in the covered agreements are listed hereunder : Agreement on Rules of Origin Article 7; Agreement on Preshipment Inspection, Article 7; Agreement on Implementation of Article VI of the GATT, Article 18.6; Agreement on Technical Barriers to Trade, Article 14.1; Agreement on Import Licensing Procedures, Article 6; Agreement on Subsidies and Countervailing Measures, Articles 13 and 30; Agreement on Agriculture, Article 18.1, and Part C, Agreement on Sanitary and Phytosanitary Measures, paragraph 35; Trade-Related Aspects of Investment Measures, Article 8; Agreement on Textiles and Clothing Article 8.4; Agreement on Trade-Related Aspects of Intellectual Property Rights, including Trade in Counterfeit Goods, Article 64; Agreement on Trade in Civil Aircraft, Article 8.8; Agreement on Government Procurement, Article VII:3; International Diary Arrangement, Article VIII:7; Arrangement Regarding Bovine Meat, Article VI:6.

shall be confidential, and without prejudice to the rights of either party in any further proceedings under these procedures.

5.3 Good offices, conciliation and mediation may be requested at any time by any party to a dispute. They may begin at any time and be terminated at any time. Once terminated, the complaining party can then proceed with a request for the establishment of a panel.

5.4 When good offices, conciliation or mediation are entered into within sixty days of a request for consultations, the complaining party must allow a period of sixty days from the date of the request for consultations before requesting the establishment of a panel. The complaining party may request a panel during the sixty days if the parties to the dispute jointly consider that the good offices, conciliation or mediation process has failed to settle the dispute.

5.5 If the parties to a dispute agree, procedures for good offices, conciliation or mediation may continue while the panel process proceeds.

5.6 The Director-General may, acting in an *ex officio* capacity, offer good offices, conciliation or mediation with the view to assisting Members to settle a dispute.

6. *Establishment of Panels*

6.1 If the complaining party so requests, a panel shall be established at the latest at the DSB meeting following that at which the request first appears as an item on the DSB's agenda, unless at that meeting the DSB decides by consensus not to establish a panel.[178]

6.2 The request for the establishment of a panel shall be made in writing. It shall indicate whether consultations were held, identify the specific measures at issue and provide a brief summary of the legal basis of the complaint sufficient to present the problem clearly. In case the applicant requests the establishment of a panel with other than standard terms of reference, the written request shall include the proposed text of special terms of reference.

7. *Terms of Reference of Panels*

7.1 Panels shall have the following terms of reference unless the parties to the dispute agree otherwise within twenty days from the establishment of the panel :

"To examine, in the light of the relevant provisions in (name of the covered agreement/s cited by the parties to the dispute), the matter referred to the DSB by (name of party) in document DS/... and to make such findings

---

[178] If the complaining party so requests, a meeting of the Dispute Settlement Body shall be convened for this purpose within fifteen days of the request, provided that at least ten days' advance notice of the meeting is given.

as will assist the DSB in making the recommendations or in giving the rulings provided for in that/those agreement/s."

7.2 Panels shall address the relevant provisions in any covered agreement/s cited by the parties to the dispute.

7.3 In establishing a panel, the DSB may authorize its Chairman to draw up the terms of reference of the panel in consultation with the parties to the dispute subject to the provisions of paragraph 7.1 above. The terms of reference thus drawn up shall be circulated to all Members. If other than standard terms of reference are agreed upon, any Member may raise any point relating thereto in the DSB.

8. *Composition of Panels*

8.1 Panels shall be composed of well-qualified governmental and/or non-governmental individuals, including persons who have served on or presented a case to a panel, served as a representative of an **WTO** Member or of a contracting party to the GATT 1947 or as a representative to a council or committee of any covered agreement or its predecessor agreement, or in the Secretariat, taught or published on international trade law or policy, or served as a senior trade policy official of a Member.

8.2 Panel members should be selected with a view to ensuring the independence of the members, a sufficiently diverse background and a wide spectrum of experience.

8.3 Citizens of Members whose governments[179] are parties to the dispute or third parties as defined in paragraph 10.2 shall not serve on a panel concerned with that dispute, unless the parties to the dispute agree otherwise.

8.4 To assist in the selection of panelists, the Secretariat shall maintain an indicative list of governmental and non-governmental individuals possessing the qualifications outlined in paragraph 1 above, from which panelists may be drawn as appropriate. That list shall include the roster of non-governmental panelists that was established by the GATT CONTRACTING PARTIES on 30 November 1984 (BISD 31S/9), and other rosters and indicative lists established under any of the covered agreements, and shall retain the names of persons on those rosters and indicative lists at the time of entry into force of this Understanding. Members may periodically suggest names of governmental and non-governmental individuals for inclusion on the indicative list, providing relevant information on their knowledge of international trade and of the sectors or subject matter of the covered agreements, and those names shall be added to the list upon approval by the DSB. For each of the

[179] In the case where customs unions or common markets are parties to a dispute, this provision applies to citizens of all member countries of the customs unions or common markets.

individuals on the list, the list shall indicate specific areas of experience or expertise of the individuals in the sectors or subject matter of the covered agreements.

8.5 Panels shall be composed of three panelists unless the parties to the dispute agree, within ten days from the establishment of the panel, to a panel composed of five panelists. Members shall be informed promptly of the composition of the Panel.

8.6 The Secretariat shall propose nominations for the panel to the parties to the dispute. The parties to the dispute shall not oppose nominations except for compelling reasons.

8.7 If there is no agreement on the panelists within twenty days from the establishment of a panel, at the request of either party, the Director-General in consultation with the Chairman of the DSB, and the Chairman of the relevant committee or council, shall form the panel by appointing the panelists whom he or she considers most appropriate in accordance with any relevant special or additional procedure of the covered agreement,after consulting with the parties to the dispute. The Chairman of the DSB shall inform the Members of the composition of the panel thus formed no later than ten days from the date he or she receives such a request.

8.8 Members shall undertake, as a general rule, to permit their officials to serve as panelists.

8.9 Panelists shall serve in their individual capacities and not as government representatives, nor as representatives of any organization. Governments shall therefore not give them instructions nor seek to influence them as individuals with regard to matters before a panel.

8.10 When a dispute is between a developing country Member and a developed country Member the panel shall, if the developing country Member so requests, include at least one panelist from a developing country Member.

8.11 Panelists' expenses, including travel and subsistence allowance, shall be met from the WTO budget in accordance with criteria to be adopted by the General Council of the WTO, based on recommendations of the Committee on Budget, Finance and Administration.

9. *Procedures for Multiple Complainants*

9.1 Where more than one Member requests the establishment of a panel related to the same matter, a single panel may be established to examine these complaints taking into account the rights of all Members concerned. A single panel should be established to examine such complaints whenever feasible.

9.2 The single panel will organize its examination and present its findings to the DSB so that the rights which the parties to the dispute would have enjoyed had separate panels examined the complaints are in no way impaired. If one of the parties to the dispute so requests, the panel will submit separate reports on the dispute concerned. The written submissions by each of the complainants will be made available to the other complainants, and each complainant will have the right to be present when one of the other complainants presents its view to the panel.

9.3 If more than one panel is established to examine the complaints related to the same matter, to the greatest extent possible the same persons shall serve as panelists on each of the separate panels and the timetable for the panel process in such disputes shall be harmonized.

10. *Third Parties*

10.1 The interests of the parties to a dispute and those of other Members[180] of a covered agreement at issue in the dispute shall be fully taken into account during the panel process.

10.2 Any Member, of a covered agreement at issue in a dispute, having a substantial interest in a matter before a panel and having notified its interest to the DSB (hereinafter referred to as a "third party") shall have an opportunity to be heard by the panel and to make written submissions to the panel. These submissions shall also be given to the parties to the dispute and shall be reflected in the panel report.

10.3 Such third parties shall receive submissions of the parties to the dispute for the first meeting of the panel.

10.4 If a third party considers a measure already the subject of a panel proceeding nullifies or impairs benefits accruing to it under any covered agreement, that Member may have recourse to normal dispute settlement procedures under this Understanding. Such a dispute shall be referred to the original panel wherever possible.

11. *Function of Panels*

11.1 The function of panels is to assist the DSB in discharging its responsibilities under this Understanding and the covered agreements. Accordingly, a panel should make an objective assessment of the matter before it, including an objective assessment of the facts of the case and the

[180] With respect to disputes arising under covered agreements contained in Annex 4 to the WTO Agreement, the term "Member" as used herein shall refer only to those Members that are parties to the relevant Annex 4 Agreements. Where the DSB administers the dispute settlement provisions of a covered agreement contained in Annex 4, only those Members that are parties to that agreement may participate in decisions or actions taken by the DSB with respect to that dispute.

applicability of and conformity with the relevant covered agreements, and make such other findings as will assist the DSB in making the recommendations or in giving the rulings provided for in the covered agreements. Panels should consult regularly with the parties to the dispute and give them adequate opportunity to develop a mutually satisfactory solution.

12. *Panel Procedures*

12.1 Panels shall follow the Working Procedures appended hereto unless the panel decides otherwise after consulting the parties to the dispute.

12.2 Panel procedures should provide sufficient flexibility so as to ensure high-quality panel reports, while not unduly delaying the panel process.

12.3 After consulting the parties to the dispute, the panelists shall, as soon as practicable and whenever possible within one week after the composition and terms of reference of the panel have been agreed upon, fix the timetable for the panel process, taking into account the provisions of paragraph 4.9, if relevant.

12.4 In determining the timetable for the panel process, the panel shall provide sufficient time for parties to the dispute to prepare their submissions.

12.5 Panels should set precise deadlines for written submissions by the parties and the parties should respect those deadlines.

12.6 Each party to the dispute shall deposit its written submissions with the Secretariat for immediate transmission to the panel and to the other party or parties to the dispute. The complaining party shall submit its first submission in advance of the responding party's first submission unless the panel decides, in fixing the timetable referred to in paragraph 12.3 'above and after consultations with the parties to the dispute, that the parties should submit their first submissions simultaneously. When there are sequential arrangements for the deposit of first submissions, the panel shall establish a firm time period for receipt of the responding party' s submission. Any subsequent written submissions shall be submitted simultaneously.

12.7 Where the parties to the dispute have failed to develop a mutually satisfactory solution, the panel shall submit its findings in a written form. In such cases, the report of a panel shall set out findings of fact, the applicability of relevant provisions and the basic rationale behind any findings and recommendations that it makes. Where a settlement of the matter among the parties to the dispute has been found, the report of the panel shall be confined to a brief description of the case and to reporting that a solution has been reached.

12.8 In order to make the procedures more efficient, the period in which the panel shall conduct its examination, from the time the composition and terms of reference of the panel have been agreed upon to the time when the final report is provided to the parties to the dispute, shall, as a general rule, not exceed six months. In cases of urgency, including those relating to perishable goods, the panel shall aim to provide its report to the parties to the dispute within three months.

12.9 When the panel considers that it cannot provide its report within six months, or within three months in cases of urgency, it shall inform the DSB in writing of the reasons for the delay together with an estimate of the period within which it will submit its report. In no case should the period from the establishment of the panel to the submission of the report to the Members exceed nine months.

12.10 In the context of consultations involving a measure taken by a developing country Member, the parties may agree to extend the periods established in paragraphs 4.7 and 4.8. If, after the relevant period has elapsed, the consulting parties cannot agree that the consultations have concluded, the Chairman of the DSB shall decide, after consultation with the parties, whether to extend the relevant period and, if so, for how long. In addition, in examining a complaint against a developing country Member, the panel shall accord sufficient time for the developing country Member to prepare and present its argumentation. The provisions of paragraphs 20.1 and 21.4 are not affected by any action pursuant to this paragraph.

12.11 Where one or more of the parties is a developing country Member, the panel's report shall explicitly indicate the form in which account has been taken of relevant provisions on differential and more-favourable treatment for developing country Members that form part of the covered agreements which have been raised by the developing country Member in the course of the dispute settlement procedures.

12.12 The panel may suspend its work at any time at the request of the complaining party for a period not to exceed twelve months. In the event of such a suspension, the time flames set out in paragraphs 12.8, 12.9, 20.1 and 21.4 shall be extended by the amount of time that the work was suspended. If the work of the panel has been suspended for more than twelve months, the authority for establishment of the panel shall lapse.

13. *Right to Seek Information*

13.1 Each panel shall have the right to seek information and technical advice from any individual or body which it deems appropriate. However, before a panel seeks such information or advice from any individual or body within the jurisdiction of a Member it shall inform the authorities of that Member. A Member should respond promptly and fully to any request by a panel for such information as the panel considers necessary and appropriate.

Confidential information which is provided shall not be revealed without formal authorization from the individual, body, or authorities of the Member providing the information.

13.2 Panels may seek information from any relevant source and may consult experts to obtain their opinion on certain aspects of the matter. With respect to a factual issue concerning a scientific or other technical matter raised by a party to a dispute, a panel may request an advisory report in writing from an expert review group. Rules for the establishment of such a group and its procedures are set forth in Appendix 4.

14. *Confidentiality*

14.1 Panel deliberations shall be confidential.

14.2 The reports of panels shall be drafted without the presence of the parties to the dispute in the light of the information provided and the statements made.

14.3 Opinions expressed in the panel report by individual panelists shall be anonymous.

15. *Interim Review Stage*

15.1 Following the consideration of rebuttal submissions and oral arguments, the panel shall submit the descriptive (factual and argument) sections of its draft report to the parties. Within a period of time set by the panel, the parties shall submit their comments in writing.

15.2 Following the deadline for receipt of comments from the parties, the panel shall issue an interim report to the parties, including both the descriptive sections and the panel's findings and conclusions. Within a period of time set by the panel, a party may submit a written request for the panel to review precise aspects of the interim report prior to circulation of the final report to the Members. At the request of a party, the panel shall hold a further meeting with the parties on the issues identified in the written comments. If no comments are received from any party within the comment period, the interim report shall be considered the final panel report and circulated promptly to the Members.

15.3 The findings of the final panel report shall include a discussion of the arguments made at the interim review stage. The interim review stage shall be conducted within the time period set out in paragraph 12.8.

16. *Adoption of Panel Reports*

16.1 In order to provide sufficient time for the Members of the DSB to consider panel reports, the reports shall not be considered for adoption by the DSB until twenty days after they have been issued to the Members.

16.2 Members having objections to panel reports shall give written reasons to explain their objections for circulation at least ten days prior to the DSB meeting at which the panel report will be considered.

16.3 The parties to a dispute shall have the right to participate fully in the consideration of the panel report by the DSB, and their views shall be fully recorded.

16.4 Within sixty days of the issuance of a panel report to the Members, the report shall be adopted at a DSB meeting[181] unless one of the parties to the dispute formally notifies the DSB of its decision to appeal or the DSB decides by consensus not to adopt the report. If a party has notified its intention to appeal, the report by the panel shall not be considered for adoption by the DSB until after completion of the appeal. This adoption procedure is without prejudice to the right of Members to express their views on a panel report.

17. *Appellate Review*

Standing Appellate Body

17.1 A standing Appellate Body shall be established by the DSB. The Appellate Body shall hear appeals from panel cases. It shall be composed of seven persons, three of whom shall serve on any one case. Persons serving on of the Appellate Body shall serve in rotation. Such rotation shall be determined in the working procedures of the Appellate Body.

17.2 The DSB shall appoint persons to serve on the Appellate Body for a four-year term, and each person may be reappointed once. However, the terms of three of the seven persons appointed immediately after the entry into force of this Understanding shall expire at the end of two years, to be determined by lot. Vacancies shall be filled as they arise. A person appointed to replace a person whose term of office has not expired shall hold office for the remainder of his or her predecessor's term.

17.3 The Appellate Body shall be comprised of persons of recognized authority, with demonstrated expertise in law, international trade and the subject matter of the covered agreements generally. They shall be unaffiliated with any government. The Appellate Body membership shall be broadly representative of membership in the WTO. All persons serving on the Appellate Body shall be available at all times and on short notice, and shall stay abreast of dispute settlement activities and other relevant activities of the WTO. They shall not participate in the consideration of any disputes that would create a direct or indirect conflict of interest.

---

[181] If a meeting of the DSB is not scheduled within this period at a time that enables the requirements of paragraphs 16.1 and 16.4 to be met, a meeting of the DSB shall be held for this purpose.

17.4 Only parties to the dispute, not third parties, may appeal a panel decision. Third parties which have notified the DSB of a substantial interest in the matter pursuant to paragraph 10.2 may make written submissions to, and be given an opportunity to be heard by, the Appellate Body.

17.5 As a general rule, the proceedings shall not exceed sixty days from the date a party to the dispute formally notifies its intent to appeal to the date the Appellate Body issues its decision. In fixing its timetable the Appellate Body shall take into account the provisions of paragraph 4.9, if relevant. When the Appellate Body considers that it cannot provide its report within sixty days, it shall inform the DSB in writing of the reasons for the delay together with an estimate of the period within which it will submit its report. In no case shall the proceedings exceed ninety days.

17.6 An appeal shall be limited to issues of law covered in the panel report and legal interpretation developed by the panel.

17.7 The Appellate Body shall be provided with appropriate administrative and legal support as it requires.

17.8 The expenses of persons serving on the Appellate Body, including travel and subsistence allowance, shall be met from the WTO budget in accordance with criteria to be adopted by the General Council of the WTO, based on recommendations of the Committee on Budget, Finance and Administration.

Procedures for Appellate Review

17.9 Working procedures shall be drawn up by the Appellate Body in consultation with the Chairman of the DSB and the Director-General, and communicated to the Members for their information.

17.10 The proceedings of the Appellate Body shall be confidential. The reports of the Appellate Body shall be drafted without the presence of the parties to the dispute and in the light of the information provided and the statements made.

17.11 Opinions expressed in the Appellate Body report by individuals serving on the Appellate Body shall be anonymous.

17.12 The Appellate Body shall address each of the issues raised in accordance with paragraph 17.6 during the appellate proceeding.

17.13 The Appellate Body may uphold, modify or reverse the legal findings and conclusions of the panel.

Adoption of Appellate Reports

17.14 An appellate report shall be adopted by the DSB and unconditionally accepted by the parties to the dispute unless the DSB decides by consensus not to adopt the appellate report within thirty days following its issuance to the Members.[182] This adoption procedure is without prejudice to the right of Members to express their views on an appellate report.

18. *Communications with the panel or Appellate Body*

18.1 There shall be no *ex parte* communications with the panel or Appellate Body concerning matters under consideration by the panel or Appellate Body.

18.2 Written submissions to the panel or the Appellate Body shall be treated as confidential, but shall be made available to the parties to the dispute. Nothing in this Understanding shall preclude a party to a dispute from disclosing statement of its own positions to the public. Members shall treat as confidential, information submitted by another Member to the panel or the Appellate Body which that Member has designated as confidential. A party to a dispute shall also, upon request of a Member, provide a non-confidential summary of the information contained in its written submissions that could be disclosed to the public.

19. *Panel and Appellate Body Recommendations*

19.1 Where a panel or the Appellate Body concludes that a measure is inconsistent with a covered agreement, it shall recommend that the Member concerned[183] bring the measure into conformity with that Agreement.[184] In addition to its recommendations, the panel or Appellate Body may suggest ways in which the Member concerned could implement the recommendations.

19.2 In accordance with paragraph 3.2 above, in their findings and recommendations, the panel and Appellate Body cannot add to or diminish the rights and obligations provided in the covered agreements.

20. *Time-Frame for DSB Decisions*

20.1 Unless otherwise agreed to by the parties to the dispute, the period from the establishment of the Panel by the DSB until the DSB considers the panel or appellate report for adoption shall not as a general rule exceed nine months where the report is not appealed or twelve months where the report is appealed. Where either the panel or the Appellate Body has acted, pursuant to paragraph 12.9 or 17.5, to extend the time of providing its report, the additional time taken shall be added to the above periods.

---

[182] If a meeting of the DSB is not scheduled during this period, such a meeting of the DSB shall be held for this purpose.

[183] The "Member concerned" is the party to the dispute to which the panel or Appellate Body recommendations are directed.

[184] With respect to recommendations in cases not involving a violation of the GATT and any other covered agreement, see section 26.

21. *Surveillance of Implementation of Recommendations and Rulings*

21.1 Prompt compliance with recommendations or rulings of the DSB is essential in order to ensure effective resolution of disputes to the benefit of all Members.

21.2 Particular attention should be paid to matters affecting the interests of developing country Members with respect to measures which have been subject to dispute settlement.

21.3 At a DSB meeting held within thirty days[185] of the adoption of the panel or Appellate Body report, the Member concerned shall inform the DSB of its intentions in respect of implementation of the recommendations and rulings of the DSB. If it is impracticable to comply immediately with the recommendations and rulings, the Member concerned shall have a reasonable period of time in which to do so. The reasonable period of time shall be:

(a) the period of time proposed by the Member concerned, provided that such period is approved by the DSB; or, in the absence of such approval

(b) a period of time mutually agreed by the parties to the dispute within forty-five days following adoption of the recommendations and rulings; or, in the absence of such agreement,

(c) a period of time determined through binding arbitration within ninety days following adoption of the recommen-dations and rulings.[186] In such arbitration, a guideline for the arbitrator[187] should be that the reasonable period of time to implement panel or Appellate Body recommen-dations should not exceed fifteen months from the adoption of a panel or Appellate Body report. However, that time may be shorter or longer, depending upon the particular circumstances.

21.4 Except where the panel or the Appellate Body has extended, pursuant to paragraph 12.9 or 17.5, the time of providing its report, the period from the date of establishment of the panel by the DSB until the determination of the reasonable period of time shall not exceed fifteen months unless the parties to the dispute agree otherwise. Where either the panel or the Appellate Body has acted to extend the time of providing its report, the additional time

[185] If a meeting of the DSB in not scheduled during this period, such a meeting of the DSB shall be held for this purpose.

[186] If the parties cannot agree on an arbitrator within ten days after referring the matter to arbitration. the arbitrator shall be appointed by the Director-General within ten days, after consulting the parties.

[187] The expression "arbitrator" shall be' interpreted as referring either to an individual or a group.

taken shall be added to the fifteen-month period; provided that unless the parties to the dispute agree that there are exceptional circumstances, the total time shall not exceed eighteen months.

21.5 Where there is disagreement as to the existence or consistency with a covered agreement of measures taken to comply with the recommendations and rulings such dispute shall be decided through recourse to these dispute settlement procedures, involving resort to the original panel wherever possible. The panel shall issue its decision within ninety days of referral of the matter to it. When the panel considers that it cannot provide its report within this time frame, it shall inform the DSB in writing of the reasons for the delay together with an estimate of the period within which it will submit its report.

21.6 The DSB shall keep under surveillance the implementation of adopted recommendations or rulings. The issue of implementation of the recommendations or rulings may be raised at the DSB by any Member at any time following their adoption. Unless the DSB decides otherwise, the issue of implementation of the recommendations or rulings shall be on the agenda of the DSB meeting after six months following the establishment of the reasonable period of time pursuant to paragraph 21.3 and shall remain on the DSB's agenda until the issue is resolved. At least ten days prior to each such DSB meeting, the Member concerned shall provide the DSB with a status report in writing of its progress in the implementation of the recommendations or rulings.

21.7 If the matter is one which has been raised by a developing country Member the DSB shall consider what further action it might take which would be appropriate to the circumstances.

21.8 If the case is one brought by a developing country Member, in considering what appropriate action might be taken, the DSB shall take into account not only the trade coverage of measures complained of, but also their impact on the economy of developing country Members concerned.

22. *Compensation and the Suspension of Concessions*

22.1 Compensation and the suspension of concessions or other obligations are temporary measures available in the event that the recommendations and rulings are not implemented within a reasonable period of time. However, neither compensation nor the suspension of concessions or other obligations is preferred to full implementation of a recommendation to bring a measure into conformity with the covered agreements. Compensation is voluntary and, if granted, shall be consistent with the covered agreements.

22.2 If the Member concerned fails to bring the measure found to be inconsistent with a covered agreement into compliance therewith or otherwise comply with the recommendations and rulings within the reasonable period of time determined pursuant to paragraph 21.3 above, such Member shall, if so requested, and no later than the expiry of the reasonable period of time, enter into negotiations with any party having invoked the dispute settlement procedures, with a view to developing mutually acceptable compensation. If no satisfactory compensation has been agreed within twenty days after the expiry of the reasonable period of time, any party having invoked the dispute settlement procedures may request authorization from the DSB to suspend the application to the Member concerned of concessions or other obligations under the covered agreements.

22.3 In considering what concessions or other obligations to suspend, the complaining party shall apply the following principles and procedures:

(a) The general principle is that the complaining party should first seek to suspend concessions or other obligations with respect to the same sector(s) as that in which the panel or Appellate Body has found a violation or other nullification or impairment.

(b) If that party considers that it is not practicable or effective to suspend concessions or other obligations with respect to the same sectors, it may seek to suspend concessions or other obligations in other sectors under the same agreement.

(c) If that party considers that it is not practicable or effective to suspend concessions or other obligations with respect to other sectors under the same agreement, and that the circumstances are serious enough, it may seek to suspend concessions or other obligations under another covered agreement.

(d) In applying the above principles, that party shall take into account:

(i) the trade in the sector or under the agreement under which the panel or Appellate Body has found a violation or other nullification or impairment, and the importance of such trade to that party;

(ii) the broader economic elements related to the nullification or impairment and the broader economic consequences of the suspension of concessions or other obligations.

(e) If that party decides to request authorization to suspend concessions or other obligations pursuant to (b) or (c) above, it shall state the reasons therefor in its request. At the same time as the request is forwarded to the DSB, it also shall be forwarded to the relevant Councils and also, in the case of a request pursuant to (b), the relevant sectoral bodies.

(f) For purposes of this paragraph, "sector" means:

– With respect to goods, all goods;

- With respect to services, a principal sector as identified in the current "Services Sectoral Classification List" which identifies such sectors;[188]
- With respect to trade-related intellectual property rights, each of the categories of intellectual property rights covered in Section 1, or Section 2, or Section 3, Or Section 4, or Section 5, or Section 6, or Section 7 of Part II, or the obligations under Part III, or Part IV of the Agreement on Trade-Related Aspects of Intellectual Property Rights, including Trade in Counterfeit Goods ("Agreement on TRIPS").

(g) For purposes of this paragraph, "agreement" means :

- With respect to goods, the agreements listed in Annex 1A of the WTO Agreement taken as a whole as well as the agreements listed in Annex 4 of the WTO Agreement in so far as the relevant parties to the dispute are parties to these agreements;
- With respect to services, the GATS;
- With respect to intellectual property rights, the Agreement on TRIPs.

22.4 The level of the suspension of concessions or other obligations authorized by the DSB shall be equivalent the level of the nullification or impairment.

22.5 The Dispute Settlement Body shall not authorize suspension of concessions or other obligations if a covered agreement prohibits such suspension.

22.6 When the situation described in paragraph 22.2 above occurs, the DSB, upon request, shall grant authorization to suspend concessions or other obligations within thirty days of the expiry of the reasonable period of time unless the DSB decides by consensus to reject the request. However, if the Member concerned objects to the level of suspension proposed, or claims that the principles and procedures set forth in paragraph 22.3 above have not been followed where a complaining party has requested authorization to suspend concessions or other obligations pursuant to paragraph 22.3(b) or (c) above, the matter shall be referred to arbitration. Such arbitration shall be carried out by the original panel, if members are available, or by an arbitrator[189]

---

[188] The list in document MTN.GNS/W/120 identifies eleven sectors.

[189] The expression "arbitrator" shall be interpreted as referring either to an individual or a group.

appointed by the Director-General and shall be completed within sixty days of the expiry of the reasonable period of time. Concessions or other obligations shall not be suspended during the course of the arbitration.

22.7 The arbitrator[190] acting pursuant to paragraph 22.6 above shall not examine the nature of the concessions or other obligations to be suspended but shall determine whether the level of such suspension is equivalent to the level of nullification or impairment. The arbitrator may also determine if the proposed suspension of concessions or other obligations is allowed under the covered agreement. However, if the matter referred to arbitration includes a claim that the principles and procedures set forth in paragraph 22.3 above have not been followed, the arbitrator shall examine that claim. In the event the arbitrator determines that those principles and procedures have not been followed, the complaining party shall apply them consistent with paragraph 22.3 above. The parties shall accept the arbitrator's decision as final and the parties concerned shall not seek a second arbitration. The DSB shall be informed promptly of the decision of the arbitrator and shall upon request, grant authorization to suspend concessions or other obligations where the request is consistent with the decision of the arbitrator, unless the DSB decides by consensus to reject the request.

22.8 The suspension of concessions or other obligations shall be temporary and shall only be applied until such time as the measure found to be inconsistent with a covered agreement has been removed, or the Member that must implement recommendations or rulings provides a solution to the nullification or impairment of benefits, or a mutually satisfactory solution is reached. In accordance with paragraph 21.6 above, the DSB shall continue to keep under surveillance the implementation of adopted recommendations or rulings, including those cases where compensation has been provided or concessions or other obligations have been suspended but the recommendations to bring a measure into conformity with the covered agreements have not been implemented.

22.9 The dispute settlement provisions of the covered agreements may be invoked in respect of measures affecting their observance taken by regional or local governments or authorities within the tenitory of a Member. When the DSB has ruled that a provision of a covered agreement has not been observed, the responsible Member shall take such reasonable measures as may be available to it to ensure its observance. The provisions of the covered agreements and this Understanding relating to compensation and suspension of concessions

---

[190] The expression "arbitrator" shall be interpreted as referring either to an individual or a group or to the members of the original panel when serving in the capacity of arbitrator.

or other obligations apply in cases where it has not been possible to secure such observance.[191]

23. *Strengthening of the Multilateral System*

23.1 When Members seek the redress of a violation of obligations or other nullification or impairment of benefits under the covered agreements or an impediment to the attainment of any objective of the covered agreements, they shall have recourse to, and abide by, the rules and procedures of this Understanding.

23.2 In such cases, Members shall:

(a) not make a determination to the effect that a violation has occurred, that benefits have been nullified or impaired or that the attainment of any objective of the covered agreements has been impeded, except through recourse to dispute settlement in accordance with the rules and procedures of this Understanding, and shall make any such determination consistent with the findings contained in the panel or Appellate Body report adopted by the DSB or an arbitration award rendered under this Understanding;

(b) follow the procedures set forth in Section 21 of this Understanding to determine the reasonable period of time for the Member concerned to implement the recommendations and rulings; and

(c) follow the procedures set forth in Section 22 of the Understanding to determine the level of suspension of concessions or other obligations and obtain DSB authorization in accordance with those procedures before suspending concessions or other obligations under the covered agreements in response to the failure of the Member concerned to implement the recommendations and rulings within that reasonable period of time.

24. *Special Procedures involving Least-Developed Country Members*

24.1 At all stages of the determination of the causes of a dispute and of dispute settlement procedures involving a least-developed country Member, particular consideration shall be given to the special situation of least-developed country Members. In this regard, Members shall exercise due restraint in raising matters under these procedures involving a least developed country Member. If nullification or impairment is found to result from a measure taken by a least developed country Member, complaining parties shall exercise

---

[191] Where the provisions of any covered agreement concerning measures taken by regional or local governments or authorities within the territory of a Member contain provisions different from the provisions of this paragraph, the provisions of such covered agreement shall prevail.

due restraint in asking for compensation or seeking authorization to suspend the application of concessions or other obligations pursuant to these procedures.

24.2 In dispute settlement cases involving a least-developed country Member where a satisfactory solution has not been found in the course of consultations the Director-General or the Chairman of the DSB shall, upon request by a least-developed country Member offer their good offices, conciliation and mediation with a view to assisting the parties to settle the dispute, before a request for a panel is made. The Director-General or the Chairman of the DSB, in providing the above assistance, may consult any source which they deem appropriate.

25. *Arbitration*

25.1 Expeditious arbitration within the WTO as an alternative means of dispute settlement can facilitate the solution of certain disputes that concern issues that are clearly defined by both parties.

25.2 Except as otherwise provided in this Understanding, resort to arbitration shall be subject to mutual agreement of the parties which shall agree on the procedures to be followed. Agreements to resort to arbitration shall be notified to all Members sufficiently in advance of the actual commencement of the arbitration process.

25.3 Other Members may become party to an arbitration proceeding only upon the agreement of the parties which have agreed to have recourse to arbitration. The parties to the proceeding shall agree to abide by the arbitration award. Arbitration awards shall be notified to the DSB and the council or committee of any relevant agreement where any Member may raise any point relating thereto.

25.4 Sections 21 and 22 of this Understanding shall apply *mutatis mutandis* to arbitration awards.

26. *Non-Violation*

26.1 *Complaints of the Type Described in Article XXIII : 1 (b) of GATT 1994* : Where the provisions of Article XXIII : 1(b) of the GATT 1994 are applicable to a covered agreement, a panel or the Appellate Body may only make rulings and recommendations where a party to the dispute considers that any benefit accruing to it directly or indirectly under the relevant covered agreement is being nullified or impaired or the attainment of any objective of that Agreement is being impeded as a result of the application by a Member of any measure, whether or not it conflicts with the provisions of that Agreement. Where and to the extent that such party considers and a panel or the Appellate Body determines that a case concerns a measure that does not conflict with the provisions of a covered agreement to which the provisions of Article

XXIII: l(b) of GATT 1994 are applicable, the procedures in this Understanding shall apply, subject to the following:

(a) The complaining party shall present a detailed justification in support of any complaint relating to a measure which does not conflict with the relevant covered agreement.

(b) Where a measure has been found to nullify or impair benefits under, or impede the attainment of objectives, of the relevant covered agreement without violation thereof, there is no obligation to withdraw the measure. However, in such cases, the panel or the Appellate Body shall recommend that the Member concerned make a mutually satisfactory adjustment.

(c) Notwithstanding the provisions of paragraph 21, the arbitration provided for in paragraph 21.3, upon request of either party, may include a determination of the level of benefits which have been nullified or impaired, and may also suggest ways and means of reaching a mutually satisfactory adjustment; such suggestions shall not be binding upon the parties.

(d) Notwithstanding the provisions of paragraph 22.1, compensation may be part of a mutually satisfactory adjustment as final settlement of the dispute.

26.2 *Complaints of the Type Described in article XXIII: 1 (c) of GATT 1994* : Where the provisions of Article XXIII:1(c) of the GATT 1994 are applicable to a covered agreement, a panel may only make rulings and recommendations where a party considers that any benefit accruing to it directly or indirectly under the relevant covered agreement is being nullified or impaired or the attainment of any objective of that Agreement is being impeded as a result of the existence of any situation other than those to which the provisions of Article XXIII:1(a) and (b) of GATT 1994 are applicable. Where and to the extent that such party considers and a panel determines that the matter is covered by this paragraph, the procedures of this Understanding shall apply only up to and including the point in the proceedings where the panel report has been issued to the Members. The dispute settlement rules and procedures contained in the Decision of the GATT Council of Representatives of 12 April 1989 (BISD 36S/61) shall apply to consideration for adoption, and surveillance and implication of recommendations and rulings. The following shall also apply :

(a) The complaining party shall present a detailed justification in support of any argument made with respect to issues covered under this paragraph.

(b) In cases involving matters covered by this paragraph, if a panel finds that cases also involve dispute settlement matters other than those covered by this paragraph, the panel shall issue a report addressing any such matters and a separate report on matters falling under this paragraph.

27. *Responsibilities of the Secretariat*

27.1 The WTO Secretariat shall have the responsibility of assisting the panels, especially on the legal, historical and procedural aspects of the matters dealt with, and of providing secretarial and technical support.

27.2 While the Secretariat assists Members in respect of dispute settlement at their request, there may also be a need to provide additional legal advice and assistance in respect of dispute settlement to developing country Members. To this end, the Secretariat shall make available a qualified legal expert from the WTO technical co-operation services to any developing country Member which so requests. This expert shall assist the developing country Member in a manner ensuring the continued impartiality of the Secretariat.

27.3 The Secretariat shall conduct special training courses for interested Members concerning these dispute settlement procedures and practices so as to enable Members' experts to be better informed in this regard.

APPENDIX 1

Agreements Covered by the Understanding

(A)	Agreement Establishing the Multilateral Trade Organization	
(B)	Annex IA:	Agreements on trade in goods
	Annex lB:	General Agreement on Trade in Services
	Annex 1 C:	Agreement on Trade-Related Aspects of Intellectual Property Rights, including Trade in Counterfeit Goods
	Annex 2 :	Understanding on Rules and Procedures Governing the Settlement of Disputes
(C)	Annex 4 :	Agreement on Trade in Civil Aircraft
		Agreement on Government Procurement
		International Dairy Arrangement
		Arrangement Regarding Bovine Meat

The applicability of this Understanding to Annex 4 Agreements shall be subject to the adoption of a decision by the Signatories of each Agreement setting out the terms for the application of the Understanding to file individual agreement, including any special or additional rules or procedures for inclusion in Appendix 2, as notified to the Dispute Settlement Body.

APPENDIX 2

Special or Additional Rules and Procedures Contained in the Covered Agreements

Agreement	*Rules and Procedures*
Anti-Dumping	17.4 to 17.7
Technical Barriers to Trade	14.2 to 14.4, Annex 2
Subsidies and Countervailing Measures	4.2 to 4.12, 6.6, 7.2 to 7.10, 8.5, footnote 33, 25.3 to 25.4, 28.6, Annex V
Customs Valuation	19.3 to 19.5, Annex II.2(f), 3, 9, 21
Sanitary and Phytosanitary Regulations	36
Textiles	2.14, 2.21, 4.4, 5.2, 5.4, 5.6, 6.9, 6.10, 6.11, 8.1 to 8.12
General Agreement on Trade in Services	XXII:3, XXIII:3
Financial Services	4.1
Air Transport Services	4
Ministestrial Decision on Services Disputes	1 to 5

The list of rules and procedures in this Appendix includes provisions where only a part of the provision may he relevant in this context.

Any special or additional rules or procedures in ANNEX 4 Agreements as determined by the competent bodies of each Agreement and as notified to the DSB.

APPENDIX 3

Working Procedures

1. In its proceedings the panel will follow the relevant provisions of the Understanding on Rules and Procedures Governing the Settlement of Disputes. In addition, the following working procedures will apply.

2. The panel will meet in closed session. The parties to the dispute, or other interested parties, will be present at the meetings only when invited by the panel to appear before it.

3. The deliberations of the panel and the documents submitted to it will be kept confidential. Nothing in this Understanding shall preclude a party to a dispute from disclosing statements of its own positions to the public. Members shall treat as confidential, information submitted by another Member to the panel which that Member has designated as confidential. Where a party to a dispute submits a confidential version of its written submissions to the panel, it shall also, upon request of a Member, provide a non-confidential summary of the information contained in its submissions that could be disclosed to the public.

4. Before the first substantive meeting of the panel with the parties, both parties to the dispute shall transmit to the panel written submissions in which they present the facts of the case and their arguments.

5. At its first substantive meeting with the parties, the panel will ask the party which has brought the complaint to present its case. Subsequently, and still at the same meeting, the party against which the complaint has been brought will be asked to present its point of view.

6. All third parties which have notified their interest in the dispute to the DSB shall be invited in writing to present their views during a session of the first substantive meeting of the panel set aside for that purpose. All such third parties may be present during the entirety of this session.

7. Formal rebuttals will be made at a second substantive meeting of the panel. The party complained against will have the right to take the floor first to be followed by the complaining party. Both parties shall submit, prior to that meeting, written rebuttals to the panel.

8. The panel may at any time put questions to the parties and ask them for explanations either in the course of a meeting with the parties or in writing.

9. The parties to the dispute and any third party invited to present its views in accordance with Section 8 of the Understanding shall make available to the panel a written version of their oral statements.

10. In the interest of full transparency, the presentations, rebuttals and statements referred to in paragraphs 5 to 9 above will be made in the presence of both parties. Moreover, each party's written submissions, including any comments on the descriptive part of the report and responses to questions put by the panel, will be made available to the other party.

11. Any additional procedures specific to the panel.

12. The panel proposes the. following timetable for its work:

(a) Receipt of first written submissions of the Parties :

(1) complaining Party:	3-6 weeks
(2) Party complained against;	2-3 weeks
(b) Date, time and place of first substantive meeting with the Parties; Third Party session :	1-2 weeks
(c) Receipt of written rebuttal of the Parties:	2-3 weeks
(d) Date, time and place of second substantive meeting with the Parties:	1-2 weeks
(e) Submission of descriptive part of the report to the Parties :	2-4 weeks
(f) Receipt of comments by the Parties on the descriptive part of the report:	2 weeks
(g) Submission of the interim report, including the findings and conclusions, to the Parties:	2-4 weeks
(h) Deadline for Party to request review of part(s) of report:	1 week
(i) Period of review by panel, including possible additional meeting with Parties:	2 weeks
(j) Submission of final report to Parties to dispute:	2 weeks
(k) Circulation of the final report to the Members:	3 weeks

The above calendar may be changed in the light of unforeseen developments. Additional meetings with the Parties will be scheduled if required.

APPENDIX 4
Expert Review Groups

The following rules and procedures shall apply to expert review groups established in accordance with the provisions of Article 13.2:

1. Expert review groups are under the panel's authority. Their terms of reference and detailed working procedures shall be decided by the panel, and they shall report to the panel.

2. Participation in expert review groups shall be restricted to persons of professional standing and experience in the field in question.

3. Citizens of parties to the dispute shall not serve on an expert review/ group without the joint agreement of the parties to the dispute, except in exceptional circumstances when the panel considers that the need for specialized scientific expertise cannot be fulfilled otherwise. Government officials of parties to the dispute shall not serve on an expert review group. Members of expert review groups shall serve in their individual capacities and not as government representatives, nor as representatives of any organization. Governments or organizations shall therefore not give them instructions with regard to matters before an expert review group.

Expert review groups may consult and seek information and technical advice from any source they deem appropriate. Before an expert review group seeks such information or advice from a source within the jurisdiction of a Member, it shall inform the government of that Member. Any Member shall respond promptly and fully to any request by an expert review group for such information as the expert review group considers necessary and appropriate.

5. The parties to a dispute shall have access to all relevant information provided to an expert review group, unless it is of a confidential nature. Confidential information provided to the expert review group shall not be released without formal authorization from the government, organization or person providing the information. Where such information is requested from the expert review group but release of such information by the expert review group is not authorized, a non-confidential summary of the information will be provided by the government, organization or person supplying the information.

6. The expert review group shall submit a draft report to the parties, to the dispute with a view to obtaining their comments, and taking them into account, as appropriate, in the final report, which shall also be circulated to the parties to the dispute when it is submitted to the panel. The final report of the expert review group shall be advisory only.

TRADE POLICY REVIEW MECHANISM

A. *Objectives*

(i) The purpose of the Trade Policy Review Mechanism is to contribute to improved adherence by all Members to rules, disciplines and commitments made under the Multilateral

Trade Agreements and, where applicable, the Plurilateral Trade Agreements, and hence to the smoother functioning of the multilateral trading system, by achieving greater transparency in, and understanding of, the trade policies and practices of Members. Accordingly, the review mechanism will enable the regular collective appreciation and evaluation by the Ministerial Conference of the full range of individual Members' trade policies and practices and their impact on the functioning of the multilateral trading system. It is not, however, intended to serve as a basis for the enforcement of specific obligations under the Agreements or for dispute settlement procedures, or to impose new policy commitments on Members.

(ii) The assessment to be carried out under the review mechanism will, to the extent relevant, take place against the background of the wider economic and developmental needs, policies and objectives of the Member concerned, as well as of its external environment. However, the function of the review mechanism is to examine the impact of a Member's trade policies and practices on the multilateral trading system.

B. *Domestic transparency*

Members *recognize* the inherent value of domestic transparency of government decision-making on trade policy matters for both Members' economies and the multilateral trading system, and agree to encourage and promote greater transparency within their own systems, acknowledging that the implementation of domestic transparency must be on a voluntary basis and take account of each Member's legal and political systems.

C. *Procedures for review*

(i) Trade policy reviews will be carried out by the Trade Policy Review Body (TPRB).

(ii) The trade policies and practices of all Members will be subject to periodic review. The impact of individual Members on the functioning of the multilateral trading system, defined in terms of their share of world trade in a recent representative period, will be the determining factor in deciding on the frequency of reviews. The first four trading entities so identified (counting the European Communities as one) will be subject to review every two years. The next sixteen will be reviewed every four years. Other Members will be reviewed every six years, except that a longer period may be fixed for least-developed country Members. It is understood that the review of entities having a common external policy covering more than one Member shall cover all components of policy affecting trade including relevant policies and practices of the individual Members. Exceptionally, in the event of changes in a Member's trade policies or practices which may have a significant impact on its trading partners, the Member concerned may be requested by the TPRB, after consultation, to bring forward its next review.

(iii) In the light of the objectives set out in A above, discussions in the meeting of the TPRB will, to the extent relevant, take place against the background of the wider economic and developmental needs, policies and objectives of the Member concerned, as well as of its external environment. The focus of these discussions will be on the Member's policies and practices which are the subject of the assessment under the review mechanism.

(iv) The TPRB will establish a basic plan for the conduct of the reviews. It may also discuss and take note of update reports from Members. The TPRB will establish a programme of reviews for each year in consultation with the Members directly concerned. In consultation with the Member or Members under review, the Chairman may choose discussants who, in their personal capacity, will introduce the discussions in the TPRB.

(v) The TPRB will base its work on the following documentation:

(a) A full report, referred to in paragraph D(i) below, supplied by the Member or Members under review.

(b) A report, to be drawn up by the Secretariat on its own responsibility, based on the information available to it and that provided by the Member or Members concerned. The Secretariat should seek clarification from the Member or Members concerned of their trade policies and practices.

(iii) the cost of production;

(vi) The reports by the Member under review and by the Secretariat, together with the minutes of the respective meeting of the TPRB, will be published promptly after the review.

(vii) These documents will be forwarded to the Ministerial Conference, which will take note of them.

D. *Reporting*

(i) In order to achieve the fullest possible degree of transparency, each Member shall report regularly to the TPRB. Full reports will describe the trade policies and practices pursued by the Member or Members concerned, based on an agreed format to be decided upon by the TPRB. This format initially shall be based on the Outline Format for Country Reports established by the Decision Of the GATT 1947 CONTRACTING PARTIES of 19 July 1989, amended as necessary to extend the coverage of reports to all aspects of trade policies covered by the Multilateral Trade Agreements in Annex 1 and, where applicable, the Plurilateral Trade Agreements. This format may be revised by the TPRB in the light of experience. Between reviews, Members will provide brief reports when there are any significant changes in their trade policies; an annual update of statistical information will be provided according to the agreed format. Particular account will be taken of difficulties presented to least developed country Members in compiling their reports. The Secretariat shall make available technical assistance on request to developing country Members, and in particular to the least-developed country Members. Information contained in reports should to the greatest extent possible be coordinated with notifications made under provision of the Multilateral Trade Agreements and, where applicable, the Plurilateral Trade Agreements.

E. *Relationship with the balance-of-payments provisions of the GATT 1994 and the GATS*

Members *recognize* the need to minimize the burden for governments also subject to full consultations under the balance-of-payments provisions of the GATT 1994 or the GATS. To this end, the Chairman of the TPRB shall, in consultation with the Member or Members concerned, and with the Chairman of the Committee on Balance-of-Payments Restrictions, devise administrative arrangements which would harmonize the normal rhythm of the trade policy reviews with the time-table for balance-of payments consultations but would not postpone the trade policy review by more than twelve months.

F. *Appraisal of the Mechanism*

The TPRB will undertake an appraisal of the operation of the TPRM not more than five years after the entry into force of the Agreement Establishing the WTO. The results of the appraisal will be presented to the Ministerial

Conference. It may subsequently undertake appraisals of the TPRM at intervals to be determined by it or as requested by the Ministerial Conference.

G. *Overview of Developments in the International Trading Environment*

An annual overview of developments in the international trading environment which are having an impact on the multilateral trading system will also be undertaken by the TPRB. It will be assisted by an annual report by the Director-General setting out major activities of the WTO and highlighting significant policy issues affecting the trading system.

ANNEX 4

Plurilateral Trade Agreements

ANNEX 4 (a)

Agreement on Trade in Civil Aircraft

The text of this Agreement is reproduced in BISD 26S/162 and later amendments. A revision of this text is under negotiation.

ANNEX 4 (b)

Agreement on Government Procurement

The text in force is contained in BISD 26S/33. A revised text, expected to enter into force on 1 January 1996, is contained in document GPP/Spec/77, dated 15 December 1993.

ANNEX 4 (c)

International Dairy Arrangement

The text of this Agreement is reproduced in BISD 26S/91.

ANNEX 4 (d)

Arrangement Regarding Bovine Meant

The text of this Agreement is reproduced in BISD 26S/84.

SIGNATURES

For the People's Democratic Republic of Algeria:

For Antigua and Barbuda:

For the Argentine Republic:

For Australia:

For the Republic of Austria:

For the State of Bahrain:
For the People's Republic of Bangladesh:
For Barbados:
For the Kingdom of Belgium:
For Belize:
For the Republic of Benin;
For the Republic of Bolivia:
For, the Republic of Botswana:
For the Federative Republic of Brazil:
For Brunei Darussalam:
For Burkina Faso:
For the Republic of Burundi:
For the Republic of Cameroon:
For Canada:
For the Central African Republic:
For the Republic of Chad:
For the Republic of Chile:
For the People's Republic of China:
For the Republic of Colombia:
For the Republic of the Congo:
For the Republic of Costa Rica:
For the Republic of Côte d'Ivoire:
For the Republic of Cuba:
For the Republic of Cyprus:
For the Czech Republic:
For the Kingdom of Denmark:
For the Commonwealth of Dominica:
For the Dominican Republic:
For the Arab Republic of Egypt:
For the Republic of El Salvador:
For the Republic of Fiji:
For the Republic of Finland:
For the French Republic:
For the Gabonese Republic:
For the Republic of the Gambia:
For the Federal Republic of Germany:

For the Republic of Ghana:

For the Hellenic Republic:

For the Republic of Guatemala

For the Republic of Guyana:

For the Republic of Haiti:

For the Republic of Honduras:

For Hong Kong:

For the Republic of Hungary:

For the Republic of Iceland:

For the Republic of India:

For the Republic of Indonesia:

For Ireland:

For the State of Israel:

For the Italian Republic:

For Jamaica:

For Japan:

For the Republic of Kenya

For the Republic of Korea:

For the State of Kuwait:

For the Kingdom of Lesotho:

For the Grand Duchy of Luxembourg:

For Macau:

For the Republic of Madagascar:

For the Republic of Malawi:

For Malaysia:

For the Republic of Maldives:

For the Republic of Mali:

For the Republic of Malta:

For the Islamic Republic of Mauritania:

For the Republic of Mauritius:

For the United Mexican States:

For the Kingdom of Morocco:

For the Republic of Mozambique:

For the Union of Myanmar:

For Republic of Namibia:

For the Kingdom of the Netherlands:

For New Zealand:
For the Republic of Nicaragua:
For the Republic of the Niger:
For the Federal Republic of Nigeria:
For the Kingdom of Norway:
For the Islamic Republic of Pakistan:
For the Republic of Paraguay:
For the Republic of Peru:
For the Republic of the Philippines:
For the Republic of Poland:
For the Portuguese Republic:
For Romania:
For the Rwandese Republic:
For Saint Lucia:
For Saint Vincent and the Grenadines:
For the Republic of Senegal:
For the Republic of Sierra Leone:
For the Republic of Singapore:
For the Slovak Republic:
For the Republic of South Africa:
For the Kingdom of Spain:
For the Democratic Socialist Republic of Sri Lanka:
For the Republic of Suriname:
For the Kingdom of Swaziland:
For the Kingdom of Sweden:
For the Swiss Confederation
For the United Republic of Tanzania:
For the Kingdom of Thailand:
For the Togolese Republic:
For the Republic of Trinidad and Tobago:
For the Republic of Tunisia:
For the Republic of Turkey:
For the Republic of Uganda:
For the United Kingdom of Great Britain and Northern Ireland:
For the United States of America:
For the Eastern Republic of Uruguay:

For the Republic of Venezuela:

For the Republic of Zaire:

For the Republic of Zambia:

For the Republic of Zimbabwe:

For the European Communities:

PART III : MINISTERIAL DECISIONS AND DECLARATIONS

DECISION ON MEASURES IN FAVOUR OF LEAST-DEVELOPED COUNTRIES

Ministers,

Recognizing the plight of the least-developed countries and the need to ensure their effective participation in the world trading system, and to take further measures to improve their trading opportunities;

Recognizing the specific needs of the least-developed countries in the area of market access where continued preferential access remains an essential means for improving their trading opportunities;

Reaffirming their commitment to implement fully the provisions concerning the least-developed countries contained in paragraphs 2(d), 6 and 8 of the Decision of the CONTRACTING PARTIES of 28 November 1979 on Differential and More Favourable Treatment, Reciprocity and Fuller Participation of Developing Countries;

Having regard to the commitment of the participants as set out in Section B (vii) of Part I of the Punta del Este Declaration;

1. *Decide* that, if not already provided for in the instruments negotiated in the course of the Uruguay Round, notwithstanding their acceptance of these instruments, the least-developed countries, and for so long as they remain in that category, while complying with the general rules set out in the aforesaid instruments, will only be required to undertake commitments and concessions to the extent consistent with 'their individual development, financial and trade needs, or their administrative and institutional capabilities. The least-developed countries shall be given additional time of one year from the date of the Special Ministerial Session concluding the Uruguay Round of Multilateral Trade Negotiations to submit their schedules as required in Article XI of the Agreement Establishing the **World Trade Organisation**

2. *Agree* that :

   (i) Expeditious implementation of all special and differential measures taken in favour of least-developed countries including those taken within the context of the Uruguay Round shall be ensured through *inter alia*, regular reviews.

(ii) To the extent possible, MFN concessions on tariff and non-tariff measures agreed in the Uruguay Round on products of export interest to the least-developed countries may be implemented autonomously, in advance and without staging. Consideration shall be given to further improve GSP and other schemes for products of particular export interest to least-developed countries.

(iii) The rules set out in the various agreements and instruments and the transitional provisions in the Uruguay Round should be applied in a flexible and supportive manner for the least-developed countries. To this effect, sympathetic consideration shall be given to specific and motivated concerns raised by the least-developed countries in the appropriate Committees and Councils.

(iv) In the application of import relief measures and other measures referred to in Article XXXVII:3(c) of GATT 1947 (and the corresponding Article of GATT 1994), special consideration shall be given to the export interests of least-developed countries.

(v) Least-developed countries shall be accorded substantially increased technical assistance in the development, strengthening and diversification of their production and export bases including those of services, as well as in trade promotion, to enable them to maximize the benefits from liberalized access to markets.

Agree to keep under review the specific needs of the least-developed countries and to continue to seek the adoption of positive measures which facilitate the expansion of trading opportunities in favour of these countries.

DECLARATION ON THE CONTRIBUTION OF THE WTO TO ACHIEVING GREATER COHERENCE IN GLOBAL ECONOMIC POLICY-MAKING

1. Ministers *recognize* that the globalization of the world economy has led to ever-growing interactions between the economic policies pursued by individual countries, including interactions between the structural, macroeconomic, trade, financial and development aspects of economic policy-making. The task of achieving harmony between these policies falls primarily on governments at the national level, but their coherence internationally is an important and valuable element in increasing the effectiveness of these policies

at national level. The Agreements reached in the Uruguay Round show that all the participating governments recognize the contribution that liberal trading policies can make to the healthy growth and development of their own economies and of the world economy as a whole.

2. Successful cooperation in each area of economic policy contributes to progress in other areas. Greater exchange rate stability, based on more orderly underlying economic and financial conditions, should contribute towards the expansion of trade, sustainable growth and development, and the correction of external imbalances. There is also a need for an adequate and timely flow of concessional and non-concessional financial and real investment resources to developing countries and for further efforts to address debt problems, to help ensure economic growth and development. Trade liberalization forms an increasingly important component in the success of the adjustment programmes that many countries are undertaking, often involving significant transitional social costs. In this connection, Ministers note the role of the World Bank and the IMF in supporting adjustment to trade liberalization, including support to net food-importing developing countries facing short-term costs arising from agricultural trade reforms.

3. The positive outcome of the Uruguay Round is a major contribution towards more coherent and complementary international economic policies. The results of the Uruguay Round ensure an expansion of market access to the benefit of all countries, as well as a framework of strengthened multilateral disciplines for trade. They also guarantee that trade policy will be conducted in a more transparent manner and with greater awareness of the benefits for domestic competitiveness of an open trading environment. The strengthened multilateral trading system emerging from the Round has the capacity to provide an improved forum for liberalization, to contribute to more effective surveillance, and to ensure strict observance of multilaterally agreed rules and disciplines. These improvements mean that trade policy can in future play a more substantial role in ensuring the coherence of global economic policy-making.

4. Ministers *recognize,* however, that difficulties whose origins lie outside the trade field cannot be redressed through measures taken in the trade field alone. This underscores the importance of efforts to improve other elements of global economic policy-making to complement the effective implementation of the results achieved in the Uruguay Round.

5. The interlinkages between the different aspects of economic policy require that the international institutions with responsibilities in each of these areas follow consistent and mutually supportive policies. The WTO should therefore pursue and develop cooperation with the international organizations responsible for monetary and financial matters, while respecting the mandate,

the confidentiality requirements and the necessary autonomy in decision-making procedures of each institution, and avoiding the imposition on governments of cross-conditionality or additional conditions. Ministers further invite the Director-General of the WTO to review with the Managing Director of the International Monetary Fund and the President of the World Bank, the implications of the WTO's responsibilities for its cooperation with the Bretton Woods institutions, as well as the forms such cooperation might take, with a view to achieving greater coherence in global economic policy-making.

DECISION ON NOTIFICATION PROCEDURES

Ministers recommend approval by the Ministerial Conference of the improvement and review of notification procedures as set out below.

Members,

Desiring to improve the operation of notification procedures under the MTO, and thereby to contribute to the transparency of Members' trade policies and to the effectiveness of surveillance arrangements established to that end,

Recalling obligations under the WTO to publish and notify, including obligations assumed under the terms of specific Protocols of Accession, waivers, and other agreements entered into by Members,

Agree as follows:

1. *General obligation to notify*

Members affirm their commitment to obligations under the Multilateral Trade Agreements and, where applicable, the Plurilateral Trade Agreements, regarding publication and notification.

Members recall their undertakings set out in the Understanding Regarding Notification, Consultation, Dispute Settlement and Surveillance adopted by the CONTRACTING PARTIES to the GATT 1947 on 28 November 1979. With regard to their undertaking therein to notify, to the maximum extend possible, their adoption of trade measures affecting the operation of the GATT 1994, such notification itself being without prejudice to views on the consistency of measures with or their relevance to rights and obligations under the Multilateral Trade Agreements and, where applicable, the Plurilateral Trade Agreements, Members agree to be guided, as appropriate, by the annexed list of measures. Members therefore agree that the introduction or modification of such measures is subject to the notification requirements of the 1979 Understanding.

II. *Central registry of notifications*

A central registry of notifications shall be established under the responsibility of the WTO Secretariat. While Members will continue to follow existing notification procedures, the Secretariat shall ensure that the registry records such elements of the information provided on the measure by the Member as its purpose, its trade coverage, and the requirement under which it has been notified. The registry shall cross-reference its records of notifications by Member and obligation.

The central registry shall inform each Member annually of the regular notification obligations to which that Member will be expected to respond in the course of the following year.

The central registry shall draw the attention of individual Members to regular notification requirements which remain unfulfilled.

Information in the central registry regarding individual notifications shall be made available on request to any Member entitled to receive the notification concerned.

III. *Review of notification obligations and procedures*

The Council for Trade in Goods will undertake a review of notification obligations and procedures under the Agreements in Annex IA. The review will be carried out by a working group, membership in which will be open to all Members. The group will be established immediately after the entry into force of the Agreement establishing the WTO.

The terms of reference of the working group will be:

— to undertake a thorough review of all existing notification obligations of Members established under the Agreements in Annex IA, with a view to simplifying, standardizing and consolidating these obligations to the greatest extent practicable, as well as to improving compliance with these obligations, bearing in mind the overall objective of improving the transparency of the trade policies of Members and the effectiveness of surveillance arrangements established to this end, and also bearing in mind the possible need of some developing Members for assistance in meeting their notification obligations;

— to make recommendations to the Council for Trade in Goods not later than two years after the entry into force of the Agreement establishing the WTO.

ANNEX

Indicative List[192] of notifiable Measures

Tariffs (including range and scope of bindings, GSP provisions, rates applied to members of free-trade areas/customs unions, other preferences)

---

[192] This list does not alter existing notification requirements in the Multilateral Trade Agreements in Annex 1A to the Agreement establishing the WTO.

Tariff quotas and surcharges

Quantitative restrictions, including voluntary export restraints and orderly marketing arrangements affecting imports

Other non-tariff measures such as licensing and mixing requirements; variable levies

Customs valuation

Rules of origin

Government Procurement

Technical barriers

Safeguard actions

Anti-dumping actions

Countervailing actions

export taxes

export subsidies, tax exemptions and concessionary export financing

Free-trade zones, including in-bond manufacturing.

export restrictions, including voluntary export restraints and orderly marketing arrangements

Other government assistance, including subsidies, tax exemptions

Role of State-trading enterprises

Foreign exchange controls related to imports and exports

Government-mandated countertrade

Any other measure covered by the Multilateral Trade Agreements in Annex IA to the Agreement establishing the WTO

DECISION REGARDING CASES WHERE CUSTOMS ADMINISTRATIONS HAVE REASONS TO DOUBT THE TRUTH OR ACCURACY OF THE DECLARED VALUE

Ministers invite the Committee on Customs Valuation to take the following decision:

Reaffirming that the transaction value is the primary basis of valuation under the Agreement on Implementation of Article VII of the GATT 1994 (the Agreement);

Recognizing that the customs administration may have to address cases where it has reason to doubt the truth or accuracy of the particulars or of documents produced by traders in support of a declared value;

Emphasizing that in so doing the customs administration should not prejudice the legitimate commercial interests of traders;

Taking into account Article 17 of the Agreement, paragraph 6 of Annex III to the Agreement, and the relevant decisions of the Technical Committee on Customs Valuation;

The Committee on Customs Valuation decides as follows:

1. When a declaration has been presented and where the customs administration has reason to doubt the truth or accuracy of the particulars or of documents produced in support of this declaration, the customs administration may ask the importer to provide further explanation, including documents or other evidence, that the declared value represents the total amount actually paid or payable for the imported goods, adjusted in accordance with the provisions of Article 8. If, after receiving further information, or in the absence of a response, customs still has reasonable doubts about the truth or accuracy of the declared value, it may, bearing in mind the provisions of Article 11, be deemed that the customs value of the imported goods cannot be determined under the provisions of Article 1, Before taking a final decision, the customs administration shall communicate to the importer, in writing if requested, its grounds for doubting the truth or accuracy of the particulars or documents produced and the importer shall be given a reasonable opportunity to respond. When a final decision is made, the customs administration shall communicate to the importer in writing its decision and the grounds therefor.

2. It is entirely appropriate in applying the Agreement for one Member to assist another Member on mutually agreed terms.

TEXTS RELATING TO MINIMUM VALUES AND IMPORTS BY SOLE AGENTS, SOLE DISTRIBUTORS AND SOLE CONCESSIONAIRES

Ministers refer the following texts to the committee on Customs Valuation for adoption:

***

Where a developing country Member makes a reservation to retain officially established minimum values within the terms of paragraph 2 of Annex III and shows good cause, the Committee shall give the request for the reservation sympathetic consideration.

Where a reservation is consented to, the terms and conditions referred to in paragraph 2 of Annex III shall take full account of the development, financial and trade needs of the Member concerned.

***

A number of developing countries considering accession to the Agreement have expressed concern that problems may exist in the valuation of imports by sole agents, sole distributors and sole concessionaires. Under paragraph 1 of Article 20, developing country Members have a period of delay of up to five years prior to the application of the Agreement. In this context, Members availing themselves of this provision could use the period to conduct appropriate studies and to take such other actions as are necessary to facilitate application.

In consideration of this, the Committee recommends that the Customs Co-operation Council assist developing country Members, in accordance with the provisions of Annex II, to formulate and conduct studies in areas identified as being of potential concern, including those relating to importations by sole agents, sole distributors and sole concessionaires.

PROPOSED UNDERSTANDING ON MTO-ISO STANDARDS INFORMATION SYSTEM

Ministers *recommend* that the WTO Secretariat reach an understanding with the ISO to establish an information system under which:

1. ISONET members shall transmit to the ISO/IEC Information Centre in Geneva the notifications referred to in paragraphs C and J of the Code of good practice for the preparation, adoption and application of standards in Annex 3 to the Agreement on Technical Barriers to Trade, in the manner indicated there;

2. the following (alpha)numeric classification systems shall be used in the work programmes mentioned above:

(a) *a standards classification system* which would allow standardizing bodies to give for each standard mentioned in the work programme an (alpha)numeric indication of the subject matter;

(b) *a stage code system* which would allow standardizing bodies to give for each standard mentioned in the work programme in paragraph J of Annex 3 an (alpha)numeric indication of the stage of development of the standard; for this purpose, at least five stages of development should be distinguished: (1) the stage at which the decision to develop a standard has been taken, but technical work has not yet begun; (2) the stage at which technical work has begun, but the period for the submission of comments has not yet started; (3) the stage at which the period for the submission of comments has started, but has not yet been completed;. (4) the stage at which the period for the submission of comments has been completed, but the standard has not yet been adopted; and (5) the stage at which the standard has been adopted;

(c) *an identification system* covering all international standards which would allow standardizing bodies to give for each standard mentioned in the work programme an (alpha)numeric indication of the international standard(s) used as a basis;

3. the ISO/IEC Information Centre shall promptly convey to the MTO Secretariat copies of any notifications referred to in paragraph C of the Code of good practice;

4. the ISO/IEC Information Centre shall regularly publish the information received in the notifications made to it under paragraphs C and J of the Code of good practice; this publication, for which a reasonable fee may be charged, shall be available to-ISONET members and through the WTO Secretariat, to the Members of the WTO.

DECISION ON REVIEW OF THE ISO/IEC INFORMATION CENTRE PUBLICATION

Ministers *decide* that in conformity with paragraph 1 of Article 13 the Committee on Technical Barriers to Trade shall, without prejudice to provisions on consultation and dispute settlement, at least once a year review the publication provided by the ISO/IEC Information Centre on information received according to the Code of good practice in Annex 3 of the Agreement, for the purpose of affording Members opportunity of discussing any matters relating to the operation of that Code.

In order to facilitate this discussion, the MTO Secretariat is requested to provide a list by Member of all standardizing bodies that have accepted the Code of good practice, as well as a list of those standardizing bodies that have accepted or withdrawn from the Code since the previous review.

The WTO Secretariat is also requested to distribute promptly to the Members copies of the notifications it receives from the ISO/IEC Information Centre.

DECISION ON MEASURES CONCERNING THE POSSIBLE NEGATIVE EFFECTS OF THE REFORM PROGRAMME ON LEAST-DEVELOPED AND NET FOOD-IMPORTING DEVELOPING COUNTRIES

1. Ministers *recognize* that the progressive implementation of the results of the Uruguay Round as a whole will generate increasing opportunities for trade expansion and economic growth to the benefit of all participants.

2. Ministers *recognize* that during the reform programme leading to greater liberalization of trade in agriculture least-developed and net food-importing developing countries may experience negative effects in terms of the availability of adequate supplies of basic foodstuffs from external sources on reasonable terms and conditions, including short-term difficulties in Financing normal levels of commercial imports of basic foodstuffs.

3. Ministers accordingly *agree* to establish appropriate mechanisms to ensure that the implementation of the results of the Uruguay Round on trade

in agriculture does not adversely affect the availability of food aid at a level which is sufficient to continue to provide assistance in meeting the food needs of developing countries, especially least developed and net food-importing developing countries. To this end Ministers agree:

(i) to review the level of food aid established periodically by the Committee on Food Aid under the Food Aid Convention and to initiate negotiations in the appropriate forum to establish a level of food aid commitments sufficient to meet the legitimate needs of developing countries during the reform programme;

(ii) to adopt guidelines to ensure that an increasing proportion of basic foodstuffs is provided to least developed and net food-importing developing countries in fully grant form and/or on appropriate concessional terms in line with Article IV of the Food Aid Convention;

(iii) to give full consideration in the context of their aid programmes to requests for the provision of technical and financial assistance to least developed and net food-importing developing countries to improve their agricultural productivity and infrastructure.

4. Ministers further *agree* to ensure that any agreement relating to agricultural export credits makes appropriate provision for differential treatment in favour of least developed and net food-importing developing countries.

5. Ministers *recognize* that as a result of the Uruguay Round certain developing countries may experience short-term difficulties in financing normal levels of commercial imports and that these countries may be eligible to draw on the resources of international financial institutions under existing facilities, or such facilities as may be established, in the context of adjustment programmes, in order to address such financing difficulties. In this regard Ministers take note of paragraph 37 of the report of the Director-General of the GATT (MTN.GNG/NG 14/W/35) on his consultations with the Managing Director of the International Monetary Fund and the President of the World Bank.

6. The provisions of this Decision will be subject to regular review by the Ministerial Conference, and the follow-up to this Decision shall be monitored, as appropriate, by the Committee on Agriculture.

DECISION ON INSTITUTIONAL ARRANGEMENTS FOR THE GENERAL AGREEMENT ON TRADE IN SERVICES

Ministers *recommend* that the Council for Trade in Services at its first meeting shall adopt the decision on subsidiary bodies set out below.

INSTITUTIONAL ARRANGEMENTS FOR THE GENERAL AGREEMENT ON TRADE IN SERVICES

The Council for Trade in Services, acting pursuant to Article XXIV with a view to facilitating the operation and furthering the objectives of the General Agreement on Trade in Services,

Decides as follows :

1. Any subsidiary bodies, that the Council may establish shall report to the Council annually or more often as necessary. Each such body shall establish its own rules of procedure, and may set up its own subsidiary bodies as appropriate.

2. Any sectoral committee shall carry out responsibilities as assigned to it by the Council, and shall afford Members the opportunity to consult on any matters relating to trade in services in the sector concerned and the operation of the sectoral annex to which it may pertain. Such responsibilities shall include:

(a) to keep under continuous review and surveillance the application of the Agreement with respect to the sector concerned;

(b) to formulate proposals or recommendations for consider-ation by the Council in connection with any matter relating to trade in the sector concerned;

(c) if there is an annex pertaining to the sector, to consider proposals for amendment of that sectoral annex, and to make appropriate recommendations to the Council;

(d) to provide a forum for technical discussions, to conduct studies on measures of Members and to conduct examinations of any other technical matters affecting trade in services in the sector concerned;

(e) to provide technical assistance to developing country Members and developing countries negotiating accession to the Agreement establishing the WTO in respect of the application of obligations or other matters affecting trade in services in the sector concerned; and

(f) to cooperate with any other subsidiary bodies established under this Agreement or any international organizations active in any sector concerned.

3. There is hereby established a Committee on Trade in Financial Services which will have the responsibilities listed in paragraph 2 above.

DECISION ON INSTITUTIONAL ARRANGEMENTS FOR THE GENERAL AGREEMENT ON TRADE IN SERVICES

Ministers *recommend* that the Council for Tráde in Services at its first meeting shall adopt the decision set out below.

DISPUTE SETTLEMENT PANELS

The Council for Trade in Services,

Taking into account the specific nature of the obligations and specific commitments of the Agreement and of trade in services with respect to dispute settlement under Articles XXII and XXIII,

Decides as follows :

1. A roster of panelists shall be established to assist in the selection of panelists.

2. To this end, Members may suggest names of individuals possessing the qualifications referred to in paragraph 3 below for inclusion on the roster, and shall provide a curriculum vitae of their qualifications including, if applicable, indication of sector-specific expertise.

3. Panels shall be composed of well-qualified governmental and/or non-governmental individuals who have experience in issues related to the General Agreement on Trade in Services and/or trade in services, including associated regulatory matters. Panelists shall serve in their individual capacities and not as representatives of any government or organisation.

4. Panels for disputes regarding sectoral matters shall have the necessary expertise relevant to the specific services sectors which the dispute concerns.

5. The WTO Secretariat shall maintain the roster and shall develop procedures for its administration in consultation with the Chairman of the Council.

DECISION CONCERNING PARAGRAPH (B) OF ARTICLE XIV OF THE GENERAL AGREEMENT ON TRADE IN SERVICES

Ministers *recommend* that the Council for Trade in Services at its first meeting shall adopt the decision set out below.

WORKING PARTY ON TRADE IN SERVICES AND THE ENVIRONMENT

The Council for Trade in Services,

Acknowledging that measures necessary to protect the environment may conflict with the provisions of the Agreement, and

Noting that since measures necessary to protect the environment typically have as their objective the protection of human, animal or plant life or health, it is not clear that there is a need to provide for more than is contained in paragraph (b) of Article XIV.

Decides as follows:

1. In order to determine whether any modification of Article XIV of the Agreement is required to take account of such measures, a Working Party shall be established and shall examine and report, with recommendations if any, on the relationship between services trade and the environment including the issue of sustainable development. The Working Party shall also examine the relevance of intergovernmental agreements on the environment and their relationship to the Agreement.

2. The Working Party shall report the results of its work within three years of the entry into force of the Agreement establishing the WTO.

DECISION ON NEGOTIATIONSON BASIC TELECOMMUNICATIONS

Ministers, meeting on the occasion of the conclusion of the Uruguay Round,

Decide as follows :

1. Negotiations shall be entered into on a voluntary basis with a view to the progressive liberalization of trade in telecommunications transport networks and services (hereinafter called "basic telecommunications") within the framework of the General Agreement on Trade in Services.

2. Without prejudice to their outcome, the negotiations shall be comprehensive in scope, with no basic telecommunications excluded *a priori.*

3. A Negotiating Group on Basic Telecommunications (NGBT) is established to carry out this mandate. The NGBT shall report periodically on the progress of these negotiations.

4. The negotiations in the NGBT shall be open to all governments and the European Community signing the Final Act of the Uruguay Round which announce their intention to participate. To date, the following governments have announced their intention to take part in the negotiations:

> Australia, Canada, Finland, Hungary, Japan, Korea, Mexico, New Zealand, Norway, Sweden, Switzerland, United States.

Further notifications of intention to participate shall be addressed to the depositary of the Agreement establishing the WTO.

5. The NGBT shall hold its first negotiating session no later than one month from the date of this Decision. It shall conclude these negotiations and make a final report no later than 30 April 1996. The final report of the NGBT shall include a date for the implementation of results of these negotiations.

6. Any commitments resulting from the negotiations, including the date of their entry into force, shall be inscribed in the schedules annexed to the General Agreement on Trade in Services and be subject to all the provisions of the Agreement.

7. Commencing. immediately and continuing until the date (referred to in paragraph 5 above) of implementation of the results of these negotiations, it is understood that no participant shall apply any measure affecting trade in basic telecommunications in such a manner as would improve its negotiating position and leverage. It is understood that this provision shall not prevent the pursuit of commercial and governmental arrangements regarding the provision of basic telecommunications services.

8. The implementation of paragraph 7 above shall be subject to surveillance in the NGBT. Any participant may bring to the attention of the NGBT any action or omission which it believes to be relevant to the fulfilment of paragraph 7. Such notifications shall be deemed to have been submitted to the NGBT upon their receipt by the Secretariat.

UNDERSTANDING ON COMMITMENTS IN FINANCIAL SERVICES

Participants in the Uruguay Round have been enabled to take on specific commitments with respect to Financial Services under the General Agreement on Trade in Services on the basis of an alternative approach to that covered by the provisions of Part III of the Agreement. It was agreed that this approach could be applied subject to the following understanding:

- it does not conflict with the provisions of the Agreement;
- it does not prejudice the right of any Member to schedule its specific commitments in accordance with the approach under Part III of the Agreement;
- resulting specific commitments shall apply on a most-favoured-nation basis;
- no presumption has been created as to the degree of liberalization to which a Member is committing itself under the Agreement.

Interested Members, on the basis of negotiations, and subject to conditions and qualifications where specified, have inscribed in their schedule specific commitments conforming to the approach set out below.

Standstill

Any conditions, limitations and qualifications to the commitments noted below shall be limited to existing non-conforming measures.

Market Access

Monopoly Rights

1. In addition to Article VIII of the Agreement, the following shall apply :

> Each Member shall list in its schedule pertaining to financial services existing monopoly rights and shall endeavour to eliminate them or reduce their scope. Notwithstanding paragraph 1.2 of the Annex on Financial Services, this paragraph applies to the activities referred to in sub-paragraph 1.2.3 of tl : Annex.

Financial Services purchased by Public entities

2. Notwithstanding Article XIII of the Agreement, each Member shall ensure that financial service suppliers of any other Member established in its territory are accorded most-favoured-nation treatment and national treatment as regards the purchase or acquisition of financial services by public entities of the Member in its territory.

Cross-border Trade

3. each Member shall-permit non-resident suppliers of financial services to supply, as a principal, through an intermediary or as an intermediary, and under terms and conditions that accord national treatment the following services :

(a) insurance of risks relating to:

(i) maritime shipping and commercial aviation and space launching and freight (including satellites), with such insurance to cover any or all of the following: the goods being transported, the vehicle transporting the goods and any liability arising therefrom; and

(ii) goods in international transit;

(b) reinsurance and retrocession and the services auxiliary to insurance as referred to in sub-paragraph 5.1 (d) of the Annex;

(c) provision and transfer of financial information and financial data processing as referred to in sub-paragraph 5.1(o) of the Annex and advisory and other auxiliary services, excluding intermediation, relating to banking and other financial services as referred to in sub-paragraph 5.1(p) of the Annex.

4. each Member shall permit its residents to purchase in the territory of any other Member the financial services indicated in:

(a) sub-paragraph 3(a);

(b) sub-paragraph 3(b); and

(c) sub-paragraphs 5.l(e) to (p) of the Annex.

Commercial Presence

5. each Member shall grant financial service suppliers of any other Member the right to establish or expand within its territory, including through the acquisition of existing enterprises, a commercial presence.

6. A Member may impose terms, conditions and procedures for authorization of the establishment and expansion of a commercial presence in so far as they do not circumvent the Member's obligation under paragraph 5 and they are consistent with the other obligations of this Agreement.

New Financial Services

7. A Member shall permit financial service suppliers of any other Member established in its territory to offer in its territory any new financial service.

Transfers of Information and Processing of Information

8. No Member shall take measures that prevent transfers of information or the processing of financial information, including transfers of data by electronic means, or that, subject to importation rules consistent with international agreements, prevent transfers of equipment, where such transfers of information, processing of financial information or transfers of equipment are necessary for the conduct of the ordinary business of a financial service supplier. Nothing in this paragraph restricts the right of a Member to protect personal data, personal privacy and the confidentiality of individual records and accounts so long as such right is not used to circumvent the provisions of the Agreement.

Temporary entry of Personnel

9. (a) Each Member shall permit temporary entry into its territory of the following personnel of a financial service supplier of any other Member that is establishing or has established a commercial presence in the territory of the Member:

(i) senior managerial personnel possessing proprietary information essential to the establishment, control and operation of the services of the financial service supplier; and

(ii) specialists in the operation of the financial service supplier.

(b) Each Member shall permit, subject to the availability of qualified personnel in its territory, temporary entry into its territory of the following personnel associated with a commercial presence of a financial service supplier of any other Member:

(i) specialists in computer services, telecommunication services and accounts of the financial service supplier; and

(ii) actuarial and legal specialists.

Non-discriminatory Measures

10. each Member shall endeavour to remove or to limit any significant adverse effects on financial service suppliers of any other Member of :

(a) non-discriminatory measures that prevent financial service suppliers from offering in the Member's territory, in the form determined by the Member, all the financial services permitted by the Member;

(b) non-discriminatory measures that limit the expansion of the activities of financial service suppliers into the entire territory of the Member;

(c) measures of a Member, when such a Member applies the same measures to the supply of both banking and securities services, and a financial service supplier of any other Member concentrates its activities in the provision of securities services; and

(d) other measures that, although respecting the provisions of this Agreement, affect adversely the ability of financial service suppliers of any other Member to operate, compete or enter the Member's market;

provided that any action taken under this paragraph would not unfairly discriminate against financial service suppliers of the Member taking such action.

11. With respect to the non-discriminatory measures referred to in sub-paragraphs 10(a) and (b), a Member shall endeavour not to limit or restrict the present degree of market opportunities nor the benefits already enjoyed by financial service suppliers of all other Members as a class in the territory of the Member, provided that this commitment does not result in unfair discrimination against financial service suppliers of the Member applying such measures.

National Treatment

1. Under terms and conditions that accord national treatment, each Member shall grant to financial service suppliers of any other Member established in its territory access to payment and clearing systems operated by public entities, and to official funding and refinancing facilities available in the normal course of ordinary business. This paragraph is not intended to confer access to the Member's lender of last resort facilities.

2. When membership or participation in, or access to, any self-regulatory

body, securities or futures exchange or market, clearing agency, or any other organization or association, is required by a Member in order for financial service suppliers of any other Member to supply financial services on an equal basis with financial service suppliers of the Member, or when the Member provides directly or indirectly such entities, privileges or advantages in supplying financial services, the Member shall ensure that such entities accord national treatment to financial service suppliers of any other Member resident in the territory of the Member.

Definitions

For the purposes of this approach :

1. A non-resident supplier of financial services is a financial service supplier of a Member which supplies a financial service into the territory of another Member from an establishment located in the territory of another Member, regardless of whether such a financial service supplier has or has not a commercial presence in the territory of the Member in which the financial service is supplied.

2. "Commercial presence" means an enterprise within a Member's territory for the supply of financial services and includes wholly- or partly-owned subsidiaries, joint ventures, partnerships, sole proprietorships, franchising operations, branches, agencies, representative offices or other organizations.

3. A new financial service is a service of a financial nature, including services related to existing and new products or the manner in which a product is delivered, that is not supplied by any financial service supplier in the territory of a particular Member but which is supplied in the territory of another Member.

DECISION ON FINANCIAL SERIVCES

Ministers, meeting on the occasion of the conclusion of the Uruguay Round,

Noting that commitments scheduled by participants on Financial Services at the conclusion of the Uruguay Round, shall enter into force on an m.f.n. basis at the same time as the General Agreement on Trade in Services.

Decide as follows :

1. At the conclusion of a period ending no later than six months after the entry into force of the Agreement Establishing the WTO, without offering compensation, Members shall be free to improve, modify or withdraw all or part of their commitments in this sector without offering compensation, notwithstanding the provisions of Article XXI of the GATS. At the same time Members shall finalize their positions relating to m.f.n. exemptions in these sectors, notwithstanding the provisions of the Annex on Article II Exemptions.

From the date of entry into force of the Agreement and until the end of the period referred to above, exemptions listed in the Annex on Article II Exemptions which are conditional upon the level of commitments undertaken by other participants or upon exemptions by other participants will not be applied.

2. The Committee on Trade in Financial Services shall monitor the progress of any negotiations undertaken under the terms of this Decision and shall report thereon to the Council for Trade in Services no later than four months after the entry into force of the Agreement.

DECISION CONCERNING PROFESSIONAL SERVICES

Ministers recommend that the Council for Trade in Services at its first meeting shall adopt the decision set out below.

WORKING PARTY ON PROFESSIONAL SERVICES

The Council for Trade in Services,

Recognizing the impact of regulatory measures relating to professional qualifications, technical standards and licensing on the expansion of trade in professional services,

Desiring to establish multilateral disciplines with a view to ensuring that, when specific commitments are undertaken, such regulatory measures do not constitute unnecessary barriers to the supply of professional services,

Decides as follows:

1. The work programme foreseen in Article VI, paragraph 4 on domestic Regulations should be put into effect immediately. To this end, a Working Party shall be established to examine and report, with recommendations, on the disciplines necessary to ensure that measures relating to qualification requirements and procedures, technical standards and licensing requirements in the field of professional services do not constitute unnecessary barriers to trade.

2. As a matter of priority, the Working Party shall make recommendations for the elaboration of multilateral disciplines in the accountancy sector, so as to give operational effect to specific commitments. In making these recommendations, the Working Party shall concentrate on:

- developing multilateral disciplines relating to market access so as to ensure that domestic regulatory requirements are: (a) based on objective and transparent criteria, such as competence and the ability to supply the service; (b) not more burdensome than necessary to ensure the quality of the service, thereby facilitating the effective liberalization of accountancy services;
- the use of international standards and, in doing so, it shall encourage

the cooperation with the relevant international organizations as defined under Article VI, paragraph 5(b), so as to give fully effect to Article VI, paragraph 5;

- facilitating the effective application of Article VI, paragraph 6, of the Agreement by establishing guidelines for the recognition of qualifications.

In elaborating these disciplines, the Working Party shall take account of the importance of the governmental and non-governmental bodies regulating professional services.

DECISION ON MOVEMENT OF NATURAL PERSONS

Ministers meeting on the occasion of the conclusion of the Uruguay Round,

Noting the commitments resulting from the Uruguay Round negotiations on the movement of natural persons for the purpose of supplying services.

Mindful of the objectives of the General Agreement on Trade in Services including, *inter alia,* the increasing participation of developing countries in trade in services and the expansion of their service exports.

Recognizing the importance of achieving higher levels of commitments on the movement of natural persons, in order to provide for a balance of benefits under the General Agreement on Trade in Services.

Decide as follows :

1. Negotiations on further liberalization of movement of natural persons for the purpose of supplying services shall continue beyond the conclusion of the Uruguay Round, with a view to allowing the achievement of higher levels of commitments by participants under the General Agreement on Trade in Services.

2. A negotiating group on movement of natural persons is established to carry out the negotiations. The group shall establish its own procedures and shall report periodically to the Council on Trade in Services.

3. The negotiating group shall hold its first negotiating session no later than one month from the date of this Decision. It shall conclude these negotiations and. produce a final report no later than six months after the entry into force of the Agreement establishing the **WTO**.

4. Commitments resulting from these negotiating shall be inscribed in Members' schedules of specific commitments.

DECISION ON IMPLEMENTATION OF ARTICLE XXIV : 2 OF THE AGREEMENT ON GOVERNMENT PROCUREMENT

1. Ministers *invite* the Committee on Government Procurement to clarify that :

(i) a Member interested in accession according to Article XXIV:2 would communicate its interest to the Director-General, submitting relevant information, including an offer by way of a list of entities having regard to the relevant provisions of the Agreement, in particular Article I and, where appropriate, Article V;

(ii) the communication would be circulated to Parties to the Agreement;

(iii) the Member interested in accession would hold consultations with the Parties on the terms for its accession to the Agreement;

(iv) with a view to facilitating accession, the Committee would establish a working party if the Member in question, or any of the Parties to the Agreement, so requests. The working party should examine: (a) the offer made by the applicant Member; and (b) relevant information pertaining to export opportunities in the markets of the Parties, taking into account the existing and potential export capabilities of the applicant Member and export opportunities for the Parties in the market of the applicant Member;

(v) upon a decision by the Committee agreeing to the terms of accession including the list of entities, the acceding Member would deposit with the Director-General of the **WTO** an instrument of accession which states the terms so agreed. Until the entry into force of the Agreement Establishing the **WTO**, the instrument would be deposited with the Director-General to the CONTRACTING PARTIES to the GATT. The text of the acceding Member's list of entities in English, French and Spanish would be annexed to the Agreement.

2. It is noted that the Committee decisions are arrived at on the basis of consensus. It is also noted that the non-application clause of Article XXIV: 11 is available to any Party.

DECISION ON THE APPLICATION AND REVIEW OF THE UNDERSTANDING ON RULES AND PROCEDURES GOVERNING THE SETTLEMENT OF DISPUTES

The Ministers,

Agree that existing rules and procedures of the GATT 1947 in the field of dispute settlement shall remain in effect until the date of entry into force of the Understanding on Rules and Procedures Governing the Settlement of Disputes under the **World Trade Organisation** It is further agreed that in respect of disputes for which the request for consultation was made before the date of entry into force of the said Understanding, the relevant Councils or Committees shall remain in operation for the purpose of dealing with those disputes.

Agree that a full review of dispute settlement rules and procedures under the **World Trade Organisation** as set out in the said Understanding, shall be completed within four years after its entry into force, and a decision shall be taken on the occasion of the first meeting at Ministerial level after the completion of the review, whether to continue, modify or terminate such dispute settlement rules and procedures.

DECISION ON IMPROVEMENTS TO THE GATT DISPUTE SETTLEMENT RULES AND PROCEDURES

The Ministers,

Recalling the CONTRACTING PARTIES' Decision of 12 April 1989,

Noting that the improvements to the GATT dispute settlement rules and procedures are being applied on a trial basis until the end of the Uruguay Round and that a decision on their adoption should be taken before the end of the Round,

Considering that the continuation of the improved rules and procedures is necessary for the effectiveness of the dispute settlement mechanism,

Decide,

To invite the CONTRACTING PARTIES to keep the above-mentioned improvements in effect until the entry into force of the Understanding on Rules and Procedures Governing the Settlement of Disputes contained in Annex 2 of the Agreement establishing the **World Trade Organisation** .

AGREEMENT ON IMPLEMENTATION OF ARTICLE VI OF GATT 1994

STATEMENT ON ANTI-CIRCUMVENTION

"The problem of circumvention of anti-dumping duty measures formed part of the negotiations which preceded this Agreement. Negotiators were, however, unable to agree on specific text, and, given the desirability of the applicability of uniform rules in this area as soon as possible, the matter is referred to the Committee on Anti-Dumping Practices for resolution."

AGREEMENT ON IMPLEMENTATION OF ARTICLE VI OF GATT 1994

STATEMENT ON STANDARD OF REVIEW FOR DISPUTE SETTLEMENT PANELS

'The standard of review in Article 17.6 of the Agreement will be reviewed after a period of three years with a view to considering the question of whether it is capable of general application."

STATEMENT ON DISPUTE SETTLEMENT PURSUANT TO THE AGREEMENT ON IMPLEMENTATION OF ARTICLE VI 1994 OR PART V OF THE AGREEMENT ON SUBSIDIES AND COUNTERVAILING MEASURES 1994

With respect to dispute settlement pursuant to the Agreement on Implementation of Article VI of GATT 1994 or Part V of the Agreement on Subsidies and Countervailing' Measures 1994. Ministers recognize the need for the consistent resolution of disputes arising from anti-dumping and countervailing duty measures.

